Radical Claims in Freudian Psychoanalysis

Radical Claims in Freudian Psychoanalysis

Point/Counterpoint

Edited by M. Andrew Holowchak, PhD

JASON ARONSON
Lanham • Boulder • New York • Toronto • Plymouth, UK

Published by Jason Aronson
A wholly owned subsidiary of The Rowman & Littlefield Publishing Group, Inc.
4501 Forbes Boulevard, Suite 200, Lanham, Maryland 20706
http://www.rowmanlittlefield.com

Estover Road, Plymouth PL6 7PY, United Kingdom

John Cottingham's essay incorporates material from his previously published books, *Philosophy and the Good Life* and *The Spiritual Dimension*, which is included here by kind permission of Cambridge University Press.

British Library Cataloguing in Publication Information Available

Library of Congress Cataloging-in-Publication Data
Holowchak, Mark, 1958–
Radical claims in Freudian psychoanalysis : point/counterpoint / M. Andrew Holowchak.
p. cm.
Includes index.
ISBN 978-0-7657-0821-2 (cloth : alk. paper) — ISBN 978-0-7657-0908-0 (electronic)
1. Freud, Sigmund, 1856-1939. 2. Psychoanalysis. I. Title.
BF173.F85H62 2011
150.19'52—dc23 2011044592

The paper used in this publication meets the minimum requirements of American National Standard for Information Sciences-Permanence of Paper for Printed Library Materials, ANSI/NISO Z39.48-1992.

Printed in the United States of America

Contents

Preface

SIGMUND FREUD WROTE IN AN 1896 LETTER to Wilhelm Fliess, "You have taught me that a kernel of truth lurks behind every absurd popular belief." Throughout his long and distinguished career, some of Freud's psychoanalytic claims—e.g., those claims relating to the Oedipus complex, the unconscious, and the use of free association as a reliable etiological method in clinic practice—are acknowledged to be absurd even by many of his stoutest defenders. Yet, as Freud's letter to Fliess indicates, acknowledgement of absurdity is not necessarily acknowledgement of untruth. A claim can be labeled "absurd" simply because it belies common sense. One has only to consider Galileo's defense of a moving Earth in his brilliant *Dialogues concerning Two Chief World Systems*, Darwin's defense of the non-fixity of species in *Origin of Species*, or Einstein's posits of the relativity of space and time in his Theory of Relativity. Moreover, even if many of Freud's claims are false, it might still be the case that a "kernel of truth" lurks behind them. Are at least some of Freud's most radical claims true? If not, then do they contain, at least, a "kernel of truth" and, if so, what can be salvaged? This anthology explores those questions.

Radical Claims in Freudian Psychoanalysis: Point/Counterpoint, as the title suggests, is non-trivially unique. It is the first book to feature pro and con essays on some of the most extreme Freudian claims—e.g., the Freudian unconscious and the Oedipus complex. It also employs a good blend of critical scholars from psychology and philosophy—all of whom have distinguished themselves in the area through prior publications. Moreover, all the essays, with one exception, are new.

Radical Claims in Freudian Psychoanalysis is structured to accommodate each separate topic, comprising a pro and con essay of modest length, as a separate part of the book. Each topic is introduced by a quote from Freud that contributors can use as a prompt for their essays. After each pro-and-con coupling on a particular topic, the contributor of the pro essay offers a brief reply to the con essay, and likewise for the contributor of the con essay.

The book comprises six parts that take up the topics—the Oedipus complex, dreams and wish-fulfillment, religion as an illusion, free association, the Freudian unconscious, and Freudian psychoanalysis as a *Weltanschauung*—seriatim.

In the first part, "The Oedipus Complex," begins with the following questions. Why did Freud think the Oedipus complex was an essential element of psychoanalysis? Is psychoanalysis better off without it? Philosopher M. Andrew Holowchak in "Freud's Oedipus Complex: Shibboleth or Canard?" gives insight into the development of Freud's Oedipus complex and seeks to salvage some key elements of it. He maintains that critical discussion and salvaging are made difficult by Freud's own accounts of the issue over the years, which invite only polar discussion. Psychoanalyst Joel Kupfersmid in "The Oedipus Complex: It Made No Sense Then, It Makes No Sense Now" argues that neither is Freud's ontogenetic account—i.e., his general account of sexual development in boys and girls—worth salvaging nor is his phylogenetic account—i.e., his infamous story of the beginnings of culture by the killing of the primal father—worth salvaging.

The questions tackled in the second part, "Freud's Theory of Dreams," are these: Is Freud's theory of dreams tenable? To what extent has it received experimental confirmation today? Philosopher Michael Michael in "The Puzzle of Dreams" examines those questions from the perspective of Freud's methods of dream interpretation and essays to defend Freud's "primary thesis" that dreams do have a discoverable meaning. Michael ends by claiming that primary thesis merits consideration as a "lively hypothesis." In the con essay, psychoanalyst Rosemarie Sand, claims that Freud's theory of dreams is too often mistakenly construed ahistorically—i.e., as if Freud was the first person to declare that dreams had a meaning. When Freud wrote *Interpretation of Dreams,* another theory, the picture theory, was prevalent and "moved into the shadows." Her analysis of the picture theory and Freud's wish-fulfillment theory essays to show that the former is actually preferable to the latter, because Freud's method of gleaning the data of dreams, free association, is itself a flawed procedure.

"Religion as Illusion" is the third part. Here the two scholars tackle the questions: What was Freud's view of religious doctrines in *The Future of an Illusion* and later works, like *Civilization and Its Discontents* and *Moses and Monotheism*? Do religious doctrines have any claim to veridicality? Philosopher John Cottingham in "Freud's Critique of Religion" offers a spirited defense of Freud and his notion of naturalistic explanation in science. In doing so, he asks whether Freud's critique of religion is based on the notion that only naturalistic explanations are valid explanations. If so, then Freud's critique is flawed. Paul Vitz, in "Freud and the Psychology of Atheism," essays to show that Freud's genealogical account is untenable. In doing so, he cleverly turns the tables on Freud by addressing Freud's atheism and exploring the psychopathology of atheism.

The fourth part is titled "Free Association." It addresses these questions: Is free association a viable scientific tool for psychoanalytic investigation? What sort of wide experiential confirmation has it received? Philosopher and practicing analyst Michael Lavin argues in his "On Behalf of Free Association" that, though Freud's etiological conception of free association is untenable, free association is still a valued tool in analytic therapy. Arguing from an ego-psychology perspective, Lavin opts for a more modest use of free association—helping a therapist through use of transference make conscious what was formerly unconscious and, thereby, giving patients the freedom afforded by knowledge. Adolf

Grünbaum in his essay on free association offers a vigorous condemnation of the etiological worth of Freud's use of the method. It cannot guarantee that the inferences made by a Freudian therapist are causally linked to presumed childhood pathogens and not due to suggestion. Thus, the overall worth of the avowed "data" of the psychoanalytic clinical setting is dubious.

The next part, "The Unconscious," is introduced with the following questions: What precisely is Freud's view of the unconscious? What sort of "proofs" did he give and are they incontrovertible? Can and should psychoanalysis do without the unconscious? Philosopher Grant Gillett, in "Freud's *Wunderblock*: The Unconscious as Neural Palimpsest," makes savvy use of two of Freud's metaphors to shed light on the Freudian unconscious. He suggests that Freud's unconscious is still relevant in neuro-scientific work on the brain. Philosopher Edward Erwin begins by exploring the anti-unconscious thinking of William James and Franz Brentano. He concludes that Freud was correct to assert a layer of mentation beneath consciousness, but Freud's notion of a dynamic unconscious, coupled with his the notion of repression, is unsustainable.

The final part, "Psychoanalysis as *Weltanschauung*," takes on the issue of the scientific status of psychoanalysis. Freud consistently argued that psychoanalysis was not a *Weltanschauung* (roughly, "world view"), but part of the scientific *Weltanschauung*. He also argued that the scientific *Weltanschauung* was radically different from the *Weltanschauungen* of religion and philosophy. The question here addressed is the cogency of Freud's arguments. Philosopher Andreas De Block begins with his essay "Freud's Psychoanalysis: A Project for a Genuinely Scientific Psychology?" Conceding numerous overlaps between science and philosophy, he argues that psychoanalysis should be construed as science, not *Weltanschauung*, because Freud's "interests were in particular things" and he used both clinical data to drive his hypotheses and the hypothetico-deductive method. Philosopher Douglas Kirsner argues that Freudian psychoanalysis is more of a *Weltanschauung* in the manner of religion and philosophy, than of a science. Freud's clinical discoveries were semantic, not causal; his work had an ineliminable normative dimension; psychoanalysis was more of a movement than a science; and Freud was hell-bent on developing an overarching, single explanatory theory.

Overall, the format of *Radical Claims in Freudian Psychoanalysis* allows for a close examination of contentious issues from more than one viewpoint—what the ancients called arguing *in utrumque partes* (roughly, "both sides of an issue"). The format enables readers to see that there are (often wide) differences of opinion on contentious issues and, thereby, allows for a broader perspective for critical engagement with them. Moreover, by addressing some of the most radical claims of Freud's psychoanalysis, this collection is proof that even many radical Freudian claims are still taken very seriously by prominent scholars. Not only is Freud still relevant today, so too is *Extreme Freud*.

Acknowledgments

I would like to thank the many exceptional scholars whose efforts made this compilation possible. I would especially like to thank Professor Adolf Grünbaum, former teacher and present colleague, whose passion for Freudian scholarship, Trojan-like work ethic, and insistence on analytic accuracy inflamed a preexisting interest in the writings of Sigmund Freud.

PART I
The Oedipus Complex

"To [a child's] choice of his mother as a love-object everything becomes attached which, under the name of the 'Oedipus complex'", Freud says in one of his *Introductory Lectures on Psycho-Analysis,* "has attained so much importance in the psycho-analytic explanation of the neuroses and has played no less a part, perhaps, in the resistance to psycho-analysis" (1917, *S.E.,* XVI: 329).

Why did Freud think the Oedipus complex was an essential element of psychoanalysis? Is psychoanalysis better off without it?

Pro: M. Andrew Holowchak, Ph.D., *Rider University,* "Freud's Oedipus Complex: Shibboleth or Canard?"

Con: Joel Kupfersmid, Ph.D., Private Practitioner, "The Oedipus Complex: It Made No Sense Then, It Makes No Sense Now"

Chapter 1
Freud's Oedipus Complex
Shibboleth or Canard?

M. Andrew Holowchak
Rider University, U.S.A.

"Childhood love is boundless; it demands exclusive possession, it is not content with less than all. . . . [I]t has, in point of fact, no aim and is incapable of obtaining complete satisfaction; and principally for that treason it is doomed to end in disappointment and to give place to a hostile attitude." Sigmund Freud, "Female Sexuality"

PSYCHOANALYSIS HAS A LONG HISTORY of being charged with insularity.[1] While other sciences progress by attending to the advances in and criticisms of other sciences, many believe that psychoanalysis is content to follow uncritically the lead of its founder Freud, who laid out the groundwork for the discipline by positing unconscious mental processes, repression and resistance, and the Oedipus complex.

The Oedipus complex, which has a dubious status today, is perhaps the best illustration of psychoanalytic insularity and evokes extreme reactions, even from psychoanalysts. On the one hand, numerous papers are published in psychoanalytic journals each year that describe the Oedipal dimension of various pathological cases. There is no effort to justify the Oedipal dimension of the etiological picture. Other psychoanalysts will understand, if no one else does, and that is sufficient because the clinical data of the analytic setting is inaccessible to nonanalysts. On the other hand, there has been an abundance of critical literature, beginning with Jung and Adler in Freud's own day, in opposition—often, in violent opposition—to the Oedipus complex.[2] Critics are astonished that adherents go on at length about Oedipal etiology when, they insist, there is no scientific basis for the Oedipus complex. To their thinking, scientific evidence for the Oedipus complex is as telling as the scientific evidence for the Easter bunny. The Oedipus complex, to them, is poppycock.

The difficulty, I maintain, is that the question of status of the Oedipus complex tends to be framed in such a way that it invites only polar discussion. The fault is Freud's, for he made too great an etiological investment in the Oedipus complex—e.g., proclaiming it, in a 1920 footnote to his "Three Essays on Sexuality," to be the "shibboleth that distinguishes the adherents of psycho-analysis from its opponents" (1905, *S.E.*, VII: 226n1).

Can anything be salvaged? I think so, but salvaging can only come about by framing the question in medial terms, not in terms of shibboleth or hogwash.[3]

The Oedipus Complex

It is widely acknowledged that Freud neither ever once settled on any one conception of "Oedipus complex" nor did he settle on any one explanation of how the Oedipus complex plays out itself in the psychosexual development of males and females. He did give detailed descriptions of its occurrence in male and female psychosexual development in many places and those accounts over the years generally are mostly consistent and progressive.

Male Oedipus Conception

Freud first mentions "Oedipus" in reference to a universal event in human psycho-sexual development in a letter to Fliess (15 October 1897). He writes:

> I have found, in my own case too, being in love with my mother and jealous of my father, and I now consider it a universal event in early childhood, even if not so early as in children who have been made hysterical. . . . [T]he Greek legend seizes upon a compulsion which everyone recognizes because he senses its existence within himself. Everyone in the audience was once a budding Oedipus in fantasy and each recoils in horror from the dream fulfillment here transplanted into reality, with the full quantity of repression which separates his infantile state from his present one (Masson, 1985).

Note here several things. Freud appeals to personal experience and hints at similar experiences of others in support of Oedipal tensions. Next, he claims that it is universal in early childhood, though it might not antedate hysteria in children.

Chapter V of *Interpretation of Dreams* formally introduces the Oedipus story (1900, *S.E.*, IV: 261-3) as a factor in psycho-sexuality. It is not the futility of trying to escape our fate that grips us, but instead Oedipus' particular fate. "It is the fate of all of us, perhaps, to direct our first sexual impulse towards our mother and our first hatred and our first murderous wish against our father."[4] Being in love with one parent and hating the other is the principal part of the lives of children that become psychoneurotic (1900, *S.E.*, IV: 261-3).

"Sexual Theories of Children," eight years later, lists three prominent false views entertained by children. First is the notion, amply verified in legends and myths, that everyone possesses a penis and can lose it by castration. Second is the notion that babies are evacuated like stool and evacuation allows male children to fantasize about giving birth, as they, like female children, have an anus.

Third is the notion, entertained by children that chance to observe sexual intercourse, that coition is sadistic—e.g., confirmed by observation of blood on bedsheets or by coition seen to be parental fighting (1908, *S.E.*, IX: 213-23).

Freud first formally introduces "Oedipus complex" two years later in "Special Type of Object-Choice Made by Men." Desire for his mother and thirst for revenge against his father are the boy's two driving forces. He finds refuge in diverse masturbatory fantasies of his mother, who seems to him an unfaithful partner. "[T]he lover with whom she commits her act of infidelity," Freud adds, "almost always exhibits the features of the boy's own ego, or more accurately, of his own idealized personality, grown up and so raised to a level with his father" (1910, *S.E.*, XI: 171).

In "Totem and Taboo" in 1913, Freud explains neurosis as infantile fixation or infantile regression that is essentially Oedipal. "We have arrived," Freud says boldly, "at the point of regarding a child's relation to his parents, dominated as it is by incestuous longing, as the nuclear complex of neurosis." He appeals to Rank's study of Oedipal longings in creative writing and in the taboo of incest by savages (1913, *S.E.*, XIII: 17). The modern-day taboo of incest, he explains, has its origins in totemic law, which prohibits the killing of the totem animal and prohibits sexual intercourse with members of the opposite sex in the same totem clan (1913, *S.E.*, XIII: 32).

By 1915, Freud complains, "[I]t cannot be said that the world has shown much gratitude to psycho-analytic research for its revelation of the Oedipus complex." He adds that some have expressed "the most violent opposition," while others gloze over its significance by "twisted re-interpretations" that rob it of its value, though evidence of it abounds in dramatic writing and dreams. He also mentions here the "castration complex," a boy's reaction to threats aimed at putting a stop to childhood masturbation, which attends on the Oedipus complex. He then cites several sexual barriers—i.e., "perversions"—that exist for adults, but not for children: sex between humans and other animals, disgust, incest, sex with members of the same sex, and what might be dubbed "genitalizing" other organs or areas of the body[5] (1915, *S.E.*, XV: 207-8).

Freud gives a lengthy elaboration of the Oedipus complex, critical to the "psycho-analytic explanation of the neuroses," in *Introductory Lectures*. Describing a boy's erotic affection for his mother,[6] Freud entertains the objection that an erotic etiology is merely a confusion of eroticism for self-interest. The child's mother attends to all the boy's needs, so he has a strong selfish, though non-sexual, interest in keeping her to himself. Yet here, Freud says, egoism merely supports eroticism. The boy's behavior—e.g., sleeping beside his mother, being present while she dresses, and his attempts at seducing her—leaves no doubt that his interest is erotic (1917, *S.E.*, XVI: 329-33).

Freud then addresses two arguments proposing to evince that there is no real dread of incest. First, the fact that members of the same family have lived together for such a long time guarantees the avoidance of incest. Furthermore, the biological abhorrence of incest shows that incest is innately dreaded. The first reason is too flimsy to require a reply. The second is shot down by the existence of the "inexorable prohibition" of incest—itself evidence of strong impulses and the lack of natural barriers. Laws against incest are extant among savages. Incest in mythology is permitted to the gods. Analysis too, he adds, amply confirms incestuous wishes in patients (1917, *S.E.*, XVI: 334-5).

What, however, of the reliability of the reports of neurotics in the analytic setting, from which Freud draws for evidence of the Oedipus complex? Freud admits that when anyone gives an account of the past—even a historian—he also puts something of his present into the past. It is the same with neurotics. So, neurotics' loves and hates are reinforced by factors of adulthood through "retrospective phatasying." However, it is vain to explain the Oedipus complex thus when sturdier evidence exists. "Its infantile core and more or less of its accessories remain as they were confirmed by the direct observation of children" (1917, *S.E.*, XVI: 336).

Observation shows that all pubescent children have intense Oedipal affections, but they remain outside of consciousness. However, as an adolescent, a child must separate himself from his parents, before he can become a viable member of human society. Seldom does detachment occur neatly. With neurotics though, there is no detachment. A son, all his life, bows to his father's authority; a daughter, to her mother's. "In this sense the Oedipus complex may justly be regarded as the nucleus of all the neuroses" (1917, *S.E.*, XVI: 337).

"Beyond the Pleasure Principle" mentions that patients' behavioral repetitions of repressed material occur with "unwished-for exactitude" and "always have as their subject some portion of infantile sexual life" of the Oedipus complex and it derivatives and those allow for transference neurosis (1920, *S.E.*, XVIII: 18-20).

In "Dissolution of the Oedipus Complex," Freud says that a boy's masturbating ceases in time due to the threat of castration and observation of the "castrated" female genitals.[7] After latency, the Oedipus complex is "destroyed"[8] and the result of desexualization and sublimation is the formation of the superego.[9] In less successful cases, the libido is merely repressed and the result is neurosis (1924, *S.E.*, XIX: 175-7).

"A Short Account of Psycho-Analysis" relates that the Oedipus complex is the "psychical correlate of two biological facts": the long period of childhood helplessness and sexual diphasism (1924, *S.E.*, XIX: 208).[10]

In "Psycho-Analysis," Freud writes of the significance of sublimation for individuals as well as the human species. "The reactions against the instinctual demands of the Oedipus complex are the source of the most precious and socially important achievements of the human mind; and this holds true not only in the life of individuals but probably also in the history of the human species as a whole" (1926, *S.E.*, XX: 268).

By 1933, the Oedipus complex convinces Freud, in "Anxiety and Instinctual Life," that his view of the etiology of hysteria is mistaken. Anxiety, he has come to find, is not the result of repression, but the cause of repression. For the boy, it is the perception of danger, internalized through the threat of castration, which is the cause of anxiety. "[W]e must hold fast to the view that fear of castration is one of the commonest and strongest motives of repression and thus for the formation of neuroses," though it finds no place in women, who are motivated by loss of parental affection (1933, *S.E.*, XXII: 85-7).

Freud in his posthumously published "Outline of Psycho-Analysis" delineates how the Oedipus complex paves the way for neurosis. The ego comes to grief over handling the real Oedipal danger of castration. It is too immature to handle such dangers. He writes, "[W]e cannot escape the conclusion that neuroses could be avoided if the childish ego were spared this task—if . . . the child's sexual life were allowed free play, as happens among many primitive peoples." Instead the ego has the task of damming up the sexual drive on account of reality and the overly strict super-ego (1940, *S.E.*, XXIII: 200-5).

Here Freud also deals with the objection of resistance to the Oedipus complex in analysis. The Oedipus complex is said to be the "central experience of the years of childhood, the greatest problem of early life and the strongest source of later inadequacy," so how is it completely forgotten? The whole experience has been subject to "highly energetic repression," thus it cannot be expected that a patient will remember it. So great is this contribution to science that Freud says, "[I]f psycho-analysis could boast no other achievement than the discovery of the repressed Oedipus complex, that alone would give it a claim to be included among the precious new acquisitions of mankind" (1940, *S.E.*, XXIII: 191-3).

Female Oedipus Complex

Female sexuality was always plaguy and perplexing to Freud. His thoughts on the female Oedipus complex lagged behind his thoughts of the male Oedipus complex considerably. For instance, he mentions the female Oedipus complex briefly in "Development of the Libido"—seventeen years after *Interpretation of Dreams*. "Things happen in just the same way with little girls," he says succinctly, perhaps dismissively, "with the necessary changes: an affectionate attachment to her father, a need to get rid of her mother as superfluous and to take her place. . ." (1917, *S.E.*, XVI: 333). The account is underdeveloped and inchoate. Freud betrays no awareness of the asymmetries he would later posit between male and female psychosexual development.

In time, Freud came to recognize that the female Oedipus complex is not symmetrical with that of the male. Two features complicate it. Over time, a girl has to change both her erotogenic zone and her love-object.

In "Dissolution of the Oedipus Complex" (1924), Freud says that a girl's clitoris functions like a penis until she compares it to a penis. When she comes to see the difference in size, she feels inferior. Soon she interprets her clitoris not as an organ but a lack of one. Once she had a penis, she reasons, but she lost it to castration and, for that, blames her mother. So, a girl accepts castration as a fact, wishes for a penis, and envies boys because they have one. Penis-envy and feelings of inferiority explain a girl's overall lack of aggression. More passive than aggressive, she integrates more readily into society than does a boy (1924, *S.E.*, XIX: 177-9).

Without a penis, there can be no castration threat and no castration anxiety. Without the threat of castration, there is little motivation for desexualization and sublimation of libido. Thus, her Oedipal "resolution" comes slowly, if it comes at all, and is due more to upbringing and social factors, like the threat of loss of parental love. In time, her wish for a penis eventuates in the wish to have a baby as a gift to her father. Ultimately, both wishes go unfulfilled and are eventually strongly cathected in the unconscious (1924, *S.E.*, XIX: 177-8).

At the end of his analysis of female sexuality, Freud hedges, "It must be admitted, however, that in general our insight into these developmental processes in girls is unsatisfactory, incomplete and vague" (1924, *S.E.*, XIX: 179).

"In the Anatomical Distinction between the Sexes," one year later, Freud says that the Oedipus complex is a secondary formation in girls. In boys, the Oedipus complex is "destroyed"—not merely repressed, but "smashed to pieces"—by the castration complex, which exists in threat, though it has not been done; in girls, the Oedipus complex is made possible by the castration complex, because castration has already occurred. In boys, libidinal cathexes are abandoned, desexualized, and sublimated and their objects form a strong super-ego. The catastrophe is a loss to the individual, but a victory to the species. In girls, they are never fully abandoned, desexualized, and sublimated and, thus, girls cannot form a strong super-ego (1925, *S.E.*, XIX: 257).

"Female Sexuality," six years later, offers an extended discussion of the female Oedipus complex. The attachment of young girls to their father is something Freud claims is apparent to observation, but it begins as an attachment to her mother. When a girl's attachment to her father is extremely intense, there is always a prior and equally strong pre-Oedipal attachment to her mother. Moreover, the duration of pre-Oedipal attachment to her mother is often unexpectedly lengthy. Some girls fixate on their mothers to their fifth year and, in such time, hold their father at bay as a rival (1931, *S.E.*, XXI: 225-6).

Because both boys and girls begin with libidinal attachments to their mother, childhood sexuality has a masculine bias. Like boys, girls begin with a masculine phase of sexuality, in which the clitoris functions much in the same way as does a boy's penis. In time, she acknowledges her own castration and, thus, her own inferiority. Annoyed by her inferiority, she eventually abandons clitoral play and her masculine phase ends (1931, *S.E.*, XXI; 233).

Yet her masculine phase, without the threat of castration, does not so much end as it gradually fades away. A girl clings with defiant self-assertiveness to her threatened masculinity and clings especially to the hope of getting a penis some day.[11] She renounces her "masculinity complex" only when she takes her father as her object-choice. Without any threat to terminate a girl's masculinity complex, her pre-Oedipal phase is of far greater significance than that of a boy (1931, *S.E.*, XXI: 229-30).

Freud hedges too at the close of "Female Sexuality." "[I]t is hardly possible to give a description which has general validity. We find the most different reactions in different individuals, and in the same individual the contrary attitudes exist side by side" (1931, *S.E.*, XXI: 233). Female sexuality has become, at this point, a tarbaby.

"Femininity," an essay composed two years later, is Freud's most extended discussion of female sexuality. He begins with two expectations: first, that a female will not adapt herself to femininity without a struggle, and second, that the decisive turning-points of female sexuality are pre-Oedipal (1933, *S.E.*, XXII: 117).

"Laborious investigations" show that a girl's attachment to her mother is often very strong and of long duration. Freud adds, "[W]e get an impression that we cannot understand women unless we appreciate this phase of their pre-Oedipus attachment to their mother." As it persists through all phases of infantile sexuality—oral, sadistic/anal, and phallic—the pre-Oedipal attachment to their mother is lengthy and diverse (1933, *S.E.*, XXII: 119-20) and, consequently, it complicates female sexuality.

Overall, the attachment to the mother turns to hatred of an intense sort that manifests itself in a series of reproaches. Too little milk is a frequent complaint. So too is the short length of nurture at the breast. Another complaint is loss of nurture that accompanies the birth of a second child. Yet the most striking complaint, gleaned through analysis, is a girl's lack of a penis. For that and her subsequent feelings of inferiority, the girl holds her mother responsible and, with execration, turns from her (1933, *S.E.*, XXII: 121-3 and 126).

Again, Freud addresses the lack of castration threat. "The castration complex [with a girl] prepares for the Oedipus complex instead of destroying it; the girl is driven out of her attachment to her mother through the influence of her envy for the penis and she enters the Oedipus situation as though into a haven of refuge." Without the threat of castration, a girl dismantles her complex late and only incompletely. "In these circumstances the formation of the super-ego must suffer; it cannot attain the strength and independence which give it its cultural significance. . . ."[12] Female pathology is mainly linked to the pre-Oedipal phase. He says: "[D]evelopment of femininity remains exposed to disturbance by the residual phenomena of the early masculine period. Regressions to the fixations of the pre-Oedipus phases very frequently occur. . ." (1933, *S.E.*, XXII: 127-31).

Freud sums his findings. For female sexuality, there are two strata: one, pre-Oedipal, where a girl has an affectionate relationship with her mother and takes her mother as her model; two, Oedipal, where a girl seeks to rid of her mother and take her mother's place beside her father. Of them, the former is decisive for the girl. Thus, a man's love and a woman's love are a phase apart (1933, *S.E.*, XXII: 134).

Freud, manqué, anticipates disagreement with his account and addresses the naysayers. "Enough can be seen in the children if one knows how to look." Yet children, he adds, cannot communicate their unconscious sexual wishes, so one must "study the residues and consequences of this emotional world in retrospect, in people in whom these processes of development had attained a specially clear and even excessive degree of expansion [i.e., neurotics]. Pathology [of a non-extreme form] has always done us the service of making discernible by isolation and exaggeration conditions which would remain concealed in a normal state"[13] (1933, *S.E.*, XXII: 120-1). Study of neurotics makes sense only on assumption of an etiological link between neurosis and sexual dysfunction.

Freud ends, once again, by hedging. He grants the incomplete, bitty nature of his account. His explanation is to him, so to speak, a kludge, not because it is tenuous, but because of the unforeseen complexities of female sexuality[14] (1933, *S.E.*, XXII: 135). Awkward as it is, it seems to work.

Complete Oedipus Complex

The duality of sexuality, Freud says, is a biological concern about which psychology has "contributed nothing." Mental life offers mere traces of the duality and that is complicated by the constitutional bisexuality of all humans[15] (1939, *S.E.*, XXIII: 188).

Freud's purchase of bisexuality forced him to modify his views on the Oedipus complex. In "The Ego and the Id" (1923), Freud mentions a "simple, positive Oedipus complex," a "negative Oedipus complex," and a "complete Oedipus complex."

The positive Oedipus complex is the straightforward story, which we have already seen, of a boy's attachment to his mother and execration of his father and a girl's eventual attachment to her father and execration of her mother (1923, *S.E.*, XIX: 32).

The negative Oedipus complex accommodates bisexuality. "It is this complicating element introduced by bisexuality," Freud writes, "that makes it so difficult to obtain a clear view of the facts in connection with the earliest object-choices and identifications, and still more difficult to describe them intelligibly." A boy betrays his femininity and, desiring his father and shunning his mother, acts like a girl; a girl betrays her masculinity and, desiring her mother and shunning her father, acts like a boy (1923, *S.E.*, XIX: 33-5).

To examine the Oedipus complex in its positive and negative guises is to examine the complete Oedipus complex. To grasp neurosis completely, an analyst must assume the existence of the complete Oedipus complex and take the positive complex and negative complex as antipodes. Both complexes factor into the formation of the super-ego, which hands out both ethical prescriptions and prohibitions and is the result of the convergence of biological and historical factors (1923, *S.E.*, XIX: 34-5).

Freud's Phylogenetic Story

The Oepidus complex allows a child to surmount the sexual tensions of infancy. The payoffs are acquisition of a super-ego and admittance to human society.

Freud soon found his etiology of Oedipal ontogeny incomplete. He offered an etiology of Oedipal phylogeny[16] as a counterpart in "Totem and Taboo."

Freud's phylogenetic explanation takes him back to the primal horde—the ancestral horde of all humanity.[17] In this horde, the primal father, as the leader and the strongest male, gave free reign to his sexual impulses to the dismay of the lesser males. The impeded sexual impulses of the lesser males eventually provoked them to form a pact to kill the primal father—the first social deed.[18] After killing the primal father, they disposed of the corpse in a cannibalistic feast.[19] The magnitude of the deed was so great that it stayed with the lesser males, the killers, in the form of a "forgotten" memory, passed on to subsequent generations (1913, *S.E.* XIII: 140-6) in Lamarckian fashion.[20] Thus, the ontogenetic Oedipus complex, rooted in wishing, has as its origin a phylogenetic deed—a wish actualized.[21]

In "Totem and Taboo," Freud acknowledges "grave difficulties" with his "deduction" to the primal deed (1913, S.E. XIII: 158), but by the time of "Moses and Monotheism," over 25 years later, the grave difficulties are gone and the deed now must have been committed numerous times in numerous hordes in early human history.[22] "Since the emergence of the idea of evolution no longer leaves room for doubt that the human race has a prehistory, and since this is unknown—that is, forgotten—a conclusion of this kind [i.e., the primal deed] almost carries the weight of a postulate" (1939, *S.E.* XXIII: 80).

Strangely enough, in "Moses and Monotheism," Freud finds confirmation of the phylogenetic component of the Oedipus complex in two other ways. First, there are the reactions of patients to early trauma. Often such a reaction, especially in the cases of the Oedipus and castration complexes, is incompatible with what a subject has actually experienced, but "fits in much better with the model of a phylogenetic event and, in general, can only be explained by such an influence." The evidential value of such an archaic event is strong enough for Freud to posit that the archaic heritage comprises both dispositions and memory-traces of the killing of the primal father. Second, there is a pragmatic justification. "If we assume the survival of these memory-traces in the archaic heritage, we have bridged the gulf between individual and group psychology: we can deal with peoples as we do with an individual neurotic." In this, humans differ nowise from other animals. He sums, "I have no hesitation in declaring that men have always known (in this special way) that they once possessed a primal father and killed him" (1939, *S.E.*, XXIII: 99-101). Both "confirmations" are tenuous. The argument overall is unpersuasive.

Joel Kupfersmid in "Does the Oedipus Complex Exist?" does a fine job of analyzing analogically any evidence, actual or conceivable, on behalf of Freud's speculations on the phylogenetic acquisition of the Oedipus complex. His sober conclusions are that there is no evidence that the deed, if performed, could have been passed on from generation to generation and transmitted genetically; no evidence that the sons, if they existed in the manner described by Freud, banded together and performed the deed; and even no evidence of a primal horde of the sort described by Freud. The story, without support at any level, is pure speculation (1995, 534-6). This is a case, I add, where Freud—by looking toward biology, anthropology, and archeology—sought aidful "confirmation" for the Oedipus complex, but wound up writing wish-based cockamamie.

Attack on the Freudian Shibboleth

Early Resistance

Resistance to Freud's Oedipus complex came early, from many directions, and from a large number of critics. I begin with a sample of the early resistance.

Freud says in "History of the Psycho-Analytic Movement" that Carl Jung takes the "incest-complex" to be only "symbolic" and "without real existence," because "a savage feels no desire towards an old hag but prefers a young and pretty woman." Yet Jung's disavowal, Freud adds, is itself confirmation of the unconscious existence of desire for the old hag. Analyses "conducted in a proper manner"—especially of children—strengthen the convictions that underpin analytic therapy (1914, *S.E.*, XIV: 64-5). Elsewhere Freud says Jung treated the Oedipus complex symbolically and failed see to its phylogenetic value (1923, *S.E.*, XVIII: 248). In "Autobiographical Study," Freud says, "Jung attempted to give to the facts of analysis a fresh interpretation of an abstract, impersonal and non-historical character, and thus hoped to escape the need for recognizing the importance of infantile sexuality and of the Oedipus complex as well as the necessity for an analysis of childhood"[23] (1925, *S.E.*, XX: 53).

The key to the debate was published disagreement between Freud's phylogenetic account in "Totem and Taboo" and Jung's earlier work "Transformations and Symbols of Libido" (1912), rooted in mythology and comparative religion, which, in effect, attacked Freud's Oedipus complex.

Alfred Adler, Freud states in "Psycho-Analysis," turned away from the unconscious and the sexual drives and toward the "will to power"—i.e., the overcoming of inferiority. Yet in turning away, Freud says, he mostly stole from psychoanalysis by renaming key psychoanalytic terms (e.g., "Oedipus complex" became "masculine protest") (1923, *S.E.*, XVIII: 249). In "Autobiographical Study," Freud says Adler completely rejected the etiological significance of sexuality and "threw all the psychological discoveries of psycho-analysis to the winds" (1925, *S.E.,* XX: 53).

Object-relations pioneer W.R.D. Fairbairn trivialized the Oedipus complex by asserting famously, "Libido is primarily object-seeking, not pleasure seeking." He also coined the term "object-relations theory," which is today recognized as a branch of psychoanalysis (Fairbairn, 1954, 137). Expressing a similar sentiment, D.W. Winnicott added, "[T]here is no id before ego." He wished to demonstrate the primacy of ego-structures and the secondary nature of drives like sexuality and aggression (1966, 56). That is not to say that all objects-relation theorists do away with drives and the Oedipus complex. It is merely that objects, not drives, are their focus. Paraphrasing Fairbairn, object relations determine libidinal attitudes; libidinal attitudes do not determine object relations. Thus, object-relations theory is not an abandonment of psychosexuality, but mainly a turning away from Freud's troublesome metapsychology.

Eric Fromm offered the sort of egoistic defense of Oedipal attraction that Freud dismissed as disguised eroticism in the *Introductory Lectures*. Fromm maintains that Freud's Oedipus complex is a mistake of extrapolation. Freud was, perhaps unconsciously, intensely attracted to his mother and that intense attraction had huge implications for the new science.

> Freud explained the attachment to the mother—quite rationalistically—as being based on the sexual attraction of the little boy to the woman with whom he is most intimate. But, considering the intensity of his attachment to his own mother, and the fact that he tended to repress it, it is understandable that he interpreted one of the most powerful strivings in man, the craving for care, protection and all-enveloping love and affirmation of Mother, as the more limited wish of the little boy to satisfy his instinctual needs through Mother.

Thus, Freud's discovery was the wish to remain attached to Mother—i.e., to the womb, to nature, and to pre-conscious existence—but "he negated this very discovery by restricting it to the small sector of instinctual desires" (i.e., by eroticizing it) (Fromm, 1959, 15).

Freud, *pace* Fromm, made no mistake of extrapolation. Freud, if we are to take him at his word, based his account of the Oedipus complex not on his own experience, but on observations of children and his clinical cases.[24] His own experience of maternal eroticism was merely additional confirmations of prior observations or an illustration of it.[25]

Selected Current Criticisms

The current status of Freud's Oedipus complex is uncertain. Some psychoanalysts, through above-board loyalty to Freud that borders on piousness, defend the etiological significance of the Oedipus complex in neuroses. That comes out in publications in psychoanalytic journals in which Oedipal tensions are cited as keys to pathological disclosure and therapeutic success. Other analysts take the Oedipus complex not as straightforwardly etiological, but as something with heuristic merit in psychopathology. Most experts on psychological development, I suspect, support the notion that the Oedipus complex has neither etiological nor heuristic significance in the analytic setting.

Margaret Clark offers an argument from "relativities." The Oedipus complex, she says, is based on the historical and cultural model of the family that was characteristic of Western European middle classes in the nineteenth century. It might have been relevant in Freud's day, but it is not relevant today. "These are relativities we have the luxury of being aware of today." She concludes that we can salvage Oedipus, not as a complex, but as one of many myths that represents some aspect of psychical turmoil (Clark, 2009, 235). The complex, thus, has no claim to scientific standing.

The argument from relativities is unavailing. Clark is right to claim that the Oedipus complex was thought up by Freud during the nineteenth century and in a Western European, middle-class setting. That in itself is insufficient to show that it is false however. Every scientific hypothesis is the product of *some* cultural climate in history. No hypothesis has ever been thought up in a vacuum. Thus, no scientific hypothesis can escape that sort of relativity. Yet that sort of relativity is entirely undamaging from a scientific standpoint. What concerns us is the scientific standing of the Oedipus complex from an etiological point of view. Is there compelling evidence to show that it does not obtain today? Are Freud's observations contaminated? To assume that it is false merely because it is the product of a particular time-frame is to commit the genetic fallacy.

Howard Lerner offers a different twist to Clark's argument. He maintains that there has been a shift from Freud's drive psychology, with its focus on sexuality, and that the shift has occurred, in part, because the "complaints of patients seeking help today differ from those described in the literature 25 or 50 years ago." It is not a question today of dealing with a conflicted, infringed-on, structuralized, and cohesive personality as it was in Freud's day; it is a question of dealing with a split, malformed, and arrested personality (Lerner, 2008, 155-6). The Oedipus complex was relevant in Freud's day, but not ours.

Lerner's argument also is problematic. Because the complaints of patients today are radically different, the causes of neurosis, culturally conditioned, must be radically different. That presupposes a large degree of plasticity in human concerns and, what is most problematic, it seems to presuppose a human condition that is too elastic—e.g., humans in Freud's day were sexual beings, while today they are somehow not. Therefore, it too is ineffective.

There are meatier objections, to which I now turn.

Sharff and Sharff reject Freud's depiction of the Oedipus complex as something that occurs only to or in a child. They emphasize the effect of both parents on a child and the child's effect on both parents. Thus, the Oedipus complex is not "in the child," as it were, but exists in the interplay of forces between the family triad. Consequently, the Oedipus complex amounts to nothing more than an expression of the triad of forces at play in the sexual development of a young child.[26] As a child in the phallic stage recognizes genital differences, there is a shift of interest to "triads and their vicissitudes." Ultimately what concerns the child is not the loss of the affection of the opposite-sex parent per se, but the loss of the family unit (Scharf et al., 1987). Thus, what Sharff and Sharff show is something noted by Devereaux (e.g., 1953) in the 1950s and Klein, Laplance, and Pontalis years earlier: Freud focuses on the complex from the perspective of children alone, while children do not and cannot act in a vacuum (1973, 286).

Kupfersmid attacks the data behind the Oedipus complex. He says that the reliability of psychoanalytic data, from which the Oedipus complex is gleaned, is dependent on "the degree to which the techniques of dream interpretation, analysis of parapraxes, and the method of free association . . . yield accurate information." His focus is on the critical literature, at the front of which is Grünbaum's work, which casts doubt on the reliability of Freud's methods as means to garner uncontaminated data (1995, 538-42). He notes the critical literature cannot be ignored and Freud's clinical data are likely contaminated.

Finally, there is the difficulty of the theory-ladenness of psychoanalysis. Simon acknowledges the tendency of researchers to find what their theories tell them to find. That difficulty is especially disconcerting to psychoanalysts that depend crucially on data gleaned from the clinical setting. "The foremost is the concern that our theoretical scheme, insofar as it guides our interpretations and interventions," Simon writes, "skews, or even 'creates' the data." Though the clinic is the "ultimate court of appeal," there is such difference of opinion among clinicians about what goes on in the clinical setting that clinical data are "controvertible." He adds that there needs to be confirmation of what goes on in the clinic by persons who stand outside of it (1991, 661).

The *Ad-Baculum* Tack

A different tack taken by some critics is *ad baculum*—i.e., based on force or threat. This *ad-baculum* tack seeks to undermine credibility of the Oedipus complex, if only indirectly, by showing that Freud's published reasons for rejecting what is today commonly called the "Seduction theory" and supplanting it with wish-based Oedipal model of hysteria were spurious. The reason for rejecting seduction and turning to the Oedipus complex was not based on evidence or its lack, but instead on coercion. I give a brief sketch of the traditional view of the shift from the Seduction theory to the Oedipus complex and then cite two instances of *ad-baculum* criticisms.

The traditional view, given sanction by adherents Ernst Kris and Earnest Jones and Freud himself in his later writings, is roughly this. Freud struggled to find confirmatory evidence of early childhood seduction as a needed cause of hysteria. The reported seductions of patients could either be taken at face-value or not. If so, then, *inter alia*, the number of childhood seductions at the hands of the father would be alarmingly high. If not, then reports of actual seduction at the hands of the father would be reports of wished-for seductions. Freud found reasons to be suspicious of the reported seductions. Therefore, he was left to explain them as wished-for seductions. Freud abandoned the Seduction theory and the Oedipus complex, the only logical alternative, was formulated relatively immediate thereafter.

Masson, in his groundbreaking *The Assault on Truth,* argues that the traditional view is untenable. Freud's rejection of childhood, paternal seduction and his endorsement of the Oedipus complex were not evidence-based. Instead, Freud bowed to peer-pressure. His aim was to gain the approbation of the Austrian-German medical community, which presumably did not embrace his views on paternal seduction as a needed condition for hysteria, and thereby disingenuously advance the cause of psychoanalysis (Masson, 1984). Difficulties with this view, dubbed the "external-threat theory" by Kupfersmid (1992 and 1995), are and have been addressed by him in three telling objections in this and prior publications. I refer readers merely to the apposite section of his essay, which immediately follows.

Kupfersmid, in addressing the defects of the external-threat theory, defends an "internal-threat theory." According to this view, "only one important piece of datum influenced Freud in displacing the seduction theory with that of the Oedipus complex"—protecting himself and his family. According to the Seduction theory, early childhood seduction is a *conditio sine qua non* for hysteria and Freud, through his period of self-analysis—which roughly corresponds to the period in which he grappled with his Seduction theory—came to believe that he and several of his sisters were hysterics. As seduction was a needed condition for hysteria, it follows that he and those sisters were sexually abused at the hands of their father—something Freud, whether for conscious or unconscious reasons, was ill-inclined to accept (1994, 537). Thus, Kupfersmid concludes, Freud's motivation for the switch was not evidentiary, but wholly internally motivated.

The Kupfersmid's external-threat, *ad-baculum* tack is enticing, but it ultimately falters, because it seems to be principally "justified" on defects of the primary alternatives, not on positive evidence adduced for existence of internal threat. Kupfersmid, in rightly pointing out flaws in the received view and external-threat view of Masson, has indeed opened conceptual space for a third alternative—an internal-threat view. His reasoning seems to be driven by at least implicit use of disjunctive syllogism: *T*, *E*, and *I* are competing explanations; *T* and *E* are false; so *I* must be true. In short, Kupfersmid focuses on proving the merit of his alternative explanation principally by showing that the two most popular explanations are implausible. That is not the same as adducing cogent evidence for his explanation.

The problem with such an argument from elimination is this. One is justified in accepting the truth of an explanation in that manner only when, first, the explanations offered are exclusive and exhaustive and, two, all possible explanations, except one, have been shown impossible. In other words, while *E* and *I* might exhaust all the alternatives of a threat-based explanation, *T* itself does not exhaust all the alternatives for a non-threat-based explanation. Such an argument from elimination only works infallibly when the first premise exhausts all possible explanatory alternatives—i.e., *T*, *E*, and *I* are exclusive *and* exhaustive options. It does not. One cannot conclude, from the numerous defects of the traditional view and the external-threat view, no other non-threat-based alternatives exist. Kupfersmid's and others' (e.g., Makari, 1998, and Triplett, 2005) elaborations of the numerous defects of the traditional view allow for alternative, non-threat-based explanations. Given that he does not rule out other explanations of a non-threat-based sort, Kupfersmid needs to adduce cogent evidence that the internal-threat explanation is the most reasonable explanation. Otherwise, showing that the two most popular explanations are implausible is inadequate and unpersuasive.

As Kupfersmid notes, critics are increasingly coming to see that the traditional view is faulty. According to that view, Freud was faced with two options—early childhood seduction and seduction fantasy—and the available evidence ultimately decided in favor of seduction fantasy as early as the writing of his famous letter to Fliess on the 21st of September of 1897. However, circumspection of Freud's later letters to Fliess show roundly that Freud, years later, still held out some hope for childhood seduction. Hal Triplett argues that it is not until 1925—twenty-nine years after formal endorsement of the Seduction theory!—Freud cleans up "all nuances of assault and trauma . . . from the accounts of 1896" in favor of a wish-based, Oedipal etiology of neurosis. The deciding factor, ultimately, Triplett takes to be dearth of evidence for early sexual traumata (2005, 665-60).

George Makari has argued for what I take to be a plausible, non-threat-based alternative. He has argued, from a careful scrutiny of Freud's letters for Fliess, that there was an intermediate phase in the development of Freud's thinking on the etiology of hysteria—roughly 1899 to sometime before 1905—in which Freud at least provisionally embraced an alternative explanation for hysteria. During this period, Freud, squeamish about childhood seduction but equally squeamish about a clean break with it, argued it was not parental abuse that was etiologically linked with hysteria, but childhood self-abuse through excessive masturbation that was linked with hysteria. Hysteria was the result of the sudden cessation of excessive masturbation—i.e., of an excess of oral or genital stimulation. Writes Freud in a letter to Fliess (27 Oct. 1897), from which Makari draws:

> Longing is the main character trait of hysteria. . . . During this same period of longing fantasies are formed and masturbation is (regularly?) practiced, which then yields to repression. If it does not yield, then no hysteria develops either; the discharge of sexual excitation for the most part removes the possibility of hysteria. It has become clear to me that various compulsive movements represent a substitute for the discontinued movements of masturbation (1998, 648).

Makari asserts that it was not until 1899, when working on Dora, that Freud thought up a new two-stage model, based on masturbation, which he sketched in a letter to Fliess (9 Dec. 1899). At the lowest stage, there is autoeroticism—"a normal stage of self-directed childhood stimulation." There then follows the stage of alloeroticism, which can be homo- or alloerotic. Hysteria is alloerotic, since it follows the path of identification with the loved one. The new model plays out itself in Freud's published case study of Dora, which Makari asserts boldly, *pace* most others, is not a work in which the Oedipus complex is being showcased, but instead, through emphasis on excessive masturbation and its sudden cessation, shows continuity with Freud's take of trauma theory (1998, 655-60).

Thus, the *ad-baculum* tack is unpersuasive.

Taking Inventory

The arguments of Sharff et al., Kupfersmid, Masson, and Simon typify some of the many problems facing psychoanalysts that assign etiological significance to the Oedipus complex in the manner of Freud. Assignation of etiological significance, however, is question-begging, as it is not evidence of etiological significance. Adherents of the Oedipus complex need to come to terms with the numerous sharp criticisms, given over the years.

One common line of defense by some adherents is to argue for the universality of a (roughly) general Oedipal pattern, but cross-cultural variability of how it plays out. That is the line for instance taken by Malinowski, according to Jones, in Malinowski's famous study of the Trobriand islanders (1985). For Malinowski, in keeping with matriarchal nature of Trobriand society, it is not the father that is a sexual rival, for a father's status is not much more than a nursemaid, but the maternal uncle.[27] The chief difficulty is that assignation of cross-cultural variability merely dodges the issue of proving the universality of the general pattern. How can one be sure, for instance, that there are not numerous exceptions to the particular manifestation of the general pattern in a particular culture?

A second defense is "redefinitional."[28] That is the approach of Klein, for example, who spoke of the "Oedipal situation," not the Oedipus complex. Her reason is that the super-ego begins to function during the oral stage, much earlier than Freud thought, so it cannot be the heir to the Oedipus complex. At every stage of libidinal organization, children introject libidinal objects—the first object being the mother's breast—and, thus, the super-ego forms early and over time (Klein, 1945). Loewald (1979), who wishes to come up with an account of the Oedipus complex that is agreeable to both traditional and non-traditional psychoanalysts, also takes the redefinitional approach. The Oedipus complex is not something that people experience in a certain maturational stage of life and that gets resolved or fails to get resolved, but something—involving drives, objects, and inner representations—that waxes and wanes during different life stages.

A third, more common line of defense by psychoanalysts is to take the complex non-literally—i.e., metaphorically or heuristically. Poland, for example, speaks of the Oedipus complex as a singular "model metaphor for development"—i.e., the playing out of love, hate, and cross-generational struggle. For Poland, Sophocles' Oedipus is "a tale of humanities (*sic*) struggle shaped by the power of outside others, the individual defined by the influences of intersubjective forces" (561 and 564). The problem can be spelled out thus. Metaphors are figures of speech, where a term or phrase—e.g., "Oedipus complex"—is applied to another to which it does not straightforwardly apply—"the playing out of love, hate, and cross-generational struggle"—for the sake of suggesting a resemblance. Precisely what work does the metaphor do in the direction of scientific clarity or understanding? That question must be answered, for metaphor in science, though often needed at some level of explication, generally does more to obscure or diminish than to clarify or enhance understanding.

As I see things, what is particularly problematic for Freudian psychoanalysis is the centrality of sexuality and of the Oedipus complex. Freud makes several contentious claims about human sexuality and the Oedipus complex.

I begin by listing some claims regarding human sexuality.

S_1: Infants have a robust sexual life (e.g., 1915, *S.E.*, XV: 208).

S_2: Adults construct several barriers for sexual expression that do not exist for children (1915, *S.E.*, XV: 208).

S_3: Human sexuality is diphasic and that is peculiar to human animals (1923, *S.E.*, XVIII: 246).

S_4: Both sexes view masculinity to be superior to femininity (1924, *S.E.*, XIX: 177-8).

S_5: A child's mother is his/her first seducer (1940, *S.E.*, XXIII: 188).

S_6: A child's first object-choice is incestual (i.e., the mother) (1925, *S.E.*, XX: 37; 1926, *S.E.*, XX: 213).
S_7: All humans are constitutionally bisexual (1923, *S.E.*, XIX: 31).
S_8: Humans, greatly dependent on their parents, spend an inordinate amount of time in nurture (1924, *S.E.*, XIX: 208).

Of these four claims, S_1 and S_2 seem unproblematic.[29] S_3 and S_4 are questionable and question-begging—i.e., answers to them depend on the veracity of the Oedipus complex. S_5 and S_6 too seem unproblematic, *pace* Fromm, insofar as the intimacy between mother and child is sexual in the broad Freudian sense of "sexual" and, thus, intimacy cannot have but some seductive effect on the newborn child. S_7 is biologically unfounded. Biology shows that all humans are biological females and maleness is only chromosomally added alter to the mix in some cases. Yet if we take Freud to be speaking in a manner that echoes commonly accepted conventions of speech and not biologically, which is just what Freud says, then the claim is sensible: Masculinity and femininity merely connote tendencies toward activity and passivity vis-à-vis sexual activities (1940, *S.E.*, XXIII: 188). S_8 is beyond dispute. Overall, S_1 and S_8 are important claims, to which I shall return.

Next, there are Freud's claims specifically related to the Oedipus complex. I skip over peculiarities of the male and female complexes that should be familiar to readers by now.

OC_1: The Oedipus complex is universal (1931, *S.E.*, XXI: 251).
OC_2: Oedipal resolution is needed for normal psychosexual development (1923, *S.E.*, XVIII: 245-6).
OC_3: The Oedipus complex is the nucleus of all neuroses (1917, *S.E.*, XVI: 337; 1919, *S.E.*, XVII: 193, 204; 1926, *S.E.*, XX: 223).
OC_4: The super-ego is the heir to the Oedipus complex in normal adults (1923, *S.E.*, XVIII: 247; 1923, *S.E.*, XIX: 36).
OC_5: The Oedipus complex is the cornerstone/shibboleth of psychoanalysis (VII: 1905, *S.E.*, 226n1 and 1923, *S.E.*, XVIII: 247).
OC_6: Bisexuality complicates Oedipal resolution (1923, *S.E.*, XIX: 32).
OC_7: There is a phylogenetic correlate to the ontogenetic Oedipus complex (1913, *S.E.*, XIII: 140-6).

OC_1 through OC_6 can be taken together, as they speak to the correctness of the Oedipus complex. OC_7, I have argued, is hokum.

Even for those persons that endorse the etiological significance of the Oedipus complex in psychopathology justification is difficult. For instance, Shapiro (1977, 576-7), who maintains that the Oedipus complex is at the heart of the neuroses as well as "severe ego pathology," concedes that verification of the complex is problematic.

Grant mentions that Oedipal themes occur in numerous writers, among them, Corneille, Dryden, Voltaire, Holderin, Orff, Stravinsky, Gide, and Conteau. He also offers the evidence of Oedipal themes in myths from Greece, Finland, Ukraine, and Java (Grant, 1986).

Prevalence of Oedipal themes in literature and myths is not proof of universality however. What need to be shown are sexual diphasism and the links both of the Oedipus complex to all the various sorts of neuroses and of Oedipus-complex resolution to super-ego development. It is in just those areas, however, that evidence of universality is severely wanting.

Bemporad, following Freud's claims S_1 (implicitly) and S_8 (explicitly), argues biologically for Oedipal universality. The behavioral complexity in primates is in inverse proportion to their time in childhood nurture. The impulse to procreate occurs relatively fast, whereas other aspects need more nurturance and guidance. The process is guided by regulator genes.

> The result is that because of prolonged childhood our early sexual drives are directed toward those figures who also satisfy our dependency needs and who are so superior in strength and independence that these fledgling desires are doomed to frustration. Here is the biological rendition of the tragedy of the Oedipus complex: that we are programmed to desire the unavailable love object, the opposite sex parent, because of the unevenness of our genetic program, which apparently did not foresee the creation of so complicated a being who required inordinate lengths of time to reach maturity (1995, 498-9).

Unfortunately, though S_1 and S_8 are needed conditions for the universality of the Oedipus complex, they are not sufficient. Moreover, how is lusting for the opposite-sex parent biologically programmed? Bemporad assumes a sort of phylogenic-driven inheritance of acquired characteristics that Freud employed and was vehemently rejected by his contemporaries.

Overall, the difficulty is the centrality of the Oedipus complex in Freudian psychoanalysis—i.e., Freud's all-or-nothing approach to the Oedipus complex. Insensitive to criticisms and inflexible in his thinking, Freud it is safe to say was muleheaded.

What is my approach in this defense of Freud? The Oedipus complex is plainly not salvageable in the manner of shibboleth and certainly not without substantial redefinition.

I begin, from the perspective of a defense, rather catastrophically. I think that none of the OC claims—all of which make sense only in universal form—are salvageable, so I turn instead to the S claims, embraced by Freud.

Of the S claims, I believe that only S_1 and S_8, claims not peculiar to Freud, are universal and true. Yet the extraordinary length of human nurture in the state of dependency on the parents and the robustness of childhood sexuality make it plausible that infancy in many cases literally is a period of seduction (both mother or primary caregiver and child as mutual seducers), that mutual seduction in such cases leads to lifelong erotic bonds, that the strength of such bonds often leads sexual tension between a child and a parent or between a child and other siblings, and that clinging to or sharp and hasty severance of such bonds is often etiologically linked to later psychopathology. Because of those "plausibilities," it does not seem strange to speak of the etiological significance of certain "Oedipal tensions" in psychosexual development and psychopathology, but not of an "Oedipus complex"—e.g., Freud's delineations of male, female, and complete Oedipus complexes; his claim to their universality; and his insistence that failed resolution results in psychopathology, while proper resolution results in the super-ego. Yet "Oedipal tensions" does allow for instances of father or mother hatred as well as instances of penis envy and castration anxiety that might play out themselves pathologically.

Yet to argue for "Oedipal tensions," which amounts to acceptance of a smidgen of the universal claims to which Freud was committed, is plainly not a matter of accepting the universality of a rough, general Oedipal pattern. It is also not a matter of redefining "Oedipus complex," for the term, I think, is best left as Freud meant it to be. It is, however, more than taking "Oedipus complex" in some vague, malleable metaphorical sense out of respect to the "old master." In arguing for Oedipal tensions, I have merely endorsed two of the S claims Freud formally endorsed. Yet that allows great flexibility in approaching particular situations—especially in the clinic. It also allows us to take Freud's analysis of certain types of psychopathology seriously in essays such as "A Special Type of Object Choice Made by Men" (1910) and "On the (Universal) Tendency to Debasement in the Sphere of Love" (1912) in cases of extreme mother-attachment.

In summary, Freud's Oedipus complex is more canard than shibboleth. Nonetheless, we need not thus reject all Freud's insights into human sexuality and psychopathology on account of that. We must acknowledge that he—in spite of the untenability of the Oedipus complex as a universal phenomenon—and other early pioneers made significant contributions to our understanding of human psychosexuality and psychopathology, sexually rooted, through key insights, not all of which were universal in application.

Notes

1. A relatively recent critique that has drawn many impassioned replies is that of Bornstein (2001). For Freud's account of his own isolation on turning away from brain anatomy, see his letter to Jung, 2 Sept. 1807 (Freud, 1961).

2. I suspect too that there are a very large number of would-be critics that find the Oedipus complex so outrageous that either it is beneath them to respond formally to it or they decline to respond to it for fear of reviving an untenable, moribund view.

3. A caveat is in order. The critical literature, from Freud's day to our own, is too vast for me to do it justice. My reference to it, thus, is selective.

4. This finds confirmation in dreams (1900, *S.E.*, V: 452).

5. In "A Child Is Being Beaten," Freud suggests a general principle for perversion. Perverts exhibit both sadism and masochism, which is sadism directed toward the self,

because of perceived inferiority and guilt. First, there is a regression to the anal/sadistic stage. Second, there is a transformation of sadism into masochism, which is also narcissistic—a transformation made possible by a weakness of genital organization. Last, there is a strong sense of guilt, which seems to be a scar-like formation, due to inferiority, that sets itself over the ego and acts as a critical agency (1919, *S.E.*, XVII: 193-4).

6. In cases where there are siblings, it is not uncommon for a boy to substitute his sister as his love-object to replace his faithless mother. Likewise, a girl may take an elder brother as a love-object or may substitute her younger sister for the baby she had wished to have from her father (1917, *S.E.*, XVI: 334).

7. This is usually carried out verbally by the boy's father (1940, *S.E.*, XXIII: 190).

8. Freud's use of "destroyed" instead of "repressed" took his disciples by surprise. See, e.g., Ernest Jones, 1957, 259.

9. An abnormally developed super-ego is in large part responsible for pathology (1926, *S.E.*, XX: 223).

10. See also 1933, *S.E.*, XXII: 66.

11. Defiant self-assertiveness often leads to a homosexual object-choice.

12. Women also have greater narcissism and shame than men. The task of plaiting and weaving, a habit of women, is a result of the configuration of pubic hair that conceals genitals. He adds, "If you reject this idea as fantastic and regard my belief in the influence of lack of a penis on the configuration of femininity as an idée fixe, I am of course defenceless" (1933, S.E., XXII: 132).

13. This is contrary to what Freud said in *Introductory Lectures*.

14. Otto Rank once argued for intrauterine life as the origin of the Oedipus complex. Melanie Klein said it originate in the first year of life. Simon, 1991, 643.

15. Human bisexuality was suggested to Freud by physician and one-time friend Wilhelm Fliess.

16. The result of Freud's purchase of biological recapitulationism—the view that individual embryological development (ontogeny) retraces the same developmental pattern of its species (phylogeny). Recapitulationism found its strongest expression in the work of Ernst Haeckel, a contemporary of Freud who proposed it as a "biogenic law," expressed succinctly and famously: "ontogeny recapitulates phylogeny."

17. Driven by the research/speculations of Darwin, Atkinson, Frazer, and Robertson Smith (1913, S.E., XIII: 125-6 and 131-9).

18. That is indicative of strength in numbers.

19. In "Psycho-Analysis," Freud says that the main taboos of totemism—not to kill the tribal ancestor and not to marry a woman from one's own clan—correspond precisely to the two Oedipal wishes—to kill one's father and marry one's mother (1923, *S.E.*, XVIII: 253).

20. Freud recognized the opposition of biologists to his Lamarckianism, but insisted on the need of acquired characteristics for his phylogenetic story.

21. In "An Infantile Neurosis," his most complete and important case-study, Freud says the Oedipus complex is one of several phylogenetically inherited schemata, where the impressions of actual experience are derived. The picture is quasi-Kantian as it speaks of inborn mental schemata, but unlike Kant, Freud's schemata are precipitates of early human history (1918, *S.E.*, XVII: 119).

22. Roazen writes of this primal deed, "Freud seems not quite able to accept his own theory of the power of psychic realities; since he had not completely convinced himself

of the strength of fantasies, he had to have a 'real' trauma, a 'real' murder of the primal father" (Roazen, 1968, 155).

23. Jung notes that the fervor with which Freud clung to and asked Jung to cling to the Oedipus complex smacked of unconscious religiosity (Jung, 1983, 173-4).

24. There is perhaps good reason not to take him at his word, when it comes to observations of children. For instance, in the 1920 preface to the fourth edition of *Three Essays on the Theory of Sexuality* Freud writes: "None . . . but physicians who practice psycho-analysis can have any access whatever to this sphere of knowledge or any possibility of forming a judgement that is uninfluenced by their own dislike and prejudices. If mankind had been able to learn from a direct observation of children, these three essays could have remained unwritten" (1905, VII: *S.E.,* 133). Also, in "Femininity," recall he said his observations of children were merely the stories told by adults in therapy (1933, *S.E.*, XXII: 120-10).

25. Clark makes a similar mistake in stating "Freud generalized from his own experience and argued that the story of Oedipus has been prominent in Western society for many centuries because it represents the central psychological drama of *all* human beings"(Clark, 2009, 234).

26. This is characteristic of Kleinian approaches to psychoanalysis.

27. Strictly speaking, Malinowski takes that as a refutation of the Oedpus complex. Jones (1925) has stood in defense of Freud by arguing that this proves only a defection of fatherly feelings.

28. Many redefinitional approaches, like those of many object-relation theorists, are shifts so radical from that of Freud that "Oedipus complex" seems to be a misnomer. Marsha Levy-Warren's approach (2008) is one instance.

29. We now know that masturbation occurs in the womb. See e.g., Chalker, 2000.

References

Bemporad, Jules, "*Oedipus Rex* and Oedipus Complex," *Journal of the American Academy of Psychoanalysis,* 23(3), 1995, 493-500.

Bornstein, Robert F. "The Impending Death of Psychoanalysis," *Psychoanalytic Psychology,* Vol. 18, No. 1, 2001, 3-20.

Chalker, Rebecca, *The Clitoral Truth: The Secret World at Your Fingertips* (New York: Seven Stories Press, 2000).

Clark, Margaret, "Suppose Freud had Chosen Orestes Instead," *Journal of Analytical Psychology,* Vol. 54, 2009, 233-52.

Devereaux, G. "Why Oedipus Killed Laius: A Note on the Complementary Oedipus Complex," *International Journal of* Psychoanalysis, 34; 1953, 132-41.

Fairbairn, W.R.D. *An Objects Relations Theory of Personaility* (New York: Basic Books, 1954).

Fairbairn, W.R.D. *Psychoanalytic Studies of the Personality* (London: Routledge and Kegan Paul, 1952).

Freud, Sigmund, *The Standard Edition of the Complete Psychological Works of Sigmund Freud*, Vols. I-XXIV, ed. and trans. James Strachey (London: The Hogarth Press, 1976).

Freud, Sigmund, *Letters of Sigmund Freud,* ed. Ernst L. Freud, trans. Tania and James Stern (New York: Basic Books, Inc, 1961)

Fromm, Eric, *Sigmund Freud's Mission* (London: Allen & Unwin, 1959).

Grant, Michael, *Myths of the Greeks and Romans* (New York: Mentor, 1986).

Jones, Ernest, "Mother Right and Sexual Ignorance of Savages," *International Journal of Psychoanalysis*, VI (2), 1925, 109-30.

Jones, Ernest Jones, *The Life and Work of Sigmund Freud,* vol. 3 (New York: Basic Books, 1957).

Jung, C.G. *Memories, Dreams, Reflections* (London: Fontana Paperbacks, 1983).

Klein, Melanie, "The Oedipus Complex in the Light of Early Anxieties," *International Journal of Psycho-Analysis,* 26, 1945, 11-33.

Kupfersmid, Joel, "The 'Defense' of Sigmund Freud," *Psychotherapy,* Vol. 29, No. 2, 1992, 275-90.

Kupfersmid, Joel, "Does the Oedipus Complex Exist?" *Psychotherapy,* Vol. 32, No. 4, 1995, 535-47.

Laplanch Jean, and J.-B. Pontalis, *The Language of Psychoanalysis* (New York: W.W. Norton & Company, 1973).

Loewald, Hans, "The Waning of the Oedipus Complex," *Journal of the American Psychoanalytic Association*, 1979, 751-75.

Lerner, Howard D., "Psychodynamic Perspectives," *Handbook of Clinical* Psychology, ed. Michel Herson and Alan M. Gross (Hoboken, NJ: J. Wiley & Sons, 2008).

Levy-Warren, Marsha, "Wherefore the Oedipus Complex in Adolescence? Its Relevance, Evolution, and Appearance in Treatment," *Studies in Gender and Sexuality,* 9, 2008, 328-48.

Makari, George J., "Between Seduction and Libido: Sigmund Freud's Masturbation Hypotheses and the Realignment of his Etiologic Thinking, 1897-1905," *Bulletin of the History of Medicine,* 72.4, 1998, 638-62.

Malinowski, Bronislaw, *Sex and Repression in Savage Society* (The University of Chicago Press, 1985).

Masson, Jeffrey Moussaieff, *The Assault on the Truth* (New York: Penguin Books, 1984).

Masson, Jeffrey Moussaieff, *The Complete Letters of Sigmund Freud to Wilhelm Fliess, 1887-1904* (Cambridge: The Belknap Press, 1985).

Poland, Warren, "Oedipal Complexes, Oedipal Schemas," *American Imago*, Vol. l64, No. 4, 1997, 561-5.

Roazen, Paul, *Freud: Political and Social Thought* (New York: Alfred A. Knopf, 1968).

Rusbridger, Richard, "Elements of the Oedipus Complex: A Kleinian Account," *International Journal of Psychoanalysis*, 85, 2004, 731-48.
Scharff, D.E., and J.S. Scharff, *Object-Relations Family Therapy* (Northvale, NJ: A.J. Aronson, 1987).
Shapiro, Theodore. "Oedipal Distortions in Severe Character Pathologies: Developmental and Theoretical Considerations," *Psychoanalytic Quarterly,* 46, 1977, 559-79.
Simon, Bennett, "Is the Oedipus Complex Still the Cornerstone of Psychoanalysis? Three Obstacles to Answering the Question," *Journal of the American Psychoanalytic Association,* 39, #3, 1991, 641-68.
Triplett, Hal, "The Misnomer of Freud's 'Seduction Theory,'" *Journal of the History of Ideas,* 2005, 647-65.
Winnicott, D.W. "Ego Integration in Child Development," *The Maturational Processes and the Facilitation Environment: Studies in the Theory of Emotional Development* (New York: International Universities, 1965), 56-63.

Chapter 2
The Oedipus Complex
It Made No Sense Then, It Makes No Sense Now

Joel Kupfersmid
Private Practice

FOR SIGMUND FREUD, TO BE CONSIDERED A TRUE PSYCHOANALYST, one had to believe in the truth of the Oedipus complex (1905, *S.E.*, VII: 135-244). The nature of the Oedipus complex is the foundation for many other critical concepts in psychoanalytic theory. For the species, "Freud traced religion, civilization, law, morality . . . to man's reactions to his conflicts over the primordial Oedipus complex" ($Jones_1$, 354). The Oedipus complex is considered "the most important segment of Freud's developmental explanatory scheme" (Fisher *et al.*, 1996, 400). How the Oedipus complex is resolved affects each person's moral beliefs, potential for psychopathology, and how neurosis is manifested, if present (1913, *S.E.*, XIII: 1-161).

Freud in *Totem and Taboo*, following the recapitulationism of his day, gave an anthropological explanation for the origins of the Oedipus complex (i.e., primal horde). He presented a biological explanation to account for the content of sexual thoughts in children (ontogeny recapitulates phylogeny) and its universal transmission of the images and ideas (inheritance of acquired ideas). Also, he claimed the standard clinical method of psychoanalysis (interpretation of a patient's free associations to parapraxes and dreams) could uncover the significance the Oedipus complex played in explaining an individual's personality and psychopathology.

In this chapter I argue for the following points. First, there is no convincing anthropological evidence to support Freud's rationale for the origins of the Oedipus complex. Second, even if anthropological evidence supports Freud's view, there is no known biological mechanism to account for the transmission of oedipal thoughts throughout the species for thousands of years. Third, even if Freud's anthropological and biological evidence is tenable, the clinical method used to uncover these universal thoughts and images (i.e., free association of slips and dreams) is empirically vacuous. Consequently, Freud's explanations for law, morality, religion, and psychological development of individuals and psychopathology are seriously flawed.

Where does that leave psychoanalysis? One can reject the existence of the Oedipus complex, and all its implications, and still be a psychoanalytically orientated therapist or theoretician.

What is the Oedipus Complex?

In no single publication does Freud outline all aspects of the Oedipus complex. There is general agreement that Freud considered the Oedipus complex universal to the human species with specific fantasies becoming activated when children are between four through six years old. According to Freud's intrapsychic dynamic model, at this period in life children have no sense of morality (i.e., superego formation), because it is only with the resolution of the Oedipus complex children develop (literally, acquire) a sense of morality.

Likewise, at this period of life the development of the ego is in its very early stages. The child's intrapsychic being is primarily id. The id seeks instant gratification for its sexual and aggressive urges. This mental apparatus cannot delay gratification, cannot think rationally, and does not have a sense of past or future. With only a weakly developed ego, there are minimal inhibitions on children's impulses to fulfill their sexual and aggressive desires.

Prior to the initiation of the Oedipus complex, children primarily seek oral and anal pleasures. With the advent of the Oedipus complex, the desire for sexual pleasures predominates. For both sexes the onset of the Oedipus complex marks the desire to have sexual intercourse with the opposite-sex parent as well as feelings of hostility towards the same-sex parent that is perceived as a rival (Brenner, 1957, 171-192; English *et al.,* 1958, 355; and Paul Kline, 1981, 130-168).

Freud (1917, *S.E.*, Vol. XVI: 303-338 and 1931, *S.E.*, XXI: 223-43) maintained it is typical for children to masturbate. When children reach approximately four years old there is a species-specific fantasy they experience while masturbating—the desire to have sexual intercourse with the opposite- sex parent. Additionally, children acquire inherited knowledge of the sexual anatomy of the opposite sex.

The Oedipus complex takes on a different pattern for boys than for girls. A male child worries that his father will discover his desire for sexual relations with his mother and castrate him. Castration anxiety in young boys is a form of instinctual knowledge. This fear becomes activated whether the young male sees a vagina, is actually threatened with castration, or is spontaneously aroused in the absence of such experiences. As a consequence of this fear, the boy abruptly represses his sexual desires for his mother. A female child believes she has been castrated and wishes for the return of her penis (penis envy). This wish is replaced by the desire to be impregnated by her father. Only gradually does the young girl relinquish her sexual interest in having her father's baby (1925, *S.E.*, XX: 7-74).

The acquisition of moral values via superego formation marks the resolution of the Oedipus complex for both male and female children. Children of both sexes reason that, since their parents love each other, if they act like their opposite-sex parent (identification with the aggressor), the same-sex parent will like them better too. The moral values children internalize are predominately determined by what values their parents—especially the parent of same sex—praise and punish. With the advent of the superego, children are developmentally ready for socialization.

This conceptualization is fraught with difficulties at the most basic level. If the Oedipus complex were true, then for thousands of years, across all societies, there should be evidence of massive complaints expressed by parents (and, more recently, by pre-school teachers) that their uncivilized and impulsive child was (1) aggressively attacking the same-sex parent out of jealousy and rage, (2) being sexually provocative towards the opposite-sex parent, and (3) frequently screaming in fear that their penis will be cut off (for boys) or complaining that it has been cut off and that they want it back (for girls). This phenomenon would be especially noticeable for brothers and sisters who bathe together in their oedipal years. Yet, those concerns in any society, at any time in human history or prehistory, are non-existent or, at best, minimal.

The Oedipus complex also requires that all children have instinctual knowledge about the act of sexual intercourse, that (at least for female children) sexual intercourse causes conception (apparently, even for a pre-pubescent female), and that (for boys) fathers punish male rivals with castration. Children of both sexes, likewise, "know" that the presence of a vigina means castration has taken place. Studies of three to six years olds have failed to confirm that even a small minority have any of this knowledge (Kreitler et al., 1966, 363-378, and Moore et al., 1971, 42-61). This limitation was known to Freud. One of his colleagues, the highly respected German psychiatrist Albert Moll, noted in his book The Sexual Life of the Child (1908), "Freud's failure to investigate the sexual life of children directly, and his reliance instead on the suggestive questioning of adults was the cause of Freud's extreme views about the role of sexual factors in neurosis" (Webster, 1995, 358). Freud (1909, S.E., X: 6) responded to this criticism in print one year later, "I have for many years been urging my pupils and my friends to collect observations of the sexual life of children—the existence of which has as a rule been cleverly overlooked or deliberately denied." Psychoanalysts have continued to overlook cleverly or deliberately deny direct investigations of children's sexual thoughts for over 100 years.

Freud could be wrong about the anthropological, biological, and clinical evidence for the Oedipus complex and still have one basic premise correct—that children's morality is a result of their internalization of their parents' values, especially those of the same-sex parent. There is a difference of opinion on this topic among researchers. On the one hand, Fisher and Greenberg (1996, 155) believe there is evidence supporting Freud's position on this matter, but note that it is not fear, but parental warmth that leads to the internalization of the same-sex parent's values. On the other hand, Harris' review of the literature (xx and 337) finds no empirical confirmation. She notes there is little support that *either* parent has much influence in determining their child's values. Rather, the peer group to which one's desires to belong has the highest relationship to shaping one's moral attitudes.

There are potentially more serious problems with the developmental implications of the Oedipus complex. For many Freudians, these inferences will not be well-received. Consider the following hypothetical scenario. What if two large groups of families were studied and all relevant variables, except one, were the same. In the first group, all children between the ages of four and six years old had sexual relations with their opposite-sex parent. In the second group none of the children experienced incest. Apparently, the fantasies of children in the first group would be fulfilled with none of the male children, much to their relief, experiencing castration. For the female children, their sexual desires would be granted without impregnation. Presumably, psychoanalytic theory would predict that, as adults, children in the first group would have much *less* psychopathology than those in the second group!

In Freud's developmental theory (1917, *S.E.*, XVI: 336), the Oedipal stage is followed by a period latency. Sexual desires for the opposite-sex parent are repressed. Puberty marks the resurgence of (now unconscious) sexual desires for the opposite-sex parent (the return of the repressed). Following the logic of Freud's intra psychic model (where gratification of id desires are pleasurable), psychoanalytic theory might well predict that the reaction of female adolescents impregnated by their fathers (thus satisfying the girl's desire for sexual union with the opposite-sex parent *and* having his baby) would be joyous. The mothers might not share their daughter's enthusiasm however. Having gratified two of the most potent desires a girl has, psychoanalytic developmental psychology predicts these adolescents, as adults, should be generally well adjusted!

Recent studies of sexually abused children provide some data on the two scenarios. A meta-analysis of seven nationally representative samples, comparing those with a sexual abuse history versus those without this history, concludes there is a low incidence of harmful psychological effects of sexual abuse in the normal population for both sexes (Rind *et al.*, 1997). Those findings, however, have come under intense criticism. Even if these results are wrong, and the psychological repercussions of child sexual abuse is very damaging, the above two predictions may still be incorrect based on the findings of Paolucci, Genuis, and Violato's meta-analysis (37 studies) on samples of those sexually abused as children (2001). Each study measured one or more of seven psychological difficulties associated with being abused (e.g., depression, PTSD, suicide, etc). The authors report there is no difference in symptom severity one experiences on any of these seven dependent variables for type of sexual abuse (genital penetration vs. non-penetration), age when abuse occurred, number of incidences of abuse, or relationship of perpetuator (parent vs. non-family member) to victim.

These findings suggest that the predictions of psychoanalytic theory (at least, the ones I inferred) are wrong. Likewise, if psychoanalytic theory predicts the *exact opposite* of the above (i.e., incest does pervasive harm, those molested as children in their oedipal years by the opposite-sex parent become more disturbed than those not molested, or those molested at a different age, etc.) this, too, would most likely be unsubstantiated.

The Invention of the Oedipus Complex

For the majority of the last 100 years, Freud's report of how he "discovered" the Oedipus complex (the "classical" view) was the accepted account. This version was challenged by Masson (1984, xxiii-xxxi) in his popular book *The Assault on the Truth* (the "externalist" view) and, more recently, by Krull (1986, 68-70) and Kupfersmid (1992, 1993, and 1995) (the "internalist" view).

The classic position begins with Freud's Seduction theory (1925, *S.E.*, XX: 7-74 and 1933, *S.E.*, XXII: 7-182), which posits repression of sexual molestation in childhood causes neurosis. On this early view of neurosis, the lifting of this repression culminates in a therapeutic cure. During this time Freud used a precursor to free association, the "pressure technique" (1986, *S.E.*, III: 191-221). Freud would place his hand on the patient's forehead and *insist* all thoughts and images that become conscious be reported. Freud would continue with this procedure until satisfied that the patient reported "true" memories surround their symptoms. Freud was well aware many critics believed his method suggested to his patients sexual molestation. He addressed these concerns in his publications at the time.

The most commonly accepted reason for Freud's change is that he somehow discovered that the reports of molestation by his patients were fantasies. Yet he adamantly denied he suggested these events (1925, *S.E.*, XX: 7-74). Others, for instance Bennett Simon (1991), believe a second factor, his self-analysis, contributed to Freud's change of heart. The essence of the classic position is that Freud had an epiphany either in his discovery that his patients were fantasizing or from his self analysis (or both), and the Oedipal complex *immediately* replaced the Seduction theory as the explanation for neurosis.

There are several problems with the classic view. First, Freud never presented any explicit criteria by which he differentiated a patient's sexual fantasies from that of real sexual abuse. So, how did Freud do it? In one of his last articles (1931, *S.E.*, XXI: 223-43) on treatment, he affirmed that for some adults their psychological difficulties were a result of being sexual abused as a child, but he does not provide any specific guidelines on how a clinician is to distinguish such fantasies from reality. Second, in print, Freud gave five different reasons for why his thinking changed. An analysis of all five reasons suggests it is unlikely Freud strongly believed any were correct (1993). Third, at the time when Freud considered abandoning Seduction theory in favor of the Oedipus complex, he presented his reasons in writing to his best friend and confidant, Wilhelm Fliess (1985, 230-1). None of the reasons Freud gave in private to Fliess correspond to any reasons he presented in print. Fourth, if the Oedipus complex was a result of a discovery that his patients engaged in fantasy or was due to enlightenment during his self-analysis, then there should be evidence that Freud's belief in the supremacy of the Oedipus complex quickly supplanted his believe in the Seduction theory. Yet, the exact opposite is the case.

Freud's letter to Fliess in October of 1897 is the first indication that he believed his patients' reports were fantasies (1985, 230-1). However, Freud's letters to Fliess over the next several *years* showed him vacillating between the realities versus fantasies of his patients' reports of sexual abuse (1992). Additionally, it was not until the publication of *Three Essays on the Theory of Sexuality* in 1905 that Freud publicly retracted Seduction theory in favor of the Oedipus complex. That was very unusual behavior for Freud, who admitted to rushing into print many of his ideas before they were adequately tested (1925, *S.E.*, XIX: 243-258) and who had a history of being obsessed with establishing priority for his ideas (Sulloway, 1983, 467).

An alternative account, externalism, is presented by Masson (1984, 190-2), who argues that Freud's change of position originated from an external source—his intense desire to gain acceptance from the German-Austrian medical community.

The externalist view has three serious flaws. First, and foremost, is that there is no evidence that the Oedipus complex was any more accepted by Freud's medical peers than was the Seduction theory. Second, throughout Freud's career he took positions that were unpopular with the current views in medicine, and with his own supporters (e.g., death instinct, inheritance of acquired ideas). Third, there is no convincing evidence that Freud was shunned by the medical community. He continued to receive referrals from his fellow physicians and had little difficulty getting his papers published in medical journals (Kupfersmid, 1992, 297-307).

A third view that addresses the defects of the classical and externalist views is internalism. According to internalism, there only one major factor that changed Freud's mind about the veracity of his patients' reports of sexual abuse--the implications the validity of Seduction theory had for Freud and his family. Freud believed he and his sisters suffered from hysteria. He writes to Fliess that acceptance of Seduction theory means that "my own father was one of these perverts and is responsible for the hysteria of my brother...and those of several younger sisters" (Masson, 1985, 230-1). Regarding the implication of Seduction theory for himself, Freud's primary biographer and member of his inner circle of confidants, Ernest Jones, reports that in May of 1897 Freud had a dream about his niece Hella.

> [Freud] *had* [emphasis added] to interpret [the dream] as covering a sexual wish towards his eldest daughter. . . . Four months after this, however, Freud had discovered the truth of the matter: that irrespective of incest wishes of parents towards their children . . . what he had to concern himself with was the general Oedipus complex of incest wishes of children towards their parents, characteristically towards the parent of the opposite sex (1953, 322).

For internalism, as a way to protect himself and his family against the obvious conclusion the Seduction theory implied, "the Oedipus complex *gradually* evolved as an acceptable defense (rationalization) that Freud could intellectually believe" (1992, 197).

The externalist view and the internalist view have two points in common. Both hold the Oedipus complex *gradually* displaced Freud's belief in real childhood seduction and both imply that he *invented* (probably unconsciously) the Oedipus complex, as opposed to having *discovered* a clinical phenomenon of fantasy in his patients.

Freud's Clinical Evidence for the Oedipus Complex

According to the classic view, the Oedipus complex was a result of insights Freud gained from analysis of patients, from his self analysis, or from both. Freud's "confirmation" of the Oedipus complex was from interpretations of his patients' dreams and parapraxes (slips of the tongue) through the method of free association. The veracity of the Oedipus complex, therefore, rests on the method of free association to reveal accurate information from adults about their thoughts and feelings when they were ages of four through six.

The capacity of free association to produce scientifically legitimate data is questioned by those inside and those outside analytic circles. "Psychoanalysts who witness the events of an analytic hour (. . .in the form of a transcript) have difficulty agreeing in their interpretation of these events" (Fisher *et al.*, 1996, 8). In a sleep study, subjects were awakened during REM sleep and their dreams were recorded. There was a negligible relationship between the contents reported by the subjects when awakened and that told to their psychoanalyst later that same day (Eysenck, 1985, 126).

The quintessential limitation with free association to discover the unconscious meaning of dreams and parapaxes, or anything else, is that (1) there is no evidence that just because an individual associates A to B that, therefore, there is some hidden intrapsychic relevance to this connection (Sand, 1988, 85-93), and (2) there are no guidelines for determining when the patient should halt their associations. They may be stopped any time the therapist believes they have "uncovered" something they consider meaningful (Grünbaum, 1984, 209). A more in-depth critique of this problem is presented in the section on free association and on dreams of this volume.

The difficulty within the psychoanalytic community to determine the veracity of their concepts and the efficacy of their techniques is exemplified in Otto Rank's theory of birth trauma. Rank, one of Freud's early disciples, published a book claiming that all anxiety in adults was caused by their experiences at birth. Freud did not initially express his views on this position. For months following Rank's book, many analysts uncovered birth trauma (apparently from interpreting their patients' free association) as a cause of their patient's anxieties. Soon after Freud publicly rejected the etiological significance of this trauma, reports of birth having causal significance ceased. This example exemplifies that in psychoanalysis appeal to authority determines what is "seen" as a causal agent and its clinical methods are impotent to generate scientifically creditable data even within the analytic community.

The problem of verification for psychoanalytic concepts was acknowledged over 50 years ago by two of its most ardent proponents. Ernest Jones (1953, 129) recognized that "dissensions concerning psychoanalysis are even harder to resolve than those in other fields of science where it is not so easy to continue re-interpreting data in terms of some personal prejudice." Former director of the Research of London Institute of Psychoanalysis, Edward Glover (1952, 403-9), has cautioned analysts that "failing corroborative evidence all we are entitled to conclude . . . is that the analyst convinced himself that his interpretation was suitable or plausible, not that it was necessarily correct."

To believe that adults can accurately recall their thoughts and feelings as five year olds (while masturbating, no less) strains credibility. To believe that somehow the interpretation of adult's free associations comes close to the truth for these events is even more problematic. As previously noted, Freud (1909, *S.E.*, X: 6) claimed he repeatedly requested that psychoanalysts study children directly, but his pleas have been ignored. However, Freud had six children whose sexual thoughts and feelings could directly be studied.

The closest Freud came to exploring the mind of a child was his case presentation of "Little Hans" (1909, *S.E.*, X: 3-147). Hans was a five year old who displayed a fear of horses. His father conducted the therapy, with Freud's guidance. Freud saw the child one time. Freud's account revealed that he strenuously tried to convince Hans, in accordance with Oedipus complex theory, that the anxiety of being bitten by a horse was a displaced fear of castration. Apparently, Hans was a stubborn child. He never indicated that he had sexual feelings for his mother, that he feared his father, or that castration was evident (Wolpe, 1989, and Sulloway, 1992). In Freud words, "Hans had to be told many things that he could not say himself, that he had to be presented with thoughts which he had so far shown no signs of possessing. . ." (1909, *S.E.*, X: 104). Thus, Freud's only direct clinical study of a child fails to confirm any important aspect of the Oedipus complex.

Genetic Account of the Oedipus Complex

Freud was aware that the interpretations of patients' dreams and slips were insufficient to explain why all children of the same age have the same sexual fantasies (for sexual intercourse with the opposite-sex parent), same fears or anxieties, (castration for boys; having been castrated for girls) and the same feelings (hatred or jealousy of the same-sex parent for both genders; for girls, penis envy and desire for impregnation by the father) regardless of personal experiences. He also had to explain how the content of these universal desires and feelings originated and are transmitted over the course of thousands of years.

Freud adopted two theories of prominent nineteenth century biologists for this purpose. Ernest Haeckel proposed that a fetus and a child repeat all developmental stages of the human race from its inception (i.e., "ontogeny recapitulates phylogeny"). As a result, Freud argued, children must have instinctual knowledge of sexuality gained by eons of past primitive adults. Haeckel's theory addressed the content of oedipal thoughts and feelings. Freud borrowed Lamarck's theory of inherence of acquired characteristics to account for the transmission of oedipal thoughts and feelings through the ages (Sulloway, 1983, 274-5).

Freud in *Totem and Taboo* first formally adopted Darwin's views, in *The Decent of Man,* that claims far back in human history primitive societies consisted of one dominant male and several adult females. Freud combined Darwin's claim with that of anthropologists James Atkinson's theory that many of the younger males banded together, killed the alpha male, and ate him. This allowed the young men to have sexual relations with all the females, all of which were the mothers of these men. Freud advanced that these males all feared their father, the dominate male. They, also, agreed that none would have sexual relations with their mother, even though they greatly desired this union. Freud concluded that this primal-horde theory explains the origin of the content of children's oedipal knowledge of sex, their sexual fantasies, and their fears. Lamarck's theory accounts for its transmission. These theories, in keeping with anthropologists James Frazer's popular book in Freud's time, *The Golden Bough*, also explain why there is a universal prohibition against incest.

Again, criticisms for Freud's views were evident in his time by both those outside and those inside psychoanalytic circles. By the beginning of the twentieth century, Haeckel's theory lost favor for lack of empirical verification. Freud's insistence on the veracity of Lamarck's theory is more interesting. At the end of the nineteenth century there was wide acceptance of Weismann's work that only genetic material (germ plasm) is inherited. Max Schur (1972,

473), Freud's personal physician, notes he and three others having close ties to Freud were unsuccessful in persuading him that Lamarck was wrong.

However, even if Lamarck were right, this would not have supported Freud's position on inheritance. Larmarck's theory states that *only acquired physical characteristics* of an organism are potentially transmitted. Freud postulated that *acquired thoughts and emotions* are passed on. Additionally, even if thoughts and feeling could somehow be inherited, Freud still had the monumental task of explaining how, out of billions of thoughts and feelings humans had over thousands of years, the specific thoughts and feelings inherent in the Oedipus complex were selected and transmitted. It would be a long stretch for Freud to invoke Darwin and claim that a child lusting after one parent and fearing physical retaliation by the other promotes survival of the fittest (Daly *et al.*, 1990).

Freud's primal-horde theory has been questioned since its inception. The Darwin-Atkinson claim that primitive humans lived in small tribes with one alpha male and several wives is, according to one of the leading American anthropologists in Freud's time, a mere guess (Kroeber, 1920, 48-55). The leading German anthropologist of Freud's day, Father Schmidt, notes that patricide or cannibalism was a "sheer impossibility" in primitive societies (Wallace, 1983, 113-172). The use of Frazer's accounts of the incest taboo among all primitives to bolster Freud's claims is unconvincing. His biographer, R. Downie, describes Frazer's anthropological evidence as a "collection of traveler's tales and the experience of a vivid imagination" (Thornton, 1984, 204).

Freud's arguments for the incest taboo have also been criticized more recently. First, there is no agreement that this taboo is universal (Daly *et al.*, 1990, and Demause, 1991). Even if such a taboo is widespread, Freud's logic is suspect. He reasons "since a taboo is to prohibit an action, there must be an unconscious desire to perform the behavior the taboo was established to prohibit" (Kupfersmid, 1995, 543).

> [T]he fact that a taboo is instituted does not necessarily mean that an innate desire to perform such an action exists. Many societies have prohibitions against wanton killing [and] stealing . . . but this does not prove that humans instinctively wish to kill or steal. Even if a taboo were an unconscious projection of a desire, it would still not demonstrate that children are the bearers of such a desire. Adults in all societies establish what is to be proscribed. Thus, an innate taboo would most likely indicate that adults desire to have sexual relations with their children, and not the other way around! (Kupfersmid, 1995, 544)

Freud's primal-horde theory piles many highly improbably events on top of one another. Nonetheless, this theory and other aspects of his Oedipus complex were, however, taken seriously by many anthropologists and hotly debated in the literature for over fifty years (Wallace, 1983, 113-172). More recently, there is little discussion of the Oedipus complex or Freud's position on the incest taboo (Wolf, 2004, 1-23).

Concluding Remarks

The conclusion I reached on the scientific validity of the Oedipus complex over 15 years ago remains unchanged. There is no convincing evidence (1) of a primal horde in our distant past, (2) that any sons at any time in human history banded together, killed their father, eat him, and made a no incest pack, and (3) that thoughts can be passed on through generations. Likewise, Freud never adequately explained how sexual knowledge all children inherent from adults in the primal horde could be so mistaken. In Freud's oedipal theory, all five year old girls desire impregnation by their fathers. Did the horde believe conception was common among pre-pubescent girls? Of greater concern is Freud's claim that children, in their oedipal years, believe the rectum is the birth canal (Freud's cloaca theory). But, he fails to account for (1) how adults in the primal horde, having observed thousands of births, kept confusing the anus with the vagina, and (2) how this misinformation was transmitted, uncorrected, from the distant past to the present. Even if the above were possible, the likelihood of free association to discover fantasies an individual had when masturbating at five years old defies creditability.

To be considered psychoanalytic in orientation, Freud insisted one must accept the validity of the Oedipus complex. This criterion has essentially been ignored by many high-profile psychoanalytic therapists. As previously noted, Freud's personal physician, Max Schur (1972) rejected the Oedipus complex yet considered himself a staunch supporter of psychoanalysis. One of the foremost authorities on the psychoanalysis of adolescents, Peter Blos, has denied that the Oedipus complex is central to all neuroses (Peter Blos, 1987, 425-441). Psychoanalysis Robert Fliess, son of Wilhelm Fliess, insisted "*no one is ever made sick by his fantasies*. Only traumatic *memories* in repression can cause neurosis" (1973, 212).

More recently, Drew Westen (1998), a well-respected academic with a Freudian orientation, reviewed the psychoanalytic literature and conducted a survey of psychodynamic-oriented clinicians across the country. His research suggests there are five tenants central to current thinking among these clinicians. The Oedipus complex is *not* one of these central beliefs, though the importance of early childhood in shaping personality is.

As stated at the beginning of this chapter, Freud's theory of morality, religion, and neuroses were conceptually tied to the Oedipus complex. If the views expressed here are essentially correct, then the Oedipus complex should be discarded. Likewise, the Freudian position on morality, religion, and neurosis would require extensive rethinking. Westen's review suggests this is taking place. May the Oedipus complex rest in peace!

References

Blos, Peter. "Freud and the Father Complex." *The Psychoanalytic Study of the Child*, 42, (1987), 425-441.

Brenner, Charles. *An Elementary Textbook of Psychoanalysis*. New York: Doubleday Anchor, 1957.

Daly, Martin and Margo Wilson. "Is Parent-Offspring Conflict Sex-Linked? Freudian and Darwinian Models." *Journal of Personality,* 58, (1990), 163-189.

Demause, Lloyd. "The Universality of Incest." *The Journal of Psychohistory,* 19, (1991), 123-164.

English, Horace and Ava English, *A Comprehensive Dictionary of Psychological and*

Psychoanalytic Terms. New York: Longmans, Green and Co., 1958.

Eysenck, Hans. *Decline and Fall of the Freudian Empire.* London: Penguin, 1985.

Fisher, Seymour and Greenberg, Roger. *The Scientific Creditability of Freud's Theories and Therapy*. New York: Basic Books, 1997.

Fisher, Seymour and Roger Greenberg, *Freud Scientifically Reappraised.* New York: John Wiley, 1996.

Fliess, Robert. *Symbol, Dreams, and Psychosis.* New York: International Universities Press, 1973.

Freud, Sigmund. "The Aetiology of Hysteria." In *The Standard Edition of the Complete Psychological Works of Sigmund Freud*, ed. and trans. James Strachey, London: The Hogarth Press, Vol. 3, 1896.

Freud, Sigmund. "Three Essays on Sexuality." In *The Standard Edition of the Complete Psychological Works of Sigmund Freud*, ed. and trans. James Strachey, London: The Hogarth Press, Vol. 7, 1905.

Freud, Sigmund. "Analysis of a Phobia in a Five-Year Old Boy." In *The Standard Edition of the Complete Psychological Works of Sigmund Freud*, ed. and trans. James Strachey, London: The Hogarth Press, Vol.10, 1909.

Freud, Sigmund. "Totem and Taboo." In *The Standard Edition of the Complete Psychological Works of Sigmund Freud*, ed. and trans. James Strachey, London: The Hogarth Press, Vol. 13, 1913.

Freud, Sigmund. "Introductory Lectures on Psycho-Analysis." In *The Standard Edition of the Complete Psychological Works of Sigmund Freud*, ed. and trans. James Strachey, London: The Hogarth Press, Vol. 16, 1917.

Freud, Sigmund. "An Autobiographical Study." In *The Standard Edition of the Complete Psychological Works of Sigmund Freud*, ed. and trans. James Strachey, London: The Hogarth Press, Vol. 20, 1925a.

Freud, Sigmund. "Some Psychological Consequences of the Anatomical Distinction between the Sexes." In *The Standard Edition of the Complete Psychological Works of Sigmund Freud*, ed. and trans. James Strachey, London: The Hogarth Press, Vol.19, 1925b.

Freud, Sigmund. "Female Sexuality." In *The Standard Edition of the Complete Psychological Works of Sigmund Freud*, ed. and trans. James Strachey, London: The Hogarth Press, Vol. 21, 1931.

Freud, Sigmund. "New Introductory Lectures on Psycho-Analysis." In *The Standard Edition of the Complete Psychological Works of Sigmund Freud*, ed. and trans. James Strachey, London: The Hogarth Press, Vol. 22, 1933.

Glover, Edward. "Research Methods in Psychoanalysis." *The International Journal of Psychoanalysis*, 33, (1952), 403-409.

Grünbaum, Adolf. *The Foundations of Psychoanalysis*. Berkeley, California: University of California Press, 1984.

Harris, Judith. *The Nurture Assumption*. New York: Free Press, 2009.

Jones, Ernest. *The Life and Work of Sigmund Freud*. New York: Basic Books, 1953.

Jones, Ernest. *The Life and Work of Sigmund Freud*. New York: Basic Books, 1955.

Jones, Ernest. *The Life and Work of Sigmund Freud*. New York: Basic Books, 1957.

Kline, Paul. *Fact and Fantasy in Freudian Theory*. New York: Methuen, 1981.

Kreitler, Hans and Schulamith Kreitler. "Children's Concepts of Sexuality and Birth." *Society for Research in Child Development*, 37 (1966), 363-378.

Kroeber, Alfred. "Totem and Taboo: An Ethnologic Psychoanalysis." *American Anthropologist*, 22, (1920), 48-55.

Krull, Marianne. *Freud and His Father*. New York: W. W. Norton, 1986.

Kupfersmid, Joel. "The 'Defense' of Sigmund Freud." *Psychotherapy*, 29 (1992), 297-309.

Kupfersmid, Joel. "Freud's Rationale for Abandoning the Seduction Theory." *Psychoanalytic Psychology*, 10, (1993), 275-290.

Kupfersmid, Joel. "Does the Oedipus complex Exist?" *Psychotherapy*, 32, (1995), 535-547.

Masson, Jeffrey. *The Assault on the Truth*. New York: Penguin Books, 1984.

Masson, Jeffrey. *The Complete Letters of Sigmund Freud to Wilhelm Fliess 1887-1904*. Cambridge, Massachusetts: Harvard University Press, 1985.

Moore, James and Diane Kendall. "Children's Concepts of Reproduction." *The Journal of Sex Research*, 7, (1971), 42-61.

Paolucci, Elizabeth, Mark Genuis, and Claudo Violato. "A Meta-Analysis of the Published Research on the Effects of Childhood Sexual Abuse." *The Journal of Psychology*, 135, (2001), 17-36.

Rind, Bruce, and Philip Tromovitch. "A Meta-analytic Review of Findings from National Samples on Psychological Correlates of Child Sexual Abuse." *The Journal of Sex Research*, 34, (1997), 237-255. .

Sand, Rosemarie. "Manifestly Fallacious." In *Unauthorized Freud*, ed. Fredrick Crews, New York: Viking Press, 1998.

Schur, Max. *Freud: Living and Dying*. New York: International Universities Press, 1972.

Simon, Bennett. "Is the Oedipus Complex Still the Cornerstone of Psychoanalysis? Three Obstacles to Answering the Question." *The Journal of the American Psychoanalytic Association,* 39 (1991), 641-668.
Sulloway, Frank. *Freud, Biologist of the Mind.* New York: Basic Books, 1983.
Sulloway, Frank. "Reassessing Freud's Case Histories." In *Freud and the History of Psychoanalysis*, ed. Tony Gelfand and John. Kerr, New York: Analytic Press, 1992.
Thornton, E.M. *The Freudian Fallacy.* New York: Dial Press, 1984.
Wallace, Edwin IV. *Freud and Anthropology.* New York: International Universities Press, 1983.
Webster, Richard. *Why Freud was Wrong.* New York: Basic Books, 1995.
Westen, Drew. "The Scientific Legacy of Sigmund Freud: Towards a Psychodynamically Informed Psychological Science." *Psychological Bulletin,* 124, (1998), 333-371.
Wolf, Arthur. "Introduction." In *Inbreeding, Incest, and the Incest Taboo*, ed. Arthur Wolf and William Durham, Stanford, California: Stanford University Press, 2004.
Wolpe, Joseph and Stanley Rachman. "Psychoanalytic Evidence: A Critique based on Freud's Case of Little Hans." In *Sigmund Freud: Critical Assessment Vol. 2*, ed. Lawrence Spuring. New York: Routledge, 1989.

Chapter 3
Reply to Dr. Holowchak

Joel Kupfersmid

Dr. Holowchak presents a well-organized and extensive account of Freud's published theorizing, previously scattered throughout the literature, on the Oedipus complex. This alone makes his chapter a worthwhile read.

We agree that the Oedipus complex is empirically vacuous as an explanation of neurosis and its phylogenic origins are "wish-based cockamamie" (2011, 9) on Freud's part. Dr. Holowchak has two reservations of my position (internal-threat view). First, he notes, "Kupfersmid focuses on proving the merits of his alternative explanation principally by showing that the two most popular explanations are implausible. That is not the same as advocating cogent evidence for his explanation". Second, he offers a "plausible non-threat based alternative" (2011, 9-14) by Makari. Due to space limitations, the rest of this paper will primarily address the first of these two issues.

Why Criticize Freud and Masson

Dr. Holowchak is correct. Discrediting a theory does not substantiate an alternative one. There is, however, a good reason for demonstrating flaws in the prevailing viewpoints. Thomas Kühn notes in *The Structure of Scientific Revolutions* "that once it has achieved the status of a paradigm, a scientific theory is declared invalid only if an alternative candidate is able to take its place" (Kühn, 1970, 77). Generally, the replacement has to explain the phenomena at issue at least as well as its rival *and* account for events (i.e., "anomalies") the establish theory is unable to resolve. In criticizing the classical view and the external-threat view, I demonstrated that their positions did a poor job of explaining events, thus setting the stage for my alternative. Dr. Holowchak (2011, 14) acknowledges that my criticisms have "indeed open conceptual space for a third alternative—an internal threat view." Thus, my goal in this endeavor is accomplished.

Evidence Needed for Internal-Threat Position

The internal-threat view claims the Oedipus complex is a defense mechanism (rationalization) used by Freud to reduce the emotional discomfort caused by implications of the Seduction theory for him (i.e., as a youngster he may have sexually abused members of his family, causing their hysterical symptoms) and his family (his father may have molested several of his daughters causes their hysteria). For the internal-threat perspective to have credibility, it should meet several criteria:

1. The Oedipus complex must have little empirical support and its origins must not be a direct result of advances in Freud's clinical treatment of his patents. If the Oedipus complex has scientific creditability, it can hardly be considered a defense mechanism. Likewise, if there is evidence that Freud gleaned the Oedipus complex from the direct study of children or made reasonable clinical inferences that were readily observable by other mental health practitioners, regardless of theoretical orientation, then it would be implausible to suppose that the Oedipus complex was a defense mechanism *even if the Oedipus complex was later found to be in error.*
2. The internal-threat view must show that the implications of the Seduction theory were a psychological threat to Freud and when the Oedipus complex replaced it as the etiological explanation of neurosis, Freud's behaviors were consistent with that of a defense mechanism.
3. The internal-threat view must also demonstrate a better "fit" than the alternative explanations—i.e., it must be consistent with known historical facts and make more reasonable inferences than competing perspectives.

Evidence for Internal-Threat View

The first criterion appears satisfied. Most mental health practitioners, including a very large number of psychoanalysts, find no evidence of an Oedipus complex. There is no empirical support for its manifestations (e.g., penis envy, castration anxiety, etc.) when children are directly studied. There is little proof that the Oedipus complex was a direct result of a clinical "discovery" made by Freud. Rather, he proclaimed its reality and projected its confirmation from the interpretations of his patients' free association (Kupfersmid, 1992).

The third criterion also appears satisfied. The flaws in the major alternatives are evident, at least to Dr. Holowchak and me. I have not found any counterarguments in print. Given the above analysis, the remainder of this paper focuses on the second criteria–that the Oedipus complex served as a defense mechanism to protect Freud psychologically.

A defense mechanism is an "enduring structure of the psyche that enables a person to avoid awareness of the unpleasant or anxiety arousing" (English *et al.,* 1958, 140). Defenses are typically triggered by feelings of anxiety, guilt, disgust, or shame (Hinsie *et al.*, 1970. 180). Rationalization is an unconscious process of justifications acceptable to the individual but questionable to others. This defense often produces a secondary by-product—feelings of omnipotence and enhanced self esteem (Eidelberg, 1968, 364).

For the internal-threat view, the implications of the Seduction theory had to cause anxiety (and possibly guilt, shame, and disgust) in Freud. There are historical data to support this contention. As noted in my chapter, Freud believed that he and many of his siblings suffered from hysteria in which the prime causal agent in Seduction theory is repressed sexual abuse occurring during childhood. Freud wrote to Fliess that one of the principle reasons for rejecting this theory is "that in all cases, the *father*, not excluding my own, had to be accused of being perverse" (Masson, 1985, 265). Two weeks later, in a letter to Fliess, Freud suggests that he and his nephew John engaged in sexual activity with his sister and a niece (Kupfersmid, 1992, 301). Thus, Freud appeared very uncomfortable with the implications of the Seduction theory.

There is also historical evidence that Freud distorted events that had emotional significance for him. In his *An Autobiographical Study* Freud claimed having to visit his fiancée prevented his discovery for the use of cocaine as an anesthetic in eye surgery. There was a one month interval, however, between Freud's idea for this use and his visit to Martha, ample time to do the necessary experiments (Anzieu, 41). This suggests Freud was in denial.

A more extreme defensive maneuver is evident in Freud's behaviors regarding Emma Eckstein's nasal surgery conducted by Fliess. Shortly after this operation, Emma began hemorrhaging from her nose. Freud called in a consulting physician who found impacted gauze in her nostrils that Fliess had failed to remove. Rather than holding his friend responsible, Freud displaced the culpability on to Emma's psychological functioning. Freud wrote to Fliess, "[T]here is no doubt that her hemorrhages were due to wishes" (Masson, 1985, 191).

Having fainted three separate times at the same restaurant when meeting with colleagues, Freud also exhibited a conversion (Kupfersmid, 1992, 307-8). For other examples, and a more detailed discussion of the Oedipus complex as a defense, see Kupfersmid (Kupfersmid, 298-303).

Freud was not immune from employing defenses for psychological protection. The implications of the Seduction theory could have produced in Freud any one (or as many as all four) of the emotions that typically triggers a defense.

Rationalization best explains Freud's formulation of the Oedipus complex. This complex provides a justification for neuroses (and hysteria) that neutralizes the psychological threat to Freud. The belief that real childhood abuse occurred is transformed into a universal fantasy. Adults in a patient's past are no longer held responsible for any reported sexualized behaviors. As an added bonus, Freud did not suggest these confessions via his clinical methods.

A by-product of rationalization is a feeling of omnipotence and enhanced self-esteem. Historical evidence supports Freud having these feelings and having considerable ambivalence. In the same letter for rejecting the Seduction theory, Freud describes his current mood. He reports being "in an opposite state"—being "depressed, confused, [or] exhausted." He notes, "It's strange too, that no feeling of shame appears—for which … there could be well occasion" (Masson, 1985, 265). Freud appears to be referring to his previous claim that cocaine cures morphine addiction. His retraction of this finding resulted in "grave reproaches" (Jones, 1953, 94).

In addition to Freud's incongruent mood, his behaviors are more indicative of a defense than an epiphany of an important discovery. In Freud's correspondences to Fliess, there is about a two-and-one-half year internal were he flip-flopped between reaffirming Seduction theory and affirming the Oedipus complex (Kupfersmid, 1992, 302). This is at the same time where he briefly proposed that cessation of childhood masturbation causes hysteria, per Makari's paper (Holowchak, 2011, 15-6). Also during this time Freud claimed excessive masturbation in adolescence caused neurasthenia in adulthood (Sulloway, 1983, 307). Apparently, to sustain good mental health, one had to masturbate at a moderate frequency (however number of times a week that is) from childhood through adolescence. As with many of Freud's theories, empirical confirmation was elusive then and is elusive now.

Even when convinced of the soundness of the Oedipus complex, Freud's behaviors were incongruent with his normal functioning. He did not publicly retract Seduction theory until eight year after he "discovered" the cause of neurosis and the origins of religion, morality, law, and civilization. Freud's self-description is "one of those who are unable to hold back what seems to be a new discovery until it has been either confirmed or corrected" (Freud, 1963, 184).

Conclusion

Freud's emotional reactions and behaviors, upon rejecting Seduction theory and supplanting it with the Oedipus complex, are consistent with a defense of rationalization. The internal-threat view remains the best "fit" with the historical record and what is known about Freud. This does not preclude that other facts may become evident, or a more reasonable interpretation of current facts may be proposed, that displaces this perspective as the most credible explanation for Freud's formulation of the Oedipus complex.

References

Anzieu, Didier, *Freud's Self-Analysis* (Madison, CT.: International Universities Press, 1986).

Eidelberg, Ludwig, *Encyclopedia of Psychoanalysis* (New York: Free Press, 1968).

Freud, Sigmund, "Some Psychological Consequences of the Anatomical Distinction between the Sexes," in *Sexuality and the Psychology of Love,* ed. Philip Rieff, (New York: Collier, 1963), 184.

Hinsie, Leland, and Robert Campbell, *Psychiatric Dictionary* (New York: Oxford University Press, 1970).

Holowchak, M. Andrew, "Freud's Oedipus Complex: Shibboleth or Poppycock?" *Radical Claims in Freudian Psychoanalysis: Point/Counterpoint,* ed. Mark Holowchak, (Landam, MD: Jason Aronson, 2011).

English, Horace, and Ava English, *A Comprehensive Dictionary of Psychological and Psychoanalytic Terms* (New York: Longmans, Green and Company, 1958).

Kühn, Thomas, *The Structure of Scientific Revolutions* (1970).

Kupfersmid, Joel, "The 'Defense' of Sigmund Freud," *Psychotherapy,* 29, (1992), 297-309.

Masson, Jeffery, *The Complete Letters of Sigmund Freud to Wilhelm Fliess 1887-1904* (Cambridge, Massachusetts: Harvard University Press, 1985).

Chapter 4
Reply to Dr. Kupfersmid

M. Andrew Holowchak

In Chapter 2 of this collection, Joel Kupfersmid gives an intelligent critique of Freud's Oedipus complex, both in its ontogenic and phylogenic aspects. He essays to show that nothing is salvageable—at least, not in the manner that Freud would have wished it to be salvaged.

My essay, in the first chapter of this collection, is in substantial agreement with Kupfersmid on most of his claims in that it does not amount to much of a defense of the Oedipus complex—not as the shibboleth that Freud said it was. I too argue that the Oedipus complex, as Freud describes it in its ontogenic and phylogenic aspects, is untenable. As a universal depiction of childhood sexual development or as an historical explanation of human's acquisition of Oedipal guilt, it is a canard. To salvage something from Freud's ontogenic account, I argue for Oedipal tensions, which entails acceptance of two of the many claims to which Freud was committed—a robust sexual life in infancy and the inordinate amount of time a child spends in nurture, which is often, I recognize, highly sexual in Freud's sense of "sexual"—and recognition that Freud's Oedipal account certainly has applications in many cases of psychopathology. It should not be ruled out categorically (Holowchak, 2011).

In his reply to my essay, Chapter 3 of this collection, Kupfersmid focuses on one of the touchiest issues in Freudian thought today: Freud's abandonment of his Seduction theory. The issue is touchy because of the indispensability of the Oedipus complex to Freudian psychoanalysis and because many scholars today believe Freud's reasons for abandoning his Seduction theory were not evidence-based. Kupfersmid acknowledges my criticism of his internal-threat view—i.e., that showing the two most prominent explanations for Freud's abandonment of his Seduction theory to be unlikely is not the same thing as adducing positive evidence for his alternative explanation as true (Holowchak, 2011, 15). He writes: "In criticizing the classical view and the external-threat view, I demonstrated that their positions did a poor job of explaining events, thus setting the stage for my alternative. Dr. Holowchak acknowledges that my criticisms have 'indeed open conceptual space for a third alternative—an internal threat view.' Thus my goal in this endeavor is accomplished" (Kupfersmid, 2011_2, 41). Yet to open up conceptual space is merely to show that there is another possible explanation and that is not to say that there is any evidence for that explanation. Kupfersmid clearly wishes to do more than open up conceptual space. His aim is to show that his internal-threat explanation best fits and, thus, best explains the known facts (Kupfersmid, 2011_2, 42-4).

Kupfersmid draws on the authority of Thomas Kühn for motivation. He says, "Thomas Kühn notes in *The Structure of Scientific Revolutions* 'that once it has achieved the status of a paradigm, a scientific theory is declared invalid only if an alternative candidate is able to take its place.'" Kühn's interest lies broadly in scientific paradigms or what most call "scientific theories"—like Copernican heliocentrism versus Ptolemaic geocentrism or, more pertinently, Skinnerian Behaviorism versus Freudian depth psychology—which are large-scale propositional networks of theoretical hypotheses and models (Holowchak, 2007, 125-9). Kühn is not so much interested in hypotheses or models as parts of paradigms or theories and that is what Freud's "Seduction theory," the name given to it by Kris, is.

For the credibility of his internal-threat explanation, Kupfersmid posits three criteria. First, the Oedipus complex "must have little empirical support and its origins must not be a direct result of advances in Freud's clinical treatment of his patents." Otherwise, it cannot be considered a defense mechanism and there cannot be a threat. Second, the "internal-treat view must show that the implications of the Seduction theory were a psychological threat to Freud and when the Oedipus complex replaced it as the etiological explanation of neurosis, Freud's behaviors were consistent with that of a defense mechanism." Finally, the "internal-threat view must also demonstrate a better 'fit' than the alternative explanations" (2011_2, 42). These criteria are certainly plausible. Does Kupfersmid meet them?

Kupfersmid states that the first and third criteria are met, and so his focus is on meeting the second. I agree that the first criterion is met, as I have argued so in my essay. I am less convinced that the third criterion is met.

I have acknowledged that there are flaws with the traditional explanation and Masson's external-threat view (Holowchak, 2011, 15-6), so I will not walk that path again. Defects and the subsequent implausibility of those two explanations are not proof that Kupfersmid's internal-threat view is correct. There are other conceptual possibilities. I have introduced Makari's explanation, which says Freud entered a period, roughly 1899 to sometime before 1905, where he entertained neither parental-abuse nor wished-for abuse, but self-abuse through excessive masturbation as the cause of hysteria. I find Makari's view the most reasonable among alternatives. Kupfersmid gives no reasons why Makari's alternative is inferior to his own view, which, given his third criterion, he ought to have done.

I leave aside Kupfersmid's justification of his second criterion, as I think there is a more generic defect with his account.

Overall, there seems to be inadequate motivation for the internal-threat view. Kupfersmid states that Freud "may have sexually abused members of his family" and his father "may have molested several of his daughters." Those are weak claims about possibility. Later he essays to show that what is merely possible is plausible. Freud stated that he and siblings were said to be neurotic, neurosis via Seduction theory requires early molestation, and so he and his siblings were molested. That is the strongest evidence in argument form for molestation within the Freud family. That, Kupfersmid acknowledges, is insufficient to show that Freud's abandonment of the Seduction theory was an (unconscious) effort to protect him and his family, hence his arguments on behalf of criterion two. If Freud's unconscious impulses to protect himself and his family were so strong all along, why then did he propose the Seduction theory in the first place? Moreover, why would it "*gradually* evolve"? (Kupfersmid, 2011_1, 33) It would seem that the natural defensive posture for such early and shameful sexual practices would have been the wish-fulfillment thesis, not the Seduction theory. Kupfersmid does not address that issue.

Kupfersmid's commitment to a gradual evolution of the Oedipus complex is historically based. Freud's behavior, historians acknowledge today, is inconsistent with a quick and radical change of mind and an unwavering commitment thereafter to it.

> Even when convinced of the soundness of the Oedipus complex, Freud's behaviors were incongruent with his normal functioning. He did not publicly retract Seduction theory until eight year after he "discovered" the cause of neurosis and the origins of religion, morality, law, and civilization. Yet, Freud's self-description is "one of those who are unable to hold back what seems to be a new discovery until it has been either confirmed or corrected (2011_2, 44).

If there is one thing we can take from Freud, it is that the motivation for human behavior is complex and seldom what it seems to be. It seems impossible to rule out tout court the possibility that threats, whether internal, external, or both, did not play some role in the overall causal picture of Freud's abandonment of the Seduction theory. The difficulty is to show that an internal threat was the chief cause of Freud's abandonment of his Seduction theory and that other contending explanations are less plausible. It seems to me still that Kupfersmid has not done that.

One thing, scholars are coming to find, does seem clear: Freud's abandonment of the Seduction theory was probably not due to a thorough examination of uncontaminated case-study reports, if only because Freud was not a patient data-gatherer and because he was inclined to speculative hypotheses, based on insufficient or contaminated data. Kupfersmid apparently agrees. "[Freud] rushed into print his theories," he writes, "he was too impatient to carefully gather confirmatory data, he supported positions that ran contrary to current opinion, and he was unlikely to be moved by the prevailing attitudes of his critics or followers" (1992, 304, and 1995, 539-40).

To make matters worse, Freud's proposal of the Seduction theory was likely not due to a thorough examination of uncontaminated case-study reports. Triplett argues persuasively that Freud's endorsement of his Seduction theory in "The Aetiology of Hysteria" was likely not evidential. In published form, the paper's conclusions are based on 18 cases of neurosis and seduction that justify "universal validity." Letters to Fliess show anything but universal validity. In several subsequent letters to Fliess, Freud confesses that none of his cases have been finished (Triplett, 2005, 649-50). Eissler, a former director of the Sigmund Freud Archives, has argued, after examining Freud's letters as they relate to his Seduction theory, "[T]he seduction theory was a conjecture which would within a few months be presented as fact" (2001, 145).

References

Eissler, Kurt, *Freud and the Seduction Theory: A Brief Love Affair* (Madison, CN: International Universities Press, 2001).

Holowchak, M. Andrew, *Critical Reasoning and Science: Looking at Science with an Investigative Eye* (Lanham, MD: University Press of America, 2007).

Holowchak, M. Andrew, "Freud's Oedipus Complex: Shibboleth or Hogwash?" in *Radical Claims in Freudian Psychoanalysis: Point/Counterpoint*, ed. Mark Holowchak, (Landam, MD: Jason Aronson, 2011).

Kupfersmid, Joel, "The 'Defense' of Sigmund Freud," *Psychotherapy,* Vol. 29, No. 2, 1992, 297-309.

Kupfersmid, Joel, "Does the Oedipus Complex Exist?" *Psychotherapy,* Vol. 32, No. 4, 1995, 535-47.

Kupfersmid, Joel, "The Oedipus Complex: It Made No Sense Then, It Makes No Sense Now" in M. Andrew Holowchak, *Extreme Freud: Essays, Pro & Con, on Some of the Most Radical Claims in Freudian Psychoanalysis* (Landam, MD: Jason Aronson, 2011_1).

Kupfersmid, Joel, "Rejoinder to Dr. Holowchak," *Extreme Freud: Essays, Pro & Con, on Some of the Most Radical Claims in Freudian Psychoanalysis* (Landam, MD: Jason Aronson, 2011_2).

Triplett, Hall, "The Misnomer of Freud's 'Seduction Theory,'" *Journal of the History of Ideas,* Vol. 65, No. 65, No. 4, 2005, 647-665.

PART II

Dreams as Wish-Fulfillments

"[The theory of dreams] occupies a special place in the history of psychoanalysis", Freud writes in "Revision of the Theory of Dreams, "and marks a turning point; it was with it that analysis took the step from being a psychotherapeutic procedure to being a depth psychology. Since then, too, the theory of dreams has remained what is most characteristic and peculiar about the young science, something to which there is no counterpart in the rest of our knowledge, a stretch of new country, which has been reclaimed form popular beliefs and mysticism. ... Whenever I had doubts of the correctness of my wavering conclusions, the successful transformation of a senseless and muddled dream into a logical and intelligible mental process in the dreamer would renew my confidence of being on the right track". Freud then goes on to list several features of his theory of dreams that have stood the test of time: "the fundamental distinction between the manifest content of dreams and the latent dream-thoughts, the realization that the wish-fulfilling function of dreams is not contradicted by anxiety dreams, the impossibility of interpreting a dream unless one has the dreamer's association to it at one's disposal, and, above all, the discovery that what is essential in dreams is the process of the dream-work...".

Is Freud's theory of dreams tenable? To what extent has it received experimental confirmation today?

Pro: Michael Michael, Ph.D., *Yonsei University, South Korea,* "On the Validity of Freud's Dream Interpretations"

Con: Rosemarie Sand, Ph.D., *Private Practice,* "The Unhappy Fate of Freud's Dream Theory"

Chapter 5
The Puzzle of Dreams

Michael Michael
Yonsei University, Korea

> "It is characteristic of dreams that often they seem to the dreamer to call for an interpretation. One is hardly ever inclined to write down a daydream, or recount it to someone else, or to ask "What does it mean?" But dreams do seem to have something puzzling and in a special way interesting about them—so we want an interpretation of them" (Wittgenstein, 1987, 13).

WITTGENSTEIN WAS AMBIVALENT ABOUT FREUD and his ideas. On the one hand, he took the ideas seriously—as he recounts, "I happened to read something by Freud, and I sat up in surprise. Here was someone who had something to say" (1987, 13). On the other hand, he regarded the style of thinking embodied in psychoanalysis as something that needs "combating." This was especially so with regard to Freud's theory of dreams, which he argued against as follows:

> The fact is that whenever you are preoccupied with something, with some trouble or with some problem which is a big thing in your life—as sex is, for instance—then no matter what you start from, the association will lead finally and inevitably back to the same theme. Freud remarks on how, after the analysis of it, the dream appears so very logical. And of course it does.
>
> You could start with any of the objects on this table—which certainly are not put there through your dream activity—and you could find that they all could be connected in a pattern like that; and the pattern would be logical in the same way.
>
> One may be able to discover certain things about oneself by this sort of free association, but it does not explain why the dream occurred (Wittgenstein, 1987, 13).

Wittgenstein surely has a point. It is one, moreover, that others have noticed and expanded on at greater length, as we shall see. Most worryingly for Freudians, it poses a challenge, not to the more peripheral details of Freud's dream theory, but to the very foundation of it: that dreams have meaning that can be discovered through a process involving free association. Without this, nothing else that Freud hypothesized about dreams can be entertained. Moreover, the challenge is a worthy one. It is difficult to see how Freud could mount a credible response to it.

Freud said many things in defense of his theory of dreams, but the most intriguing of these is an analogy. Writing of the analyst's conviction as to having found the correct interpretation of a dream, he says:

> What makes him certain in the end is precisely the complication of the problem before him, which is like the solution of a jig-saw puzzle. A coloured picture, pasted upon a thin sheet of wood and fitting exactly into a wooden frame, is cut into a large number of pieces of the most irregular and crooked shapes. If one succeeds in arranging the confused heap of fragments, each of which bears upon it an unintelligible piece of drawing, so that the picture acquires a meaning, so that there is no gap anywhere in the design and so that the whole fits into the frame—if all these conditions are fulfilled, then one knows that one has solved the puzzle and there is no alternative solution (1923, *S.E.*, XIX: 116).

Anyone who has interpreted a dream in the manner that Freud suggests and felt the certainty that he speaks of here is likely to find this analogy appealing. But as it stands, it can hardly be considered an adequate response to the challenge posed by Wittgenstein. If the number of pieces is vast and the variety great, and if each piece is such that it can fit to numerous other pieces, then it is far from inconceivable that one can construct any picture, intelligible in itself, almost at will. What needs to be the case if this analogy is to have any weight is that the fitting of pieces together be not commonplace. It is the rarity of a flush fit that would make the solution of such a puzzle compelling. Unfortunately, Freud does not explain how this might translate to his interpretations of dreams.

My main aim in this essay is to provide a defense of Freud against the kind of criticism described above by making good the analogy of the jigsaw puzzle.[1] More generally, my concern is to defend that part of Freud's theory that he himself believed could be justified by examples of dream interpretation alone—namely, that dreams have a discoverable meaning. Given the many apparently more substantive claims that constitute the theory and the vast body of literature that bears on them, this is undoubtedly a narrow focus, but it nevertheless serves to concentrate attention on what I believe to be Freud's most important contribution to our understanding of dreams. Other parts of his theory may need to be revised or discarded, but this much I think will remain.[2] My strategy is thus, not primarily to review research on dreaming as it relates to the numerous details of Freud's theory, but to offer a defense of that which Freud sought to establish by his own methods.

In doing so, I review two other forms of evidence: the experiential evidence adverted to by Rachel Blass and the neuroscientific evidence presented by Mark Solms. The former strengthens the defense I make of Freud's primary thesis, the latter reveals that this thesis has not been contradicted by modern neuroscience, as many believe. In no case will the conclusion be that Freud's theory has been justified. Blass offers only a conditional justification of Freud's theory, the interpretation of the neuroscientific evidence remains controversial, and my own defense also falls short of a justification, for reasons that I will explain. But though I offer no justification, I hope to show that Freud's primary thesis should be regarded as very much a "live hypothesis" for the academic community.

The most appropriate place to begin, though, is with a delineation of Freud's theory.

Freud's Theory and Project

Freud makes many claims about dreams. How one is to delimit what counts as his 'theory of dreams' depends on how many of these claims one wishes to include. This is an important question with regard to criticism or defense of his theory, but also a somewhat controversial one. Grünbaum, perhaps the leading philosophical critic of Freud, takes the theory to be well defined by the claims that for all dreams the content is the fulfillment of a wish and the instigator is a repressed infantile wish. Consequently, it is these claims that bear the brunt of his criticism. Blass, however, argues that these claims are not the central ones. "The essence of the psychoanalytic theory of dreams is the claim that the dream contains accessible meanings. The claim that the nature of those meanings is wishes is secondary, and the claim that wishes are what instigated the dream is even further removed" (Blass, 2002, 7). Both writers have a point. It is undoubtedly true that a significant portion of *The Interpretation of Dreams*, the most authoritative exposition of Freud's theory of dreams, is spent on substantiating the claims that Grünbaum takes to be definitive of the theory. Yet Freud's own stated aims appear to be more in line with Blass's account:

> The aim which I have set before myself is to show that dreams are capable of being interpreted; and any contributions I may be able to make towards the solution of the problems dealt with in the last chapter [which reviews the literature on dreams in relation to a number of issues, including the function of dreams] will only arise as by-products in the course of carrying out my proper task (1900, *S.E.*, IV: 96).

Neither of these points, however, settles the issue. Nor perhaps is the issue settleable. Which claims are taken to be more definitive of Freud's theory may depend on from which perspective or with what interests one approaches it. Nevertheless, the claim that dreams have a discoverable meaning is primary in at least this sense: it is the more fundamental. If Freud is wrong in this claim, none of his theory of dreams can be retained, whereas if he is wrong in the other claims, then still part of his theory can remain intact.

Since this is what I will be focusing on in this essay—the primary thesis—I will have little to say about those parts of his dream theory that purport to explain why dreams take the form they do and why they occur in the first place. This includes the basic mechanisms of dreaming, namely, censorship, regression, and the dream-work. It also includes the claim that the "indispensible motive force for the formation of dreams" is repressed infantile sexual wishes. Indeed, I hold that Freud himself did not believe that these theoretical elements could be justified through dream interpretation alone, but only in relation to his more general psychoanalytic theorizing about the mind, which ostensibly derived from his work on neurosis. To see this we need to turn briefly to the justificatory project he undertakes in *The Interpretation of Dreams*.

Freud's justification of his theory begins with the analysis of a specimen dream—the famous dream of Irma's injection. The primary aim of this is to demonstrate that he has a valid method of interpreting dreams. According to him, the interpretation reveals that the content of the dream "was the fulfilment of a wish and its motive was a wish" (1900, *S.E.*, IV: 119). Though he goes on to assert that this is general to all dreams, he acknowledges that this has yet to be justified. Later he states, "The fact that dreams really have a secret meaning which represents the fulfilment of a wish must be proved afresh in each particular case by analysis" (1900, *S.E.*, IV: 146). One problem for the general claim is that there are many dreams that appear to represent entirely the opposite of what is hypothesized—the frustration of wishes. To deal with this, Freud proceeds to offer interpretations of a number of such apparently counter-wish dreams and concludes in each case that it is wish-fulfilling after all. In this context he remarks, "I hope the foregoing examples will be enough (till the next objection is raised) to make it seem plausible that even dreams with a distressing content are to be construed as wish-fulfilments" (1900, *S.E.*, IV: 159). With this comment he seems to reject a possible move that he could have made here: to claim that he now has enough inductive support to draw the general conclusion. Instead he claims only that the examples make this claim plausible. This is reinforced by a footnote (added in 1925) that he makes to the above sentence, "I must point out that the subject is not yet finally disposed of; I shall return to it later on" (*Ibid.*). This "later on" is a reference to Chapter VII of his book. There he asserts, "Analysis is able to demonstrate that . . . unpleasurable dreams are wish-fulfilments no less than the rest" (1900, *S.E.*, V: 557). He explicates this assertion with an account of the psychical processes involved in unpleasurable dreams that draws heavily on his more general theorizing about the mind, that is, theorizing that goes beyond what can be established on the basis of the analysis of dreams alone (as he himself acknowledged to Fliess in 1898, writing: "All its [i.e. Chapter VII's] themes come from the work on neurosis, not from that on dreams" (Bonaparte *et al*, 1954, 257). It therefore appears that, at least in his more cautious moments, he holds his claim that all dreams are wish-fulfillments to be justified only with the support of such general theorizing about the mind.

His claim that the instigator of dreams is always a repressed infantile wish is still further removed from his main justificatory aims. The interpretations of dreams he gives rarely uncover an infantile wish. In the section in which he does attempt to provide evidence for the claim, the conclusion he draws is tentative:

> My experiences in analysing dreams have drawn my attention to the fact that trains of thought reaching back to earliest childhood lead off even from dreams which seem at first sight to have been completely interpreted, since their sources and instigating wish have been discovered without difficulty. I have therefore been compelled to ask myself whether this characteristic may not be a further essential precondition of dreaming. . . . It is still extremely hard to demonstrate the truth of this suspicion; and I shall have to return in another connection (Chapter VII) to a consideration of the probable part played by the earliest experiences of childhood in the formation of dreams (1900, *S.E.*, IV: 218).

In Chapter VII, in relation to this claim, he speaks of the "indications derived from the psycho-analysis of the neuroses" (1900, *S.E.*, V: 553) and that he is "aware that [the assertion that the wish represented in a dream must be an infantile one] cannot be proved to hold universally" (1900, *S.E.*, V: 554). These comments clearly illustrate both the role played by his general psychoanalytic theorizing and the still tentative nature with which he is treating the claim. Indeed, even while writing the book, Freud appears to have been undecided as to whether or not to include the claim about the instigator of dreams, as revealed by his letter to Wilhelm Fliess in March 1898:

> Biologically dream-life seems to me to proceed directly from the residue of the prehistoric stage of life (one to three years), which is the source of the unconscious and alone contains the aetiology of all the psychoneuroses. . . . [A] recent wish leads to a dream only if it can be associated with material from that period, if the recent wish is a derivative of a prehistoric wish or can get itself adopted by such a wish. I do not know yet to what extent I shall be able to stick to this extreme theory, or let it loose in the dream book (Bonaparte *et al.*, 1954, 246-247).

The "extreme theory" did find its way into the book, but as we have seen, in an appropriately tentative way. That Freud himself labeled it "extreme" is another indication of the remoteness it bares to the core of his justificatory project.

What emerges from the above is that Freud himself did not think he could justify much of his theory of dreams by examples of dream interpretations alone. Yet he clearly does set out to justify *some* aspect of his theory on this basis. In which case we may ask, which part of his theory would he have held to be justified in this way?

The obvious candidate is his primary thesis that *all dreams have meaning*. The generality of this claim, though, itself raises suspicions, for if Freud was not content with an enumerative induction to justify the claim that all dreams are wish-fulfillments, why should he be content with one to justify the claim that all dreams have meanings? One suspects that this claim too owes to his general theorizing about the mind. What is left to defend without recourse to such theorizing needs to be more limited.

A second candidate would be the claim that *at least many dreams have meaning*. This however is too limited. Given that, as Freud himself observed, many dreams—such as thirst, hunger, or sex dreams—seem straightforwardly to be wish-fulfillments, it seems trivial to claim that at least many dreams have meaning. Something more substantial is required. A third candidate is the far more interesting claim that *at least many dreams have hidden meaning that can be revealed by a process involving free association*. This is both fundamental to Freud's theory and appropriately circumscribed. It is, I think, a claim that Freud would have believed to be justified on the grounds of his dream interpretations alone and to be the most minimal claim worthy of such justification. I will therefore henceforth take this, rather than the general claim, as his *primary thesis*.

Epistemological Prelude

Though I think the case Freud makes for his primary thesis is far stronger than his critics claim, it nevertheless falls short of a justification. This is because the kind of evidence needed to justify the conclusion reached in any particular dream interpretation is not unambiguously available to anyone other than the analysand and his/her analyst. That it is so means that a defense on the basis of dream interpretations alone cannot take the form of a *justification*, but of something less, namely, a *validation*.

Let me explain the distinction I have in mind. On the one hand, to *justify* a theory or claim is to provide grounds that show that it is right to believe the theory or claim. Stated without qualification, these grounds should in principle be accessible to any agent in such a way that that agent would, if operating rationally, come to see the rightness of believing the theory or claim. On the other hand, a method of inference is *methodologically valid* just in case, for any particular application of it, if the input is of the right kind then the output will be of the right kind. The model for this is *inductive validity* (often simply called inductive strength). An argument is *inductively valid* just in case if the premises are true then the conclusion is probably true (though can be false). However, I am extending this model in one important respect: It need not simply be that the input consists of true propositions that matters for methodological validity, but that it (perhaps) has additional properties. Consider, for example, inductive generalization. Any particular inductive generalization is cogent (or inductively sound) as long as the data on which it is based is not only veridical, but also constitutes a large enough and representative enough sample. We can say of any *particular* inductive generalization that is based on a large enough and representative enough sample that it is inductively valid, meaning, if the data is veridical then the conclusion is probably true. But we can say more generally that the *method* of inductive generalization is valid, meaning, for any particular application of it, if the data is veridical *and* constitutes a large enough and representative enough sample then the conclusion is probably true. The cogency of any application of a valid method thus depends, in a principled way, on the qualities of the input. My defense of Freud consists in my showing that there is a valid method of inference from the data (dream contents, free associations on these, and background details about the dreamer) to the interpretation. This entails showing that there is a principled account of the characteristics of the data such that an application of the method of inference on data with such characteristics is inductively valid. What I mean, then, by 'validation' of the claim that dreams can have hidden meanings is simply that this claim is based on a valid method of inference.

Given that it falls short of justification, one may legitimately ask what the value of such validation is. The chief value of it in the context of this essay is that it refutes what I consider to be the most serious criticism of Freud's theory, that the method of inference that Freud employs in reaching his interpretations is inherently fallacious. Once this criticism is defeated, I do not think there remains a meaningful rebuttal to Freud's primary thesis. This is not, of course, to say that the thesis has been proven; only that it has been shown that it has not been disproven. In addition, such validation implies that one who has interpreted dreams in the manner Freud suggests can be *personally justified* in believing that those interpretations are correct, and hence in believing the primary thesis. Furthermore, such validation elucidates Freud's method of inference and the qualities of the evidence that are important to it. Such elucidation can pave the way towards a general justification.

The Case against Freud's Primary Thesis

The case against Freud's primary thesis is most thoroughly developed by Clark Glymour. The main criticism he makes has been endorsed by a number of critics, and, as alluded to in the introduction, was anticipated, albeit in a different form, by Wittgenstein. Most of these critics take the criticism to be decisive. The tone Glymour adopts indicates that he himself does not think that the problems he identifies are merely expository. Witness: "The method itself is worthless . . . the objections to it are obvious ones. . . . It is hard to believe that they did not occur to Freud himself. The whole business seems the cheapest of rhetorical tricks" (Glymour, 1983, 65).

The general theme of Glymour's paper is that Freud's justificatory project fails because he fails adequately to justify his method. Glymour puts the failure down to three things. Firstly, the method that Freud describes does not correspond with the method that he practices. Secondly, there is an obvious objection to his method to which Freud fails to respond. Thirdly, the method is in fact fallacious.

Freud describes his method as involving the analysand engaging in free association with elements of the content of his dream. This requires his starting with a particular element of the dream and simply reporting whatever comes to mind on the basis of this on the condition that he does not critically appraise or hold back any thoughts. Here is what Freud himself says in this regard: "The self-observer ... need only take the trouble to suppress his critical faculty. If he succeeds in doing that, innumerable ideas come into his consciousness of which he could otherwise never have got hold. The material which is in this way freshly obtained for his self-perception makes it possible to interpret . . . his dream-structures" (1900, *S.E.*, IV: 102).

Glymour objects that though this is all that Freud says in describing his method, it does not correspond to how Freud's actual dream interpretations proceed:

> Freud gives us several pages of report of his associations with elements of the dream; though in fact what he gives us is not that at all, but something much more complex. For Freud's 'associations' include conclusions as to what dream elements mean or represent, queries regarding such conclusions, associations from such conclusions, that is, associations starting from elements of the interpretation of the dream, and, of course, associations with the dream elements themselves. . . . Very little of what we get sounds like the free association procedure that Freud has described to us (Glymour, 1983, 63).

Moreover, the way that the associations generated by these complex processes are selected and sorted seems even more complicated, and nowhere does Freud help his reader understand this process:

> Freud gives us no rules for stopping the dreamer's associations, or for insisting that he continue, or for coming back again and demanding new associations with an element of the dream previously subjected to association, and with his own. It is pretty clear that in dealing with his patient's dreams, and with his own, Freud did all of these things (*Ibid.*, 62).

Freud's method is thus both under-described and poorly illustrated.

This much seems true enough, though there is nothing here to indicate that it is anything other than an expository failing on Freud's part. But Glymour thinks that there are deeper problems. Freud fails to respond to the following obvious objection:

> We know *before-hand* that, if a person is asked to associate his thought with elements of a dream, and report his associations, after a while we will be able to make up a cogent story, thought, fear, wish, or whatever from the resulting associations. We know that simply from our elementary psychological knowledge

> of people. There is nothing special about dreams in this regard; much the same could be done with rock formations or with blotches of ink or Thematic Apperception Tests or whatever. Unless he or she is enormously stupid, the person doing the associating can make up such a story from the elements of his or her associations. Indeed if the associater is clever, many such stories can be made up. Now the production of such associations from dream elements and the resulting stories will do nothing to establish that the dreams are expressing that story, that thought, anymore than the stories that result from people observing random ink blots or rock formations and then associating freely give evidence that the ink blots or rock formations are expressing those stories (*Ibid.*, 60-1).

This is similar to the objection which Wittgenstein made in that both think that through free association one can end up with a plausible "interpretation" that nevertheless has nothing to do with how the dream content actually arose. It presents a serious challenge to the validity of Freud's method. It is clear, though, that Glymour does not regard it as just a challenge to which Freud needs to respond, but that as one to which he *cannot* respond. As he later remarks about Freud's alleged interpretations of counter-wish dreams:

> [I]f his patients were convinced of his thesis by the interpretations Freud offers of their recalcitrant dreams, then they cannot have been very clever people. For by Freud's method every dream could be made out to be an expression of a wish just as every dream could, with almost equal ease, be made an expression of disgust or regret or fear or . . . (*Ibid.*, 66).

Freud's failings are thus not merely expository; they are elemental.

Glymour takes the point a step further by implying that Freud's method actually involves a fallacy. He does this in the context of an example of one of Freud's interpretations. The dream in question, by a woman patient, is as follows:

> 'I wanted to give a supper-party, but I had nothing in the house but a little smoked salmon. I thought I would go out and buy something, but remembered then that it was Sunday afternoon and all the shops would be shut. Next I tried to ring up some caterers, but the telephone was out of order. So I had to abandon my wish to give a supper-party' (1900, *S.E.*, IV: 147).

The woman was then asked to produce associations based on this dream, and eventually she came up with the following:

> [S]he went on to tell me that the day before she had visited a woman friend of whom she confessed she felt jealous because her (my patient's) husband was constantly singing her praises. Fortunately this friend of hers is very skinny and thin and her husband admires a plumper figure. I asked her what she had talked about to her thin friend. Naturally, she replied, of that lady's wish to grow a lit-

tle stouter. Her friend had enquired, too: 'When are you going to ask us to another meal? You always feed one so well.'

The meaning of the dream was now clear, and I was able to say to my patient: 'It is just as though when she made this suggestion you said to yourself: "A likely thing! I'm to ask you to come and eat in my house so that you may get stout and attract my husband still more! I'd rather never give another supper-party." ... The fact that what people eat at parties makes them stout had been brought home to you by your husband's decision not to accept any more invitations to supper in the interests of his plan to reduce his weight.' All that was now lacking was some coincidence to confirm the solution. The smoked salmon in the dream had not yet been accounted for. 'How,' I asked, 'did you arrive at the salmon that came into your dream?' 'Oh,' she replied, 'smoked salmon is my friend's favourite dish.' I happen to be acquainted with the lady in question myself, and I can confirm the fact that she grudges herself salmon no less than my patient grudges herself caviare (1900, *S.E.*, IV: 148).

Glymour claims that the association the woman makes with the dream, the thought of her skinny friend, is caused by two elements of the dream: the supper-party and the smoked salmon. That is, the causal links are as follows:

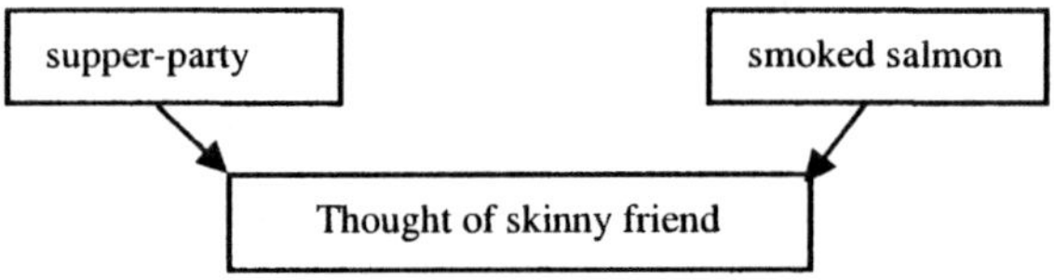

And that Freud "transposes the causal relation", to give this:

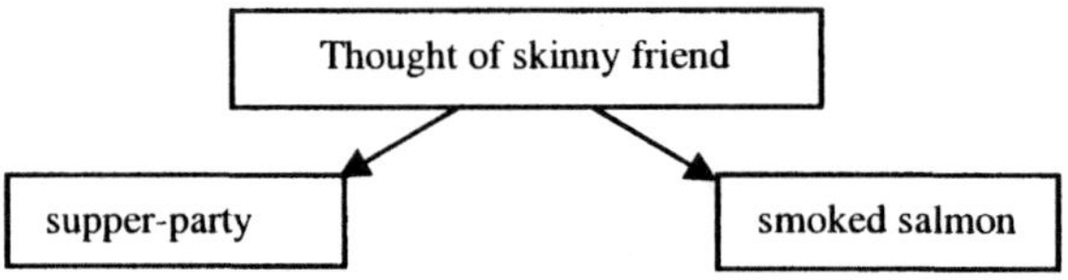

"What," Glymour asks, "are the grounds of the transposition? Evidence for the first causal model is not necessarily evidence for the second" (1983, 68).

He goes on to argue that the first causal model is indeed not genuine evidence for the second:

> If we think simply in terms of the second causal picture, the fact that the dream both contains a failed attempt at a supper-party and mentions smoked salmon, and both of these elements lead to the remembrance of features of the patient's friend, seems an amazing coincidence that demands explanation. The best explanation seems to be that these elements of the dream have a common cause, and that cause has to do with a thought about the friend in question. But if we stand back for a moment we see that this coincidence is manufactured: one associates, at Freud's direction, until one thinks of something which has connection with several elements in one's dream; the several elements cause the com-

> mon thought, not vice versa, and the coincidence requires no further explanation (*Ibid.*, 68).

In other words, Freud's inference is fallacious because he purports to explain an "amazing coincidence" which was in fact engendered by his own methods. Grünbaum, in his influential critique of Freud's theory, endorses Glymour's argument wholeheartedly, "Indeed, Freud thus argues fallaciously from the confluence of associations to a causal reversal in *explicitly generalized* form" (Grünbaum, 1984, 234).

Rosemarie Sand makes a related though slightly different criticism:

> I will refer to this . . . as the "free association fallacy." . . . The fallacy occurs, for instance, when it is assumed that something—a thought, a feeling, a motive—which turns up during free association to a dream, merely because it turns up, must be a background thought of the dream. In other words . . . if I associate from *A* to *B*, then *B* must have been a determinant of *A* (Sand, 1993, 531).

The difference is that Sand does not consider that Freud is purporting to explain any coincidences, but that he simply assumes "that *B* is a determinant of *A* because *B* occurred in the series of associations" (*Ibid.*, 532). If it is true that Freud assumes that an element is the cause of the dream content *merely* because it emerged through free association, then this does seem to be a fallacy, somewhat similar to the kind called *post hoc, ergo propter hoc*. One line of defense against this accusation is to point out that Freud is not assuming such a causal relation merely because the reverse of it emerged through free association, but holds that it is a legitimate move on the grounds of his deeper psychoanalytic theorizing about the mind. This, however, does not save his justificatory project, or whatever can be rescued from it. The criticism, at the very least, appears to completely undermine the idea that any part of Freud's theory can be defended on the grounds of dream interpretations alone.

A Defense of Freud's Primary Thesis

Before I address the criticisms described above, I need to make a couple of distinctions. The first is that between *method of analysis* and *method of inference*. The method of analysis that Freud uses in interpreting dreams is the entire procedure by which he goes from the report of the dream content to the interpretation of the dream. This process of course includes the inference to the interpretation, but it also includes more than this. As such, though free association is part of the method of analysis, it need not be part of the method of inference. Indeed, this is the implication of Glymour's first criticism, for as he points out, in his specimen dream interpretations Freud is manifestly selecting and sorting among the associations (and other material generated) in coming up with his interpretations. As Glymour puts it, "[W]e learn that [Freud] did not hesitate to reject associations, even those which led to an intelligible and plausible interpretation, if he disliked their direction" (Glymour, 1983, 66). Glymour's observation thus points to a distinction between free association and the method of inference. This may be in keeping with Freud's own account, for, as we have seen, upon describing the process of free association, Freud states, "The material which is in this way freshly obtained for his self-perception makes it possible to interpret both his pathological ideas and his dream-structures." The material does not constitute or necessitate the interpretation, but merely "makes it possible to interpret," suggesting that work still needs to be done in order to infer the correct interpretation. Free association therefore seems to be a procedure for generating material from which an inference can be made. Though it is part of the method of analysis, it need not be part of the method of inference.

The second distinction is that between *method of heuristic inference* and *method of logical inference*.[3] The first refers to that by which a result is obtained, the second to that by which a result is considered warranted. The two can, of course, coincide—the method of logical inference can be the method of heuristic inference—but they need not. It is with the latter that I will be primarily concerned. To see why this is so, observe the context of our interpretation of what Freud is doing. Freud presents his specimen dream interpretations as a way of validating his method of analysis. As such, it is reasonable to hold that he considers that the dream interpretations he gives would be seen as warranted by those who do not already assume that his method is valid, for otherwise he would be guilty of begging the question. Of course, critics may uncharitably interpret him as committing this fallacy, but it would be a violation of the "principle of charity" that should guide any interpretation to make this judgment too hastily. Rather, we should begin with the question, "why would he think that this dream interpretation is warranted?"—that is, "what is his method of logical inference?" So when I speak about method of inference *simpliciter*, where there is a chance that heuristic inference and logical inference are not the same, it is specifically logical inference that I am concerned about.

Armed with these distinctions, let us first examine Sand's criticism. The accusation is that Freud merely assumes that items associated with elements from the dream caused the dream content. As already observed, that this is not an accurate description of his general method of inference is suggested by Glymour's observation that Freud is selecting and sorting among the associations made. Something more seems to be going on then the mere assumption that an item associated with the dream content caused the dream content. The more pertinent point, however, is that even if the accusation were in some sense true, it need only be so of his method of heuristic inference, not of his method of logical inference. Indeed, I hold that, in the case of his specimen dream interpretations, it is not the case that Freud considers his positing of certain associations as causes of the dream content as warranted merely by the fact of their having been freely associated with elements of that content. This much I think should be held on the grounds of the "principle of charity," as explained above. But Freud also provides us with plenty of clues as to what his method of logical inference is. Such are contained, for example, in his jigsaw puzzle analogy that we saw in the introduction, in which he explains that confidence in an interpretation has to do with something analogous to the "absence of gaps" and the "fit into the frame" of a completed puzzle. Such are also contained in his specimen dream analyses. Consider, for example, what Freud says in rejecting a potential interpretation of one of his dreams:

> Anyone who interprets this dream without regard for my rules will conclude that I was worried about my friend's health and that this worry was realized in the dream. But I should be glad if anyone interpreting the dream in this way would be good enough to explain to me why my fears on Otto's behalf should have lighted on *Basedow's* disease—a diagnosis for which his actual appearance gives not the slightest ground (1900, *S.E.*, IV: 269).

What is noteworthy here is that Freud's objection to the suggested interpretation is that it fails to explain the dream content accurately enough. This accords with the jigsaw puzzle analogy: Here the suggested interpretation is rejected because it leaves unsatisfactory "gaps." More generally, this quote suggests that Freud's concerns, from a logical point of view, are precisely such explanatory considerations. That is, he considers his positing of certain associations as causes of the dream content as warranted because they offer "fitting" explanations of the content. This is different from asserting that he considers it warranted merely by the fact of their having been freely associated with elements of that content.[4]

None of this, of course, vindicates Freud. Though Freud's method of inference may have been an attempt at inference to the best explanation rather than that of merely assuming that a thought associated with the dream content is a cause of it, this does not entail that any of his inferences are in fact valid. Inference to the best explanation is a valid method of inference, but it is frequently misapplied. Can we have any confidence that Freud's explanations are best?

This brings us to Glymour's criticism that the fallacy Freud commits is that he purports to explain something that he himself has engendered. Consider this in the context of the example that Glymour provides—the supper-party dream. Recall that Glymour begins with the claim that there were two elements that caused the thought of the skinny friend, both the supper-party and the smoked salmon. As it stands, this claim is a mere assumption. There is no indication in Freud's account that the smoked salmon element of the dream was a cause of the thought of the skinny friend. Indeed, it is misleading for Glymour to make this claim, for by presenting the smoked salmon element as a cause, he diminishes without argument the confirmatory value of the subsequent discovery of a connection between the skinny friend and smoked salmon. According to Freud's report, it was only after the theory that the thought of the skinny friend was a cause of the dream content had been proposed that Freud brought up the smoked salmon element, to which the patient immediately responded by connecting the element with her skinny friend. That was why Freud considered this connection as *confirmation* of the theory—that is, as supporting the theory in a way similar to that in which a successful prediction supports a theory. Why then does Glymour make the apparently groundless assumption that the patient was associating with the smoked salmon element of the dream to begin with?

As we proceed with his argument it becomes clear. Glymour realizes that there is a fact that demands explanation, namely, the coincidence that the thought of the skinny friend connects two distinct elements of the dream. Since he wants to reject Freud's own purported explanation on the grounds that the coincidence is manufactured, he needs to posit that it is indeed manufactured. The most charitable interpretation of Glymour's reasoning here, then, is that it is based on the premise that that the two elements were joint causes of the thought is part of a better explanation of the coincidence than Freud's explanation that the elements of the dream had a common cause. The other part of this "better explanation" is that Freud was consciously selecting, among a large number of associations, one that happened to have connections of content with both elements of the dream. However, Glymour's explanation fits poorly with Freud's account of what happened. As already remarked, Freud offers no indication that the patient was associating with the smoked salmon element of the dream. Neither does he offer any indication that he himself was consciously selecting among a large number of associations one that happened to have two connections. Rather, what he reports is that he was impressed enough by the connection of the supper-party conversation and the dream content to posit this as the cause, and that the smoked salmon element was considered only after this. So Glymour's explanation is not supported by the facts as reported.

There is, though, something more telling here. Even if the patient had been consciously or unconsciously looking for connections with both the supper-party and the smoked salmon element, it is surely a remarkable coincidence that she was so successful. That is, it is a remarkable coincidence that there existed an emotionally salient association that had such striking connections with at least two elements of the dream. (Note in this regard that the connection between the conversation with the skinny friend and the supper-party element of the dream was more striking for the fact that the patient's husband had, just the day before, stated his intention to avoid supper-party invitations so as not to put on weight, thereby alerting her to this potential that supper-parties have.) The probability that Glymour's explanation is true can only be as high as the expectation beforehand that there would be an emotionally salient thought that has such striking connections with two elements of the dream. The probability of Freud's explanation being true, however, does not depend on this expectation. Considering the nature of the concerns and of the connections, it seems reasonable to hold that Freud's explanation is more probable than Glymour's.

It is important in this respect to take into account what is initially plausible. We know on the basis of many straightforward dreams that thoughts from the previous day can be causes of the dream content. What Freud is positing is that this was the case with the supper-party dream as well. This is a plausible enough claim. If the explanandum here is the content of the dream, then the hypothesis that the thoughts of the skinny friend were a cause of this content is at least a candidate for explanation. What is then left is to compare the likelihood of this explanation with alternatives. As stated above, since no alternative can have a higher likelihood than the prior expectation that there would be an emotionally salient association with such connections to the dream content, and given that it seems reasonable to estimate that this expectation would be relatively low, it seems reasonable to infer that the thoughts of the skinny friend were a cause of the dream content.

Glymour goes on to concede that the explanation Freud gives is indeed quite likely:

> The *real* coincidence is that on the one hand, on one day the dreamer was visited by a friend, whose favourite dish is smoked salmon, and who had asked her when she, the dreamer, planned to have another supper-party, and, on the other hand, that night she dreamed of a supper-party and smoked salmon. Is this coincidence evidence of a causal connection between the encounter with her skinny friend in the dream? Perhaps it is, in the case at hand, for the real event and the dream are proximate in time and share a number of independent features, and one doubts that any event so proximate would share those features. (Glymour, 1983, 69)

Given his previous argument, this seems to me a remarkable admission. If it is conceded that it is likely that the thought of the skinny friend caused the dream content, then there is no ground for maintaining that the coincidence that the thought of the skinny friend connects two distinct elements of the dream is manufactured. But Glymour's point now changes. The problem for Freud is that the case was meant to be illustrative of his method, yet the features which here suggest that he has made a successful interpretation do not seem generalizable. Glymour takes this as indicating that Freud has failed in his purpose of demonstrating the general validity of his method. However, though I agree that Freud has failed to demonstrate that his method of analysis will *always* yield successful interpretations, if this interpretation is successful, he has nevertheless shown that the method of analysis *can* yield successful interpretations. More importantly with regard to the validation of his primary thesis, it indicates his method of logical inference. Freud infers that a particular interpretation is correct on the basis that it explains both the dream content and the existence of a coherent set of concerns in the agent that happen to have several striking connections with the dream content, something the expectation of which would have been low prior to the process of interpretation. In the case of the supper-party dream, the facts that Glymour alludes to, the proximity of events and the shared independent features, are part of what renders the connections in question as particularly striking. In other cases what renders the connections as striking may be different, but as long as there is something that does so, the proposed interpretation can nevertheless be deemed successful on the basis of the same pattern of inference.

Let me elaborate on this idea. In an example Sand gives, she imagines somebody associating with the dream element "I was driving alone in the car" as follows: "automobile," "autoerotic," "masturbation" (Sand, 1993, 538). There are obvious connections of content between consecutive words in this series, but those connections would strike most of us as tenuous with regard to their potential meaningfulness. Why then, in his specimen dream interpretations does Freud see it as warranted to hold certain associations as likely causes of the dream content?

The example of the supper-party dream suggests that there are two considerations.

One is that the connections he finds are not tenuous, at least, not for the dreamer. Rather they are *striking* connections, that is, they are ones that have a felt significance with respect to their potential meaningfulness, again, at least for the dreamer. More specifically, they are ones for which it can be reasonably inferred, often on the basis of an intimate acquaintance with the dreamer, that they would have struck the dreamer as significant prior to the interpretative process. Not all, or indeed many, connections of content proposed to somebody would be felt by her as significant in this way. A test of this is to observe one's response to those connections that somebody else experiences as significant for idiosyncratic reasons—I venture that one is likely to experience these, as one would of Sand's examples, as tenuous rather than as significant. (For another example, consider the connection between 'baboon' and 'barbarian' on the basis of the internal alliteration of the words. Does that feel like a significant connection or a tenuous one? I venture the latter; or at least, that the felt significance which this connection has for others would be much less than that which it had for me at a particular period in time).

The other consideration is that the association posited as a cause often has more than one striking connection to the dream content. Both strikingness and number of connections are of course a matter of degree, and that degree is important to the validity of the inference. But the key observation is this: There is surely a point where, when the strikingness of the connections is high enough and/or there are enough such connections, it is reasonable to judge that the prior expectation that there would be an emotionally salient thought with such connections to the dream content is low, that is, that the probability that that there is an association with such connections is just a coincidence is small. People may differ as to where they think that point would occur, but this is a difference of judgment, not of principle. If the judgment is that this expectation is significantly low, then the inference that the element thus connected was a cause of the dream content is reasonable. The method of logical inference is therefore valid, even if any particular application of it is not.

It is also worth pointing out that many of the connections Freud picks out have a high felt significance because of the distinctive similarity of the contents thus connected. For example, in his analysis of one of his own dreams, Freud comes up with the following memory. "A gentleman, with unmistakable signs of Basedow's disease—incidentally, just as in the dream, only the brown discoloration of the skin of the face and the protruding eyes, but no goitre—placed himself entirely at our disposal and asked what he could do for us" (1900, *S.E.*, IV: 270). Here it seems that the memory of the gentleman in question matched the image in the dream in precise detail—brown discoloration and protruding eyes but, unusually for Basedow's disease, no goitre. In another dream of his that he analyses, he observes: "[T]here was the face which I saw in the dream with its elongated features and yellow beard. My uncle did in fact have a face like that, elongated and framed in a handsome fair beard. . . . The face that I saw in the dream was at once my friend R.'s and my uncle's. It was like one of Galton's composite photographs" (1900, *S.E.*, IV: 138-9). Again, there is a striking connection between an association—thoughts of his uncle—and the dream content. This feature, distinctive similarity, occurs most poignantly in images, but it need not be restricted to them. For instance, a phrase heard in a dream might match exactly a phrase in the agent's memory, not just in terms of the words spoken, but also the manner and mood with which they are spoken. Elements thus associated with dream content are very likely to be the sources of the dream content, for the distinctiveness of the details makes it highly implausible that there are other such elements in memory, and it is also considerably less likely that such a distinctive image or episode was constructed from other elements than it is that the associated element is the source. Just how likely depends on the details in question: the more distinct the image or episode and the more similar the match in detail, the more likely that the associated element is the source. So in the case of connections of distinctive similarity, the inference that the associations in question are sources of the dream content is particularly cogent.

Thus far we have established that there is a valid method of inference to the conclusion that certain associations are causes of dream content. This, I think, is a sufficient response to accusations that Freud's method is inherently fallacious. I do not claim that Freud never commits the "free association fallacy" or that he always applies the method of inference described above correctly. I only claim that his specimen dream interpretations can be reasonably interpreted as involving this method of logical inference, and that whether or not this method has been applied correctly depends on subtle judgments about how striking the connections are and whether this degree of strikingness is high enough to warrant the conclusion drawn. There is, however, more to Freud's thesis than just that certain associations are the causes of the dream content. Uncovering sources of the dream content would not necessarily uncover a coherent meaning for the dream, for the sources may be just as arbitrary as the manifest content of the dream appears to be. So now we need an account of how Freud arrives at the overall interpretation of the dream.

What Freud proceeds to do in his interpretations is to uncover a coherent set of concerns of the dreamer that are related to the sources thus far uncovered in that they are what render these sources emotionally salient, and it is from these that he reads off the meaning of the dream. The method of logical inference here is not essentially different from that which we saw before. The concerns may be posited as the cause of the dream content in that they provide a unified explanation of the following: (1) the content of the dream in its entirety, and (2) the fact that there happens to be a coherent set of concerns that render emotionally salient the thoughts already inferred as causes of the dream content. That there should be a set of concerns that are coherent among themselves and are connected to the dream content in the way described is once again something the expectation of which could be reasonably judged to be low, depending on the nature and number of the connections. The alternative to this explanation compatible with the thesis that dreams do not have meaning is that the dream content was generated arbitrarily *and* that it is just a coincidence that there exists a set of concerns with such connections. The question then is which is the likelier of these two explanations. The latter explanation—indeed *any* alternative to the first explanation—cannot be more probable than the prior expectation of the purported coincidence. This expectation will, of course, depend on subtle judgments about the connections. But the point is this: Depending on how such judgments go, one may be justified in concluding that the first explanation is significantly likelier. In such a case, one will be justified in drawing the conclusion that the concerns identified caused the dream content—that is, that they are the meaning of the dream.

This provides an answer to Glymour's earlier criticism, that from one's associations with random arrangements—such as ink blots, rock formations, or (as Wittgenstein suggests) the arrangements of objects on a table—one can posit just about any meaning one wants on to these arrangements. The objection makes out Freud's procedure to be gratuitous, whereas, on the interpretation of it that I have given above, it is not. Firstly, there is, as we have seen, a principled method by which associations are judged to be the causes of the dream content—namely, by that being the likeliest explanation of why there should be emotionally salient thoughts with such striking connections to the dream content. Secondly, there is a principled method by which a meaning may be derived from these associations—namely, by being those concerns that render the associations in question emotionally salient. The supper-party dream exemplifies this, for the conversation with the skinny friend to which the patient associated was emotionally salient precisely because of the patient's jealousy about her husband's high opinion of that friend and her consequent wish that the friend should not grow stouter so as not to attract her husband more. The interpretation that Freud gives of this dream is thus far more plausible than one would expect if Freud's procedure was as gratuitous as Glymour makes out. There are therefore subtle differences between gratuitously assigning a plausible meaning to a set of associations and Freud's process of interpretation, but ones which nevertheless make all the difference with regard to the validity of his method.

This account of Freud's method of logical inference makes good the jigsaw puzzle analogy that we saw in the introduction to this essay. The pieces of the puzzle correspond to elements of the dream content and to associated thoughts and memories. The fit of tabs and blanks corresponds to striking connections. The epistemological insight that can be gleaned from consideration of jigsaw puzzles is that one knows that a puzzle has been solved when there is a flush fit between the pieces joined together, when all the pieces have been accounted for, and when a coherent meaning can be read off the completed puzzle: that the pieces can be brought together in this way is sufficient evidence for their having been constructed accordingly. Something similar holds for dreams. That the dream content and associations can be brought together by striking connections, that all the elements of the dream content can be accounted for in this way, and that a coherent meaning can be read off the elements thus connected, can be sufficient evidence that the proposed meaning is the true meaning of the dream. As long as the judgment about the strikingness of the connections is in order, one is justified in holding that that dream has been correctly interpreted.

This last point, though, contains the reason why I cannot go all the way and say that Freud has provided a general justification of his primary thesis through his dream interpretations. The warrant for the judgment that a particular connection is of high enough felt significance often depends on an intimate acquaintance with the analysand. When this is so, only those who have such an acquaintance—the analysand himself and the analyst—may be justified in concluding that the dream has been interpreted. Those who do not are not justified in so concluding, for without this acquaintance it is reasonable to doubt whether and to what extent the connections picked out were of a kind that is relatively rare. In brief, validation falls short of general justification because some of the data can be inaccessible to other rational agents. Nevertheless, as I think we have seen from the example of the supper-party dream, Freud has come far closer to justifying the primary thesis than his critics would admit.

Blass's Experiential Evidence

The arguments of the previous section provide a strong enough defense of the primary thesis against the objections brought against it. However, the case can be strengthened still further by considering a form of evidence that has always been present in dream interpretations but has not always been explicitly recognized. The only systematic account of this form of evidence to date is that provided by Rachel Blass in *The Meaning of the Dream in Psychoanalysis* (Blass, 2002, 170). A proper introduction to it is best given in the context of a summary of her own justificatory project.

Blass attempts to provide a conditional justification of Freud's primary thesis, that is, to show that it is justified as long as the general principles of psychoanalysis are justified. There is a problem however: Freud has given us no good reason to believe that the general principles of psychoanalysis are applicable to dreams. The principles are concerned with what Blass calls "networks of meaning"—integrated sets of causally related psychic elements within an agent with respect to which we can interpret his or her intentions. The assumptions that underlie psychoanalysis, she argues, are reasonable with regard to those networks operative when we are awake, for then we have introspective and intuitive evidence for them. But the same evidence does not apply to dreams. It follows that we cannot know that there are networks of meaning for dreams in the same way as we can know this for wakeful states, and even if there were, we cannot know that they are continuous with those which are operative at the time of analysis in the same way as we do for wakeful states. Unless there is any other evidence available, we would have no reason to apply the principles of psychoanalysis to dreams, hence Freud's primary thesis would remain unjustified even for those who accept the general principles of psychoanalysis.

Blass, however, goes on to argue that there is alternative evidence available. It comes from an experience with a particular quality: "the experiential quality of meaningfulness" (henceforth, *EQOM*). This experience has three manifestations. The first is that there is a meaningful connection between two known psychic entities, *A* and *B*. Formally, this is represented as E[*A* M *B*], standing for the EXPERIENCE THAT [*A* is MEANINGFULLY CONNECTED TO *B*]. The second is that "psychic entity *A* has some meaningful connection to something," though the agent does not know to what. Formally, this is represented as E[*A* M *x*], where *x* is a variable standing for some unknown entity. The third is that "something meaningful has happened or been stated," but the agent knows not what. Formally, this is represented as E[*x* M *y*], where *x* and *y* are both variables standing for an unknown entity (Blass, 2002, 170-1).[5]

The quality of the experiences thus described is, according to Blass, "a feeling of connectedness of psychic entities or ideas" (2002, 171). She takes pains to distinguish this experience from that of a judgment, implying that an agent can have the experience without being committed to the truth of any proposition. The quality of the experience has two aspects to it. One is "immediacy and contentlessness," which means, first, that it *falls upon* the agent—that is, is not mediated by reflection or any other process of thought—and second, that it is not *about* anything in the way that, for example, the states of belief and desire are about something, but rather is simply a particular quality of experience. The other aspect is "judgmentalness." Though the experience is not that of a judgment, it nevertheless bears some similarity to the experience of making a judgment. Blass compares it in this respect with the experience of *déjà vu*—the "judgmental" feeling that one has been here before. As such, *EQOM* differs from the "immediate and contentless" experience of anxiety, which does not have the "judgmental" aspect to it.

Blass argues that the "experiential quality of meaningfulness" provides evidence that the general principles of psychoanalysis are applicable to dreams as follows. She first argues that the fact that a person *experiences* a meaningful connection is good reason for believing that there *is* a meaningful connection. This is so because (a) it would be difficult to explain why someone would experience an *illusion* of meaningfulness and (b) clinical experience indicates that "contents that are felt to be connected for reasons unknown to the patient emerge as significantly tied to each other" (2002, 182) She then observes that it is common for people to experience *EQOM* in relation to their dreams—that is, to have an unmediated feeling that the dream is meaningful. Since *EQOM* is a reliable indicator of meaning, we may conclude that, in such instances, the dream does have meaning. Moreover, Blass argues, just as one can experience only one's own pain, so one can experience only one's own meanings—that is, those that relate to one's currently operating network of meaning. It follows that the network of meaning of a dream must be the same as the network of meaning of an awake individual at the time of this experience, thereby justifying the application of the principles of psychoanalysis to dreams. Thus we have a conditional justification of Freud's primary thesis.

As Blass herself acknowledges, her argument is not watertight, as there is room to dispute the inference that *EQOM* is a reliable indicator of meaningfulness—for example, by giving an account of how the experience may be illusory after all. More significantly, for those who do not already accept the general principles of psychoanalysis, the argument will be of no consequence. Nevertheless, I think that the experiential evidence that Blass presents has value beyond that of making good her conditional justification of Freud's thesis. Specifically, it can be utilized to support the argument of the previous section. Recall that I argued that the justification that the analyst has for his interpretation is that it is the best explanation of both the content of the dream and the existence of a coherent set of concerns with several striking connections to the dream content. There are several places where the "experiential quality of meaningfulness" can strengthen this inference by providing additional facts that the analyst's account explains but that explanations that do not invoke meaning do not; or at least, do so only *ad hoc*. What matters here is, not so much that we are warranted in inferring that the experience of a meaningful connection indicates that there is a meaningful connection, but that it is a phenomenon that, because of its immediacy and distinctiveness, demands an explanation.

There are three manifestations of *EQOM* that can serve as such evidence. The first is the one that Blass refers to in her argument: that people often have the immediate experience that their dream, or some part of it, is meaningful. This is the manifestation of *EQOM* formally denoted as E[*A* M *x*], where *A* here is either the dream as a whole or some element within it. This also seems to be the phenomenon that Wittgenstein observed in the quote that heads this essay, in which he notes that dreams are often experienced as *calling* for an interpretation. Since the analyst provides a meaning for the dream through his interpretation, he also thereby provides an explanation of why this experience should be present. It is, however, difficult to see how any explanation of a particular dream content that holds that that content is meaningless could explain this phenomenon; or at least, explain it in anything other than an *ad hoc* manner.

The second manifestation is the following: The analysand often experiences an element that emerges during free association as meaningfully connected to an element of the dream. This is the experience of *EQOM* denoted by E[*A* M *B*], where *A* is the an element of the dream and *B* is an element associated with it. When this experience is present it either constitutes or contributes to the strikingness of a connection. Any alternative explanation to that in which *B* is posited as the cause of *A* is not only limited in likelihood by the prior expectation that there would be an element with such a striking connection to the dream content, but must also explain why the analysand's experience of the connection would have *that* particular quality. Again, it is difficult to see what such an explanation could be; and even more difficult to see how it could be anything other than *ad hoc*.

The third manifestation is that, when provided with an interpretation of her dream, the analysand often comes to experience the concerns thus uncovered as meaningfully connected to the dream content as a whole. That is, the interpretation strikes her as being the meaning of the dream. This is the experience of *EQOM* denoted by E[*A* M *B*], where *A* is the dream as a whole and *B* is the meaning of it provided by the interpretation. There are in Freud hints that this is the case with at least some of his dream interpretations. For example:

> I was able to give her the correct interpretation of the dream, which she afterwards confirmed (1900, *S.E.*, IV: 152).

> [S]he no longer denied that the dream-picture corresponded to a wish of hers (1900, *S.E.*, IV: 154).

I differ from Glymour in taking these, not as evidence that the patients in question were not clever, but rather as evidence that the patients experienced an *immediate* conviction that many people who have had their dreams interpreted (either by themselves or others) have also experienced and which seems independent to any case that has been made for that particular conclusion. If we suppose that a dream interpretation is accompanied in this way by the distinctive experience of meaningfulness, then we have another datum that is explained by the correctness of the interpretation. Here, though, there is an obvious alternative explanation, namely, that which Glymour offers, that the analysand is convinced by the analyst that his interpretation is indeed the meaning of the dream. This explanation, however, does not do justice to the phenomenology of the experience—as remarked, the experience has an immediacy which is absent from that of becoming convinced by the case made for it by the analyst. The explanation offered by the correctness of the interpretation, on the other hand, does do justice to the phenomenology. So once again, when present, this is evidence in favor of the analyst's interpretation.

Overall, the experience of *EQOM* in any one or more of these three manifestations considerably strengthens the argument that the analyst's interpretation is correct because its being so is the best explanation of the facts under view. As with the felt significance of connections, we are dealing here with evidence not available to anyone outside of the analytical setting. For this reason I think that, as before, we can only speak of this evidence as contributing to the validation of Freud's method of inference, rather than to the justification of his thesis.

The Neuroscientific Evidence

The arguments presented above make the primary thesis plausible, but if it turns out that neuroscientific evidence shows that the content of dreams cannot be generated in the way that Freud suggests, then the thesis must nevertheless be abandoned. For a time, it seemed that this was indeed the case. In a paper published in 1977, Hobson and McCarley challenged many aspects of Freud's theory of dreams on neurophysiologial grounds and proposed an alternative theory that they regarded as incompatible with Freud's. The basis of their challenge was that neurophysiological evidence pointed towards the pons, on the brainstem, as the instigator of dreams rather than the forebrain, thereby rendering it impossible that ideas are the progenitors of dreams: "If we assume that the physiological substrate of consciousness is in the forebrain, these facts [i.e. that the trigger, the power supply, and the regulating biological clock of dream sleep are pontine] completely eliminate any possible contribution of ideas (or [of] their neural substrate) to the primary driving force of the dream process" (1977, 1338). This posed a direct challenge to Freud's theory, and led to widespread skepticism about its tenability.[6]

Even at the time, however, the challenge was not seen by all as decisive. Objections were raised by the sleep physiologist Vogel, who argued that, not only is there neurophysiological evidence that the forebrain is also involved in the genesis of dreams, but that Hobson and McCarley's critique fails also for methodological reasons (Vogel, 1978, 1531-5). If the findings that the authors refer to are to serve as evidence against Freud's theory, then they need to show empirically that the physiological processes they theorize as the actual generators do not correspond to the psychological processes of which Freud speaks. Vogel went on to argue that they had failed to do so. These arguments prompted even Grünbaum to admit that "In the light of Vogel's critique of Hobson and McCarley it would seem at best premature to suppose that their significant elucidation of the neurophysiology of dreaming has obviated appraisal of Freud's clinical arguments for his psychological dream theory" (Grünbaum, 1984, 219).

As it turns out, there is now considerably more evidence that forebrain processes are essentially involved in dreaming. Solms points out that Hobson and McCarley's case rested on the assumption that "dreaming and the REM state are synonymous." But subsequent evidence has emphatically proved this false. Sleep-lab subjects reported dreams upon awakening from NREM sleep, including during the sleep-onset phase of sleep, before the first episode of REM sleep. Moreover, patients with damage to the REM-generating regions that Hobson and McCarley speak of, the pons, reported that they still had dreams, whereas patients with damage to specific areas of the forebrain reported a cessation of dreaming (Solms and Turnball, 1993, 193-196). Solms goes on to argue, "good evidence exists that suggests that dreams *can* be causally generated by *forebrain* mechanisms" (*Ibid.*, 197). Evidence from both lesioning and imaging studies suggests that the two areas essential to dreaming are the occipito-tempero-parietal junction and limbic frontal white matter. On Solms's view, these two areas play a more constitutive role in dreaming than the REM-generating regions. The occipito-tempero-parietal junction is "heavily implicated in the generation of visuospatial imagery," whilst, more tellingly as far as Freud's theory is concerned, the limbic system has to do with emotions. More specifically, pharmacological evidence implicates the basic-emotion command system that Solms calls the dopaminergic "seeking" system, "a nonspecific motivational system engaged in looking for something to satisfy needs … linked to the pleasure/lust subsystem" (*Ibid.*, 201). The evidence for this as follows:

> Ernest Hartmann conducted a study that might be considered a direct test of the hypothesis that the mesocortical-mesolimbic dopamine (SEEKING) system is the "primary driving force" behind dreams (Hartmann et al., 1980). He administered either L-dopa or a placebo to neurologically and psychiatrically normal subjects, shortly after the first REM period. The effect was immediate and dramatic. The subjects who received L-dopa experienced a massive increase in the frequency, vivacity, emotional intensity, and bizarreness of dreaming. The frequency, density, and length of their REM periods was, by contrast, completely unchanged (*Ibid.*, 207).[7]

This result is especially interesting seen in the context of a particular criticism of Freud's theory. Grünbaum argues that, given that Freud compares dreams to the symptoms of neurotic patients, "his dream theory predicts a reduction in the *frequency* of dreaming among extensively psychoanalyzed patients"

(Grünbaum, 1993, 370-376). However, as Blass points out, this argument does not go through because the correspondence between dreams and neurotic symptoms is not exact, and indeed elsewhere Freud held that a dream was "a thought like any other," hence hardly something that we would expect to decrease in frequency with time spent in therapy (Blass, 2002, 60). The study by Hartmann that Solms quotes above nevertheless offers something in the spirit of Grünbaum's desired test of Freud's theory: the frequency of dreams is affected by a variable—not extent of psychoanalysis undertaken, but administration of L-dopa. Thus we have a correlation with frequency of dreaming, though one that turns out to be favorable to the Freudian idea that motivational states are the driving force of dreams. Overall, Solms considers the evidence uncovered by modern neuroscience to be "broadly consistent with Freud's psychoanalytic theory of dreams—although it would be inappropriate to say that his theory has been directly *proven*" (Solms and Turnball, 1993, 215).

Solms views are, however, controversial, and we must wait to see the outcome of subsequent debates in neuroscience before subscribing to them. In particular, Hobson has been prominent in continuing to take an antagonistic attitude towards Freud's theory. However, this antagonism concerns those aspects of the theory that I earlier argued were secondary, such as the censorship mechanism. Hobson's most recent version of his "activation-synthesis" model seems to leave room for the thesis that is the primary focus of this essay, that dreams can have a hidden meaning.[8] As he states: "Putting it all together—integrating all of these disparate elements into a credible dream plot—is the job of what's left of the executive 'I'. Here we are on thin ice because we don't really know how the dream scenarios are composed, any more than we know how ideas are generated in waking" (2002, 131). This seems compatible with the claim that dream scenarios may be brought about by underlying thoughts and concerns that are not manifest in the dream content itself; that is, that the dream can have a hidden meaning. In sum, what appears the case from neuroscience is that the evidence does not incontrovertibly contradict Freud's main claims about dreams and may indeed actually support them.

Conclusion

Let me outline what I think has been accomplished in this discussion. Firstly, I set out to demarcate which parts of Freud's theory of dreams can be defended on the basis of his dream interpretations alone. Much of his theory of dreams cannot be defended in this way because it depends essentially on his general theorizing about the mind, which was ostensibly developed through his work on neurosis. In this respect, Blass is right to aim at a holistic justification of Freud's theory. The part of the theory that can be defended without recourse to the rest of psychoanalytic theory is the fundamental thesis that dreams can be interpreted by a method involving free association. Even for this limited claim, though, the defense cannot take the form of a general justification because the data with which Freud works in his dream interpretations are not unambiguously accessible to anyone other than the analysand and the analyst. As such, the best that we can do by way of a defense is to show that his method of inference is valid. This is what I have attempted to do.

An important distinction I make is that between method of analysis and method of logical inference. Free association is part of the first but need not be part of the second. This clarification is useful in responding to the argument that some critics have set forth that Freud's method involves the fallacy of assuming that material associated by the analysand with the dream content is the source of the dream content. In his specimen dream interpretations at least, Freud is not merely assuming that associations are sources of the dream, but inferring that they are on the basis that this best explains the dream content and the existence of material with connections to it. Here we run against another objection: that one can surely associate to whatever material one wants. My response to this is that the connections that matter in Freudian dream interpretation are principled in being *striking* connections. The more striking these connections, and the more striking connections there are between an association and the dream content, the less likely it is that it is simply a coincidence that there exists such an element with such connections. On this basis, it could turn out that the likelier explanation is that the dream content was caused by this element. A set of concerns that has several striking connections to the dream content and which accounts for all this content can thus be rationally inferred as the cause of it. This captures the spirit of Freud's famous jigsaw puzzle analogy.

If we trust that the connections that Freud uncovers in his dream interpretations are striking ones, then we have reason to hold that the interpretations he offers are probably correct. In a large part, what we are trusting is that those connections are ones that had a high felt significance for the dreamer. That this is so may not be something that we could verify. As such, Freud has not provided us with a justification of his theory. But, his expository failings notwithstanding, he has brought us as close as he could have done. My defense of Freud is therefore limited by necessity. But I think it is valuable nevertheless, for it shows how perhaps the most serious challenge to it misses the mark. Freud's method is not fallacious and his interpretations are not gratuitous. Moreover, his method is one that, with discernment, we may follow in order to make those subtle judgments for ourselves. If we follow Freud's method to a satisfactory interpretation of our own dreams, we are justified in our conclusion insofar as it is the case that the connections we uncover are of the appropriate kind.What more is required for a general justification? I think that certain of the considerations presented in this essay are not matters beyond empirical testing. Blass herself has called for systematic empirical research into the "experiential quality of meaningfulness," and I think related research into what I have called the "felt significance" of connections is also in order. Additionally, the case for Freud's theory would undoubtedly be strengthened by a convergence of findings within psychology and neuroscience that are in line with it; and as we have seen, there are favorable signs, at least in the case of the latter.[9] However, though empirical research is germane to the question, it is difficult to envisage a set of findings within psychology and neuroscience that would issue something approaching a clear verdict on the claim that many dreams have a hidden but discoverable meaning. This does not entail that the thesis should be rejected. The claim that a particular set of concerns was the cause of a given dream content is a historical claim, hence the thesis is a summary of a collection of historical claims. We do not reject historical claims merely because they do not easily lend themselves to direct empirical test; rather, we make the best inference we can from the available evidence, and often this is good enough to warrant belief in the claim. Though the evidence from dream interpretations is not yet of a form that can provide a general warrant for belief in the primary thesis, it seems to me that, perhaps due to understandable concerns about the scientificity of the claim (in conjunction with too close an adherence to a questionable criterion of such scientificity), it has nevertheless been considerably underestimated by many. Well-documented cases of dream interpretation already provide important evidence, and when combined with empirical studies along the lines suggested above, would bring us yet closer to a general justification. Overall, I hope that the arguments set forth in this essay have shown that Freud's primary thesis about dreams at least merits being regarded as a "live hypothesis"[10]—that the thought that there is a "royal road to the unconscious" should not be dismissed as merely a dream.

Notes

1. I treat the analogy as a metaphor of Freud's method of inference and not as justificatory in itself—cf. M. Holowchak, 2010.

2. Freud himself famously revised his claim that all dreams are wish-fulfillments in the light of evidence from the dreams of those who had suffered traumas.

3. I do not of course mean logic merely in the sense of deductive reasoning, but in the broader sense that encompasses also inductive reasoning.

4. See Michael, 2008, 58-63, for a fuller discussion.

5. Blass (2002, 170) quotes Daniel 2: 3-10 to illustrate this third manifestation of *EQOM*. In this, King Nebuchadnezzar demands that his servants interpret a dream that he has forgotten but is nevertheless sure has a meaning.

6. After a presentation by Hobson at the 1976 annual meeting of the American Psychiatric Association (APA), a vote was taken as to whether Freud's theory was scientifically tenable, with the vote going overwhelmingly against Freud (Solms *et al.*, 2002, 190).

7. Study cited is from E. Hartmann *et al.*, 1980.

8. Cf. Hobson *et al.*, 2002.

9. Though it has not been my aim here to review the psychological evidence bearing on Freud's theory, one prominent study that perhaps should be mentioned is that of Wegner *et al.*, in which it was found that suppression of thoughts of a target person before sleep increased dreaming about the person. This can be interpreted as consistent with the Freudian thesis that repressed thoughts manifest in dreams.

10. As William James defines it, a live hypothesis is a proposal for belief "which appeals as a real possibility to him to whom it is proposed" (James, 2006, 2).

References

Blass, R. *The Meaning of the Dream in Psychoanalysis* (New York: State University of New York Press, 2002).

Bloom, H. (ed.), *Sigmund Freud's The Interpretation of Dreams* (New York, New Haven, & Philadelphia: Chelsea House Publishers, 1987).

Bonaparte, M.; A. Freud; and E. Kris (eds.), *The Origins of Psycho-Analysis, Letters to Wilhelm Fliess, Drafts and Notes: 1887-1902* (New York: Basic Books; London: Imago Publishing, 1954).

Freud, S. *The Standard Edition of the Complete Psychological Works of Sigmund Freud*, ed. James Strachey (London: The Hogarth Press, 1964).

Glymour, C. "The Theory of Your Dreams." In R. S. Cohen & L. Lauden (eds.), *Physics, Philosophy and Psychoanalysis (Boston Studies in the Philosophy of Science,* Vol. 76*)* (Dordrecht: D. Reidel Publishing Company, 1983), 57-71.

Grünbaum, A. *The Foundations of Psychoanalysis* (Berkeley and Los Angeles: University of California Press, 1984).

Grünbaum, A. *Validation in the Clinical Theory of Psychoanalysis: A Study in the Philosophy of Psychoanalysis* (Madison, Connecticut: International Universities Press, 1993).

Hartmann, E.; D. Russ; M. Oldfield; R. Falke; and B. Skoff, "Dream Content: Effects of L-DOPA," *Sleep Research*, 9, 1980, 153.

Hobson, J.A. *Dreaming: A Very Short Introduction* (Oxford: OUP, 2002).

Hobson, J.A., and R.W. McCarley, "The Brain as a Dream State Generator: An Activation-Synthesis Hypothesis of the Dream Process." *American Journal of Psychiatry*, 134, 1977, 12.

Hobson, J.A.; E. Pace-Schott; and R. Stickgold, "Dreaming and the Brain: Toward a Cognitive Neuroscience of Conscious States," *Behavioral and Brain Sciences*, 23, 2002, 783-842.

Holowchak, M. "The Problem of Unassailability: Analogy and the Adequacy of Constructions in Freudian Psychoanalysis," *Psychoanalytic Psychology* (forthcoming).

James, W. *The Will to Believe and Other Essays in Popular Philosophy* (New York: Cosimo Classics, 2006).

Michael, M. "On the Validity of Freud's Dream Interpretations." *Studies in History and Philosophy of Biological and Biomedical Sciences*, 39, 2008, 52-64.

Sand, R. "On a Contribution to a Future Scientific Study of Dream Interpretation." In J. Earman et al (eds.), *Philosophical Problems of the Internal and External Worlds: Essays on the Philosophy of Adolf Grünbaum* (Pittsburgh: University of Pittsburgh Press, 1993), 527-546.

Solms, M. and O. Turnball, *The Brain and the Inner World: An Introduction to the Neuroscience of Subjective Experience* (New York: Other Press, 2002).

Vogel, G.W. "An Alternative View of the Neurobiology of Dreaming." *American Journal of Psychiatry*, 135, 1978, 12, 1531-1535.

Wegner, D.M.; R.M. Wenzlaff; and M. Kozak, "Dream Rebound: The Return of the Suppressed Thoughts in Dreams," *Psychological Science*, 15, 2004, 232-236.

Chapter 6
The Unhappy Fate of Freud's Dream Theory

Rosemarie Sand
Psychoanalyst, Member of Institute of Psychoanalytic Training and Research

ON THE FIRST PAGE OF *THE INTERPRETATION OF DREAMS,* Freud's introduction of a new theory was accompanied by a rejection of what he deemed the useless accumulated conceptions of the ages. "In spite of many thousands of years of effort, the scientific understanding of dreams has made very little advance," he asserted. The older literature contained "little or nothing that touches upon the essential nature of dreams or that offers a solution of any of their enigmas." He, on the other hand, was offering a psychological technique which, if properly employed, would reveal that every dream had a meaning, every dream could be "inserted in an assignable point in the mental activities of waking life" (1900, *S.E.*, IV: 1).

These remarks, and others like it, suggest that Freud, creating a theory featuring the supposedly unheard-of concept that dreams were meaningful, abandoned the whole of the past and made an entirely new beginning. A belief of this kind is still sometimes voiced. It is said that "Freud discovered the meaning of dreams," under the assumption that, before Freud, dreams were universally regarded as senseless. However, Freud did not design his theory in a wasteland; another theory already occupied the field. The Freudian hypothesis therefore ought to be appraised, not against the background of a supposed historical vacuum, but against the conception he attempted to replace.

In this chapter I will briefly describe the two theories, the old and the new, both founded on the premise that dreams were meaningful, both offering a method by which the meanings of dreams could be discovered. I will show that the earlier theory was superior in that results of its method were trustworthy, while Freud's principle procedure, free association, was based on a fallacy that undermines the theory. Freud also employed symbol interpretation to discover dream meanings but this method always remained subordinate to free association. Freud's various attempts to answer critics will be examined. In conclusion, attention will be paid to the relatively unexplored origin of the fallacy. I will suggest that Freud's lifelong persistence in this error can be attributed to his strange belief about the nature of free association.

The Picture Theory

According to the tradition which moved into the shadows during the years of Freud's ascendancy, dreams are pictures. The contents of such dreams, their imagery, actions and the emotions and thoughts that appear in them, reflect a dreamer's mental states. In the words of the twentieth-century American psychologist Calvin Hall: "[Dreams] are pictures of what the mind is thinking. . . . The images of a dream are the concrete embodiments of the dreamer's thoughts; these images give visible expression to that which is invisible, namely, conceptions" (Hall, 1953, 85 and 95).

From the most ancient times, it was assumed that dreams were depictions and that discovering their meaning depended upon matching their content with what they depicted, their source. In superstitious ages, sources were supernatural; dreams were regarded as messages sent by gods or demons and they served to warn or to predict. The Biblical Joseph dreamed that the sheaves of wheat bound by his brothers stood up in the field one day and bowed down to his sheaf. His brothers immediately understood that this imagery symbolically pictured a future event and expressed their indignation: "Shalt thou indeed rule over us?" (Genesis, 37.8)

When faith in otherworldly messages gradually diminished, the dream had to be regarded as a product of the dreamer's mind. It was then supposed that the dream reflected a mental state of the dreamer. In the case of a modern Joseph the presumption might be that he had been thinking of his standing in the family, perhaps hoping to surpass his brothers.

In spite of the momentous shift from a mystical to a secular view of the dream, the principle of interpretation did not change. Discovering the meaning of a dream depended upon the recognition of a correspondence—a similarity or thematic affinity—between the dream content and a source which it could be regarded as representing.[1]

Tradition allowed the representation of any mental state in a dream: wishes, worries, fears, perceptions, premonitions, or reflections. Occasionally, a dream, replete with details taken from waking life, could be very realistic. In many other dreams, a few realistic details served to suggest the origin of an otherwise puzzling dream. Figurative dreams, like that of Joseph, were also recognized, particularly when the symbolism in which they were expressed lent itself to commonsense interpretation.

Dreams, it was believed, might occasionally reveal unconscious mental states; they might provide glimpses of thoughts, feelings and motives of which the dreamer was unaware. They did this by picturing states of mind which the dreamer did not recognize, or did not recognize immediately. A person who was not conscious of a feeling of resentment might discover that feeling by noticing their manifestly resentful behavior in a dream. Nathaniel Hawthorne was referring to this tradition when he wrote, "Truth often finds its way to the mind close muffled in robes of sleep, and then speaks with uncompromising directness of matters in regard to which we practice an unconscious self-deception during our waking moments" (Hawthorne, 1970, 51-2).

In the nineteenth century, champions of this theory were looking forward to the scientific study of its basic premise, the picturing principle. The dreams that were expected to lend themselves to research were those which appeared in response to stimuli occurring during sleep. The dreamer seems to be under cannon fire on the battlefield of Waterloo; waking reveals that the intermittent roar of the cannon correlates with the banging of a shutter. Such dreams were appealing because they could be artificially produced by stimulating a sleeping subject and because the influence of the stimulus on the responding dream could often be recognized, with good agreement between researchers. At the end of the century, experiments were already being conducted; in the twentieth, however, with a few notable exceptions, such studies have not been pursued (Dement, 1976, 66-9).

Freud's contemporaries were familiar with these traditional beliefs about dreams. Literature and the plastic arts just then were being drawn to revelations of the inner life and dreams were often called upon to aid in these revelations. A sophisticated public took the appearance of dreams in plays and novels in stride. In 1899, while Freud was writing *The Interpretation of Dreams,* Arthur Schnitzler was drafting a play the plot of which hinged on a dream revealing an unrecognized sexual desire.[2]

The strength of the picture theory was that, when dreams reflected mental states in a transparent fashion, one could with some assurance attribute the dream to a particular source; one could maintain that one knew what the dream was about. The great drawback of the picture theory was that dreams that clearly instantiated it were not common. Moreover, many dreams, having no recognizable connection with their dreamer's life, were incomprehensible. These, necessarily, were inexplicable.

Freud's Dream Theory

In contrast to the picture theory, Freud proposed a theory and a mode of interpretation that promised that few, if any, dreams would remain mysterious. To do this, he took a step which had never been taken before: He eliminated the picturing principle. In a complete break with the past, he asserted that dreams ordinarily did *not* reflect a mental state. In place of the traditional form of interpretation, which depended upon the finding of a resemblance between the dream and a state of mind, he proposed a method that would locate mental origins that bore no resemblance to the dreams attributed to them. This liberation from the traditional demand for a recognizable link between a dream and what it represented, promised to widen the scope of the search and would free him to look for previously unsuspected sources.

This may well have seemed to be a significant insight and complete break, comparable perhaps to that of the astronomer Kepler, who, by overriding the ancient Aristotelian dictum that all heavenly motions were circular, was able to discover the elliptical orbits of the planets. In Freud's case, the theoretical advantage offered by relinquishing the picturing principle was that it cleared the way for his wish-fulfillment theory. He would be able to show not only that dreams were caused by wishes, but also that most of these wishes were sexual and unconscious.

Clearly, if Freud had succeeded, he would have produced a superior theory. The traditional conception could not have competed with a hypothesis that successfully brought to light the mental origins of most dreams. The question to be answered, therefore, is whether or not Freud was able to get along without the picturing principle as he supposed he could. In order to do this, he would have had to be able to demonstrate that particular wishes produced particular dream scenes without appealing to any likeness between them. As we will see, he failed in the attempt.

Freud allowed that a few "innocent" dreams, like those of children, might be pictured in dreams. However, according to his theory, most of the dreams of adults were stimulated by desires which, having originated in the Oedipal situation in childhood, were morally objectionable. These had to be kept out of the conscious mind by repression. In this repressed state, they retained their energy and continuously strove to break into consciousness. During waking hours, a moral counterforce, exercising "censorship," prevented this emergence. In sleep, however, when censorship weakened, the forbidden wishes threatened to make their way into dream consciousness, thereby disturbing the sleeper. This eventuality was prevented by the "dream-work," a process which altered the appearance of the objectionable wish; in an unrecognizable form, it was allowed to appear in the dream.

In Freud's exploratory procedure, the search for the meaning of a dream would not focus on the dream as remembered by the dreamer even when it seemed to make sense. This dream, he asserted, was not "the genuine thing." It was a disguise which concealed the dream's real meaning. Calling it the "manifest dream," he noted: "Every attempt that has hitherto been made to solve the problem of dreams has dealt directly with their *manifest* content as it is presented in our memory. . . . We are alone in taking something else into account" (1900, *S.E.*, IV: 277).

Analysis began with the dismemberment of the manifest dream. Explaining the process, Freud said: "If I say to a patient who is still a novice: 'What occurs to you in connection with this dream?', as a rule his mental horizon becomes a blank. If, however, I put the dream before him cut up into pieces, he will give me a series of associations to each piece, which might be described as the 'background thoughts' of that particular part of the dream" (1900, *S.E.,* IV: 103-104). The dreamer was asked to relax and, starting off from one of the dream's segments, was to let thoughts wander in any direction, exercising no control, immediately putting all of the ideas that came to mind into words however, irrelevant, meaningless, or unimportant they might seem to be. A series of these "background thoughts," also known as "latent dream thoughts," would culminate in the revelation of the repressed wish that had prompted the dream. This was the procedure which came to be known as "free association."

The Free Association Fallacy

The novelty of Freud's approach lay in his claim that the manifest dream, being a deliberate disguise, did *not* picture the wish that produced it. Most of the dream analyses that Freud offered, his own dreams and those of patients, begin with this condition; the content of the dream does not reveal the determining wish. For instance, when Freud dreamed that his friend Otto seemed ill, because "his face was brown and he had protruding eyes," his associations led him to conclude that the dream was the result of two wishes: He wanted to become a professor and to lead a long life. An elderly female patient dreamed that when she tried to help trapped may-beetles escape, one managed to fly out the open window but the other was crushed. Her associations supposedly led to the wish that her husband would have an erection. But what justified this assumption?[3]

Critics protested vehemently against the proposition that a wish that turned up in a series of associations to a dream could be regarded as cause of a dream merely because it had turned up. What was being asserted was that if one began with A (for instance, the images of the escaped and crushed beetles) and, through free association, reached B (a wish for her husband to have an erection), one could legitimately accept that B had caused A. Free association, opponents charged, was being assigned a power that it simply did not have.

One facet of the ensuing argument, a failure to define its terms, kept it simmering for years and should be eliminated at the outset. Two different kinds of free association have not been distinguished. In one sense, "free association" is used to discover what is on a person's mind. When people let thoughts come to them, expressing them freely—deliberately not monitoring the flow—they may well gain information about themselves. According to a pre-Freudian expectation, this liberated form of "association" may yield valuable insights and bring back memories; it has also been credited with opening the door to creativity. Free association of this sort is not at issue.

Free association, as Freud understood it, was something quite different. He turned it into an exploratory instrument—a tool to be used in the excavation of unconscious wishes. He trusted that associating to a component of a dream would often bring the origin of this component to light. Opponents argued that free association to a dream, carried on for a while, would always eventuate in the appearance of a wish of some kind or other, but this appearance did not signify that this wish had caused the dream.

Freud responded to this objection. Accurately reporting the argument against his method of free association, he noted:

> We allow ourselves to be led on by our thoughts regardless of the direction in which they carry us and drift on in this way from one thing to another. But we cherish a confident belief that in the end, without any active intervention on our part, we shall arrive at the dream-thoughts from which the dream originated. Our critics argue against this along the following lines. There is nothing wonderful in the fact that a single element of the dream should lead us *somewhere;* every idea can be associated with *something*. What *is* remarkable is that such an aimless and arbitrary train of thought should happen to bring us to the dream-thoughts.

Critics concluded, "[T]he whole thing is completely arbitrary . . . in this way anyone who cares to take such useless pains can worry out any interpretation he pleases from any dream" (1900, *S.E.,* V: 527)

Freud answered confidently that he could "cut the ground from under" this objection. Conscious thought was ordinarily guided by purposes. In free association, purposes were deliberately set aside and thoughts were allowed to wander. Freud warned, however, that this wandering was not as aimless as it might appear to be, because when conscious control was abandoned, unconscious guidance took its place. He explained, "[A]ll that we can ever get rid of are purposive ideas that are *known* to us. . . ." When we free associate, *unknown ideas*—that is unconscious, purposive ideas—"take charge and thereafter determine the course" of the ideas (1900, *S.E.*, V: 528).

Freud was persuaded that unconscious purposive ideas would take a "course" leading to the origin of the dream. At this critical point, he and his adversaries parted company. They insisted that the course of such ideas was unknown. One might grant that the flow of free associations was unconsciously determined, but one could know nothing about the heading the flow might take. It could by no means be supposed that it would necessarily gravitate towards the dream's origin.

What evidence was there that free association was unconsciously guided at all? Freud maintained that the very complexity of the patterns it produced suggested unconscious creation. Free association to separate components of the manifest dream did not simply produce a number of unrelated trains of thought. As the process continued, intricate relations between these trains were established. The final result often consisted of a "tissue" of ideas—a fertile soil in which a dream was rooted.

In response to this, critics pointed to the way in which such intricate, interconnecting networks came about. The dreamer, associating to a dream segment

A, produces a series of thoughts. Then making a "new start" takes up another segment of the dream, B. But this is *not* a new start. At this point the dreamer is not associating only to B, but also to A and to everything that has come up in association so far. Themes that emerged during association to A are likely to turn up again in association to B, and then again, in connection to C, and so forth. An intricate network is quickly produced.

Freud was aware of this analysis, but he insisted that the results of free association were so rich and meaningful that they could not be attributed to the waking associations but had to have been produced unconsciously by the dream-work. He appealed to "the impression made by our interpretations, to the surprising connections with other elements of the dream which emerge in the course of our pursuing a single one of its ideas, and to the improbability that anything which gives such an exhaustive account of the dream could have been arrived at except by following up psychical connections which had already been laid down" (1900, *S.E.*, V: 528). The waking associations merely brought the achievement of the dream-work to light.

However, meaningful networks could be produced without the assistance of the dream-work—that is, without having been previously "laid down." They could be created at any time, in association to *anything*. One could pick a sentence from a newspaper, cut it into pieces, and associate to the segments and in no time one would have assembled a meaningful tissue of thoughts. Moreover, Freud's adversaries pointed out that association to *anything* could result in the appearance of an important wish. For example, in 1920, when the issue was being hotly debated, a physician, testing the hypothesis, asked a patient to associate to a number that he had chosen for her at random. She complied and in a little while was confessing that she was in an embarrassing predicament. Fearing she was pregnant, she was anxiously wishing that her period would start soon (Schneider, 1920, 250-1).

Taking another tack, Freud appealed to the results of psychoanalytic practice to bolster his claim about free association. He maintained that when free association was used to trace a neurotic symptom back to the unconscious memory that had caused it, the symptom immediately disappeared, thus validating the exploratory procedure. Dreams could be treated like symptoms, he averred. The procedure which revealed unconscious pathogenic memories could be relied upon to uncover the unconscious dream-producing wishes. In actuality, Freud soon gave up the claim that retrieving the pathogenic memory was followed by immediate symptom removal. However, even if it had been true that symptoms disappeared, the evidence offered by this observable event would not have carried over to justify the unconscious wish detection that had no comparable perceptible consequence.

None of Freud's responses over the years satisfied his critics. No meeting of minds ever took place on this issue. To the end of his days, Freud insisted that free association led to the excavation of wishes, although objections continued to rain down on him. It was as though he was selectively deaf to the protest that a wish could not be regarded as having caused a dream just because it turned up during free association to that dream. His inability to get his mind around this essential admonition served as a roadblock to any reconciliation between Freud and his scientific contemporaries.

The Root of the Fallacy

Explanations for Freud's stubborn adherence to this fallacy have rarely been sought in recent times. Unless I am mistaken, expositors of the fallacy, once they have established to their own satisfaction that Freud was embroiled in this peculiar error, have not gone on to look for possible sources of the error. Such sources can be found, however, not only in *The Interpretation of Dreams,* but also in Freud's later publications.

Freud revealed in all frankness that he was convinced that when he free associated he was "following up psychical connections which *had already been laid down"* (emphasis added; 1900, *S.E.*, V: 528). While associating, he did not merely discover an unconscious wish, but the associations themselves constituted a *preexisting unconscious road* that led to the wish. The first few associative steps that he took put him on a previously prepared track. Thereafter, while associating consciously, he was simultaneously moving back along this unconscious pathway.

Freud was in the grip of a conviction that never wavered, a subjective certainty that most of the ideas that occurred to him when he free associated were thoughts that had been active in his mind earlier when the dream was produced. They were not "fresh daytime material"; they were returnees (1900, *S.E.,* V: 532). The dream-work left a trail that led from the wish to the dream. When he free associated, he began with the dream and followed the path back to the unconscious wish.

Freud believed some "fresh" material might make its way into a series of associations, for instance, thoughts relating to events which had occurred between the time of dreaming and analysis. He supposed that not every idea that appeared had necessarily previously had "a share in the formation of the dream" (1900, *S.E.*, IV: 311). However, such new associations would not be essential, although they might provide additional "shafts" down to the deeper-lying dream thoughts. Freud insisted, "It must be allowed that *the great bulk of the thoughts which are revealed in analysis* [by free association] *were already active during the process of forming the dream. . .*" (emphasis added; 1900, *S.E.*, IV: 280).

With the exception of occasional fresh material, Freud declared, "It is true that in carrying out the interpretation in the waking state we follow a path which leads back from the elements of the dream to the dream-thoughts and that the dream-work followed one in the contrary direction" (1900, *S.E.*, V: 532). The dream-work had started with the hidden wish and had completed its task with the production of the manifest dream. When Freud free associated, he started with the manifest dream and supposed that he was retracing the steps taken by the dream work to arrive at the starting point—the hidden, unconscious wish.

This concept, that free association consisted of a sort of back-tracking, enabled Freud to construct long, causal trails from a dream element to a significant dream-thought—the construction facilitated by the loose connections permitted between thoughts.

Looking back, for example, at a series of associations he had produced to a lengthy dream, Freud believed that he had traced the steps that the dream-work had taken to get from "favorite flower" to "a gaseous excretion known by the name of '*flatus.*' I now saw that the path leading to *flatus* had been prepared far ahead: from *flowers,* through the *Spanish* couplet, *Isabelita, Isabella* and Ferdinand, *Henry VIII, English* history, and the Armada which sailed against *England,* after whose defeat a medal was struck, bearing the inscription '*Flavit* et dissipati sunt' [L., "He blew and they had scattered'], since the storm-blast had scattered the Spanish fleet." And so, from "flavit," he arrived at "flatus" (1900, *S.E.*, IV: 213-214).

Freud supposed the very irrationality of these sequences was evidence of their unconscious production by the dream work. In connection with a convoluted series of associations—"*Pélagie—plagiarizing—plagiostomes* or sharks" which led ultimately to "overcoats" (i.e., condoms)—Freud said, "No doubt it was a very far-fetched and senseless chain of thought; but *I could never have constructed it in waking life unless it had already been constructed by the dream-work*" (emphasis added; 1900, *S.E.*, IV: 206).

In order to sustain this belief, Freud had to hold on to the conviction that most of the thoughts that occurred to him while he was free associating were repetitions of thoughts that had been active earlier—that the series that was coming to his mind *now* was a series created *previously.* This conviction allowed him to suppose that he was uncovering what had happened in the past when the dream was produced. It permitted him to trust that he was actually investigating unconscious operations when he free associated.

In spite of important modifications of other aspects his dream theory in later years, Freud never changed his mind about the efficacy of free association to uncover the wishes behind dreams. Fifteen years after the publication of *The Interpretation of Dreams*, he reiterated: "And let me remind you once again that the work which transforms the latent dream into the manifest one is called the *dream-work.* The work *which proceeds in the contrary direction* (emphasis added), which endeavours to arrive at the latent dream from the manifest one, is our work of interpretation" (1915, *S.E.*, XV: 170).

In the last presentation of his ideas, posthumously published in 1940, he reaffirmed his faith in the procedure with a bit of caution, "[I]t is not to be wondered at if *this work of interpretation (acting in a direction opposite to the dream-work)* fails occasionally to arrive at complete certainty" (emphasis added) (1940, *S.E.*, XXIII: 169).

Freud's Reception

Freud complained bitterly about the reception of *The Interpretation of Dreams*. According to his biographer, Ernest Jones, it had been "annihilating" (1953, 361). Psychoanalysis had met with a "storm of protest" (155, 107). Looking back on his career, Freud recalled that "German science was united in rejecting it." He accused his opponents of "barbarism" and declared that "for the degree of arrogance which they displayed, for their conscienceless contempt of logic, and for the coarseness and bad taste of their attacks there could be no excuse" (1925, *S.E.*, XX: 49). He added years later, "The situation recalled what was actually put in practice in the Middle Ages" when a person was "put in the pillory and given over to maltreatment by the mob" (1933, *S.E.*, XXII: 137).

When historians first looked at some reviews of his dream book, they were surprised to find that these were quite favorable (Bry *et al.*, 1962, 20-4). Thus, Freud's angry response to what seemed to have been a relatively friendly welcome was puzzling. However, investigation subsequently revealed that Freud's theories had elicited two kinds of reaction: The favorable was found chiefly in literary and general interest journals; the scientific press, on the other hand, had been almost universally hostile. Freud was bitter about lack of acceptance by the scientific community.

From about 1906, when Freud's theories were beginning to attract widespread attention, until the First World War, numerous protests, often penned by men illustrious in their fields, appeared in scientific publications. These critics, who have been described as constituting a "Who's Who" of German science, did not typically engage in crude polemics (Shakow *et al.*, 1964, 20). They were Freud's scientific colleagues, publishing in professional journals. They were generally civil. Sometimes they softened their commentary with a few kind phrases (e.g., "stimulating ideas"), but then concluded with a condemnation of psychoanalytic hypotheses as unsupported by satisfactory evidence.

The focus of Freud's opponents was almost entirely on what were deemed his faulty methods and their inability to supply reliable evidence for his theories. The free-association fallacy and the irresponsible use of symbolism regularly came in for negative appraisal.

When psychoanalysis began to make inroads in lands outside of Germany, similar assessments appeared there. In America, an essay by Robert Sessions Woodworth, professor of psychology at Columbia University, resembled continental evaluations in both mood and content. Woodworth, a student of William James—philosopher, experimenter, and author of influential textbooks—admitted that, so far as psychoanalysis was concerned, he was one of the "skeptics." He added, "There is scarcely a page in the writings of the school that does not contain assertions that arouse the suspicion of the psychologist" (1917, 186). When his review appeared in 1917, Freud had extended the use of free association to the discovery of the unconscious origins of "lapses" of all kinds—the forgetting of names, slips of the tongue, bungled actions, and so forth. Jung had used it to locate psychological "complexes." Woodworth's comments encompassed all of these efforts.

Woodworth said, "[T]he first concern of the psychologist confronted with the numerous assertions put forward by the Freudian school is with the *methods* employed to reach these conclusions" (1917, 176). The first method Freud had used had been free association. Woodworth took note of the fallacy:

> [I]f the subject has dreamed of a person A, and on letting his mind move freely from the thought of A comes more or less directly to think of a significant person B, then A in the dream was really a representative of B. By such reasoning, the conclusions are reached that dreams have a hidden meaning very different from their manifest content, and that lapses and hesitations in the process of thinking or acting are due to the stirring of submerged complexes.
>
> Now what is the logic of this inference? Can the psychoanalyst seriously uphold the proposition that, whenever the thought of A has come into my mind, if I then let my mind move freely from A and reach B (sooner or later), B must have been operative in making me think of A in the first place? (1917, 176-7)

Woodworth also rejected the psychoanalytic theory of "fixed" symbolism. "My conclusion is that fixed symbolism . . . is worthless as a method of scientific psychology, and cannot support the conclusions that are based on it." It followed that "There is actually no evidence that dreams in general have a 'latent content', or are the fulfilment of deep-seated and ordinarily repressed wishes" (1917, 183 and 186).

Logical objections like these were swept away in the general enthusiasm for psychoanalysis. For several decades at the beginning of the twentieth century, Freud's dream theory ruled supreme: The manifest-latent distinction was regarded as his solution to the dream's mysteries; the manifest dream was derided.

Gradually, however, enthusiasm waned. References to the critical distinction appeared less frequently, even in journals which had championed it. At some point, interest seems to have dwindled away entirely. After a hiatus, which must seem exceedingly brief in a history that stretches across millennia, the traditional picture theory of dreams has reasserted itself.

Notes

1. In the twentieth century, dream science changed in one important particular. The premise had always been that there was a causal relationship between the dream and what

it pictured. For instance, when an agitated man whose car had been damaged in an accident dreamed about this accident that night, it would have been supposed that the psychological stimulus, the agitation, had caused him to dream. It has turned out that this is not so. Psychological stimuli, physical or mental, do not cause dreams. Dreams occur only when the sleeping brain is in a particular state; this state is the cause of dreams.

Scientists have learned that during the night the brain is repeatedly in a condition which is manifested externally by the rapid eye movements of the sleeper. Wakened at such times of "rapid eye movement" ("REM") sleep, people generally report that they have been dreaming; at other times, they rarely do. Although the correlation between REM sleep and dreaming is not perfect, the theory now accepted is that a brain state triggers dreaming.

Traditional dream interpretation, however, has not been much affected by this important scientific discovery. Granted that the dreamer's agitation about the accident did not cause the dream to occur, yet it caused the dream's *content*. The man may have dreamed because he was in a REM state, but he dreamed about the accident because that was what was on his mind. To avoid confusion between these two different kinds of causes, I have reserved the word "cause" for the production of the dream and the use of the word "source" for the mental state which determines the dream content. It appears that a psychological stimulus can only function as source for a dream content if it is sensed while the individual is in REM sleep. However, some REM periods are very long, giving stimuli ample opportunity to shape the content of dreams.

2. In Schnitzler's *The Veil of Beatrice,* a young woman foolishly tells her lover that she dreamed that she was the duchess, married to the duke, and that in the surroundings, he, Filippo, appeared merely as a face in the crowd. When he is enraged, she protests that it was "only a dream," but he interprets it as a wish: "But dreams are desires without courage/Shameless wishes, which the light of day/Drives back into the corners of the soul/From which they dare to creep only at night."

3. Notably, the wishes in these two instances can hardly be regarded as having been unconscious in Freud's usual sense of the word. They do not exemplify the repressed desires which, according to his hypothesis, are beyond the reach of the conscious mind. Unfortunately, it is difficult to find in Freud's works any dream analysis which perfectly illustrates his use of his method, that is, an instance in which the uninterrupted flow of associations culminates in the discovery of a repressed wish. His practice allowed the insertion of helpful interpretations and his own associations, as well as interventions in the case of blocking caused by repression. Nevertheless, he maintained that free association often resulted in the discovery of hidden motives and that the method opened the door to the exploration of the unconscious mind.

References

Bry, Ilse, and Alfred H. Rifkin, "Freud and the History of Ideas: Primary Sources, 1886-1910," *Science and Psychoanalysis,* Vol. V, *Psychoanalytic Education,* Jules H. Masserman (ed.) (New York: Grune and Stratton, 1962).

Dement, William, *Some Must Watch While Some Must Sleep* (New York: W.W. Norton & Company, 1976).

Hall, Calvin S., *The Meaning of Dreams* (New York: McGraw-Hill Book Company, 1953).

Hawthorne, Nathaniel, "The Birthmark," *Mosses from and Old Manse* (Freeport, N.Y. Books for Libraries Press [1854] 1970), 47-69.

Jones, Ernest, *The Life and Work of Sigmund Freud, Volume l: The Formative Years and the Great Discoveries, l856-1900* (New York: Basic Books, 1953).

Jones, Ernest, *The Life and Work of Sigmund Freud, Vol. II: Years of Maturity, 1901-1919* (New York: Basic Books, 1955).

Schneider, Rudolf, "Zu Freuds Untersuchungsmethode des Zahleneinfalls," *Internationale Zeitschrift für Psychoanalyse,* 1920, VI, 75, 250-1.

Schnitzler, Arthur, *Der Schleier der Beatrice.* In *Gesammelte Werke, Vol. II* (Berlin: S. Fischer Verlag, 1915), 129-325.

Shakow, David and David Rapaport, *Psychological Issues,* Vol. IV, No. 1; Monograph 13, *The Influence of Freud on American Psychology* (New York: International Universities Press, 1964).

Woodworth, R.S. "Some Criticisms of the Freudian Psychology," *The Journal of Abnormal Psychology*, Vol. XII, August, 1917, 174-94.

Chapter 7
Reply to Dr. Michael

Rosemarie Sand

RECENTLY, I HAD THE FOLLOWING DREAM: I opened the door to the terrace and stepped out and there I found a number of rabbit-size coyotes tumbling about; I had a broom with which I chased them away. The dream was amusing; in a busy morning, I gave it no thought. Several hours later, however, I recalled the episode responsible for the dream. I had opened the same door, stepped out onto the same terrace and had come face-to-face with what seemed to be quite a large animal—a real, live coyote. I had never seen a coyote before and now I was confronted with one at a distance of no more than ten feet. We looked into each other eyes for a few tense moments and then it turned and loped away.

This episode was the source of the dream. Once I had recalled it, I knew why I had dreamed this particular dream. The recognizable, meaningful connection between the source—my memory of the event—and the dream attested to a causal link between them. This very ancient mode of commonsensical dream interpretation depends upon the perception of a significant link between a mental state—something in the mind of the dreamer—and the content of the dream.

The discovery of this link can come about in a variety of ways; in my case, I simply spontaneously recalled the source of the dream. But suppose that I had not done so and that I was in psychoanalysis; the episode then might have come to my mind while I was free associating. Under these circumstances, it would be recognized as the source of the dream, not because it was recalled during free association, but because it had an identifiable connection with the dream's content.

The long-acknowledged drawback of the traditional mode of dream study is that suitable dream sources are often hard to find; in those cases, dreams are uninterpretable. Nevertheless, some nineteenth-century scientists valued this ancient method because it could be modified for scientific use. Studies showed that sleepers, stimulated by a sensation, dreamed about the sensation in recognizable form about half the time. Researchers, examining the resultant dreams, were thereby accorded a unique view of the amazing creativity of the sleeping brain.

Freud was aware of this kind of dream interpretation but he believed that he had a superior method, one that would permit the analysis of most dreams. He supposed that the "great majority" of the dreams of adults were stimulated by repressed wishes. The dream recalled by the dreamer was a facade, a disguise which concealed the real significance of the dream. In the theory that he constructed, Freud called this facade the "manifest" dream. He supposed that free association—letting thoughts come to the mind beginning with an element of the dream but thereafter flowing without guidance from the conscious mind—would result in the discovery of the dream's real meaning—the "latent dream thoughts" or "latent dream." Freud justifiably regarded this theory and the method which implemented it as uniquely his own and his authorship has been universally recognized.

Freud illustrated the use of the method with analyses of his own dreams. In one of these examples, he reported a dream in which he saw his friend Otto looking ill; his face was brown and he had protruding eyes as though he had Basedow's disease. Freud associated to this dream until he arrived at two wishes: that he himself would become a professor and that he would lead a long life. These wishes, he supposed, were responsible for the dream.

The very first scientific reviewers of *The Interpretation of Dreams* pointed out that the method was invalid because it was based on a serious logical error. One could not rationally suppose that a person associating to a dream was following "a path which leads back from the elements of the dream to the [latent] dream thoughts. . ." (1900, *S.E.*, V: 532). One could not reasonably accept that a wish, merely because it occurred during free association, was the source of the dream. Doubtless the wishes arrived at in this faulty manner were genuine wishes. Freud really did want to become a professor and lead a long life but the assumption that these wishes had produced the dream about Otto's illness was altogether unjustified.

Michael agrees that Freud sometimes committed this "free association fallacy," but points out that Freud made use of more than one method when interpreting dreams.

Freud undoubtedly employed a variety of interpretative techniques. Free association, which matches the description Freud gave of it when describing his theory, rarely occurs in anything like the pure form in his book. Occasionally, Freud even resorted to the traditional technique, apparently unaware that he was doing so. The first dream analysis in the book, the so-called "specimen dream," is of this type. Unfortunately, the dream which Michael chose to illustrate his presentation—the "smoked salmon" dream—is also subject to commonsense interpretation. The dream clearly reflects the dreamer's state of mind.

On the day before she had the dream, a woman, Freud's patient, conversed with an acquaintance of whom she was jealous because her husband was constantly singing her praises. This woman said to her "When are you going to ask us to another meal? You always feed one so well." That night, Freud's patient dreamed that, for several reasons, she *could not* give a dinner party—there was nothing in the house, the shops were closed because it was Sunday, and the caterers could not be reached because the phone was out of order. Alas, she would not be able to feed her rival.

If we knew only so much, it seems that, given the identity of the subject matter of the episode and the dream, we could plausibly conclude that the dream appeared in response to the episode. This conclusion is supported, as Michael points out, by a number of details. For instance, the rival's favorite food was *smoked salmon*. This item appears in the dream and the point is made there that only a little smoked salmon was available—not enough for a dinner party. Clark Glymour, the critic of Freud's theory whose objections Michael examines in detail, opined that this dream interpretation was "enormously plausible." Its credibility, however, was due to the commonsense connection between the episode and the dream and it therefore supported the pre-Freudian conception and not any theory of Freud's.

Michael's use of the dinner party dream to illustrate various points obscures his defense of Freud's method because the method he describes is not based a traditional analysis. One wishes that he had picked a dream whose interpretation did not lie on the surface, one of the many analyses which have been challenged by critics over the years—the dream about his friend Otto looking as though he had Basedow's disease, for instance.

Following Freud's lead, Michael aims to justify a method of dream interpretation which Freud himself compared to the solution of a jig-saw puzzle. Freud asserted, "If one succeeds in arranging the confused heap of fragments, each of which bears upon it an unintelligible piece of drawing, so that the picture acquires a meaning, so that there is no gap anywhere in the design and so that the whole fits into the frame—if all these conditions are fulfilled, then one knows that one has solved the puzzle and there is no alternative solution" (1923, *S.E.* XIX: 116).

Michael begins his exposition by pointing out that one can validly infer that certain associations appear in the dream—the dream image of Basedow's disease for instance, matched a memory in precise detail. As I understand it, Michael means that we can know that the Basedow image was in Freud's mind when the dream was produced. This is true enough, but an early warning may be called for here: We cannot simply assume that an image pictured in a dream is what the dream is about; we do not know how the image is being used. A dream featuring an image of "Uncle Bob" may be about the real Uncle Bob, of course, but not necessarily. Joseph dreamed that sheaves of wheat bowed down to another sheaf but this dream was not about wheat, or even about farming, it was about a family relationship.

However, Michael is certainly right that an image like that of Basedow's disease which appears in a dream must have been previously in the dreamer's mind. One might want to add that *every* image in the dream must have been in this mind. Michael, however, proposes that *some* of these images are salient. Adopting a novel approach, he focuses on the *emotions* which accompany the associations. Those associations, pictured in the dream, are salient and stand out because of their emotional significance. These salient associations are the pieces of the puzzle that the interpreter must solve. The dreamer's free associations have provided him or her with a number of salient associations; a dream meaning has to be derived from this cluster.

The puzzle can be solved, according to Michael, by reliance on the emotions that accompany the associations. Suppose that we discover that the feelings of the individual associations cohere—that they come together harmoniously in a central meaning. When this point has been reached, the puzzle has been solved, Michael maintains. From this cohering set of emotional concerns, Freud was reasonably entitled to "read off" the meaning of the dream.

The probability that such a set of coherent concerns, connected to the dream content, could come into being fortuitously, was low, Michael maintains. The alternative to the explanation he offers "was that the dream content was generated arbitrarily" and that the dream had no meaning. This conclusion by no means follows, since at least one alternative theory of dream meaning is available.

Michael's thesis is open to a number of objections, some of them quite serious, but the "puzzle" solution is rendered irrelevant by one of these: the whole of the construction which Michael describes, the organization of meaningful associations and associated concerns, and their coherence, remains on the wrong side of the fence so far as the meaning of the dream is concerned.

We do not know if the individual associations pictured in the dream shed light on the origins of the dream and we are not in a position to decide that the emotional concerns tied to these associations, individually or in a group, are the concerns which prompted the appearance of the dream. In spite of the cohesion of emotions, which might be impressive, we cannot logically stipulate that this cluster has anything at all to do with the meaning of the dream, which could be concerned with entirely different matters and rise out of a different set of feelings.

It is important to keep in mind that the objections both to free association and to puzzle-solving as Michael describes it are aimed only at the fallacious attempt to present them as revealing dream meanings. Both may serve another purpose—the examination of the mind of the individual. The possibility that free association and puzzle solving may lead to important discoveries is not being ruled out. This is the place where feelings can be offered as evidence. The person being studied has privileged access to her own mind; often only she will be in a unique position to point out what matters to her ("this is a painful memory" or "this upsets me for such-and-such reason").

However, the dreamer cannot "feel" the causal connection between the mental state of the dreamer and the dream. It is true that in common parlance, "feel" is often used as a synonym for "think" or "believe," but, strictly speaking, it signifies "emotion"—how one "feels" about a thing. An emotion cannot be offered as evidence for an objective fact. The decision that my dream about the small coyotes was caused by a mental state—my memory of the encounter with a large coyote—is the product of a judgment, the result of a cognitive, not an emotional act.

Moreover, logic does not stop at the door of the analyst's office. Analyst and patient, working together, however much else they may be able to accomplish, cannot determine the cause of a dream except by discovering a meaningful connection between the dream and a recognizable source in the mind of the dreamer.

Finally, Michael cites an authority who supports the scientific standing of Freud's dream theory on the basis of recent research: the evidence uncovered by modern neuroscience is "broadly consistent with Freud's psychoanalytic theory of dreams. . . ." The same research is also broadly consistent with the ancient theory that a dream can be interpreted when its content reflects a mental state of the dreamer.

Chapter 8
Reply to Dr. Sand

M. Michael

I WOULD LIKE TO THANK DR. SAND for her clearly written and informative essay. It raises two main questions. First, does Freud's method of dream analysis involve a fallacy? Second, how does Freud's theory of dreams compare to the "picture theory"? The first question is one that I have already addressed at length. Nevertheless, I will reprise my answer here. The second question is interesting, but I do not think of central importance, as I am unconvinced that the "picture theory" as described is in direct competition with Freud's primary thesis. I will nevertheless offer the beginning of an answer to it. I start with the first question.

The Free-Association-Fallacy Fallacy

Sand's charge is that Freud *merely* assumes that elements freely associated with the dream content are sources of the dream content (87 and 1993, 531). My response is the one that I made in my essay. This is that this charge makes Freud's justificatory project seem pointless. Freud set out, through specimen cases of dream interpretations, to show that he has a valid method of interpreting dreams. Unless his purported justification is trivially question-begging, it cannot be correct that he is *merely assuming* that associations are sources of the dream content. It seems more reasonable to suppose that he considers that his interpretations can be seen as warranted by those who do not yet trust his method. Only then can he hope to have justified his method.

Sand herself acknowledges that Freud gave a number of reasons in support of the method of free associations. But she does not seem to recognize that if he had reasons, then it is no *mere* assumption, regardless of whether or not one accepts the reasons. Sand clearly does not accept the reasons. The first reason given is that the complexity of the patterns that emerge from free association suggests that the process is being unconsciously guided. Sand dismisses this by offering an alternative explanation of the purported complexity, along the lines of the one given by Glymour (as discussed in my essay). She writes, "The dreamer, associating to a dream segment *A*, produces a series of thoughts. Then making a 'new start' takes up another segment of the dream, *B*. But this is *not* a new start. At this point the dreamer is not associating only to *B*, but also to *A* and to everything that has come up in association so far." This is an assumption. Why, when asked to associate with segment *B*, would one still be associating with segment *A*? "Themes that emerged during association to *A* are likely to turn up again in association to *B*. An intricate network is quickly produced." Perhaps, but again this is just an assumption. When your line of argument is that of criticizing someone for making mere assumptions, one would have expected a little more circumspection. Nevertheless, assumption or not, it is possible that that is the case, so it represents an alternative explanation that Freud has failed to consider. If this alternative is at least as good Freud's, then he is open to the charge of committing a fallacy, not on the grounds of his making a mere assumption, but on the grounds of making a weak attempted inference to the best explanation.

However, if one is to accuse Freud of a fallacy on these grounds, then one has to take up the burden of showing that the alternative explanation is at least as good as the one Freud gives. I cannot see that Sand has done this. Firstly, is what Sand describes really what is taking place in Freud's dream interpretations? The supper-party example suggests not. As we saw in my earlier discussion, Freud posited the thought of the skinny friend as a source of the dream even before the patient had associated with the smoked-salmon element. The patient, as far as we can glean from the report, had not been associating with the smoked-salmon element until then. Rather, that the patient subsequently brought out a connection between the smoked salmon and the thought of the skinny friend was taken to *confirm* the earlier posit. So this example does not fit in with Sand's alternative explanation. "Perhaps," an uncharitable critic might argue, "Freud is an untrustworthy reporter of what actually took place." Still, this is the evidence we have of how the interpretative process unwrapped in the case in question, and it does not match the pattern the critics propose.

The important observation about the above case is this: That the thought of the skinny friend was judged a likely source of the dream even before its connection to the smoked-salmon element was considered indicates that there is something about the connection between this thought and the dream element that was particularly impressive. In other words, not all possible connections are equal: Some are more striking than others. It is the quality of the connection between the thought and the dream element that renders it a likely source of the dream, and the subsequent discovery of another striking connection between the thought and the dream *reinforces* this estimation. This is typical of Freud's interpretations. It is not a pattern that can be explained away as easily as Sand suggests.

This observation relates to the chief objection to Sand's argument. As she herself reports, Freud in his defense pointed out that the associations produced during dream analysis are "so rich and meaningful" that they could not have come about by the alternative process suggested. He spoke of "the impression made by our interpretations" and the "surprising connections with other elements" and the "improbability that anything which gives such an exhaustive account of the dream could have been arrived at" by means other than the ones he postulated. These are good points. It does indeed seem improbable that an "intricate network" of associations, composed of apparently meaningful and often surprising connections—or as I put it, connections that are striking in their potential meaningfulness—and that impressively and exhaustively accounts for the dream content, could have emerged by accident. If one accepts that the connections in question are as striking and the network so produced as "fitting," as Freud suggests, then his explanation that this network is behind the dream seems better than the one that Sand offers. It seems unlikely that such a network could emerge merely as a result of the analysand effortlessly and unwittingly associating with several elements of the dream at once. At least, there must be some degree of strikingness, intricateness, and exhaustiveness for which this is so. In which case, Sand has failed to show that her explanation is as good as Freud's in general, and hence that his method is fallacious.

Sand is nevertheless dismissive of Freud's defense. She claims that "meaningful networks . . . could be created at any time, in association to *anything*." With some effort and with low enough standards as to what counts as "meaningful" this is undoubtedly so. But Freud's point, I take it, in speaking of "surprising" connections, is that the degree of apparent meaningfulness in question is much higher than one could expect from "associating to *anything*." Sand continues, "[A]ssociation to anything could result in the appearance of an important wish." Again, undoubtedly it could, but this says nothing of the quality of the connections involved. Sand recounts the example of a patient who associates with a randomly chosen number to the wish that her period would start soon. But what does this prove? It certainly does no t prove that the kinds of "rich and meaningful" networks that Freud alludes to could arise by association to any set of elements and account for them in an impressive and exhaustive way. Again, my point is that, whatever one thinks of any of Freud's actual dream interpretations, the charge that his method of logical inference is fallacious has not been proven.

I am repeating myself, of course, but there is nothing new in Sand's argument. She is right that many people have made the same criticism, though this certainly does not show that it is correct. I hope that the arguments I have given here and in my essay can help put to bed the charge that Freud's method is inherently fallacious, or at least show that it remains unproven.

An Interlude: Carts and Horses

What is new in Sand's paper is her purported explanation of Freud's "error." Unsatisfied with the reasons that Freud provides, she instead claims that Freud was "in the grip of a conviction" that "most of the ideas that occurred to him when he free associated were thoughts that had been active in his mind earlier when the dream was produced." This is her explanation of Freud's belief in the efficacy of free associations.

As it stands, it is not much of an explanation. One would surely want to know *why* he had this "conviction" in order to understand his belief. Moreover, in order to prove that this is an explanation of Freud's belief in the efficacy of the method, she needs to provide evidence that this "conviction" *preceded* this belief. For it is plausible to suppose that Freud became convinced that thoughts free associated were ones previously active *from* the perceived efficacy of free associations. That is, it seems that she may have got the explanatory order wrong. Sand, however, provides no evidence for her version of events.

Here is a rough outline of how inference to the best explanation works. One observes a phenomenon—say, that free association enables the interpretation of dreams. One then posits an explanation of this—say, that, in general, thoughts free-associated with a dream are ones that were causally active at the time the dream was formed. Supposing that this is a good enough explanation and that no better exists, one then infers it as the correct explanation. Notice the direction of the inference in the example given: One starts with observing the efficacy of free association, and *then* one infers from this that thoughts that occur during free association were ones causally active at the time of the dream formation. I do not suppose that this is quite the path Freud took, as it is from the efficacy of free associations in uncovering the sources of neurotic symptoms that he would have first come to trust in this method. But in any case, the direction of the inference is from efficacy to theoretical posit (first taken in the case of neurotic symptoms, then retaken and hence reinforced in the case of dreams). This seems to me a more plausible account of what happened than to suppose that Freud began with an ungrounded conviction in the theoretical posit from which he inferred the efficacy. If one wishes to argue for the latter account, then one at least needs to supply some evidence that events happened in that order.

The Picture of a Theory

In my essay I argued that the minimal thesis that Freud would take to be justified by dream interpretations alone is that dreams have a hidden meaning discoverable by a method involving free association. But what does "hidden" mean? Perhaps it means "disguised by the censor," for that is what Freud ultimately thought. However, this is not how he sets about justifying his thesis. When he presents his first example dream interpretation—the "specimen dream" of Irma's injection—he makes no mention of the censor or disguise. He begins with a dream that appears to be about the medical examination of Irma—a patient, who in the dream displays a number of physical symptoms unrelated to her actual condition—and, using his method, he uncovers as the meaning of that dream the wish that it is not he but his friend Otto who is responsible for Irma's real-life symptoms (1900, *S.E.*, IV: 106-120). It is not obvious on the face of it that this wish was the cause of the dream content.[1]

So "hidden" can be given the neutral, pre-theoretic meaning of "unobvious" (or, "not immediately accessible to view"). Considerable work needs to be done to uncover the meaning of the dream, and the conclusion of this work could not have been determined by one not undertaking this work. There need be no commitment to the theoretical notion of a censor that is "disguising" the dream. That notion, rather, need only be entertained as an explanation of aspects of the relationship between the manifest dream content ("manifest" also being understood pre-theoretically) and the dream meaning, including the hiddenness of the latter. One may reject the explanans without rejecting the explanandum.

Freud knew and admitted that he was not the first to posit that dreams have hidden meanings. As he puts it, "[L]ay opinion . . . seems to assume that, in spite of everything, every dream has a meaning, though a hidden one" (1900, *S.E.*, IV: 96). The difference between his thesis and lay opinion lies in the method employed to uncover the hidden meaning. He describes the lay world as employing two methods: that of "symbolic" dream interpretation and that of "decoding," using a dream key (1900, *S.E.*, IV: 96-99). It is the first of these that seems closest to Sand's "picture theory." Freud describes the method as that of considering "the content of the dream as a whole and [seeking] to replace it by another content which is intelligible and in certain respects analogous to the original one" (1900, *S.E.*, IV: 96-97). He goes on to say, "[I]t is of course impossible to give instructions upon the *method* of arriving at a symbolic interpretation" (*ibid.*), and later on, "the symbolic method is restricted in its application and incapable of being laid down on general lines" (1900, *S.E.*, IV: 99-100). He is not here saying that the method cannot work, only that it cannot be described.

Insofar as Sand's "picture theory" can be identified with the "symbolic method," it does not conflict with Freud's thesis. They can both be correct. Sand, however, sharply draws the distinction: "He eliminated the picturing principle. In a complete break with the past, he asserted that dreams ordinarily did *not* reflect a mental state" (85). If it is a complete break, then it is one based on a rather obvious observation, indeed one that Sand herself makes in the paragraph immediately before, "The great drawback of the picture theory was that dreams that clearly instantiated it were not common." So, then, considerable evidence that dreams "ordinarily" do not "reflect a mental state"! It seems to me that Sand is over-dramatizing the degree to which these approaches are in competition.

A problem in drawing a suitable contrast between Sand's "picture theory" and Freud's is the vagueness of the key notion of the former. Terms like "reflect," "depict," and "picture" are sufficiently broad to cover also aspects of Freud's theory. To use Sand's own example, why cannot the dream element "I was driving alone in the car" (1993, 538) not "reflect/ depict/ picture" masturbation? More generally, one can say that Freud's thesis is that the manifest content of a dream does "reflect/ depict/ picture" a mental state—namely, the wish that is fulfilled. To be sure, the relationship between the picture and what is pictured is not straightforward, but that is also true of many great works of art.

Undoubtedly it is this idea of "straightforwardness" that Sand intends to demarcate her notion of "picturing" from that which may be applied to Freud's theory. Though much remains to make it more precise, it seems to me to consist of two main characteristics, both pertaining to the methodology of interpretation. The first is that the manifest content must be interpreted as a whole, rather than being cut into smaller elements as per Freud's method. In this it resembles the "symbolic method." The second is that, as least insofar as it would render the dream amenable to interpretation on Sand's view, the relationship between picture and pictured must be more or less transparent (85). In this it differs from the "symbolic method."

The difference can be brought out by two dreams related to the Biblical Joseph. The first, the one that Joseph himself had, of his brothers' sheaves of wheat bowing to his sheaf, is given by Sand to illustrate the "picture theory" (82). The second, one that Pharaoh had, of seven fat kine followed by seven lean kine, which Joseph interpreted as symbolizing seven years of plenty followed by seven years of famine, is given by Freud to illustrate the "symbolic method." They are similar in that they both employ "metaphorical symbolization" (Sand, 1993, 540). However, one may draw a difference on the grounds that the first was easily interpreted by Joseph's brothers—they "immediately understood this imagery," as Sand puts it—whereas the second was not easily interpreted, requiring divine revelation to do so (Genesis 41: 8). The difference, of course, is not one of kind, but of degree: The second is less obvious than the first. It is not entirely clear where Sand would draw the line in delimiting what is and what is not an acceptable picture-theoretic interpretation. It seems that she holds that, though a dream may have an unobvious interpretation, there is no justification for believing in such, hence only obvious interpretations should be entertained. But, of course, between the obvious and the unobvious there is much grey ground. One may ask, "Was Joseph's dream as obvious as his brothers' seemed to think? Might it not represent, instead of an "elevation of Joseph over his brothers" (Sand, 1993, 540), simply a wish for them to admire his handiwork? Does this dream really reflect its meaning "in a transparent fashion" (85)?"

This relates to the following important question that can be posed of Sand's theory: How is the "similarity" that is supposed to underpin the concept of "reflecting/ depicting/ picturing" to be determined? There are many ways in which two things can said to be similar, but how is one to determine which matter for interpretation? In the absence of an answer, it seems to me that Freud's point about the lack of instruction upon the "symbolic method" applies also to Sand's "picture-theoretic" method. As such, I suspect that what Sand has given us is not yet fully a theory, but rather a sketch of one. Nevertheless, I will try to make a meaningful observation about it, focusing on the path to which Sand appears to be committed in answering the above question. I will of necessity be brief and perhaps somewhat oblique.

Suppose that a number of respondents, upon hearing of a dream, immediately draw the same conclusion as to its meaning, just as Joseph's brothers did. Why this interpretation and not others? The bowing of a sheaf of wheat is similar to the bowing of a subject to his ruler. But it can also be similar to one bowing in admiration. So why do the respondents agree on one rather than the other? A full answer will be complex, but I think it has to do, at least in part, with something like a shared "background" between the respondents. One suspects, for example, that those with a shared cultural background are more likely to give the same interpretation. Now if an interpretation is to have any chance of being correct, whose "background" matters? It is surely the dreamer's. Whatever the overlap between the dreamer's "background" with those of other people from the same culture, there will also be aspects of his background that are not shared, that is, there will be idiosyncratic elements. Indeed, there will be aspects of his background that are private to him—ones that represent the secret by-ways of his mind, viz., his own unique interests and feelings and memories and concerns and so forth. Joseph's brothers may well have misinterpreted his dream for lack of an intimate acquaintance with these by-ways of his mind. It is in this respect that the analyst who has this intimate acquaintance, or at least is in a position to gain it, can make a better judgment than a lay observer. And it is in this respect that focusing on "transparency" seems to me to miss the point. Yes, one gains the subjective certainty of general agreement. But what matters is not general agreement, but that the connections of similarity picked out are the right ones with respect to the dreamer's own "background" (hence the phrase I use in my essay, "have a felt significance . . . at least for the dreamer"). Freud's method makes ample use of this observation, while Sand's does not. It is in this that the superiority of Freud's method lies.

Notes

1. A number of Freud's critics have argued that the meaning Freud uncovers is an obvious one that can be read off the manifest content of the dream (e.g. Glymour, 1983, 65). This is false. There are a plethora of details in the dream which do not have any obvious connection to the wish that Freud claims was fulfilled in the dream. These include, but are by no means limited to, Irma's complaint about "the pains in her throat and abdomen and stomach," her looking pale and puffy, her recalcitrance at having her throat examined, the "white patch and turbinal bones with scabs in them" that Freud sees, the skin of her shoulder being infiltrated, Dr. M's statement that "Dysentery will supervene and the toxin will be eliminated', the "preparation of propyl . . . propyls . . . propionic acid," and the "Trimethylamin." To say that it is far from obvious that these details are related to the wish that Freud identifies is an understatement. Yet this is of central impor-

tance to what Freud means by "the meaning of the dream," for this must be something that accounts, as far as possible, for all the details of the dream content. Given this, it is wrong to say that the meaning of the dream is obvious.

PART III
Religion as Illusion

In *The Future of an Illusion,* Freud says, "We can now repeat that all [religious doctrines] are illusions and insusceptible of proof. No one can be compelled to think them true, to believe in them. Some of them are so improbable, so incompatible with everything we have laboriously discovered about the reality of the world, that we may compare them ... to delusions. Of the reality value of the most of them we cannot judge; just as they cannot be proved, so they cannot be refuted" (1927, *S.E.,* XXI: 31).

What was Freud's view of religiosity and religious doctrines in *The Future of an Illusion* and later works, like *Civilization and Its Discontents* and *Moses and Monotheism*? Do religious doctrines have any claim to veridicality?

Pro: John Cottingham, Ph.D., *University of Reading,* "Freud's Critique of Religion: How Damaging is his Account?"

Con: Paul Vitz, Ph.D., "Freud and the Psychology of Atheism," *New York University*

Chapter 9
Freud's Critique of Religion
How Damaging is his Account?

John Cottingham
University of Reading, U.K., Emeritus
Heythrop College, University of London, U.K.

"We can now repeat that all [religious doctrines] are illusions and insusceptible of proof. No one can be compelled to think them true, to believe in them. Some of them are so improbable, so incompatible with everything we have laboriously discovered about the reality of the world, that we may compare them . . . to delusions. Of the reality value of the most of them we cannot judge; just as they cannot be proved, so they cannot be refuted." Sigmund Freud, *The Future of an Illusion*

What is Freud's Attack?

A popular picture portrays Freud as "driving the last nails in the coffin of Divinity" (White, 1960, 29). The picture assigns him to a trio of thinkers responsible for undermining religion. First Copernicus shifted the Earth from its central place, so that it becomes more difficult to see our planet as the special focus of the Creator's concern. Then Darwin demoted humanity from its unique status, making it harder to see humans as God's special image-bearers, set apart from the animal kingdom. And lastly Freud administers the *coup de grace*,[1] arguing that the very idea of God, so far from being the divine image shining in the human soul, is a sign of arrested development—an infantile illusion that humanity needs to outgrow if we are ever to come of age (1917, *S.E.* XVII: 139-41 and 1917, *S.E.* XVI: 284-5).

But our opening quotation from *The Future of an Illusion* does not quite match this prevailing interpretation of Freud's view of religion. Yes, the disparaging characterization of religious doctrine as *illusions* is certainly prominent (and I shall discuss its exact import in Section Four, below). But we also find Freud making another, quite distinct, point about religious doctrines, namely that they are *insusceptible of proof*. This is not in itself a hostile or damaging point; on the contrary, it is one that most religious adherents would be happy to accept. The traditional Christian view, as found for example in Thomas Aquinas, is that rational proof yields only a very minimal idea of the Deity—that there exists something that is the first cause, prime mover and so on, "which all men call God," but that we cannot comprehend God or know what God is (1266-73, Part I, Qu. 2, art 3, and Preface to Part I, Qu. 3.) What is required for salvation is not proof but faith, and this, Aquinas asserts, is quite unlike rational proof, since it involves a deliberate voluntary act of assent on the part of the subject (1266-73, Part II, Second Part, Qu. 1, art. 5.)

So it is probably fair to say that the "insusceptibility of proof" that Freud stresses can readily be taken on board by the average religious believer. And Freud goes on to make an additional point, which, again, does not in itself seem damaging to religion, indeed quite the contrary—namely that religious doctrines cannot be *disproved* either. Freud is here much more clear-sighted than some of our contemporary militant atheists who assert or imply that science has somehow disproved religion—as if a complete scientific account of the natural world, however full and compelling, could somehow logically rule out the existence of a divine reality beyond the natural world. In short, Freud's assertion that the existence of God cannot be proved or disproved is a relatively mild claim that in itself places no stumbling block in the path of religious belief.

But things are not quite as simple as this. What comes across from the general tone of our opening quotation is a highly sceptical attitude to religion, and in this context the reference to disproof takes on a particular significance. For Freud is evidently suggesting that his sceptical stance is entirely reasonable, and does not *need* to be bolstered by offering a disproof of God. Here he would surely have agreed with Bertrand Russell that the onus does not lie on the sceptic to disprove outlandish dogmas, whether of a religious or any other kind. As Russell put it, "[I]f I were to suggest that between the Earth and Mars there is a china teapot revolving about the sun in an elliptical orbit, nobody would be able to disprove my assertion" (Dawkins, 2006, 52). Russell's argument is that the teapot hypothesis, though not actually disprovable, is something we have not the slightest reason to believe in, and Freud evidently takes the same view about God. The impossibility of proof or disproof does not close the matter, since we can still go on to inquire about the *probability* of there being a God, and here Freud declares that the notion of God is "so improbable, so incompatible with everything we have laboriously discovered about the nature of the world" that it may be compared to a delusion (1927, *S.E.,* XXI: 31).

With his usual brilliance, Freud here cuts to the chase. The chief obstacle to religious belief is not the question of proof or disproof (and one may add that the ideal of watertight, demonstrative knowledge in this or any other area, except perhaps pure logic and mathematics, has long since ceased to have the hold on us that it did in the classical and medieval epochs); rather it is the question of whether the religious outlook *coheres with the modern scientific worldview*—the framework for understanding and interpreting reality that has been laboriously, and very successfully, developed since the Enlightenment. Many of the items commonly associated with traditional religious belief—spirits, souls, angels, miraculous supernatural inventions, immaterial entities and forces, and personal consciousness not grounded in any material substrate—seem incapable of being fitted into the naturalistic framework in terms of which during the past two or three hundred years we have all learned to reconceive the world at large and our human predicament in particular. Freud has thus anticipated what has since become a standard criticism of religious belief in contemporary anglophone philosophy, namely that it is irreparably contaminated with outmoded supernatural or "spooky" elements.[2] As Owen Flanagan has recently put it, "Naturalism is impressed by the causal explanatory power of the sciences. Science typically denies the truth—or at least the testability—of theories that invoke non-natural, occult or supernatural causes or forces" (2009, 2).

But just how damaging is this? Science clearly proceeds on the assumption that whatever happens in the world is to be explained naturalistically. What, though, is the status of this assumption? Construed one way, naturalism is simply a *methodological recommendation*: that science should always continue the search for natural explanations and avoid invoking anything 'spooky' or supernatural. Such methodological naturalism, as we may call it, is clearly a crucial part of our modern scientific framework—and, one may add, it has turned out to be extremely fruitful in encouraging scientists to seek for natural physical causes of otherwise mysterious or baffling phenomena. But there is another way of understanding naturalism, namely as a *metaphysical doctrine*: that there are, and can be, no other causes beyond those contained within the natural world. Construed this way, the principle amounts to an insistence that the universe is a closed system—impermeable, as it were, to any possible supernatural influence; or, if you prefer, a complete self-contained totality such that no putative "outside" influence is even conceivable. Now of course the universe may indeed be "closed" in this way: the complete set of physical events since the Big Bang, and all the various properties and occurrences arising out of those events, may comprise absolutely everything that there is. But such a claim is clearly a piece of metaphysics, not a piece of science. Since science, by definition, deals only with natural phenomena it could never establish the truth of this kind of metaphysical claim. No scientific procedure could conceivably establish that there is or can be nothing that transcends the natural world.

The upshot is that Freud's claim that religion is "incompatible with what science has discovered about the reality of the world" is ambiguous. If religion is understood as a set of supernatural explanations of the world or of events in the world, then it evidently violates the methodological principle of modern science, that we should invoke only naturalistic explanations; and in that sense Freud is right. But if Freud is making the further point that the claims of religion are incompatible with the supposed truth that there is *no reality whatever* except the natural phenomena studied by science, then this alleged truth is far from self-evident. As we have just seen, it is a metaphysical principle, not a scientific claim, and it is certainly not established by the success story of modern science, impressive though that story undoubtedly is.

Freud's Methods

Freud was clearly keen to present himself as a scientist; indeed, he is in some ways the arch-rationalist, bent on dispelling mystery through the tools of careful clinical observation and rational reflection. His famous slogan "where Id was, there shall Ego be" (1933, *S.E.*, XXII: 80) implies that the way to achieve understanding is to drag what is hidden and occult into the clear light of day. But Freud also acknowledged, perhaps most explicitly in his *General Introduction to Psychoanalysis* [1920] that his methods of medical treatment diverged very significantly from those which are typical of standard scientific procedure. He points to two important differences. First, conventional scientific medicine looks to "establish the functions and disturbances of the organism on an anatomical basis, to explain them in terms of chemistry and physics, and to regard them from a biological point of view", whereas Freud's own approach, he concedes, focuses on a much more elusive aspect, namely the "psychological attitude of mind". And second, Freud acknowledges the oddity of the fact that the processes involved are not susceptible of public investigation under normal observer conditions, since the psychotherapeutic process takes place in a private consulting room and "only under the conditions of a special affective relationship to the physician". In view of these two radical divergences from normal scientific method, Freud accepts that the critic has every right to be concerned that "no objective evidence for psychoanalysis exists, and no possibility of demonstrating the process" (Freud, 1952, 22-4).

Set against these comments, our opening quotation, with its implied stark contrast between the religious and the scientific outlooks, appears in a rather different light. So far from there being an objective scientific template to which all valid discourse and all legitimate human inquiry must conform, Freud in the *General Introduction* appears ready to allow that there are phenomena whose nature is such that quite different modes of understanding are appropriate. Indeed, he goes further, and acknowledges that "psychoanalysis is learnt first of all on oneself, through the study of one's own personality" (1952, 23). These concessions are most significant, since—whether Freud himself drew such an inference or not—they militate strongly against critiques of religion that would dismiss the validity of religious experiences on the grounds that they resist external verification by detached or non-involved observers.

Despite the prevalence of scientistic modes of thinking in our contemporary culture and in some parts of Freud's own thinking, we need to take seriously the idea that there may be phenomena which do not manifest themselves "cold," as it were, but require involvement and commitment on the part of the subject in order to be apprehended. The scientistic outlook tends to assume that truth or reality ought to be accessible *irrespective of the character and state of mind of the aspirant to truth*. That is an assumption of modern scientific inquiry— that the truth is simply available for discovery, given sufficient ingenuity and the careful application of the appropriate techniques, and that the dispositions and moral character of the inquirer are entirely irrelevant.[3] But while this assumption may be correct enough when inquiring into truths within meteorology, say, or chemical engineering, there is no reason to accept it when we are dealing with central truths of our human experience—for example truths about how a poem or symphony may be appreciated, or how a loving relationship may be achieved and fostered. In these latter areas, the impartial application of a mechanical technique is precisely the wrong approach: The truth yields itself only to those who are already to some extent in a state of receptivity and trust.[4]

In short, there may be phenomena, or parts of reality, whose detection or apprehension is subject to what I have elsewhere called *accessibility conditions*: the requirements for getting in touch with them include certain requirements as to the subjective attitude and psychological, and perhaps moral, state of the subject (Cottingham, 2009, ch. 5). And Freud himself seems clearly to acknowledge this when he speaks of the insights arising from the psychotherapeutic process making themselves available "only under the conditions of a special affective relationship to the physician" (Freud, 1952, 23).[5] Yet once this is allowed, it is a short step to applying the same principle to religious phenomena, or the realities—if such there be—that are the object of traditional religious belief. It is precisely this kind of consideration that has led the contemporary American philosopher Paul Moser to question the terms of the current debate in the philosophy of religion about the evidence for God's existence, where there is often an insistence on the kind of evidence that might meet the normal standards of objective scientific inquiry:

> For purposes of cognitively rational belief that God exists, skeptics and philosophers generally demand that God provide us with *spectator evidence* of divine reality. In doing so, they miss what would be the main redemptive . . . aim of the Jewish and Christian God. . . . Spectator evidence from God would allow God to be . . . domesticated and taken for granted by us in our selfish ways, because it would lack corrective judgement toward us and our selfishness. Given spectator evidence, the topic of divine reality would readily become a matter for casual, speculative discussion, and would thereby be trivialized. . . . Opposing selfish human pride, authoritative divine evidence would work by *cognitive grace*, a free, unmerited gift from God, rather than by any human earning that supposedly obligated God to redeem a person or to give divine self-revelation to a person. . . . The God of perfectly authoritative evidence would therefore not fit well with the docile gods of the philosophers and natural theologians (2008, 47-9).

Irrespective of whether one subscribes to the Judaeo-Christian concept of a redemptive God that is invoked here by Moser, the general philosophical point stands: We need to allow the possibility that there may be some phenomena that are not such as to be apprehended under the standard scientific conditions for what counts as objective evidence, but which require receptivity by the subject, and possibly even internal transformation, in order to make themselves manifest. Something very close to this seems to be what Freud has in mind regarding what counts as "evidence" in the psychotherapeutic case. And it may be worth adding that anyone familiar with the psychoanalytical process is likely to agree. The kinds of insight gained in therapy are not achieved via objective and detached scrutiny; on the contrary, the patient who maintains a sceptical and detached stance is already in a condition that tends to block the healing effects of the process, or even prevent it getting off the ground in the first place. Only by allowing oneself to be vulnerable and open to the images dredged up from the depths of the unconscious—a process which itself requires a certain vulnerability and openness to the terms of the "affective relationship" with the therapist—will the work of healing be able to make itself felt. The affective dimension, including the painfulness and the vulnerability, is quite simply part of the process; and the subject's entering into such a state is a precondition for the confirmatory evidence to be manifested. As Carl Jung, here as often following Freud's lead, aptly describes it:

> The psychoanalytic aim is to observe the shadowy presentations—whether in the form of images or of feelings—that are spontaneously evolved in the psyche and appear, without his bidding, to the man who looks within. In this way we find once more what we have repressed or forgotten. Painful though it may be, this is itself a gain—for what is inferior or even worthless belongs to me as my shadow, and gives me substance and mass. How can I be substantial if I fail to cast a shadow. I must have a dark side if I am to be whole; and inasmuch as I become conscious of my own shadow, I also remember that I am a human being like any other (1933, 40).

Reaching into an Anomalous Domain

It should by now be apparent that there are certain significant parallels between the psychotherapeutic and the religious domains—parallels that Freud does not himself draw, but which are strikingly consistent with what he does say about the nature and evidential structure of psychoanalytic process. I want now to explore a further parallel, which arises from the central tenet of psychoanalytic thinking, namely its positing the existence of unconscious mental processes. The notion of unconscious mentality is one that tends to generate a lot of initial scepticism; this was certainly the case when Freud originally proposed it, and to some extent it remains so. For as Freud admits, it seems to go against all our preconceived opinions:

> Consciousness [to our normal ways of thinking] appears positively the characteristic that defines mental life, and we regard psychology as the study of the content of consciousness. This even appears so evident that any contradiction of it seems obvious nonsense to us; and yet it is impossible for psychoanalysis to avoid this contradiction, or to accept the identity between the conscious and the psychic. . . . [In maintaining] that there are such things as unconscious thinking and unconscious wishing . . . psychoanalysis has forfeited at the outset the sympathy of the sober and scientifically minded, and incurred the suspicion of being a fantastic cult, occupied with dark and unfathomable mysteries (1952, 25-6).

Freud here anticipates what has come to be a common criticism, especially among the numerous opponents of psychoanalytic theory in the community of anglophone analytic philosophers, namely that the very idea of the unconscious mind is a contradiction in terms, since what cannot be brought within the domain of mental awareness cannot, by definition, count as a mental phenomenon. One way of expressing the difficulty is to say that the principal object posited by psychoanalytic theory, namely the Unconscious, is *anomalous* with respect to our ordinary conceptual scheme, which tends to equate the mind with the contents of consciousness.[6]

There are various ways of responding to this criticism, of which the most promising seems to me that outlined by the British philosopher Sebastian Gardner. Gardner accepts the broad conceptual link between mentality and conscious awareness or manifestability, but argues that this condition can in a certain (albeit complicated) way be satisfied in the case of unconscious states:

> The data of clinical practice . . . suggest [that] the unconscious can . . . be epistemically fixed through something that we could call the "quasi-manifestability" of unconscious states. To some degree the Unconscious is introspectable. People who have undergone analysis for a certain length of time come to be able to recognise events in their unconscious—activations of impulses, onsets of [phantasy] activity and so forth—as they occur. They are then aware of these movements of their mind in such a way that they can identify their content and direction, and can perhaps do something to hinder them, but without being able to fully control (let alone initiate) them (1991, 156).

Gardner concludes, appropriately enough, that unconscious mentality need not be understood in terms of mental states that lack any possibility of manifestation; rather, manifestation is still possible, though in a finer and more conditional sense: the contents of the unconscious mind can be brought to conscious awareness, though with great difficulty and subject to a complex guided process of rediscovery. This accords quite closely with the line taken in some of his writings by Freud himself, who asserted, in effect, that manifestability was not only possible, but that its actualization was the very essence of the therapeutic process: "the task of psychoanalytic treatment can be summed up in this formula: everything pathogenic in the unconscious must be transferred into consciousness" (1917, *S.E.*, XVI: 239). In the famous case of the "table-cloth lady"—a patient subject to compulsive and obsessive behaviour, namely the summoning of her maid again and again to witness a supposed spot on the tablecloth—the patient had responded to initial questioning by insisting that the ritual was meaningless, and she really didn't know why she did it. But when analysis slowly brought to light the painful events of her wedding night—an impotent husband who after repeated unsuccessful attempts to consummate the marriage, ended the night by marking the sheets with red ink, to avoid, as he put it, "being disgraced in the eyes of the maid"—the patient, after prolonged embarrassment and hesitation, suddenly came to see that she did, after all, know what her obsession about the stained tablecloth meant (1917, *S.E.*, XVI: 223). As it appears in psychoanalytic theory, the unconscious is a shadowy area, often stocked with fearful and dark images which the subject initially perceives only dimly, if at all; but the notion that these contents are nonetheless in some sense in the subject's mind is made plausible precisely by the process of guided discovery whereby what is dark is brought into the light. Whether the resulting explanations are satisfying will depend, as with any claim about the human mind, on a host of complex theoretical and empirical considerations. But the charge that the very notion of unconscious mentation is conceptually incoherent can confidently be met.[7]

Notwithstanding this successful rebuttal of the charge of conceptual incoherence, what I have called the anomalousness of the concept of the Unconscious still in part remains. By its very nature, the principal object and focus of psychoanalytic theory, the Unconscious, is such as to resist the complete and transparent grasp of the conscious mind. This is part of the reason why its investigation, as we noted earlier, is not subject to ordinary scientific standards of evidence; for it is an object that in virtue of its very nature cannot be brought entirely within the arena of ordinary human understanding. Yet the fact that the Unconscious is anomalous, outside the framework of ordinary mentation, need not be a fatal objection to positing it; for what cannot be fully encompassed may nonetheless be something we can reach towards. The "shadowy presentations" of the unconscious mind, as Jung (1933, 40) termed them, while remaining beneath the threshold of what is consciously registered, can nevertheless leave their traces in the forgotten memories of childhood, or the in weird and only partly recoverable deliverances of dreams; and they can make sense, as Freud so brilliantly showed, of a whole range of similar phenomena, thereby illuminating and transforming aspects of our affective life that would otherwise be wholly baffling.

There is a close analogy here with what the religious adherent holds with regard to God—the elusive and mysterious source of being who, as St.

Augustine declared, can never be brought fully within the grasp of the human mind. This resistance to being mentally encompassed is in the very nature of the divine: *si comprehendis, non est Deus* ("if you grasp him, he is not God"), wrote Augustine (392-430, 52, 16). For the very fact of our encompassing him, bringing him entirely within the horizon of our human understanding, would be the best evidence that what was so grasped was not God but a mere idol of our own construction. Hence, to use a striking image from Descartes, God is like the mountain which we can never comprehend or grasp, never put our arms round, but which we can nevertheless touch; we can somehow reach towards him in our thought.[8] This anomalous aspect, which applies both to God and to the Unconscious—their resistance to the encompassing grasp of human inquiry—is only an obstacle to their acceptance for those who make the mistake of equating the limits our conscious apprehension with the limits of reality.

Religion as Illusion

It is now time to turn to the important element in our opening quotation which we have so far postponed considering, namely Freud's famous idea of religion as *illusion*. The starting point, developed most strikingly by Freud in his essay *Civilization and its Discontents*, is the human helplessness we all experience in the face of "the majestic, cruel and inexorable powers of nature". These powers include both external forces (storms, floods, disease, death) and the internal forces of our own nature (lust, anger, brutality and so on), which may be just as frightening and threatening. Religion is, consciously or unconsciously, an attempt to mitigate our defencelessness by endeavouring to "adjure, appease, bribe" or otherwise influence those various powers. Freud famously links all this with mankind's universal longing for a father figure, one who will protect us from suffering, and impose justice on a seemingly chaotic and terrifying universe (Freud, 1991, 195).[9]

The longing for celestial protection is identified by Freud as essentially *infantile*. "The derivation of religious needs form the infant's helplessness and the longing for the father aroused by it seems to me incontrovertible. . . . I cannot think of any need in childhood as strong as the need for a father's protection" (Freud, 1991, 260). The general line, incidentally, is prefigured in David Hume, though in a more matter–of–fact form, rather than via the idea of unconscious drives. What prompts humans to suppose there is a God, according to Hume is "the ordinary affections of human life" such as the dread of misery and the terror of death (1757, Sectn. 2).[10] The upshot is the same: Religion is an illusion born of helplessness and fear.

It is important to note, however, that an "illusion," in Freudian usage, is not necessarily erroneous. Freud at one point explicitly concedes this (*The Future of an Illusion* [*Die Zukunft einer Illusion*, 1927], *PFL* Vol. 12, p. 213. distinguishing "illusion" from "delusion," though his terminology is not always consistent. Cinderella may have the fantasy that a prince will come and marry her—and in a few cases it may actually happen. But Freud argues that it is characteristic of illusions in his sense that they are held without regard for rational justification; further, they characteristically stem from, indeed are generated by, the wishes or needs of the believer. And again the conclusion at which Freud is aiming is all too clear: Religion is something we need to grow out of (1991, Vol. 12, 213).[11]

Can the religious adherent find a response to this seemingly devastating criticism? It seems to me that there is unmistakeable truth in Freud's account of our human needs and fears in the face of a dangerous and often hostile world, and that to take issue with him here is a very unpromising strategy. So instead of going this route, I argue, consistently with the general strategy of this paper, that we should recognize the force of the points Freud makes, but recognize also that they are not as damaging to religious belief as he tends to assume.

First, Freud's own remarks, in the Cinderella case, make it clear that he does not intend his psychoanalytic diagnosis of our longing for protection to be a logical demonstration of the falsity of the religious worldview. That would be to commit the Genetic Fallacy (the logical fallacy of supposing that giving an account of the causal genesis of a belief is enough to show it is false); yet Freud clearly shows he is innocent of that charge. He correctly allows that an illusion, born of longing, might actually turn out to correspond to reality. Once that is recognized, however, it is not clear that the religious adherent need find Freud's analysis as threatening as it might initially seem to be. On the contrary, the believer might well be happy to agree with Freud that human beings do indeed have a longing for security and protection—a powerful wish for an authoritative source of meaning and purpose in whom they can put their trust. One has to look no further than St. Augustine's famous pronouncement: "You have made us for Yourself, and our heart is restless until it finds repose in You" (398, Bk I, Ch. 1). Notice however that the Augustinian thought is not just that religious devotion provides peacefulness of mind, in the sense of securing some kind of tranquillizing or calming effect; rather, the idea is that God is the source of genuine value, and that orienting ourselves toward that source bestows meaning on our human existence and enables us to find true contentment. This is surely the meaning of Dante's famous lines, which are a clear echo of the Augustinian dictum:

> For blessedness, for any creature, lies
> In keeping fast within the will of God . . .
> And in His will alone our peace belongs.[12]

Augustine and Dante acknowledge our dependency, but manage to construe it as a corollary of our creatureliness, so to speak, so they can end up celebrating it as a cause for joy. Freud by contrast sees our dependency as a condition which scares us so much that we desperately need some way of appeasing it. The two positions, though from radically different orientations, share a great deal of common ground. Most significantly, they start from an explicit acknowledgment of the vulnerability of the human condition. As to which of the two stances corresponds to the truth, that is something—Freud himself implicitly acknowledges—that cannot be determined by philosophical argument alone.

The Beneficial Function of Fantasy

Whatever the objective truth may be with regard to whether there is a genuine divine reality that is the goal of our needs and longings, the Freudian account of illusion still has the power to unsettle many believers, since at the very least it raises the possibility that the loving father of traditional Christian faith is in the end not much more than a fantasy. But this in turn prompts us to inquire into the nature and moral status of fantasy thinking (Cottingham, 2005, ch. 4.2). The tendency of many psychoanalytic thinkers after Freud has been to absorb much of his work on fantasy thinking, but to subject it to a fundamental re-appraisal from the evaluative point of view. So far from being a necessary indicator of neurosis or immaturity, the capacity for fantasising turns out, on the analysis of post-Freudians like Donald Winnicott (1971), to be a fundamental part of natural human creativity. Compare the following assessment by William Meissner, as quoted by Michael Palmer:

> Man needs to create, to shape and transform his environment, find vehicles for expressing his inner life, or rather the constant commerce between the ongoing worlds of his external experience and his inner psychic reality. . . . It is through illusion, then, that the human spirit is nourished. . . . The man without imagination, without the capacity for play or for creative illusion, is condemned to a sterile world of harsh facts without color or variety, without the continual enrichment of man's creative capacities (Palmer, 1997, 73).

In a rather more complex, but essentially similar vein, the work of Carl Jung stresses the importance of *symbolic thought* for the health of the psyche. The integration of conscious and unconscious elements of the self is a precondition for wholeness, and religious imagery and symbolism performs a vital function here. The struggle for "individuation" as Jung terms it, the process of achieving internal balance and integration, requires just those modes of thought and expression which the religious archetypes provide. Thus the figure of Christ, for example, can be seen as representing the archetype of the Self, "the completest expression of that fateful combination we call individuality" (1966-77, Vol. 9.2, 183).[13]

This is not the place to attempt an assessment of the controversial Jungian theory of the archetypes that is presupposed here, let alone of Jung's specific account of the Christ-archetype. For present purposes, the general message to be gleaned from the work of psychoanalytic thinkers as diverse as Winnicott and Jung is that Freud's dismissive characterization of the religious impulse as infantile does not do full justice to the imaginative and symbolic role of religious modes of thought and expression, and their possible role in the healthy development of the human personality. As Michael Palmer has put in discussing the way Freudian ideas are developed and transformed in the work of Carl Jung, "Religion, far from being neurotic, is revealed as a constant and evolving process in the development of the psychic personality. . . . Religious symbols . . . open up a psychic level . . . that is primordial and . . . of supreme value for the present and future development of the human psyche" (1997, 110-1).

It could be objected that this more sympathetic strand in psychoanalytic thinking about religion does not provide quite the life-raft for the defender of the religious outlook that might at first appear. Despite all the talk of the valuable role of religious symbols in the integration of the self, do we not end up with a kind of psychologizing or subjectivizing of religion—in the words of Michael Palmer, "a retreat into a self-justifying psychic world, in which the validity of God's image is established by its psychic effect, this effect making it indistinguishable from any other image having the same transforming power" (1997, 187 and 196). Jung's own response to this type of criticism was that his role as a psychologist was not to make pronouncements about the existence or non-existence of transcendent realities, but simply to describe the role of certain fundamental and universal images and symbols in human development.

> We know that God-images play a great role in psychology, but we cannot prove the [actual] existence of God. As a responsible scientist, I am not going to preach my personal and subjective convictions which I cannot prove. . . . To me, personally speaking, the question whether God exists at all or not is futile. I am sufficiently convinced of the effects man has always attributed to a divine being. If I should express a belief beyond that . . . it would show that I am not basing my opinion on facts. When people say they believe in the existence of God, it has never impressed me in the least. Either I know a thing and then I don't need to believe it; or I believe it because I'm not sure that I know it. I am well satisfied with the fact that I know experiences which I cannot avoid calling numinous or divine (Palmer, 1997, 125).[14]

This is an essentially Kantian position, of the kind that also informs much of Freud's thinking: Scientific knowledge is confined to the phenomenal world, and any attempt to step outside that world takes us beyond the domain of what can be known or established by reason. Just as Freud, as we have seen, declared that God's existence is not susceptible of proof or of disproof, so it is no part of

Jung's project to pronounce directly on the standard arguments for God's existence. What the Jungian approach does show, if it is plausible from a psychological point of view, is that religious concepts and images play a crucial role in the development of the human personality and its search for integration. Whether there is an external reality corresponding to those concepts, an "objective correlative," in T.S. Eliot's phrase (1950, 100),[15] is left beyond the bounds of empirical psychology. What matters is the possibility that emerges of accepting the Freudian idea of the dynamic role of religious notions in the individual psyche without having to take on board Freud's additional assessment of their damaging and neurotic nature.

Conclusion

There is a strangely paradoxical aspect to Freud's attitude to religion. His official position is unquestionably that of a dismissive sceptic. But the apparatus he brilliantly deploys in his seminal account of the unconscious mind actually yields the materials for a more sympathetic assessment of the religious outlook. What, after all, Freud is telling about the Unconscious is (1) that it resists complete rational apprehension; (2) that its workings cannot be objectively confirmed in the way required for normal scientific research; (3) that they nevertheless become manifest in the context of an committed affective relationship; and finally, in spite of all these potentially problematic features, (4) that there is good reason to accept it, in the light of the healing afforded by the psychic processes that invoke it and presuppose it.

What is striking about this quartet of claims concerning the Unconscious is how closely, point for point, they match what the religious adherent will say about God. The God who (1) is beyond the reach of complete rational apprehension (2) eludes objective scientific ratification, yet (3) manifests himself in the committed relationship of the worshiper, is, for the religious adherent (4) the being whom we have good reason to accept in the light of the salvific power afforded by the process of seeking him. This latter quartet of claims takes us into the realm of spiritual rather than psychotherapeutic praxis, and so might initially seem worlds away from the austere scientific framework of Freud's thinking. But it was Freud's genius to reach beyond current conventions and boundaries of thought, and despite so often presenting himself in the white coat of the medical researcher, he also had the insight to see that the rigid confines of orthodox empiricism have to be escaped if we are to reach forward to understand the complexities of our human nature. All of us who embark on the quest for spiritual and psychological wholeness, irrespective of whether we accept or reject the religious framework for understanding the human condition, would do well to listen to what he has to say.

Notes

1. It should be added this picture is in no small measure due to Freud himself. At the end of Chapter 18 of the *Vorlesungen zur Einführung in die Psychoanalyse*, 1916-17, having mentioned Copernicus and Darwin as the authors of "two great outrages upon humanity's naïve self-love," he then adds "But man's craving for grandiosity is now suffering the . . . most bitter blow from present-day psychological research which is endeavouring to prove to the 'ego' of each one of us that he is not even master in his own house, but that he must remain content with the veriest scraps of information about what is going on unconsciously in his own mind.'(1952, 296).

2. The present paper is not the place to discuss the interesting question of whether traditional religious belief must necessarily be framed in supernaturalist terms (or indeed the question of what precisely the term 'supernatural' is supposed to mean). But if we take two of the most significant entities in the Judaeo-Christian worldview, God and the soul, it is worth remembering that not all believers have construed these as 'spooky', i.e. immaterial, entities. St. Paul, for example, argues that we are resurrected not as incorporeal souls but with transformed 'spiritual bodies' (I Corinthians 16:42-4: "So also is the resurrection of the dead. It is sown in corruption, yet raised in incorruption . . . . It is sown a biological body [*soma psychikon*] and raised a spiritual body [*soma pneumatikon*]." The Apostles' Creed, moreover, speaks of the resurrection of the *body* (not the survival of an incorporeal soul). And with regard to God, the seventeenth-century philosopher and Oratorian priest Nicolas Malebranche argued that just as we should not imagine God to be corporeal, so we should not really describe him as a Mind or Spirit, since that invites comparison with a human mind. Rather, Malebranche suggested, we should think that "just as He includes the perfections of matter without being material, so He includes the perfections of created spirits without being spirit—at least in the manner we conceive spirit" (Malebranche, 1674, Bk. 3, Ch. 9).

3. For more on this theme, see Foucault, 2000, 143ff. See also Cottingham, 2003, 40-54, and 2005, chs. 5 and 7.

4. Compare Cottingham, 2005, ch. 1, §3 and §4.

5. For more on Freud's departure from a standard third-personal approach, see Cottingham, 2007, esp. 253-5.

6. This equation is often said to go back to Descartes, but this is an oversimplification of Descartes's actual position. See Cottingham, 1998, chs. 3 and 4.

7. For more, see Cottingham, 1998, Ch. 4.

8. René Descartes, letter to Mersenne of 27 May 1630: "I say that I know [that God is the author of everything, including the eternal truths], not that I conceive it or grasp it; because it is possible to know that God is infinite and all powerful although our soul, being finite, cannot grasp or conceive him. In the same way we can touch a mountain with our hands but we cannot put our arms around it as we could put them around a tree or something else not too large for them. To grasp something is to embrace it in one's thought; to know something it is sufficient to touch it with one's thought" (Descartes, 1995, 25).

9. Jean-Paul Sartre, though he presented himself as a sharp critic of Freudian theory, describes certain defence mechanisms whereby humans respond to stress in ways that seem highly reminiscent of Freud: "When the paths traced out become too difficult, or when we see no path, we can no longer live in so urgent and difficult a world. All the

ways are barred. However, we must act. So we try to change the world, that is, to live as if the connection between things and their potentialities were not ruled by deterministic procedures, but by magic"' (Martin, 2002, 67).

10. I am here indebted to Michael Palmer's fascinating study (1997).

11. Cf. Palmer, 1997, Ch. 3.

12. Anzi è formale ad esto beato esse/tenersi dentro a la divina voglia.../E'n la sua volontade è nostra pace. (1310, Bk iii, lines 79ff). The translation provided is my own.

13. In similar vein, Jung observes that "the living and perceptible archetype ... has been projected onto the man Jesus, and ... has historically manifested itself in him" (1966-77, Vol. 11, 95). These and other significant passages are quoted in Palmer (1997, 121 and 135), who summarizes Jung's thought as asserting that "what the individual identifies in Christ ... is the archetype expressing his own need for wholeness and unity."

14. This is from the correspondence with H.L Philp of 1956.

15. The term is defined, by Eliot, as the set of objects that will set off a specific emotion in the reader.

References

Alighieri, Dante, *The Divine Comedy* [*La Divina Comedia*] (1300-1310), *Paradiso*. References provided are not to pages but to the original book, canto and line numbers, which are common to all editions and translations.

Aquinas, Thomas, *Summa theologiae* (1266-73). References provided are not to pages but to the original part and section numbers, which are common to all editions and translations.

Augustine of Hippo, *Confessions* (398). References provided are not to pages but to the original chapter and section numbers, which are common to all editions and translations.

Augustine of Hippo, *Sermons* (430). References provided are not to pages but to the original chapter numbers, which are common to all editions and translations.

Cottingham, John, *Philosophy and the Good Life: Reason and the Passions in Greek, Cartesian and Psychoanalytic Ethics* (Cambridge: Cambridge University Press, 1998).

Cottingham, John, "Spirituality, Science and Morality," *Essays on Spirituality and Education,* ed. D. Carr and J. Haldane (London: Routledge, 2003).

Cottingham, John, *The Spiritual Dimension* (Cambridge: Cambridge University Press, 2005).

Cottingham, John, "The Self, the Good Life and the Transcendent", *The Moral Life: Essays in Honour of John Cottingham,* N. Athanassoulis and S. Vice, eds., (Oxford: Blackwell, 2007).

Cottingham, John, *Why Believe?* (London: Continuum, 2009).

Dawkins, Richard, *The God Delusion* (London: Bantam Press, 2006).

Descartes, René, *The Philosophical Writings of Descartes*, *Vol. III, The Correspondence*, trans. J. Cottingham, R. Stoothoff, D. Murdoch, and A. Kenny, (Cambridge: Cambridge University Press, 1995).

Eliot, T.S., "Hamlet and His Problems," (1919), repr. in *The Sacred Wood* (London: Methuen, 1950), p. 100.

Flanagan, Owen, *The Really Hard Problem: Meaning in a Material World* (Cambridge, Mass: MIT Press, 2009).

Foucault, Michel, "Subjectivité et Vérité;" *Cités*, vol. 2, ed. Y.C. Zarka (Vendôme: Presses Universitaires de France, March 2000).

Freud, Sigmund, *The Standard Edition of the Complete Works of Freud,* Vol. XXII, ed. James Strachey (London: The Hogarth Press Ltd., 1964).

Freud, Sigmund, *A General Introduction to Psychoanalysis,* trans. J. Riviere (New York: Washington Square Press, 1952).

Freud, Sigmund, *The Penguin Freud Library* (London: Penguin, 1991), Vol. 12.

Gardner, Sebastian, "The Unconscious," *The Cambridge Companion to Freud,* ed. Jerome Neu (New York: Cambridge University Press, 1991).

Hume, David, *The Natural History of Religion* (1757). References are to the original section numbers, which are common to all editions.

Jung, Carl, Modern Man in Search of a Soul: Essays from the 1920s and 1930s, trans, C.F. Baynes (London: Routledge, 1933).

Jung, C.J. *Aion*, *Collected Works* (London: Routledge, 1967-77).

Malebranche, Nicholas, *Recherche de la Vérité* (1674). References provided are not to pages, but to the original book and chapter numbers, which are common to all editions and translations.

Moser, Paul, *The Elusive God* (Cambridge: Cambridge University Press, 2008).

Martin, T, *Oppression and the Human Condition* (Lanham, MD.: Rowman & Littlefield, 2002).

Palmer, Michael, *Freud and Jung on Religion* (London: Routledge, 1997).

White, Victor, *God and the Unconscious* (London: Collins, 1960).

Winnicott, Donald, *Playing and Reality* (London: Routledge, 2005 (first published 1971).

Chapter 10
Freud and the Psychology of Atheism[1]

Paul C. Vitz
Institute for the Psychological Sciences
New York University, U.S.A., Emeritus

I WILL ADDRESS PRIMARILY THE DEEP PERSONAL PSYCHOLOGY of the greater—at least the passionate and influential—atheists, with a focus on Freud. Atheism has not simply been the expression of a personal psychology of important atheists: It has received much support from social, economic, and cultural forces. Yet atheism began in the personal lives of particular people, many of them the leading intellectuals of the modern period, such as Friedrich Nietzsche, Sigmund Freud, Bertrand Russell, and Jean-Paul Sartre. *I propose that atheism of the strong or intense type is to a substantial degree generated by the peculiar psychological needs of its advocates.*

But why should one study the psychology of atheists at all? Is there any reason to believe that there are consistent psychological patterns in their lives? To begin, it should be noted that self-avowed atheists tend, to a remarkable degree, to be found in a somewhat narrow range of social and economic strata: in the university and intellectual and media world and in certain professions. Today, as a rule, they make up a significant part of the governing class. (By contrast, believers are found much more widely throughout the entire social spectrum.) Given the relatively small numbers of intense unbelievers and the limited number of social settings in which they are found, there is certainly reason for expecting regularity in their psychology.

Nevertheless, the reader might ask if this is not unfair—even uncalled for. Why submit atheism to psychological analysis at all? Is this relevant to the issue of unbelief? Here we must remember that it is atheists themselves who began the psychological approach to the question of belief. Indeed, many atheists are famous for arguing that believers suffer from illusions, from unconscious and infantile needs, and from other psychological deficits. A significant part of an atheist's position has been an aggressive interpretation of religious belief as arising from psychological factors, not from the nature of reality. Furthermore, this interpretation has been widely influential. In short, the theory that God is a projection of our own needs is a familiar modern position and is, for example, presented in countless university courses. Nonetheless, the psychological concepts used so effectively to interpret religion by those who reject God are double-edged swords that can also, as we will see, easily be used to explain their unbelief.

Finally, a valid reason for exploring the psychology of atheism is to give us some understanding of why certain historical forces common in the modern period have so reliably promoted an atheistic attitude. By identifying psychological factors in the lives of prominent rejecters of God, we will observe how social and economic conditions which fostered a similar psychology also promoted the spread of atheism. By starting with the psychological, we will be able to see how the personal became political. In short, there has been a synchrony between the psychology and the sociology of atheism.

Before beginning, I wish to make two points bearing on the underlying assumptions of the present analysis. First, I assume that the major barriers to belief in God are not rational but can be called, in a general sense, psychological. I am quite convinced that for every person strongly swayed by rational argument, there are countless others more affected by non-rational, psychological factors such as those I will discuss here. One of the earliest theorists of the unconscious, St. Paul, wrote: "I can will what is right, but I cannot do it. . . . I see in my members another law at war with the law of my mind" (*Rom.* 7:18, 23). The explicit comments of perhaps the most famous atheist Friedrich Nietzsche are to the point. Nietzsche wrote, "I have absolutely no knowledge of atheism as an outcome of reasoning, still less as an event; with me it is obvious by instinct" (1979, 51). He also wrote, "Gradually it has become clear to me what every great philosophy so far has been: namely the personal confession of its author and a kind of involuntary and unconscious memoir" (1966, 13-4).

Therefore, it seems to me sound psychology to accept that psychological factors can be impediments to belief and that these factors are often unconscious. To know the human heart—though no one can truly fathom it or know all its deceits—is the proper task of a psychologist. I propose, consequently, that irrational, often neurotic, psychological barriers to belief in God are of great importance. This is most likely true in the case of intense and dogmatic atheists.

Second, irrespective of various difficulties, all of us still have a free choice to accept or reject God. This qualification is not a contradiction of the first. A little elaboration will make this clearer. As a consequence of particular past or present circumstances some may find it much harder to believe in God. But presumably they can still choose to move toward God or to move away from God. Likewise, those persons born without psychological barriers to belief can choose either path. Although the ultimate issue is one of the will, it is nevertheless possible to investigate those psychological factors that predispose many persons to unbelief.

The Projection Theory of Belief in God

As is generally known, Freud's criticism of belief in God is that such a belief is untrustworthy because of its psychological origins. That is, God is a projection of our own intense, unconscious desires. He is a wish-fulfillment derived from childish needs for protection and security. Since these wishes are largely unconscious, any denial of such an interpretation is to be given little credence. It should be noted that in developing this kind of critique, Freud raises the *ad hominem* argument to a new importance. It is in *The Future of an Illusion* that Freud makes his position clearest: "Religious ideas have arisen from the same need as have all the other achievements of civilization: from the necessity of defending oneself against the crushing superior force of nature." Therefore, religious beliefs are "illusions, fulfillments of the oldest, strongest and most urgent wishes of mankind. . . . As we already know, the terrifying impression of helplessness in childhood aroused the need for protection—for protection through love—which was provided by the father. . . . Thus the benevolent rule of a divine Providence allays our fear of the dangers of life" (1961, 30).

Looking at this argument carefully, we see that in spite of its enthusiastic acceptance by so many, it is very weak. In the first passage, Freud notes that his arguments against religious belief are equally valid against many of the achievements of civilization, including psychoanalysis itself. Although aware of this problem, he fails to relate the logic of his critique of religion to a critique of the various achievements of civilization—e.g. psychoanalysis.

In the second passage Freud makes another strange claim—namely that the oldest and most urgent wishes of mankind are for the loving protection and guidance of a powerful father. However, if these wishes were as strong as he claims, one would expect the religions that immediately preceded Christianity to have strongly emphasized God as a benevolent father. An emphasis on the father does seem to be characteristic of the most primitive religions. In general, however, this was not the case for the pagan religions of the Mediterranean world and for such major religions as Buddhism, Hinduism, and Islam. For example, for Muslims to refer to almighty God as father is a kind of blasphemy. Indeed, Christianity is in many respects *distinctive* in its emphasis on God as a loving Father. Apparently Freud seems to think that Christianity is representative of all religions (Schmidt, 1935, 267).

Let us set aside the preceding weaknesses and turn to another aspect of Freud's projection theory. It can be shown that his theory is not really a part of psychoanalysis—and hence cannot claim support from psychoanalytic theory. To put it differently, Freud's argument is essentially *autonomous*. His critical attitude toward and rejection of religion are rooted in his personal predilections, and his interpretation of religion is a kind of meta-psychoanalysis, or framework, that is not supported by specifically clinical concepts. Indeed, the lack of theoretical connection of the projection theory to psychoanalysis probably accounts for its wide general influence outside the psychoanalytic world. There are two strong pieces of evidence for this interpretation of the projection theory.

First, Freud's theory had been clearly articulated many years earlier by Ludwig Feuerbach in his book *The Essence of Christianity*, first published in 1841. Feuerbach's interpretation was well known in European intellectual circles and Freud, as a youth, read Feuerbach avidly. Illustrative quotations from Feuerbach's work make his influence on Freud clear: "What man misses—whether this be articulate and therefore conscious, or an *unconscious* need—that is his God"; "Man projects his nature into the world outside himself before he finds it in himself"; "To live in *projected dream-images* is the essence of religion. Religion sacrifices reality to the *projected dream*" (emphasis added; 1957, 33 and also 11 and 49). Throughout the work, Feuerbach describes religion in "Freudian" terms such as "wish-fulfillment" and the like. What Freud did, years later, was to revive Feuerbach's position, articulate it more eloquently, and publish it at a time when the audience for such a theory was much larger. (Between 1841 and 1927, atheistic attitudes had made substantial headway in Western society.) And because Freud is the author, somehow the findings of psychoanalysis are assumed to support the theory. The Feuerbachian character of Freud's position in *The Future of an Illusion* is also revealed by his use of such key phrases as the "crushing superior force of nature" and the "terrifying impression of helplessness in childhood," which are not psychoanalytic, either in terminology or in meaning.

Second, Freud himself states that projection theory does not arise from psychoanalytic evidence. In a letter of 1927 to his friend Oskar Pfister, an early psychoanalyst and believing Protestant pastor, Freud wrote: "Let us be quite clear on the point that the views expressed in my book [*The Future of an Illusion*] form no part of analytic theory. They are my personal views."

Nevertheless, Freud states in *The Future of an Illusion* that he is very familiar with the psychological origins of belief in God. Such, however, is not the case. In fact, Freud had very little psychoanalytic experience with patients who believed in God or were genuinely religious. None of his published cases deals with a patient who believed in God at the time of the psychoanalysis. That is, *nowhere did Freud publish a psychoanalysis of the belief in God based on clinical evidence provided by a believing patient.* He never presented publicly any serious psychological evidence for his projection theory or for his other ideas about religion. Instead, Freud's peculiar personal obsession with religion is primarily focused on texts and issues drawn from anthropology, history, and literature—not from any cited psychoanalytic experience. In short, Freud's general projection theory is an interpretation of religion that stands on its own, unsupported by psychoanalytic theory or clinical evidence.

It is important to add that, to the best of my knowledge, there is still no systematic empirical evidence to support the thesis that religious belief is a neurotic projection. Instead, there is now much research showing that a serious and committed religious life is associated with greater physical health and psychological well-being.[2]

Freud's Overlooked Theory of Unbelief

Nevertheless, Freud is quite right to consider that a belief might be an illusion because it derives from powerful wishes or unconscious, childish needs. The irony is that he inadvertently provides a powerful new way to understand an illusion as the psychological basis for rejecting God—that is, a projection theory of atheism.[3]

The central concept in Freud's work, aside from the unconscious, is the well-known Oedipus complex. In the case of male personality development, the essential features of this complex are the following. Roughly at age three, the boy develops a strong sexual desire for his mother. At the same time, he develops an intense hatred and fear of his father and a desire to supplant him—a "craving for power." This hatred is based on the boy's knowledge that his father, with his greater size and strength, stands in the way of his desire. The child's fear of his father may be explicitly a fear of castration by the father, but more typically it has a less specific character. The son does not really kill his father, of course, but patricide is assumed to be a common preoccupation of his unconscious fantasies and dreams. The "resolution" of the complex is supposed to occur through the boy's recognition that he cannot replace his father and through fear of castration which eventually leads the boy to identify with his father—with the aggressor—and to repress the original frightening components of the complex. This resolution is normally completed around age five.

It is important to keep in mind that, according to Freud, the Oedipus complex is never truly resolved, and is capable of activation at later periods—almost always, for example, at puberty. Thus, the powerful ingredients of murderous hate and of incestuous sexual desire within the family are never in fact removed; they are merely covered over and re-pressed. The adult continues to fear his now-internalized father, who has been incorporated into his super-ego. This fear and self-directed moral hostility are always ready to erupt from the unconscious. Freud explains the neurotic potential of the situation: "[T]he Oedipus complex is the actual nucleus of neuroses. . . . What remains of the complex in the unconscious represents the disposition to the later development of neuroses in the adult" (1919, 193). In short, in classical Freudian theory, all human neuroses derive from this complex. In many cases, this potential is not expressed in any seriously neurotic manner but shows up in critical attitudes toward God and authority, and also in slips of the tongue, transient irrationalities, and the like.

Aside from the personal dimensions of the Oedipus complex, Freud elaborated a cultural-historical model of this complex in *Totem and Taboo*. In this work, Freud proposed an Oedipal and totemic origin of religion. He begins by postulating that the earliest stage of society consisted of "a violent and jealous father who keeps all the females for himself and drives away his sons as they grow up." Freud proposed that such a primal horde, without real culture, was the initial human state. But "one day the brothers who had been driven out came together, killed and devoured their father and so made an end to the patriarchal horde. United, they had the courage to do and succeeded in doing what would have been impossible for them individually" (1950, 141). Freud explains the eating of the murdered father:

> [C]annibal savages as they were, it goes without saying that they devoured their victim as well as killing him. The violent primal father had doubtless been the feared, envied model of each one of the company of brothers; in the act of devouring him they accomplished their identification with him and each one of them acquired a portion of his strength. The totem meal, which is perhaps mankind's earliest festival, would thus be a repetition and commemoration of this memorable and criminal deed, which was the beginning of so many things—of social organization, of moral restrictions and of religion (1950, 142).

He concludes his argument with a reference to the Oedipus complex:

> In order that these latter consequences may seem plausible, leaving their premises on one side, we need only suppose that the tumultuous mob of brothers were filled with the same contradictory feelings which we can see at work in the ambivalent father-complexes of our children and of our neurotic patients. They hated their father, who presented such a formidable obstacle to their craving for power and their sexual desires; but they loved and admired him too. After they had got rid of him, had satisfied their hatred and had put into effect their wish to identify themselves with him, the affection which had all this time been pushed under was bound to make itself felt. It did so in the form of remorse. A sense of guilt made its appearance, which in this instance coincided with the remorse felt by the whole group. The dead father became stronger than the living one had been (1950, 143).

The development of this idea in *Totem and Taboo* closely parallels Freud's presentation of the Oedipus complex, for example, in *The Ego and the Id*, but with one interesting difference. In his discussion of the origin of religion in *Totem and Taboo*, Freud is more concerned with violence—with the son's hatred of and rebellion against the father—while in his other oedipal writings he places heavier emphasis on the sexual relationship with the mother.

As a statement about the origins of religion, Freud's interpretation is thoroughly rejected by anthropologists, because there is simply no evidence that culture began with anything like Freud's "primal horde." Basic family units appear from the very start. Wilhelm Schmidt presents a simple but devastating critique of Freud's Oedipal totemic theory about the origin of religion: First, there are many cultures which have not yet reached a totemic stage; nevertheless, these pre-totemic cultures have religion. Second, some rather advanced cultures do not appear to ever have had a totemic stage—yet, like all cultures, they have a religion. No totemic theory—much less an oedipal one—can account for the origin of religion. Freud's theory of how religion arose is a kind of "just-so story."

Yet in postulating a universal Oedipus complex as the origin of all our neuroses, Freud inadvertently developed a straightforward rationale for understanding the wish-fulfilling origin of the rejection of God. After all, the Oedipus complex is unconscious, it is established in childhood, and above all its dominant motive is hatred of the father (God) and the desire for him not to exist, something represented by the boy's desire to overthrow or kill the father. Freud regularly described God as a psychological equivalent to the father, and so a natural expression of Oedipal motivation would be powerful, unconscious desires for the nonexistence of God. Therefore, in the Freudian framework, atheism is an illusion caused by the Oedipal desire to kill the father (God) and replace him with oneself. To act as though God does not exist reveals a wish to kill Him, much in the same way as in a dream the image of a parent going away or disappearing can represent such a wish. The belief that "God is dead," therefore, is simply an Oedipal wish fulfillment—the sign of seriously unresolved unconscious motivation.

It is certainly not hard to grasp the oedipal character of so much contemporary atheism and skepticism. Those whose lives are characterized by sexual promiscuity and atheism are, on Freud's analysis, living out the Oedipal, primal rebellion. And of course the oedipal dream is not only to kill the father and possess the mother or other women in the group, but also to displace the father. Modern atheism has attempted to accomplish this. Man, not God, is now the consciously specified ultimate source of goodness and power in the universe. Secular philosophies glorify him and his "potential" in much the same way religion glorifies the Creator. We have *devolved* from the one god reliably found in the very primitive cultures to simple then complex polytheism and finally to modern narcissistic cultures where everyone is a god. Man, through his narcissism (pride) and oedipal wishes, has made himself divine. Thanks to Freud, we may more easily understand the deeply illusory and thoroughly neurotic oedipal psychology of this intellectual position.

One interesting example of the oedipal motivation proposed here is that of Voltaire, a leading skeptic about all things religious who denied the Judeo-Christian concept of a personal God, especially of God as a Father. Voltaire was a deist who believed in a cosmic, depersonalized God of unknown character. The psychologically important thing about Voltaire is that he strongly rejected his father—so much so that he repudiated his father's name (Arouet) and took the name "Voltaire." It is not certain where the new name came from. When Voltaire was in his twenties (in 1718), he published a play entitled *Oedipe* (Oedipus), the first of his plays to be publicly performed. The play, which was a major success, recounts the classical legend, with heavy undertones of religious and political rebellion (see Aldridge, 1975, 4 and 28-33).

Voltaire's rejection of his own father, his rejection of God as Father, and also (in his play) his political rejection of the king—an acknowledged father figure—are all reflections of the same basic need. Psychologically speaking, Voltaire's rebellion against his father and God are directly interpretable as unresolved oedipal wish-fulfillments derived from childhood. Voltaire's rejection of God is therefore a comforting illusion, and—following Freud's logic—is a belief unworthy of a mature mind.

Diderot, the great encyclopedist and avowed atheist—indeed he is one of the founding brothers of modern atheism—had both oedipal preoccupation and insight. Freud approvingly cites Diderot' s anticipatory observation, "If the little savage were left to himself, preserving all his foolishness and adding to the small sense of a child in the cradle the violent passions of a man of thirty, he would strangle his father and lie with his mother."[4]

The "Defective Father" Theory of Atheism

I am well aware that there is good reason to give only limited acceptance to Freud's Oedipal theory. In any case, it is my own view that, although the Oedipus complex is valid for some, the theory is far from a universal explanation of unconscious motivation. There is a need, therefore, for a wider understanding of atheism, especially of the intense kind. Since I know of no theoretical framework other than the oedipal one, I am forced to sketch something of a new model. But in fact I will develop an undeveloped thesis of Freud himself. In his essay on Leonardo da Vinci, Freud remarks that "psychoanalysis, which has taught us the intimate connection between the father complex and belief in God, has shown us that the personal god is logically nothing but an exalted father, and daily demonstrates to us how youthful persons lose their religious belief as soon as the authority of the father breaks down" (1947, 98).

Freud's interesting observation requires no assumptions about unconscious sexual desires for the mother, or even about presumed universal competitive hatred focused on the father. Instead, Freud makes the simple and easily understandable claim that once a child or youth is disappointed in or loses respect for his earthly father, belief in a heavenly father becomes impossible. That a child's psychological representation of his father is intimately connected to his understanding of God was assumed by Freud and has been rather well developed by a number of psychologists, especially psychoanalysts. In other words, an atheist's disappointment in and resentment of his own father unconsciously justifies his rejection of God.

There are, of course, many ways a father can lose his authority or seriously disappoint his child: he can be absent through death or abandonment; he can be present but obviously weak, cowardly, and unworthy of respect, even if he is otherwise pleasant or "nice"; or he can be present but physically, sexually, or psychologically abusive. I will call these proposed determinants of atheism, taken together, the "defective father" hypothesis and will seek evidence for it in the lives of prominent atheists, for it was in reading their biographies that this interpretation first occurred to me.

I start with two famous atheists, namely Frederick Nietzsche and Sigmund Freud.

I begin with Nietzsche (1844-1900) because he is probably the world's most famous atheist. In particular, he dramatically rejected Christianity and the Christian God. His best-known pronouncement, "God is dead," is familiar to millions. He was deeply preoccupied with religion all his life and repeatedly and obsessively denounced Christian ideas and those who believed them. In addition, Nietzsche himself provided the basis for this linkage: "Gradually it has become clear to me what every great philosophy so far has been: namely the personal confession of its author and a kind of involuntary and unconscious memoir. . . . In the philosopher, conversely, there is nothing whatever that is impersonal; and above all, his morality bears decided and decisive witness to *who he is*" (1966, 13-4). In a like vein Nietzsche claimed, "I have absolutely no knowledge of atheism as an outcome of reasoning, still less as an event; with me it is obvious by instinct" (1979, 51). We have, then, good reason to believe Nietzsche's psychology (unconscious "instinct") bears on his philosophy.

Nietzsche was born in a small village in Prussian Saxony (Germany) on October 15, 1844, the son of a Lutheran pastor. On both sides of his family there had been numerous clergymen. One of his biographers notes that although Nietzsche did not learn to speak until he was two and a half, "By then he had an extremely close relationship with his father, who even allowed him in the study while he was working" (Hayman, 1980, 18).

Friedrich's father, Pastor Ludwig Nietzsche, died on July 30, 1849, two or three months short of Nietzsche's fifth birthday. Pastor Ludwig had been sick for the previous year from a brain disease. (The postmortem spoke of a "softening" affecting as much as a quarter of his brain.) Prior to his death, and even before his illness, he occasionally suffered from what appeared to have been small epileptic seizures that were of concern to his young wife. Nietzsche often spoke positively of his father and of his death as a great loss which he never forgot. As one biographer has put it, Nietzsche was "passionately attached to his father, and the shock of losing him was profound" (Holingdale, 1965, 10). When he was in his early teens, Nietzsche wrote recollections of his childhood—*Aus meinem Leben* [*From My Life*]—which included an account of the day his father died:

> When I woke up in the morning I heard weeping all round me. My dear mother came in tearfully, wailing "Oh God! My dear Ludwig is dead!" Young and innocent though I still was, I had some idea of what death meant. Transfixed by the idea of being separated forever from my beloved father, I wept bitterly. The ensuing days were taken up with weeping and with preparation for the funeral. Oh God! I had become an orphan and my mother a widow!—On 2 August my dear father's early remains were consigned to the earth. . . . The ceremony began at one o'clock, accompanied by the tolling of the bells. Oh, I shall always have the hollow clangour of those bells in my ears, and I shall never forget the gloomy melody of the hymn *Jesu meine Zuversicht* ["Jesus My Faith"] (Hayman, 1980, 18).

In this same early autobiography, the young Nietzsche expressed strong religious feeling and identified God with his dead father.

When he was twenty-four, Nietzsche wrote that his father "[d]ied all too soon. I missed the strict and superior guidance of a male intellect" (1969, 47). But other comments of Nietzsche make it clear that although he loved and admired his father, he also saw him as weak, sickly, and lacking in the "life force." He wrote in July 1888, six months before the nervous breakdown from which he never recovered, that he is suffering "under the pressure of nervous exhaustion (which is in part heredity—from my father, who also died from the consequences of a pervasive lack of life force)" (1969, 47). Nietzsche made the connection equally clear when he wrote, "My father died at the age of thirty-six; he was delicate, lovable and morbid, like being destined to pay this world only a passing visit—a gracious reminder of life rather than life itself" (1979, 38).

The general weakness and sickness of his father was for Nietzsche also associated, naturally enough, with his father's Christianity. Nietzsche's major criticism of Christianity—of its morality, of the Jesus of Christian theology, and of the whole meaning of the Christian God—was that it suffers from an absence, even a rejection, of "life force." The God that Nietzsche chose was Dionysius—a strong pagan expression of the life force. It is therefore not hard to view Nietzsche's rejection of God and Christianity as a rejection of the weakness of his father. Nietzsche's own philosophy, with its emphasis on the "superman" (German, *Übermensch)*, on the "will to power," on "becoming hard," on the "blond beast," as well as his well-known denigration of women (He remarked, for example, "You are going to see a woman? Do not forget your whip!" and "The happiness of man is 'I will.' The happiness of woman is 'He will."), can all be seen as further expression of his attempt to identify with a masculine ideal that his father and, by association, his father's religion, were never able to provide.

His search for masculinity was further undermined by the domination of his childhood, after his father's death, by his mother and female relatives: he lived in a very Christian household with his mother, his younger sister, his paternal grandmother and two paternal aunts until he went away to school at age fourteen. It is not surprising, then, that for Nietzsche Christianity and its morality was something for women—a sign of weakness, a slave mentality. In *Ecce Homo*, his autobiography, he stated: "When I look for my profoundest opposite, the incalculable pettiness of the instincts, I always find my mother and my sister—to be related to such *canaille* [rabble, riffraff] would be a blasphemy against my divinity. The treatment I have received from my mother and my sister, up to the present moment, fills me with inexpressible horror, there is an absolutely hellish machine at work here" (1979, 41).

At the local school he attended as a young boy, Nietzsche had difficulty relating to other boys. They mocked him as "little pastor" for his serious, self-controlled, pious manners. Because of his myopia, his physically passive temperament, and his frequent illness even as a child, he did not participate in boyhood games. To compensate for his social deficiencies, Nietzsche, even at this young are, emphasized his will. Indeed, he had a real desire for self-mastery. He once demonstrated his courage to other children by taking a handful of matches, setting them alight, and holding them in the palm of his hand until a bystander forcibly knocked them to the round. His hand was badly burned.

Many have noted the strong discrepancy between Nietzsche's harsh, dramatic, and very masculine philosophy—a kind of fantasy persona which he created—and his actual temperament and behavior. "War is another thing," he wrote, "I am by nature warlike. To attack is among my instincts" (1979, 41). But in person he was reserved and intellectual, frequently ill with headaches, stomach pains, and other assorted physical problems, including symptoms of syphilis. His health was so bad that he was often bedridden and nursed by his younger sister and his mother.

His philosophy can be interpreted as an intense intellectual struggle to overcome the weakness of his Christian father, a weakness that often seemed to haunt him, as in a dream, which he had a young boy in 1850, six months after his father died and just before his baby brother died:

> I heard the church organ playing as at a funeral. When I looked to see what was going on, a grave opened suddenly, and my father arose out of it in a shroud. He hurries into the church and soon comes back with a small child in his arms. The mound on the grave reopens, he climbs back in, and the gravestone sinks back over the opening. The swelling noise of the organ stops at once, and I wake up. In the morning I tell the dream to my dead mother. Soon after that little Joseph is suddenly taken ill. He goes into convulsions and dies within a few hours (Hayman, 1980, 18).

In short, in Nietzsche we have a strong, intellectually macho reaction against a dead, very Christian father who was loved and admired but perceived as sickly and weak, a representative of what might be called a "death force"—the very opposite of the Superman figure. Nietzsche's life can be seen as a permanent "quest for the father" with the Superman interpreted as Nietzsche's idealized father figure.

Next there is Sigmund Freud (1856-1939), the focus of this anthology.

That Sigmund Feud's father, Jacob, was a disappointment or worse to his son is generally agreed upon by his biographers. Jacob Freud was a weak man, unable to provide for his family. Instead, the money seems to have come from his wife's family and others. Furthermore, Freud's father was passive in response to anti-Semitism. Freud recounts a frequently-noted episode told him by his father, in which Jacob allowed an anti-Semite to call him a "dirty Jew" and knock his hat off. Young Sigmund, on hearing the story, was mortified at his father's failure to respond strongly, at his father's weakness. Sigmund Freud was a complex and in many respects an ambiguous man, but all agree that he was a courageous fighter and that he greatly admired courage in others. As a young man, Sigmund several times physically stood up against anti-Semitism, and of course he was a great intellectual fighter.

Jacob's defectiveness as a father, however, probably went deeper than incompetence and weakness. Specifically, in two of his letters as an adult, Freud writes that his father was a sexual pervert and that Jacob's children suffered as a result. Finally, it should be recalled that in proposing the Oedipus complex, Freud placed hatred of the father at the center of his psychology. It is not unreasonable to assume that this expressed, at the least, his strong unconscious hostility to and rejection of his own father.

The connection of Jacob to God and religion was also present for his son. Jacob was involved in a kind of "reform" Judaism when Freud was a child; the two of them together spent hours reading the Bible, and later Jacob became increasingly involved in reading the Talmud and in discussing Jewish scripture. In short, for Sigmund this weak, rather passive "nice guy" was clearly connected to Judaism and God, and also to a serious lack of courage and to sexual perversion and other weaknesses very painful to young Sigmund. It is not surprising then that we owe to Freud the autobiographical insight, "Psychoanalysis . . . daily demonstrates to us how youthful persons lose their religious belief as soon as the authority of the father breaks down" (1947, 98).

Other well-known atheists who fit the pattern and documented by me (Vitz, 1999) include David Hume, whose father died when he was two and there was no subsequent substitute father; Bertrand Russell, whose father died when he was four and he was raised by a puritanical grandmother nick-named the "Deadly Nightshade"; John Paul Sartre, whose father died when he was a baby and whom he spent years repudiating; and Albert Camus, who lost his father in WW I and who, near the end of his life, began searching for what his father might have been like. Also Arthur Schopenhauer hated his mother and had a modest but weak bond with his father for whom he was working at age 16 at the time his father committed suicide. Seriously abusive or weak fathers are found in the lives of Thomas Hobbes, Voltaire, Jean D'Alembert, Ludwick Feuerbach, Samuel Butler, and H.G. Wells. Contemporary atheists with such defective fathers include Madalyn Murray O'Hair, past president of an atheist society and public atheist who was responsible in the1960s for having prayer removed from the public schools, and Albert Ellis, a famous cognitive and behavioral psychologist who very often attacked God, religion, and believers in public lectures and his published writings. Political atheists with nasty fathers include Josef Stalin, Adolf Hitler, and Mao Zedong.

In contrast, prominent theists during the same time period and in the same cultures as in the above list of atheists who had positive fathers or occasionally very positive father substitutes include Blaise Pascal, George Berkeley, Joseph Butler, Thomas Reid, Edmund Burke, Moses Mendelssohn, William Paley, William Wilberforce, Francois Rene de Chateaubriand, Friedrich Schleiermacher, John Henry Newman, Alexis de Tocqueville, Samuel Wilberforce, Sören Kierkegaard, Baron Friedrich von Hugel, G.K. Chesterton, Albert Schweitzer, Martin Buber, Karl Barth, Dietrich Bonhoeffer, and Abraham Heschel. The autobiographical comments of Kierkegaard are especially insightful and come close to stating the present position about the relevance of one's father-relationship to belief in God. In any case, it is the contrast between the fathers of major theist and atheist types of intellectuals that constitutes the best evidence for the "Defective Father" hypothesis.

It is not possible to have a genuine control group when looking at our historical group of unbelievers and believers; however I suggest that the above list of theists can be roughly considered as a control group. I have also, since the publication of my *Faith and the Fatherless*, received many personal testimonies about the barriers set up by negative fathers to belief in God, especially in the case of men.[5]

Notes

1. This paper is based heavily on Chapter 1 of my book, *Faith of the Fatherless: The Psychology of Atheism*. A fuller development and documentation of the present position can be found there.

2. See Bergin, 1983, Larson and Larson, 1981, Koenig, McCullough, and Larson, 2001.

3. Quite some time after developing this oedipal hypothesis I came across a "Freudian" comment by the well known philosopher John MacMurray, "The wish to destroy the father and to take his place is one of the common phantasies of childhood. Would it not be as good an argument as Freud's, then, if we were to conclude that adult atheism was a projection upon the universe of this phantasy" (MacMurray, 1961, p. 155).

4. From *Rameau's Nephew,* quoted by Freud, in Lecture XXI, 1916-17, 338.

5. This entire interpretation of fathers as influencing later relationships to God can be placed in the contemporary literature on attachment. Indeed there is some evidence that anxiously attached college students are more likely to be atheist or agnostic in contrast to believers who are more likely to be securely attached. Kirkpatrick, 2005.

References

Aldridge, O., *Voltaire and the Century of Light* (Princeton, NJ: Princeton University Press, 1975).

Bergin, A.E., "Religiosity and Mental Health: A Critical Reevaluation and Meta-analysis," *Professional Psychology: Research and Practice,* Vol. 14, No. 2, 1983, 170-184.

Feuerbach, Ludwig, *The Essence of Christianity,* eds. E.G. Waring and F.W. Strothemann (New York: Ungar, 1957).

Freud, Sigmund, *The Standard Edition of the Complete Psychological Works of Sigmund Freud*, ed. and trans. James Strachey (London: The Hogarth Press, Vol.16, 1916-7).

Freud, Sigmund, *The Standard Edition of the Complete Psychological Works of Sigmund Freud*, ed. and trans. James Strachey (London: The Hogarth Press, Vol.17, 1919).

Freud, Sigmund, *Leonardo da Vinci* (New York, NY: Vintage/Random House, 1947).

Freud, Sigmund, *Totem and Taboo*, trans. J. Strachey (New York: Norton, 1950).

Freud, Sigmund, *The Ego and the Id*, trans. J.R. Riviere (New York: Norton, 1960).

Freud, Sigmund, *The Future of an Illusion,* trans. James Strachey (New York: Norton, 1961).

Freud, Sigmund, and Oskar Pfister, *Psychoanalysis and Faith: The Letters of Sigmund Freud and Oskar Pfister,* eds. H. Meng and E. French (New York: Basic Books, 1962).

Hayman, R., *Nietzsche: A Critical Life* (New York, NY: Oxford University Press, 1980).

Holingdale, R.J., *Nietzsche* (Baton Rouge, LA: Louisiana State University Press, 1965).

Kirkpatrick, L.A., *Attachment, Evolution and the Psychology of Religion* (New York, NY: Guilford, 2005).

Koenig, H.G., McCullough, M. E. and Larson, D.B. *Handbook of Religion and Health* (New York, NY: Oxford University press, 2001).

Larson, D. B. and Larson, S.S. "Religious Commitment and Health: Valuing the Relationship," *Second Opinion: Health, Faith & Ethics,* Vol. 17, No. 1, 1991, 26-40.

MacMurray, J., *Persons in Relation* (Atlantic Highlands, NJ: Humanities Press, 1961).

Nietzsche, Friedrich, *Selected letters of Friedrich Nietzsche,* ed. C. Middleton (Chicago: University of Chicago Press, 1969).

Nietzsche, Friedrich, *Ecce Homo*, trans. R. Hollingdale (London: Penguin, 1979).

Nietzsche, Friedrich, *Beyond Good and Evil,* trans. W. Kaufman (New York: Vintage, 1966).

Schmidt, W., *The Origin and Growth of Religion, 2nd Ed.,* trans. H.J. Rose (London: Metheun, 1935).

Vitz, Paul C., *Faith of the Fatherless: The Psychology of Atheism* (Dallas, TX: Spence, 1999).

Chapter 11
Reply to Dr. Cottingham

Paul Vitz

JOHN COTTINGHAM'S CAREFUL AND LUCID ANALYSIS of Freud's critique of religion invites a few comments and reflections. He nicely identified Freud's own method as requiring psychoanalysis to be "learnt first of all on oneself, through the study of one's own personality." Freud's personal psychoanalysis, much of which is accessed through the well-known Freud-Fliess letters (Freud et al., 1954), demonstrates the truth of this in Freud's own case. Cottingham notes psychoanalysis is a method that requires involvement and commitment or, as he proposes more generally, "accessibility conditions." This useful expression he uses to describe the kinds of truth or knowledge that we come to have through the development of various mental attitudes that prepare the mind to receive certain kinds of truth. This preparation—the development of "accessibility conditions"—obviously is in many respects the opposite of the traditional scientific attitude of cool neutrality with respect to observation.

All psychotherapists these days are taught that the forming of a positive therapeutic alliance with the patient is necessary for healing change to take place. Empathy with the patient on the part of the therapist is a crucial requirement for the therapist to be able to understand the mental life of the other. Indeed probably all true interpersonal intimacy and the genuine knowledge of the other that comes from this requires empathy and other accessibility conditions. This kind of truth or knowledge is probably especially necessary in the development of love between persons. For a many believers, their belief in God and/or in Jesus is based on an intimate interpersonal relationship that involves love. Indeed God is described as being love. We all know that love is a great and important reality, but that it is killed or prevented by the cold, distant, abstract attitude required by naturalistically based observation.

Cottingham goes on to develop the special problem of understanding the Freudian unconscious. He rightly points out that the unconscious is mysterious, and not directly observable in any obvious way. Nevertheless, with psychoanalytical experience, certain manifestations of the unconscious can be brought into consciousness, Freud's best example being the manifest content of dreams, which must be probed for their latent meaning. Our limited but still real knowledge of the mysterious unconscious, Cottingham insightfully compares to a believer's limited and shadowy knowledge of God. This understanding is in a sense Freud's critique of religion turned on psychoanalysis itself. Perhaps this is why Freud (Freud and Pfister, 1963) wrote to his friend, colleague and Christian believer Oskar Pfister that his critique of religion in *The Future of an Illusion* was in no way part of psychoanalysis itself, but instead an expression of his personal philosophy.

In his last section Cottingham discusses the concept of illusion, and Freud's comparison of religious belief to the illusion in the Cinderella story, namely that the reader will, like Cinderella, find a prince. We will put aside the very biased choice of the Cinderella story as analogous to religious belief. (Perhaps it would be useful to see Cinderella's hope for a prince as equivalent to Freud's hope that psychoanalysis would be accepted as science.) The claim that religious belief is based on the hope of a meaningful universe with a loving God at the center has real truth to it; but that religious belief is a total comforting illusion is quite mistaken. All religious believers know that religion involves serious challenges, requiring changes in how to live that we fear to make. These challenges make the true religious life a source of joy and consolation, but also often painfully difficult. It seems to me that atheism is in fact the more comforting position since it requires no specified struggle with moral or spiritual challenges. You live however you want.

As Cottingham notes, Freud's understanding of religion as illusion meant that he and others who followed his view interpret religion as a neurosis, as a loss of contact with reality, and therefore as a kind of pathology, or at least mental unhealthiness. The recent extensive research showing that seriously religious people live longer, healthier and happier lives makes such a claim rather hard to accept scientifically speaking (Bergin, 1983, and Larson and Larson, 1991).

References

Freud, Sigmund, *The origins of Psychoanalysis: Letters to Wilhelm Fliess, Drafts and Notes: 1887-1902,* eds., A. Bonaparte, E. Freud, and E. Kris (New York, NY: Basic Books, 1954).

Freud, Sigmund and Oskar Pfister, *Psychoanalysis and Faith: The Letters of Sigmund Freud and Oskar Pfister,* eds. H. Meng and E.L. Freud (New York, NY: Basic Books, 1963).

Bergin, A.E., "Religiosity and Mental Health: A Critical Reevaluation and Meta-analysis," *Professional Psychology: Research and Practice,* Vol. 14, No. 2, 1983, 170-184.

Larson, D.B. and S.S. Larson, "Religious Commitment and Health: Valuing the Relationship," *Second Opinion: Health, Faith & Ethics,* Vol. 17, No. 1, 1991, 26-4.

Chapter 12
Reply to Dr. Vitz

John Cottingham

IT IS A PLEASURE TO COMMENT ON PAUL VITZ'S stimulating paper, in which he brilliantly turns the tables on Freud, by arguing that the anti-religious outlook of several leading atheist intellectuals of the modern period, most prominently Friedrich Nietzsche and Freud himself, can plausibly be explained in terms of the psychological history of these particular individuals. So, just as Freud famously claimed that religious belief is an infantile projection stemming from unconscious needs and drives, so the use of Freud's own framework invites the suggestion that the atheistic stance has a similar psychogenesis. Not only does this expose a vulnerability in Freud's approach, by showing that it is subject to a devastating *tu quoque*; it also neatly challenges the widespread assumption in our contemporary intellectual culture—certainly in Western Europe, and increasingly even in North America—that atheism is the natural, rational, "default" position, while theism is the pathology that needs explaining, or explaining away.

Let me first underline what I take to be three of Vitz's most telling points. First, the idea of the loving father is not, *pace* Freud, typical of religion in general, but in many ways distinctive of Christianity. To this, I would just add: with clear antecedents in Judaism. "As a father pitieth his children, so the Lord has compassion on them that fear him." (Psalms 103:13). Second, Freud's deflationary account of religion is not in fact, nor does he claim it to be, based on any psychoanalytic findings, but simply represents his personal opinion (strongly influenced by Feuerbach). And third, there is no independent evidence that religious adherents are more neurotic than the ordinary run of people; on the contrary, what data there is suggests that religious belief is correlated with psychological health.

I would suggest that the upshot of these points, which seem to me very persuasive, is that as far as the psychogenesis of religious belief is concerned, the honors are even. One may plausibly cite cases, such as those chosen by Vitz and including Freud himself, where negative images of the father in childhood and adolescence seem strongly to have influenced the subjects' fierce aversion to belief in God. But conversely, it would surely not be hard to find cases where having a defective father has produced a powerful compensatory religious allegiance. In the absence of extensive further research, it would probably be unwise to pronounce on the likely prevalence of atheists over theists, or vice versa, among those whose early family circumstances were of this untoward kind.

From a philosophical point of view, in any case, we certainly cannot invoke the psychogenesis of a belief in order to infer its falsity—a point that Freud himself implicitly concedes, when he observes that an "illusion" (in the sense of a belief generated by infantile neurosis) may in fact happen to be true. Nevertheless, the term "illusion" retains its pejorative or deflationary force: Freud clearly wants to maintain that we should not trust a belief if "wish fulfilment is a prominent factor in its motivation" (*PFL* Vol. 12, 213). Yet the difficulty here is that the notion of "prominence" is an imprecise one, and we are left wondering exactly what level of untoward psychological motivation is sufficient to cast doubt on the reliability of a belief.

Suppose, seriously worried about the catastrophic current decline in the sparrow population in the UK, I am desperate to see a sparrow feeding in my garden. I look out of the window and believe I see one. Clearly my wanting to see one is a "prominent factor in my motivation"; but that does not help much in the evaluation of the truth or otherwise of my belief. Consider a second case. The sparrow problem is keeping me awake at night and my wife hires a skilled hypnotist, who puts me into a trance and says, "The first time you look out of the window every morning, you will see a sparrow in the garden." All the following week I look out and think I see a sparrow. Even in this case, the fact of my having been hypnotized does not logically rule out the possibility that a sparrow has indeed taken up residence in the neighbourhood.

Clearly, what we ideally want is for our beliefs to *track the truth*, or to match reality. We want the actual presence of a sparrow in the garden to be part of the causal story that explains my belief that there is a sparrow out there. Now in the case of an ordinary common-sense empirical belief (putting on one side far-fetched Cartesian-type sceptical scenarios) there is normally no problem establishing that a belief does indeed track the truth in this way. We can systematically check, using cameras or other observer reports, whether my belief that there is a sparrow out there corresponds with the actual presence of the bird in the garden. In more complicated scientific cases, such as my belief that there are photons bombarding my window, the verification procedure is far more elaborate, but in principle follows the same pattern. But the case of God poses unique problems. For what could be the agreed procedure for establishing whether a being, who *ex hypothesi* transcends the natural world, is actually playing a causal role in the genesis of my belief that there is such a being?

In the ordinary empirical cases, the crucial point will be that the belief-forming causal mechanism in question is operative independently of the motivational structure of the believer. Whether or not I want to see a sparrow, when I look out of the window in the right direction and the sparrow is there, the relevant belief is triggered automatically. Yet in the religious case, there is good reason to think that this kind of automatic triggering for any standard observer would not apply. On the contrary, at least according to most religious traditions, the motivational structure of the subject is expected to play a prominent, indeed an overwhelmingly important, role. As Blaise Pascal put it, God manifests himself "only to those who seek him with all their heart" (1660, no. 427). In such cases, the motives and attitude of the religious aspirant could be a very significant factor indeed in the likelihood of the belief, being formed, as is implied in the following observations of Paul Moser:

> We should ask whether there is a potentially sacred place deep within us, beneath the noise and the clutter of this dying world, for receiving divine self-revelation. This would be a place . . . where we could receive . . . the authoritative voice of a perfectly loving God who calls us to turn from selfishness and selfish fear to be remade wholeheartedly after God's morally perfect character. . . . Perhaps relatively few people have actually listened for a divine voice with an inclination to take it seriously, because it could change one's life dramatically and put worldly success and social acceptance at risk (Moser 2008, 66).

Without begging any questions in favour of the truth of theism, it seems fair to conclude that none of Freud's arguments are sufficient to justify discounting the possibility of a genuine reality at work in those cases where the subject is motivationally receptive, in Moser's sense.

This conclusion is, I believe, fully consistent with Paul Vitz's general approach to these matters, with which I am in broad agreement. The analysis and diagnosis of the psychological makeup of any given individual, whether theist or atheist, will of course always be a highly complicated matter, and there will no doubt be room for dispute about particular cases. But by raising the question of the "psychological barriers" to theistic belief, Dr. Vitz seems to me to have opened up a fascinating area of research. And his employment of a broadly psychoanalytic framework in order to investigate these barriers is perhaps yet further testimony to the fertile legacy that Freud bequeathed to our culture, even in cases such as that of religion, where Freud's particular arguments are problematic.

Let me close by offering one final reflection, prompted by Vitz's insightful paper. We know from a vast range of writings, both literary and philosophical, as well as from our own circle of friends and acquaintances, that people see the ultimate character of reality in very different lights. William Wordsworth, struck by the beauty and goodness of the natural world, spoke in his *Lines Written above Tintern Abbey* (1798) of his "cheerful faith that all which we behold is full of blessings." Arthur Schopenhauer, writing twenty years later, cried out in horror at

> the futility and fruitlessness of the struggle of the whole phenomenon [of life on earth]. . . . Instead of [any lasting final aim] we see only momentary gratification, fleeting pleasure conditioned by wants, much and long suffering, constant struggle, *bellum omnium* [war among all], everything a hunter and every-

> thing hunted, pressure, want, need and anxiety, shrieking and howling; and this goes on in *saecula saeculorum* [world without end], or until once again the crust of the planet breaks (1818, Bk. II, Ch. 28).

Wordsworth is here on the side of Plato, Aquinas and many others in seeing beauty and goodness at the heart of creation, while Schopenhauer, writing well before the Darwinian revolution, anticipates the gloom many have since come to feel about the processes of nature, "red in tooth and claw." Of the two, which is it whose vision tracks reality as it genuinely is, and which whose vision is pathological, a neurotic pessimism (or an irrational optimism), generated by unhealthy parenting or other psychic trauma? It is perhaps impossible to sit in final judgement here, for to the wholly neutral and impartial observer the universe remains in the end poker-faced—containing undoubted elements both of the Wordsworthian and of a Schopenhauerian kind. But what can surely be asserted (at the very least as a plausible hypothesis) is that the Wordsworthian response is no aberration, but that the vast majority of people of ordinary sensibilities, where these have not been blunted or distorted by deprivation or abuse or serious illness or lack of proper nurturing in their early years, are likely show a powerful and undeniable disposition to respond to the beauties of the world with joy and wonder, and something akin to gratitude. This is perhaps not "evidence" for the truth of theism in any scientific sense of that term, but it is at least strikingly consistent with it.

References

Moser, Paul, *The Elusive God* (Cambridge: Cambridge University Press, 2008).

Pascal, Blaise, *Pensées* [*c.* 1660], ed. L. Lafuma (Paris: Seuil, 1962). (References not to page numbers but to the Lafuma numbering of the *Penseés*, which has become the standard way of referring to Pascal's text.)

Schopenhauer, Arthur, *The World and Will and Representation* [*Die Welt als Wille und Vorstellung,* 1818]; transl. E.F.J. Payne (New York: Dover, 1966).

PART IV
Free Association

Freud writes in "Psychoanalysis" about the genesis of free association, "It was to be expected—though this was still unproved and not until later confirmed by wide experience—that everything that occurred to a patient setting out from a particular starting-point must also stand in an internal connection with that starting-point; hence arose the technique of educating the patient to give up the whole of his critical attitude and of making use of the material which was thus brought to light for the purpose off uncovering the connections that were being sought" (1922, *S.E.*, XVIII: 238).

Is free association a viable scientific tool for psychoanalytic investigation? What sort of wide experiential confirmation has it received?

Pro: Michael Lavin, Ph.D., *Private Practice* and *Clarke University,* "A Defense of Free Association"

Con: Adolf Grünbaum, Ph.D., *University of Pittsburgh,* "Epistemological Liabilities of the Psychoanalytic Method of Free Association"

Chapter 13
On Behalf of Free Association[1]

Michael Lavin, Ph.D.
Private Practice and Clarke University, U.S.A.

"So long as the patient's communications and ideas run on without any obstruction, the theme of transference should be left untouched. One must wait until the transference, which is the most delicate of all procedures, has become a resistance". "On Beginning the Treatment" (1913, *S.E.*, XII: 139)

DURING THE 1890S, FREUD ACKNOWLEDGED HIS LIMITATIONS as a hypnotist. The failed hypnotist then began to invent a new way of helping his patients by asking them to say whatever came into their heads while in a relaxed state. They were asked not to censor these thoughts. In their uncensored form, a patient's free associations (*freien Einfälle*) were to become the fundamental data of psychoanalysis. Rightly or wrongly, *freier Einfall*[2] is in English translated as free association. An explication of the role of free association will be the governing idea of this paper.

Accordingly, the first section of this chapter will provide an explanation of what free association is. Unlike typical accounts, special stress will be placed on the context of free association in order to better understand its peculiarity and isolation from forms of communication that occur outside a psychoanalytic hour. In particular, free association is an instrument for obtaining psychoanalytic data. Like most scientific instruments, the construction of free association is not independent of the type of rational inquiry that made its construction desirable. Free association, no more than the microscope, was not build out of idle curiosity. It was designed to further psychoanalytic investigation.

The second section of this chapter makes what a theoretical point. If the account of free association that precedes it is right, free association, like a microscope, is a tool of psychoanalytic inquiry. Its defensible employment hinges on the uses psychoanalysts make of it, especially relative to the state of psychoanalytic inquiry. Further, if free association is a data-acquisition tool, it is a tool for obtaining data. It remains for psychoanalysts and their allied inquirers to figure out the apt use of this method; however, there is no denying that these data are thought by psychoanalysts to establish distinctively psychoanalytic findings.

In this chapter's third section, I have several purposes. First, the application of context-enriched account of free association to acquire psychoanalytic data is explored. Second, limitations that are inherent in efforts to remove these data from the psychoanalytic situation are identified. Third, probable futility of attempts to give other kinds of data, rather than data from free association, to justify psychoanalytic hypotheses is endorsed. This account renders plausible Freud's notorious indifference to efforts to justify psychoanalytic discoveries through non-psychoanalytic inquires, for example work in experimental psychology.

The chapter concludes with some observations about the implication that a context-enriched account of free association has for the so-called "Freud wars." The conclusion also provides recommendation about the kind of extra analytic evidence one can in good conscience demand of psychoanalysts and other defenders of psychoanalysis regarding the credentials of the method of free association.

What is Free Association?

By 1913, Freud gave a striking metaphor for the description of free association. In one of a famed suite of papers on psychoanalytic technique, Freud compared free association to passenger's observations from a train. He recommended that a psychoanalyst instruct his patient to comply with the fundamental or basic rule by saying whatever comes into his mind, no matter how irrelevant, unimportant, or nonsensical a psychic occurrence may seem. Freud explained the patient's duty to free associate as follows:

> Act as though . . . you were a traveler sitting next to the window of a railway carriage and describing to someone inside the carriage the changing views that you see outside. . . . [N]ever forget that you have promised to be absolutely honest, and never leave anything out because, for some reason or other, it is unpleasant to tell it (1913, *S.E.*, XII: 135).

Conspicuous by absence is any reference to context of a patient's free associating. During his announcement of the fundamental rule, enjoining his patient to free associate, Freud makes no reference to the extraordinary circumstances of the psychoanalytic situation, in which a patient's free associating is to take place, or how the psychoanalyst proposes to make use of the patient's free associating in this context.

However, though the fundamental rule makes no reference to the extraordinary context of psychoanalysis, the prelude to psychoanalysis, the initial examination and selection, on Freud's account, did. He insisted that the patient pay for treatment and lie on the couch—a posture that made Freud and his expressions invisible to the patient and conditioned his responding to the patient on the patient's compliance (1913, *S.E.*, XII: 131-4). Even if one dissents from the idea that these features of the psychoanalytic context are essential to it, they are archetypical of it. But two illustrative features of what is so singular about the psychoanalytic context omit mention of what the psychoanalyst will do as the patient attempts to free associate. For example, a psychoanalyst might ask a question or, especially if the associative stream suffers an arrest, offer an interpretation, especially a defense interpretation, provided he thinks it helpful to do so. Even more important, the context of free association includes the presence of an anonymous, abstinent, neutral psychoanalyst. Once one remembers to include the context of free association, the singularity of a carefully selected person, paying to say what comes to his mind, without editing, while lying on a couch, to an anonymous, abstinent, neutral, and interpreting psychoanalyst comes into high relief, as does the centrality of free association as a tool for conducting psychoanalytic investigations.

Contemporary accounts are more elaborate than Freud's and reflect an evolution of psychoanalytic technique. In *Textbook of Psychoanalysis*, Sandberg and Marcus are explicit in how free association hinges on specific capacities of a patient, especially in the case ego psychology—a form of psychoanalysis that places special emphasis on defense analysis.

> With the advent of ego psychology, free association was understood to provide the best field for observing defensive processes in action. The patient must have the capacity to tolerate the regressive aspects of the free-associative process and then shift to a self-reflective stance. *Primary process* modes of thinking refer to all emotionally laden experience as well as their symbolic representations, as in dreams and fantasies. *Secondary process* modes of thinking refer to all more linear logic-based modes of reality-experience thinking. It is the patient's capacity for mobility between the two that is most critical (Samberg et al., 2005, 231).

The emphasis on the patient's capacities is salient, but the context remains as previously described. But free association in analysis requires the psychoanalytic situation and the capacity of a patient to move back and forth from primary process to secondary process thinking. The latter thinking is necessary for the patient to make use of the psychoanalyst's clarifications, confrontations, and interpretations. A central purpose of free association in contemporary accounts is to make the patient's defensive processes visible within the psychoanalytic dyad. In this context, one does well to remember that defensive processes—unconscious processes of the patient's Ego—occur when free association ceases. Instead of reporting what he is observing without censorship, the defended patient fends off unconscious impulses and materials in response to defense-activating escalations of signal affect. If all goes well, the interpretation of defenses against the emergence of unconscious wishes and impulses into consciousness increases the patient's ability to admit repressed material into full consciousness. In practice this means these previously resisted materials have access to the patient's consciousness without increasing signal affect to a level that triggers defense against the emergence of distressful unconscious material into consciousness. In practice, the psychoanalyst hopes to see the patient be able to go further in his associations before escalating signal affect triggers defenses.

A Theoretical Interlude

The preceding account of free association has presented it as one of the tools psychoanalysts routinely use in their work. Although paradigmatic free association's existence depends on the psychoanalytic situation, it does not by itself yield any psychoanalytic knowledge. Instead, it yields psychoanalytic data. Also it is far from clear that it is possible to export the tool from the psychoanalytic situation, though one can, of course, give persons instructions of a kind similar to those given to a patient beginning analysis. But it is anything but clear that doing so would result in psychoanalytic free association. In the psychoanalytic situation, free association provides the psychoanalyst material to work with. Tapes of psychoanalyses provide psychoanalysts and others an opportunity to learn what kind of material association generates in particular cases, while affording an opportunity to apply a researcher's codes to it to generate numerical data of the kind contemporary behavioral and social scientists prefer. Coding, thus, permits free association to be transformed into data for quantitative analysis. Without this transformation, a patient's free associations can be viewed as evidence that is typically used to help the patient and the psychoanalyst have, among other things, a clearer understanding of categories of understanding that matter in psychoanalysis, as well as information about the patient's inner world. For example, observing the patient's free associations and their arrests will, if all goes well, permit the patient and his psychoanalyst to understand what triggers a patient's anxiety, the characteristic defenses of the patient, the unconscious wishes and impulses that have triggered escalations in signal affect, and the nature of the patient's transference to the analysts, to name a few. The psychoanalyst may well cite a patient's free associations and their failures as evidence for claims he will make about the mental organization and life of his patient.

In thinking about the theory of free association, two further familiar facts about psychoanalysis are worth keeping in mind. Free association evolved as a replacement for the treatment of patients with hypnosis. Even more importantly, the greatest initial deployment of free association came about as Freud sought to unveil the secrets of dreams and the psychopathology of everyday life. Free association, as Freud conceived it, was the key to comprehending the secret, unspeakable meaning of dreams and the meaning of a variety of slips of tongue, body, and pen that permeate everyday life. A background of the project was an assumption that free association is not free. Instead, the direction to describe one's inner world without editing somehow alters a causal chain in the free associater's mental life in a way that makes the astute, attentive analyst able to discern unconscious meanings. On this picture, the secret meanings are undammed. The defensive dams that permitted them from being recognized become negligible enough to make decryption possible. *The Interpretation of Dreams* (1900, *S.E.*, IV and V) and *The Psychopathology of Everyday Life* (1901, *S.E.*, VI) are Freud's examples of the utility of the method. Further, neither of these two works imposes, as a requirement for the success of the method, that accurate interpretations have a mutative effect on the associater's life. As Freud saw it, his method could work as an aid to decryption, even if it were impotent as therapy.[3]

As the method moved towards the form described in the previous section as a device for therapeutic work in the psychoanalytic situation, Freud and some of his followers posited a curative use of the method to bring to consciousness "pathogenic" unconscious contents. Nevertheless, the vindication of free association was its (alleged) power to assist the recovery of latent contents from manifest contents dreams and parapraxes, the central topic of *The Interpretation of Dreams* and *The Psychopathology of Everyday Life*.

Without detailed argument, let it be taken as defensible that one could further believe, as Forrester asserts, that the accuracy of the decryptions of latent content obtained through the interpretations of free associations in the psychoanalytic situation is for the patient to decide. The idea that only somebody else can validate the accuracy of psychoanalytic interpretations, Forrester rejects. As he neatly puts it:

> To be convinced that one can speak from a position of critical strength on these matters without applying psychoanalysis to oneself, I would have to be convinced that I am not qualified to pass judgment on my own person, on my own body, on my own dreams, on my own destiny. . . . I would have to be convinced that *only* someone other than myself is qualified to judge these things about me. And who will convince me that I am so disqualified?[4]

And perhaps in this sense, the sense assigning primacy to each person as an appraiser of his own psychoanalytic truths is at odds with ordinary natural science. But, as Forrester also contends, there are alternatives to that view. In particular, psychoanalysis rests on naturalistic observations and inferences in the psychoanalytic situation. For although Freud claimed psychoanalysis is a natural science, he adds that it is psychology and that every person has opinions about psychological truths in a way that he does not about physics and chemistry (Forrester, 1997, 242-4).[5] Despite unresolved controversies about what conditions psychoanalysis must satisfy to deserve inclusion as a science, it could still count as a field of rational inquiry, as is naturalistic observations and inferences from them, even if it fails some litmus tests for being a science.

Free Association at Work

If all goes well, the psychoanalytic association produces free associations, as well as interruptions of free association, as a result of the patient's defenses or of his need to attend and assimilate the comments of his psychoanalyst. The psychoanalyst making these interpretations will have had special training. In particular, he will have had coursework on psychoanalysis, will have undergone psychoanalysis himself—the so-called training analysis—and will have conducted supervised psychoanalyses during his training. Also, most candidates training to become psychoanalysts already have attained qualifications as licensed physicians, psychologists, social workers, or psychiatric nurse practitioners.

In some respects, psychoanalysts receive training similar to what musicians receive. Musicians take courses on music theory. They perform music themselves. Vast portions of musicians' training involve listening with the goal of transcribing into musical notation pieces their instructors assign them to hear. The result in each case is a trained listener. Just as musicians learn to hear certain chord progressions, psychoanalysts learn to notice markers of escalating anxiety and defenses. Even if neither were counted a science, each admits of systematic treatment.[6] Nevertheless, in neither discipline does anybody lacking in the relevant praxis, no matter how comprehensive his theoretical education, attain mastery of either discipline's own brand of listening and doing.

Psychoanalysts bring to their task a trained, disciplined approach. Their goal is to foster the maintenance of the psychoanalytic situation. Psychoanalysts, like musicians, may differ in how successfully they implement the technical demands of their discipline, but it is part of a psychoanalysts training to recognize and feel the pull of the requirements of good and proper technique just a conservatory-trained musician does.[7]

If a psychoanalyst's patient has the capacity to free associate, has other strengths as well that make him "analyzable," and his analyst has the training and discipline to exercise good enough psychoanalytic technique, psychoanalysts believe the patient will begin to develop a transference (*Übertragung*) to his analyst. In non-technical language, the patient begins to adopt a stance towards his psychoanalyst that repeats, in broad outline, patterns of relating to central figures of his early life, especially in regard to the management of wishes, impulses, and their attendant emotions. The psychoanalyst's job is to analyze this transference in a way comprehensible to the patient.

What does the process of analysis look like? The psychoanalytic situation provides a framework for the psychoanalyst's activity. Nevertheless, psychoanalysts no more respond in precisely the same way to a patient's free associations than conservatory-trained musicians respond precisely the same way to a musical score, even though both bring a particular set of techniques, developed to varying degrees of excellence, to their respective situations. One way of understanding the psychoanalyst's listening is via what Menninger called the triangles of conflict and of person.[8]

Consider the following triangular scheme: the triangle of conflict.

The psychoanalyst's activity in this triangle emerges as follows. As the patient free associates, he may begin to approach unconscious wishes or impulses. One reason for attributing these unconscious wishes and impulses to the patient is that the patient's level of anxiety and other disagreeable affects climb. Psychoanalysts view this type of disagreeable affect as a signal of emerging proscribed unconscious material pressing for consciousness. However, because of the patient's developmental history, the material has been, to use an analytic word, "repressed." As the patient's signal affect escalates, he becomes likelier to rely on a defense in an effort to reduce it.

The escalation of signal affect is a visible phenomenon. Any number of signs may support the idea that signal affect has increased. The psychoanalyst might observe increases in striated muscle activity, as the patient squirms, fidgets, or drums his fingers. If the anxiety escalates still more, the patient might begin having difficulty breathing, might sweat, burp, or show other markers of physiological anxiety. If the patient's anxiety becomes extreme enough, he may begin to have difficulty keeping his associates at all coherent. To cope with his signal affect, the patient typically relies on a defense. The defense interferes with the press of prohibited unconscious wishes or impulses for expression that would have occurred, if the patient had been able to continue to free associate. The patient's psychoanalyst might, for example, proceed by interpreting the patient's defense. Take one typical type of interpretation. "When you began talking about your mother's punishing you, you mentioned your anger. As you talked about it, you got more anxious. You even began to sweat. At that point, you fell silent."

This typical interpretation of defense points out to the patient that discussing his anger at his mother made him angry, and that that anger went hand and hand with an escalation of his anxiety. The psychoanalyst has also pointed out what the patient did to reduce his anxiety. He went silent. Any number of defenses might occur. A patient might arrest his anxiety by shifting from anger at his mother to abrupt insistence that she was a marvelous woman who spanked him for his own good. The mark that a defense has begun is a reduction in the patient's signal affect as the danger of repressed wishes and impulses achieving consciousness recedes.

During the course of a patient's psychoanalysis, this triangular pattern occurs again and again. Overtime, the patient and the psychoanalyst become connoisseurs of the personal nuances of this triangle by identifying, for example, characteristic associative streams that ignite anxiety and defenses for handling it, and showing how, over time, the interpretation of defenses may delay or even eliminate the need for defenses, as repressed impulses or wishes become conscious.

There is another triangle as well: the triangle of persons.

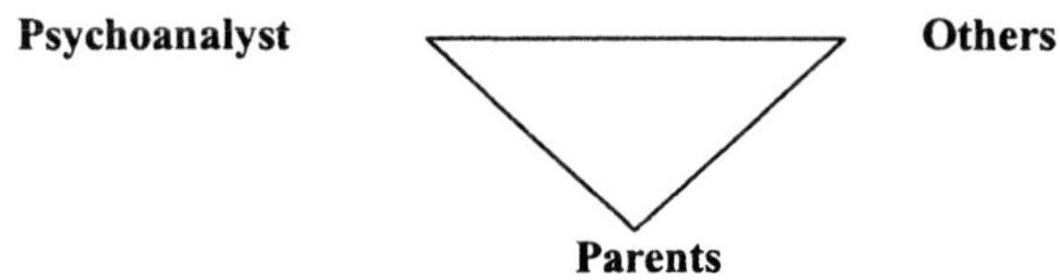

From the psychoanalytic perspective, this triangle describes interpretations focused on transferences.

To trace these transference for the patient, the psychoanalysis must listen to his associations long enough to notice certain patterns. In particular, the psychoanalyst hopes to show the patient that patterns of his responses to the psychoanalyst resemble responses to other people in his life and to his parents. To take one example, a psychoanalyst might remark to a patient, "When you begin to express angry feelings, whether toward me or your friends, you become anxious and fall silent. You do the same when you express anger at your parents. What's more you have told me that as a boy, you used to become fearful and silent whenever you got angry at your parents, especially your father." So the patient gains an opportunity to notice how pattern keeps repeating itself in his life. Although repeating past behavior may sometimes be an apt response, it is doubtful that it is always an apt response, as the patient's automaticized and stereotyped anger-generated behavior toward important people indicates.

Free associate facilitates the interventions suggested by the triangles of conflict and person because a patient's free association in the psychoanalytic situation helps highlight the nodes of each triangle. For example, in ordinary conversation, people do not associate until they begin to experience escalations of signal anxiety. Further, in ordinary conversation, the listener has no training that makes him acutely sensitive to escalations in a speaker's anxiety or in shifts in his associative pattern that represent the arrival of a defense. The ordinary listener has not had training designed to make him acutely aware of a speaker's emotional shifts, anymore than the ordinary person hears a succession A, E, G, C notes as an Am7 arpeggio, or even hears them as an A, E, G, C notes, though he does hear a succession of sounds. Identifying the chord takes musical training.

In the psychoanalytic situation, Freud and his successors have created a laboratory for the identification of affect-laden associations, for the predecessors of signal affects, for the arrival of defenses, and, as the patient's story unfolds, for his transferences to the psychoanalyst. Archaic strategies the patient employed for dealing with difficulties are, at least as psychoanalysts theorize their work, redeployed in the analysis. If a patient reports feeling that his parents were icy and uncaring, he will likely interpret the analyst's anonymity, abstinence, and neutrality in the same way. His fantasies about what he wishes from a relationship are allowed to emerge with minimal interference (suggestion) from the psychoanalyst. The constraint the psychoanalytic situation places on a patient's access to knowledge make it easier to discern unreality in a patient's free associations and posits, as well as in his general treatment of the psychoanalyst when he is not free associating—including but not limited to how he enters and leaves the office, his handling of money matters, and all the details that emerge in the course of his psychoanalysis. If, to take but one example, a patient imagines that his psychoanalyst eats kosher, it will rarely be because the psychoanalyst has stated his dietary preference or religion. Instead, what the patient imagines about his psychoanalyst likely reflects a fantasy about his psychoanalyst. His psychoanalyst, in turn, will probably entertain falsifiable conjectures about the fantasy's connections to this patient's developmental history.

The psychoanalyst's inferences from the associations of a patient are risky. A psychoanalyst's training creates sensitivity to particular features of associations. Psychoanalysts remain alert to evidence of conflict—to evidence of the great calamities (e.g., fears of physical injury, death of a loved one, loss of love, and superego driven guilt)—but inferences can go wrong, even seemingly solid ones.[9] A birdwatcher faces similar risks. A particular birdsong might lead him to infer a particular bird is in his vicinity, rather than that his birdsong-mimicking wife is in the vicinity. Still, with training, a psychoanalyst does come to learn what inferences a competent psychoanalyst might reasonably make from a set of associations. This type of reasoning feeds into the great psychoanalytic project of analyzing a patient's transferences to the psychoanalyst. If the project succeeds, the patient replaces a stereotypic response from the past with a wider repertoire of responses. The kinds of events that used to elicit reflexive, archaic responses cease to do so. The patient places these old reflexes with a capacity to select responses adapted to living well in his own terms. And even when a patient is unable to make a change he might wish to make, he may find himself better able to tolerate his ancient, unbreakable habit.[10]

To emphasize again the account just presented, free association is a source of information that psychoanalysts obtain in the psychoanalytic situation. To speak strictly, it is unclear whether free association occurs in situations outside of the psychoanalytic situation. In particular, ordinary people do not have conversations with paid, anonymous, abstinent, neutral persons who are attempting to be mirrors to the patient. Ordinary conversations are not so lopsided. Nor do ordinary conversations take place in situations designed to guard privacy so carefully. Further, ordinary conversation does not involve attempting to speak one's mind without editing to a person trained to psychoanalyze the material as well as the patient's transferences to the psychoanalyst. Patients do not ordinarily speak to persons trained as psychoanalytic listeners. Moreover, the training is rigorous in the ways that, for example, the training of a musician is rigorous, even if some may wish to insist that neither is scientific. Each of these disciplines has developed a vocabulary and body of specialist knowledge that is peculiar and internal to it. Further, neither discipline counts "book knowledge" as sufficient. Sooner or later, psychoanalysts must psychoanalyze just as musicians must create music. There is no substitute for actual engagement in the activity, if one wishes to have an adequate competency in the discipline. Finally, as is the case with any serious discipline, there are risks of error. Further, the types of understanding ultimately acquired are often idiographic rather than nomothetic. The psychoanalytic dyad's principal discoveries, in any given case, are often about the patient and, less importantly, his psychoanalyst.

Concluding Observations

Skeptics about psychoanalysis will likely continue to be skeptics about psychoanalysis. Insightful, skeptical critics like Grünbaum (1984) may well believe that the details of their criticism of the epistemic underwriting of psychoanalysis have been ignored. Anybody not convinced by sustained responses given to these types of skeptical criticisms by writers like Edelson (1984) are not going to be convinced by what I have written. It also seems unlikely that philosophical skepticism about the use free association in psychoanalytic treatment of known efficacy will assuage philosophical doubts about the method, even though there are efficacious psychoanalytic treatments.[11] These studies are indirect evidence for psychoanalysis by showing it works for treating certain patients with certain diagnoses, but that is not a direct validation of hypotheses accepted in the psychoanalytic situation. Nevertheless, if psychoanalysis has no scientific *bona fides*, whence comes the recent effort to integrate its approach into mainstream psychiatry with the publication of the *Psychodynamic Diagnostic Manual* (PDM)?[12] And noticing the existence of work like Milrod's or the PDM ought to be an antidote against extreme skepticism about the intellectual standing of psychoanalysis that likens psychoanalysts to astrologers and other quacks. Unlike astrologers, creationists, numerologists, and masters of kabala, psychoanalysts do contribute papers to scientific journals, write treatment manuals with the support of the American Psychiatric Association, and hold important chairs in major universities, as does Peter Fonagy at University College London.[13]

Despite the scientific presence of psychoanalysis in the world of psychiatry, psychoanalysis is likely to prove highly resistant to efforts to make it quantitative—a mark of unproblematic sciences.

Meehl puts it well:

> A simple model of a psychoanalytic episode, such as a parapraxis or the associations to a dream, would be to classify the analyst's interpretation in terms of needs, objects, and defenses. Some 20 Murray needs and 20 defenses yields 400 need-defense combinations; adding 40 objects gives us 16,000 configurations. With a little ingenuity and plenty of looseness, explanations abound (2006, 434).

Meehl continues by pointing out that what he calls "documentary, nonexperimental" disciplines have bleak quantitative prospects. Among these disciplines he counts psychoanalysis, paleontology, archeology, history, and biography and notes that the epistemology of these disciplines is offensive to skeptical investigators. He admits, with justice, that even if a statistical analysis established nonrandom thematic patterns in, for example, a set of free associations, those patterns, as Grünbaum has argued, would not tell investigators about the inferred latent causality guiding the associations (2006, 434). Of course this is also a true inference to latent causes in the other "cursed" disciplines. To be persuaded of putative truths from within psychoanalyses, a person may well have to see some value in the psychoanalytic outlook and its internal, expert-sanctioned inferences about psychoanalytic material. It would further help if the person were open to a higher rate of erroneous inferences about the patient and were also willing to concede the patient has a privileged epistemic position regarding the accuracy of inferences about his inner world made during psychoanalyses, but the skeptic can decline to agree to this potentially risky course. Nevertheless, there is external evidence available for Freudian hypotheses, and Drew Westen has reviewed some of it in one of psychology's premier journals, and Shaver and Mikulincer have also added to the empirical literature, as, once again, friends of psychoanalysis have responded rather differently to criticism than astrologers and their dupes (Westen, 1998).

In the preceding pages, the argument has been made that free association has a central role in the psychoanalytic situation. What's more, the use of free associations by trained psychoanalysts permits the psychoanalytic dyad to decode portions of the patient's mental life, and to understand better the patient's transference, which comprise the goal of his psychoanalysis. Some devices bring the use of free association in the psychoanalytic situation into better relief, and the triangles of defense and person are one example of a psychoanalytic heuristic. Like many cursed sciences, much of what psychoanalysts count as knowledge is part of the internal development of the discipline. Its external vindication comes from studies like Mildrod's, but it has not been this work that has to date led to psychoanalytic discoveries. Because of this, skepticism about latent causes remains an option for external critics of psychoanalysis, though within an analysis sane dyads relax the requirements for acceptable causal inferences, just as charitable readers do in biography or history. Few people expect the level of internal validity obtainable in a good psychology experiment, let alone an experiment in physics or chemistry, from biographers, historians, or psychoanalysts.

In the end, though, to achieve a deep appreciation of the power of the psychoanalytic situation and the use of free associations in it requires accepting a risk. To achieve psychoanalytic depth, one must accept Forrester's invitation to have psychoanalytic experiences or to train as a psychoanalyst. As always, some will say that psychoanalysts or historians or archeologists or paleontologists or the practitioners of cursed sciences do not have good enough science, if it is science, to make training worthwhile. And they will not train. But there are costs for caution of having exacting standards. Lost knowledge and an enriched perspective can be two.

Notes

1. I wish to thank my friend Dr. Hoffman, who is also a psychoanalyst, for change-forcing comments on this chapter. I also thank Dr. Holowchak for his comments and editing as well. In addition I wish to thank Ms. Olga Chernysheva for her assistance in editing.

2. Literally, a free falling in or free irruption, in the sense of an idea suddenly popping into one's mind.

3. Freud (1922, *S.E.* XVIII: 235) makes this point, among others, in his entry on psychoanalysis for the *Encyclopedia Britannica* 1922. He describes psychoanalysis as a theory of mind, a type of therapy, and a method of investigation.

4. Forrester's work (1997, 248) on the history of science has also exhibited a caution about whether psychoanalysis is a science, as he believes what counts as a science depends on its historical place. He also argues (1996) psychoanalysis is, unlike much modern behavioral science, a discipline of cases, not statistics.

5. This essay in the Forrester's *Dispatches* is forthright in identifying central controversial contentions that some of Freud's recent critics have relied on when lambasting his psychoanalytic science.

6. For example, in music, one has Schoenberg (1978), while in psychoanalysis could turn to Fenichel (1996).

7. For brisk, beautiful discussion of the psychoanalytic situation and its attendant technique, Leo Stone (1961) is perhaps the finest source.

8. The best account of these triangles is available in Malan (1999). One point is worth stressing. Malan's own approach differs from standard psychoanalytic approach in that he is concerned to develop an approach to brief psychodynamic therapy. The emphasis, following Davanloo (1995), is on blocking, rather than interpreting, defenses, with the goal of rapidly unlocking the patient's unconscious.

9. The centrality of conflict, as well as the importance of these four calamities in psychoanalyses, is forcefully argued by Charles Brenner (1982). The four calamities are present in Freud.

10. The late psychoanalyst, Allen Wheeler (1973), wrote movingly and beautifully of the genesis of his own discomfort with idleness and authority in a memorable chapter on having to cut grass.

11. See for example Barbara Milrod's empirical work (2007).

12. PDM Task Force. (2006). *Psychodynamic Diagnostic Manual.* Silver Spring, MD: Alliance of Psychoanalytic Organizations. Other efforts to make psychoanalytic diagnosis more rigorous include *Operationalized Psychodynamic Diagnostics: Foundations and Manual.*, (2001). (Ed.) OPD Task Force. Kirkland, WA: Hogrefe & Huber.

13. For an example of psychoanalytic authored manual, see Busch et al., 2004).

References

Brenner, C., *The Mind in Conflict* (Madison, CT: International Universities Press, 1982).

Busch, F., M. Rudden, and T. Shapiro, T., *Psychodynamic Treatment of Depression* (Arlington, VA: American Psychiatric Press, 2004).

Davanloo, H., *Unlocking the Unconscious: Selected Papers of Habib Davanloo, M.D.* (Hoboken, NJ: John Wiley & Sons, 1995).

Edelson, M., *Hypothesis and Evidence in Psychoanalysis* (Chicago, University of Chicago Press, 1984).

Edelson, M., *Psychoanalysis: Theory in Crisis* (Chicago: University of Chicago Press, 1988).

Fenichel, O., *The Psychoanalytic Theory of Neurosis with a New Introduction and Epilogue by Leo Rangell, M.D.: 50th Anniversary Edition* (New York: W.W. Norton, 1996).

Forrester. J., "If P, then What? Thinking on Cases," *History of the Human Sciences,* Vol. 9, No. 3, 1996, 1-25.

Forrester, J., *Dispatches from the Freud Wars: Psychoanalysis and its Passions* (Cambridge: Harvard University Press, 1997).

Freud, S., *The Standard Edition of the Complete Psychological Works of Sigmund Freud,* Vols. I-XXIV, ed. and trans. James Strachey (London: The Hogarth Press, 1976).

Grünbaum, A., *The Foundations of Psychoanalysis* (Berkeley: University of California Press, 1984).

Malan, D., *Individual Psychotherapy and the Science of Psychodynamics, 2nd Edition* (Oxford: Butterworth-Heinemann, 1999).

Meehl, P., "The Power of Quantitative Thinking," *A Paul Meehl Reader: Essays on the Practice of Scientific Psychology*, eds. Niels G. Waller, Leslie J. Younce, William M. Grove, David Faust, and Mark F. Lenzenweger (Mahwah, NJ: Lawrence Erlbaum Associates, 2006), 433-44.

Milrod, B., A.C. Leon, and F.N. Busch, F. N., et al., "A Randomized controlled Clinical Trial of Psychoanalytic Psychotherapy for Panic Disorder," *American Journal of Psychiatry,* 164, 2007, 265-272.

PDM Task Force, *Psychodynamic Diagnostic Manual* (Silver Spring, MD, 2006).

Samberg, E. and E.R. Marcus, "Process Resistance, and Interpretation," *Textbook of Psychoanalysis*, eds. E.S. Pearson, A.M. Cooper, and G.O. Gabbard (Washington, D.C.: American Psychiatric Publishing, 2005).
Schoenberg, A, *Theory of Harmony*, trans. Roy Carter (Berkeley: University of California Press, 1978).
Shaver, P.R. and M. Mikulincer, "Attachment Theory and Research: Resurrection of the Psychodynamic Approach to Personality," *Journal of Research in Personality*, 39, 2005, 22-45,
Stone, L., *The Psychoanalytic Situation: An Examination of Its Development and Essential Nature* (New York: International Universities Press, 1961).
Westen, D., "The Scientific Legacy of Sigmund Freud: Toward a Psychodynamically Informed Psychological Science," *Psychological Bulletin,* Vol. 124, 1997, 333-71.
Wheelis, A., *How People Change* (New York: Harper, 1973).

Chapter 14
Epistemological Liabilities of the Psychoanalytic Method of Free Association[1]

Adolf Grünbaum
University of Pittsburgh, U.S.A.

Another basic difficulty . . . [for Freud's theory of repression] lies in the epistemological defects of Freud's so-called "fundamental rule" of free association, the supposed microscope and X-ray tomograph of the human mind. This rule enjoins the patient to tell the analyst without reservation whatever comes to mind. Thus it serves as the fundamental method of clinical investigation. We are told that by using this technique to unlock the flood gates of the unconscious, Freud was able to show that neuroses, dreams and slips are caused by repressed motives. Just as in Breuer's cathartic use of hypnosis, it is a cardinal thesis of Freud's entire psychoanalytic enterprise that his method of free association has a two-fold major capability, which is both investigative and therapeutic: (i) It can identify the unconscious causes of human thoughts and behavior, both abnormal and normal, and (ii) By overcoming resistances and lifting repressions, it can remove the unconscious pathogens of neuroses, and thus provide therapy for an important class of mental disorders.

But on what grounds did Freud assert that free association has the stunning investigative capability to be causally probative for etiologic research in psychopathology? Is it not too good to be true that one can put a psychologically disturbed person on the couch and fathom the etiology of her or his affliction by free association? As compared to fathoming the causation of major somatic diseases, that seems almost miraculous, if at all true. Freud tells us very clearly (1900, 528) that his argument for his investigative tribute to free association as a means of uncovering the causation of neuroses is, at bottom, a therapeutic one going back to the cathartic method of treating hysteria. Let me state and articulate his argument.

One of Freud's justifications for the use of free association as a causally probative method of dream investigation leading to the identification of the repressed dream thoughts, he tells us (1900, 528), is that it "is identical with the procedure [of free association] by which we resolve hysterical symptoms; and there the correctness of our method [of free association] is warranted by the coincident emergence and disappearance of the symptoms. . . ." But, as I have pointed out elsewhere (Grünbaum, 1993, 25-26) his original German text here contains a confusing slip of the pen. As we know, the patient's symptoms hardly first emerge simultaneously with their therapeutic dissipation. Yet Strachey translated Freud correctly as having spoken of "the coincident emergence and disappearance of the symptoms." It would seem that Freud means to speak of the resolution (German: "Auflösung"), rather than of the emergence ("Auftauchen"), of the symptoms as coinciding with their therapeutic dissipation. Now, for Freud, the "resolution of a symptom," in turn, consists of using free association to uncover the repressed pathogen that enters into the compromise-formation which is held to constitute the symptom. This much, then, is the statement of Freud's appeal to therapeutic success to vouch for the "correctness of our method" of free association as causally probative for etiologic research in psychopathology.

To articulate the argument adequately, however, we must still clarify Freud's original basis for claiming that (unsuccessful) repression is indeed the pathogen of neurosis. Only then will he have made his case for claiming that free association is etiologically probative, because it is uniquely capable of uncovering repressions. The pertinent argument is offered in Breuer and Freud's "Preliminary Communication" (1893, 6-7). There they wrote (italics in original):

> For we found, to our great surprise at first, that each individual hysterical symptom immediately and permanently disappeared when we had succeeded in bringing clearly to light the memory of the event by which it was provoked and in arousing its accompanying affect, and when the patient had described that event in the greatest possible detail and had put the affect into words. Recollection without affect almost invariably produces no result. The psychical process which originally took place must be repeated as vividly as possible; it must be brought back to its status nascendi and then given verbal utterance.

Breuer and Freud make an important comment on their construal of this therapeutic finding:

It is plausible to suppose that it is a question here of unconscious suggestion: the patient expects to be relieved of his sufferings by this procedure, and it is this expectation, and not the verbal utterance, which is the operative factor. This, however, is not so (Breuer *et al.*, 1893, 7).

And their avowed reason is that, in 1881, i.e. in the "'pre-suggestion' era," the cathartic method was used to remove separately distinct symptoms, "which sprang from separate causes" such that any one symptom disappeared only after the cathartic ("abreactive") lifting of a particular repression. But Breuer and Freud do not tell us why the likelihood of placebo effect should be deemed to be lower when several symptoms are wiped out seriatim than in the case of getting rid of only one symptom. Thus, as I have pointed out elsewhere (Grünbaum 1993, 238) to discredit the hypothesis of placebo effect, it would have been essential to have comparisons with treatment outcome from a suitable control group whose repressions are not lifted. If that control group were to fare equally well, treatment gains from psychoanalysis would then be placebo effects after all.

In sum, Breuer and Freud inferred that the therapeutic removal of neurotic symptoms was produced by the cathartic lifting of the patient's previously ongoing repression of the pertinent traumatic memory, not by the therapist's suggestion or some other placebo factor (See Grünbaum, 1993, ch. 3 for a very detailed analysis of the placebo-concept). We can codify this claim as follows:

> T. Therapeutic Hypothesis: Lifting repressions of traumatic memories cathartically is causally relevant to the disappearance of neuroses.

As we saw, Breuer and Freud (1893, 6) reported the immediate and permanent disappearance of each hysterical symptom after they cathartically lifted the repression of the memory of the trauma that occasioned the given symptom. They adduce this "evidence" to draw an epoch-making inductive etiologic inference (1893, 6), which postulates "a causal relation between the determining [repression of the memory of the] psychical trauma and the hysterical phenomenon." Citing the old scholastic dictum "Cessante causa cessat effectus" ("when the cause ceases, its effect ceases"), they invoke its contrapositive (1893, 7), which states that as long as the effect (symptom) persists, so does its cause, (the repressed memory of the psychical trauma). And they declare just that to be the pattern of the pathogenic action of the repressed psychical trauma. This trauma, we learn, is not a mere precipitating cause. Such a mere "agent provocateur" just releases the symptom, "which thereafter leads an independent existence." Instead, "the [repressed] memory of the trauma ... acts like a foreign body which long after its entry must continue to be regarded as an agent that is still at work" (1893, 6).

The upshot of their account is that their observations of positive therapeutic outcome upon the abreactive lifting of repressions, which they interpret in the sense of their therapeutic hypothesis, spelled a paramount etiologic moral as follows:

> E. Etiologic Hypothesis: An ongoing repression accompanied by affective suppression is causally necessary for the initial pathogenesis and persistence of a neurosis. (This formulation of the foundational etiology of psychoanalysis supersedes the one I gave at the hands of a suggestion by Carl Hempel and Morris Eagle [in Grünbaum, 1984, 181, last paragraph]. The revised formulation here is faithful to Breuer and Freud's reference to "accompanying affect" [1893, 6] à propos of the traumatic events whose repression occasioned the symptoms.)

Clearly, this etiologic hypothesis E permits the valid deduction of the therapeutic finding reported by Breuer and Freud as codified in their therapeutic hypothesis T: The cathartic lifting of the repressions of traumatic memories of events that occasion symptoms engendered the disappearance of the symptoms.

And, as they told us explicitly (1893, 6), this therapeutic finding is their "evidence" for their cardinal etiologic hypothesis E.

But I maintain that this inductive argument is vitiated by what I like to call the "fallacy of crude hypothetico-deductive ("H-D") pseudo-confirmation." Thus note that the remedial action of aspirin-consumption for tension-headaches does not lend H-D support to the outlandish etiologic hypothesis that a hematolytic aspirin-deficiency is a causal sine qua non for having tension headaches, although such remedial action is validly deducible from that bizarre hypothesis. Twenty-five years ago, Wesley Salmon called attention to the fallacy of inductive causal inference from mere valid H-D deducibility by giving an example in which a deductively valid pseudo-explanation of a man's avoiding pregnancy can readily give rise to an H-D pseudo-confirmation of the addle-brained attribution of his non-pregnancy to his consumption of birth-control pills. Salmon (1971, 34) states the fatuous pseudo-explanation:

> John Jones avoided becoming pregnant during the past year, for he had taken his wife's birth control pills regularly, and every man who regularly takes birth control pills avoids pregnancy.

Plainly, this deducibility of John Jones's recent failure to become pregnant from the stated premises does not lend any credence at all to the zany hypothesis that this absence of pregnancy is causally attributable to his consumption of birth control pills. Yet it is even true that any men who consume such pills in fact never do become pregnant. Patently, as Salmon notes, the fly in the ointment is that men just do not become pregnant, whether they take birth control pills or not.

His example shows that neither the empirical truth of the deductively inferred conclusion and of the pertinent initial condition concerning Jones nor the deductive validity of the inference can provide bona fide confirmation of the causal hypothesis that male consumption of birth control pills prevents male pregnancy: That hypothesis would first have to meet other epistemic requirements, which it manifestly cannot do.

Crude H-D confirmationism is a paradise of spurious causal inferences, as illustrated by Breuer and Freud's unsound etiologic inference. Thus, psychoanalytic narratives are replete with the belief that a hypothesized etiologic scenario embedded in a psychoanalytic narrative of an analysand's affliction is made credible merely because the postulated etiology then permits the logical deduction or probabilistic inference of the neurotic symptoms to be explained.

Yet some apologists offer a facile excuse for the fallacious H-D confirmation of a causal hypothesis. We are told that the hypothesis is warranted by an "inference to the best explanation" (Harman, 1965). But in a careful new study, Wesley Salmon (2001) has argued that "the characterization of nondemonstrative inference as inference to the best explanation serves to muddy the waters ... by fostering confusion" between two sorts of why-questions that Hempel had distinguished: Explanation-seeking questions as to why something is the case, and confirmation-seeking why-questions as to why a hypothesis is credible. Thus, a hypothesis that is pseudo-confirmed by some data cannot be warranted qua being "the only [explanatory] game in town." Alas, "best explanation"-sanction was claimed for psychoanalytic etiologies to explain and treat the destructive behavior of sociopaths to no avail for years (cf. Cleckley, 1988, Section Four, esp. 238-9 and 438-9).

I can now demonstrate the multiple failure of Freud's therapeutic argument for the etiologic probativeness of free association in psychopathology, no matter how revealing the associative contents may otherwise be in regard to the patient's psychological preoccupations and personality dispositions. Let us take our bearings and first encapsulate the structure of his therapeutic argument.

First, Freud inferred that the therapeutic disappearance of the neurotic symptoms is causally attributable to the cathartic lifting of repressions by means of the method free associations. Relying on this key therapeutic hypothesis, he then drew two further major theoretical inferences: (i) The seeming removal of the neurosis by means of cathartically lifting repressions is good inductive evidence for postulating that repressions accompanied by affective suppression are themselves causally necessary for the very existence of a neurosis (1893, 6-7), and (ii) Granted that such repressions are thus the essential causes of neurosis, and that the method of free association is uniquely capable of uncovering these repressions, this method is uniquely competent to identify the causes or pathogens of the neuroses. (Having convinced himself of the causal probativeness of the method of free associations on therapeutic grounds in the case of those neuroses he believed to be successfully treatable, Freud also felt justified in deeming the method reliable as a means of unearthing the etiologies of those other neuroses—the so-called "narcissistic ones", such as paranoia—which he considered psychoanalytically untreatable.)

But the argument fails for the following several reasons: In the first place, the durable therapeutic success on which it was predicated did not materialize (Borch-Jacobsen, 1996), as Freud was driven to admit both early and very late in his career (1925, 27 and 1937, 216-253). But even in so far as there was transitory therapeutic gain, we saw that Freud failed to rule out a rival hypothesis that undermines his attribution of such gain to the lifting of repressions by free association: The ominous hypothesis of placebo effect, which asserts that treatment ingredients other than insight into the patient's repressions—such as the mobilization of the patient's hope by the therapist—are responsible for any resulting improvement (Grünbaum, 1993, ch. 3). Nor have other analysts ruled out the placebo hypothesis during the past century. A case in point is a forty-five-page study "On the Efficacy of Psychoanalysis" (Bachrach et al., 1991), published in the official *Journal of the American Psychoanalytic Association*. Another is the account of analytic treatment process by (Vaughan and Roose, 1995).

Last, but not least, the repression-etiology is evidentially ill-founded. . . . It is unavailing to the purported etiologic probativeness of free associations that they may lift repressions, since Freud failed to show that the latter are pathogenic. In sum, Freud's argument has forfeited its premises.

References

Bachrach, H., *et al.*, "On the Efficacy of Psychoanalysis", *Journal of the American Psychoanalytic Association,* Vol. 39, 1991: 871-916.

Borch-Jacobsen, M. (1996). Remembering Anna O.: 100 Years of Psychoanalytic Mystification. New York; London: Routledge.

Breuer, J., and S. Freud, "On the Psychical Mechanism of Hysterical Phenomena: Preliminary Communication," (1893, *S.E,* II: 1-17).

Cleckley, H., *The Mask of Sanity,* 5th (Augusta, GA: Emily S. Cleckley, 1988).

Freud, S., *The Interpretation of Dreams* (1900, *S.E.*, IV-V: 1-621).

Freud, S., "An autobiographical study," (1925, *S.E.*, XX: 7-74).

Freud, S., "Analysis Terminable and Interminable," (1937, *S.E.*, XXIII: 209-253).

Grünbaum, A., *The Foundations of Psychoanalysis: A Philosophical Critique* (Berkeley: University of California Press, 1984). There are German, Italian, Japanese and French Translations.

Grünbaum, A., *Validation in the Clinical Theory of Psychoanalysis: A Study in the Philosophy of Psychoanalysis* (Madison, CT: International Universities Press., 1993).

Harman, G., "Inference to the Best Explanation", *Philosophical Review*, Vol. 74, 1965: 88-95.

Salmon, W., *Statistical Explanation and Statistical Relevance* (Pittsburgh: University of Pittsburgh Press, 1971).

Salmon, W., Explanation and Confirmation: A Bayesian Critique of Inference to the Best Explanation," in G. Hon and S.S. Rackover (eds.), *Explanation: Theoretical Approaches and Applications* (Dordrecht: Kluwer, 2001).

Vaughan, S. and S. Roose, "The Analytic Process: Clinical and Research Definitions," *International Journal of Psycho-Analysis*, Vol. 76, 1995: 343-356.

[1] Taken, with permission of the author, from A. Grünbaum, "Critique of Psychoanalysis," *The Freud Encyclopedia: Theory, Therapy, and Culture,* ed. Ed Erwin (New York: Routledge, 2002), 117-136.

Chapter 15
Reply to Dr. Lavin

M. Andrew Holowchak

MY REPLY TO LAVIN HAS TWO PARTS. The first part concerns Freud: the techniques he used during his career as an analyst, his discovery of free association as a method for disclosing unconscious pathogens, and an enumeration of key defects of free association. The second part is a critique of Lavin's insightful essay in defense of free association vis-à-vis its use in contemporary ego psychology.

Freud on Free Association

The cathartic methods Freud used, for abreaction, early in his analytic career were two: hypnosis and suggestion.

Freud used hypnosis early in his career—e.g., *Studies in Hysteria*—but with limited success, as he was not good at inducing a hypnotic state in his patients (1895, *S.E.,* II: 108 and 268). In "Psychotherapy," Freud says hypnosis is suggestive and cosmetic, not etiological and substantive—i.e., it does not concern itself with the origin, strength, and meaning of hysterical symptoms. Instead, it "superimposes a suggestion" with the hope that the suggestion itself will be sufficiently strong to keep the pathogenic idea from expressing itself. It conceals the play of underlying mental forces and, thereby, conceals a patient's resistances. Consequently, hypnosis guards against his recovery. . . (1905, *S.E.,* VII: 260-1).

Shortly after *Studies on Hysteria*, Freud gave up hypnosis as a fruitful method of pathogenic disclosure, though it is likely that he never stopped tinkering with it throughout his life.

Whereas Freud had limited success with hypnosis, he professes in his case-study of Lucy R. in *Studies on Hysteria* to have found a friendlier suggestive alternative in the "pressure" technique of Bernheim. Bernheim showed Freud that memories of events, which would crop up during somnambulism, were not forgotten, while awake. Such memories could be revived during wakefulness by a mild command and slight pressure of the hand on the head of a patient. The suggestive results were similar to those results of hypnosis (1895, *S.E.* II: 108-10).

Freud goes on to relate that the suggestive technique, in all cases, yielded just those results he needed. "I can safely say that it has scarcely ever left me in the lurch. . . . It has always pointed the way which the analysis should take and has enabled me to carry through every such analysis to an end without the use of somnambulism." So cocksure was Freud of the efficacy of the suggestive technique that he could readily dismiss patients' responses such as "I see nothing" as signs of resistance, due to tension in their critical faculty. Something had surely surfaced in every case of pressure, he insisted, but was immediately judged by the patient to be unserviceable or irrelevant and so it was not related to the analyst. Overall, the suggestive method gave Freud insight into the motives behind "forgetting." It showed that "forgetting is often intentional and desired; and its success is never more than *apparent*" (1895, *S.E.* II: 110-2 and 268-70).

In spite of its avowed superiority over hypnosis,[1] the pressure technique proved laborious (1895, *S.E.* II: 111) and Freud would abandon it not long after *Studies on Hysteria*. We cannot say precisely when, but 1904 is a likely year.[2]

Problems with the cathartic method were several and did not escape Freud's notice, even in *Studies on Hysteria*. First, Freud notes that the cathartic method is symptomatic, not causal. It can remove present symptoms, but cannot prevent new ones from emerging (1895, *S.E.* II: 262). Second, given its symptomatic nature, cathartic method is time- and labor-intensive. The demands on an analyst are enormous; so too are those on a patient. An analyst's first task is to recognize the slowness of the cathartic process; success is achievable slowly and *per gradus*. Patience is required[3] (1895, *S.E.* II: 282). Third, the cathartic method might not remove all the symptoms of hysteria. To that objection, Freud notes, first, that a patient's personal circumstances, inaccessible to an analyst, might intervene to help the analyst and, second, that some symptoms, as mere residues of "complete and permanent successes," are harmless. Nonetheless, pathogenicity is, as a rule, over-determined and relapses are always possible (1895, *S.E.* II: 262-3). Fourth, during periods of acute hysteria, an analyst, like a physician faced with an acute infectious disease, is often helpless. Cure, in such instances, can come about only when malady has run its course (1895, *S.E.* II: 263-4).

The cathartic methods did not address the problem of etiology in a manner serviceable to hysterical patients. In addition, they failed to recognize the sexual origins of hysteria. "I now learned from my rapidly increasing experience that it was not *any* kind of emotional excitation that was in action behind the phenomena of neurosis but habitually one of a sexual nature, whether it was a current sexual conflict or the effect of earlier sexual experiences" (1925, *S.E.* XX: 21-22).

The cathartic methods, especially Breuer's suggestive pressure technique, quite naturally led Freud to the method of free association (*freier Einfall*[4]).

> The abandonment of hypnosis seemed to make the situation hopeless, until [I]

> recalled a remark of Bernheim's to the effect that things that had been experienced in a state of somnambulism were only *apparently* forgotten and that they could be brought into recollection at any time if the physician insisted forcibly enough that the patient knew them. [I] therefore endeavored to press [my] *unhypnotized* patients into giving [me] their associations, so that from the material thus provided [I] might find the path leading to what had been forgotten or warded off. [I] noticed later that such pressure was unnecessary and that copious ideas almost always arose in the patient's mind, but that they were held back from being communicated and even from becoming conscious by certain objections put by the patient in his own way. It was to be expected—though this was still unproved and not until later confirmed by wide experience—that everything that occurred to a patient setting out from a particular starting-point must also stand in an internal connection with that starting-point; hence arose the technique of educating the patient to give up the whole of his critical attitude and of making use of the material which was thus brought to light for the purpose of uncovering the connections that were being sought. A strong belief in the determination of mental events certainly played a part in the choice of this technique as a substitute for hypnosis (1922, *S.E.* XVIII: 237-8).

As the passage shows, three assumptions fundamental to free association are these: Mental events are (in some sense) determined; Everything occurring to a patient from a particular starting-point must stand in an internal connection to that starting-point; and Somnabulant experiences can be brought to recollection at any time through a trained analyst's persistence.

So significant was "free association" that Freud gave a new name to his analytic therapy to distinguish it from that of Breuer. He writes, "The new technique [of free association] altered the picture of the treatment so greatly, brought the physician into such a new relation to the patient and produced so many surprising results that it seemed justifiable to distinguish the procedure from the cathartic method by giving it a new name . . . *psycho-analysis.*" Free association allowed Freud to use associative links to disclose hidden pathogens (1922, *S.E.* XVIII: 238-9).

To get at the underlying "meaning" of associations, Freud argued that the analyst and the patient, as it were, had to bring something to the table—what Freud called the "fundamental rule of psycho-analysis."

> A patient must relate everything that his self-observation can detect, and keep back all the logical and affective objections that seek to induce him to make a selection from among them, while the doctor must put himself in a position to make use of everything he is told for the purposes of interpretation and of recognizing the concealed unconscious material without substituting a censorship of his own for the selection that the patient has forgone (1912, *S.E.* XII: 115).

A patient must be in a position of "attentive and dispassionate self-observer." Thus, he must relate whatever is on the surface of his conscious thoughts with utmost candor. All ostensibly disagreeable, nonsensical, unimportant, and even irrelevant thoughts are to be related to an analyst (1922, *S.E.* XVIII: 238). The analyst must meet his patient, who surrenders himself uncritically to his unconscious, halfway. His attitude too must be one of surrender to his own unconscious mental activity—in a state of "*evenly suspended attention*"—without fixating on anything in particular that a patient relates.[5] In such circumstances, a patient's associations emerge like "allusions" to one theme, which, over time and through repetition, proves to be the key to his pathology (1922, *S.E.* XVIII: 239 and 1912, *S.E.* XII: 114-6).

There are several difficulties with free association. I focus on four: neutrality, psychical determinism, etiological concatenation, and faulty constructions.

First, let us consider the principle of neutrality—the therapist's pledge, during associations, to meet his patient unconscious to unconscious. Writes psychotherapist Stephen Ellman: "[T]he analyst [like Freud] who tends to see neutrality as an essential component of the analytic situation tends to see interpretation as the main avenue of analytic communication. Interpretation stimulates insight, and insight is the vehicle of change in the analytic process" (1991, 333). Many analysts—Charles Brenner (1976) and Mark Kanzer (1853) among them—advocate neutrality, even though it may be an unobtainable ideal. Others—Ellman as well as M.M. Gill and Mark Grunes—view neutrality as impossible or undesirable.[6] Gill (1982) maintains that everything in analysis is a matter of transference and argues that neutrality is an illusion. Grunes (1984) states that neutrality is perceived by patients as a signal that a therapist is amoral and that impedes the aim of analysis—the resolution of psychical conflict.

Some variants of psychoanalytic thought view neutrality as counterproductive, as the relationship between analyst and patient is interactive, not analyst-driven. Rudnytsky (1992) considers the relationship between patient and analyst and the primary transference to be foremost in object-relations theory. Fonagy refers to an "interpersonal-relational approach" in which the analytic setting is co-constructed between therapist and patient—each an active participant that has a role in determining the success or failure of therapy. Here, with co-construction, neutrality not just obstructive; it is impossible (2001).

A second difficulty for free association is the issue of psychical determinism: All psychic events have causes. Just what does Freud mean by this? Psychotherapist Charles Brenner gives what I deem to be the canonical interpretation. He states that psychical determinism is the view that "in the mind, as in physical nature about us, nothing happens by chance. . . . Each psychic event is determined by the ones which preceded it" (1984, 2).

That interpretation is, however, not what Freud had in mind. First, it is not clear just what a "psychic event" is. Many events that Freud explained psychically were not themselves psychical events, but physical events—i.e., a nervous twitch or numbness of a particular part of one's body. Second, since Freud often states that psychical explanation will one day likely be replaced by physiological explanation, it seems likely that Freud is only essaying to explain certain types of phenomena—like dreams, neurotic symptoms, jokes, and slips of the tongue—by reference to psychical causes.

Wes Salmon corrects the confusion on psychical determinism in a watershed paper, "Psychoanalytic Theory and Evidence." Here Salmon insists that it is not that events like dreams, slips, and neuroses are determined, but rather that they are *psychically* determined—i.e., that the relevant causes of them are psychical, not physical. Behavior that "*cannot be explained on the basis of constitutional mechanisms alone constitutes indirect inductive evidence for the existence of conscious or unconscious psychic mechanisms for which other indirect inductive evidence is also theoretically available.*" Such psychical mechanisms may be deterministic or probabilistic and, as evidence has a bearing on such relationships, their existence is a matter of experience. Such psychical mechanisms are also entirely consistent with neurophysiological mechanisms, yet they are at least provisionally indispensable for psychoanalysts (1958, 256-60).

A third difficulty is the assumption of etiological concatenation—roughly the view that pathological phenomena are causally linked, cognitively and affectively, to pathogenic memories that are early and sexual and, most importantly, still operable. Given etiological concatenation, Freud believed that free association was the best method for access to these early pathogenic experiences.

Ernest Nagel attacks this point straightforwardly

> It is pertinent to ask . . . what is the evidence for the tacit assumption that none of the events that have transpired since that early traumatic experience need be considered in accounting for the patient's present neurosis. For even if one grants that such a childhood experience is an indispensable condition for an adult neurosis, the assumption that the repressed wish has continued to operate essentially unmodified in the subject's unconscious, despite the countless number of more proximate happenings in the subject's life, cannot be accepted as a matter of course (1971, 54).

Nagel's point is that Freud needs to show, not merely assume, that the precipitating event in early childhood is etiologically operative in an unmodified manner.

Adolf Grünbaum more recently has addressed etiological concatenation and the purported efficacy of free association in his well-known critique of Freudian psychoanalysis in *Foundations of Psychoanalysis* as well as in chapter 13 of this book. He maintains, for Freud, that a proper analytic assessment—one that accords with a patient's actual pathogenic situation—is necessary for remission of symptoms. Grünbaum calls this the "Tally Argument." He derives the Tally Argument principally from a large passage in a 1917 paper of Freud, "Analytic Therapy," of which I quote only two sentences. Freud writes: "[A patient's] conflicts will only be successfully solved and his resistances overcome if the anticipatory ideas he is given tally with what is real in him. Whatever in the doctor's conjectures is inaccurate drops out in the course of the analysis; it has to be withdrawn and replaced by something more correct" (1917, *S.E.* XVI: 452). According to Grünbaum, remission of pathogenic symptoms requires correct analytic assessment; it cannot come about spontaneously or by any method other than psychoanalysis (2984, 139-40).

The Tally Argument has implications for the value of free association. Grünbaum writes:

> The collapse of the therapeutic argument for the repression etiology seriously undermines the purported clinical research value of free association, which are given pride of place as an epistemic avenue to the presumed pathogens! After all, Freud had enunciated his fundamental rule of free association as a maxim of clinical research because he thought that associations governed by it had reliably certified the unconscious pathogens of the neuroses (1984, 185).

There remains the final difficulty—the problem of faulty constructions. That concerns an analyst's capacity to guarantee that his analytic constructions, gleaned through a patient's associations and the transference relationship between them, are accurate. As that is an issue that I have covered elsewhere, I shall merely refer the reader to my paper "The Problem of Unassailability: Analogy and the Adequacy of Constructions in Freudian Psychoanalysis" (Holowchak, 2011).

Critique of Lavin

Lavin begins by stating that his paper concerns an "explication of the role of free association." Free association is *sui generis* to psychoanalysis; it is an "instrument for obtaining psychoanalytic data" (Lavin, 155).

After a brief explication of the context of free association in Freudian psychoanalysis—and here Lavin concedes that free association as practiced by Freud, did not deliver what Freud had promised (Lavin, 156)—he turns to "more elaborate" contemporary use of the technique in ego psychology that enables a therapist to navigate between primary-process and secondary-process modes of thinking. Why this contemporary use is more "elaborate" than that of Freud is unclear. The aim of free association in ego psychology is a patient's defensive posture. "A central purpose of free association in contemporary accounts is to make the patient's defensive processes visible within the psychoanalytic dyad," writes Lavin. The aim is to admit unconscious material more readily into consciousness. The yield is not knowledge *per se*, but data that enable a therapist to gain information about the "mental organization and life of his patient" (Lavin, 157-8).

Lavin takes it as concedable that "the accuracy of the decryptions of latent content obtained through the interpretations of free associations in the psychoanalytic situation is for the patient to decide"—a practice that is at odds with

Freud's approach, in which the therapist is judge and jury, and with the general practice of natural science. Whatever its status as science, there seems no reason to think psychoanalysis is not a valid field of rational inquiry (Lavin, 159).

The key difficulty is Lavin's concession, following Forrester, is that patients are ultimately arbiters of the success or failure of a construction, an interpretation, and perhaps even therapy. He quotes Forrester:

> To be convinced that one can speak from a position of critical strength on these matters without applying psychoanalysis to oneself, I would have to be convinced that I am not qualified to pass judgment on my own person, on my own body, on my own dreams, on my own destiny. . . . I would have to be convinced that *only* someone other than myself is qualified to judge these things about me. And who will convince me that I am so disqualified?

Yet Forrester's customer-knows-best position is problematic. Many persons are categorically convinced of the accuracy of psychic readings that pertain to their "own person," "own body," "own dreams," and "own destiny," though there is little reason to believe psychics have the sort of "reading" capacities they profess to have. Even psychoanalysts would certainly admit to that. Yet if we allow a customer-knows-best approach to psychoanalysis, just because the judgments of therapists relate personally to clients, then why should one not allow the same standard to apply to psychic readings, which relate personally to clients?

Lavin goes on to speak of the training of a psychotherapist and draws an analogy with music.

> Just as musicians learn to hear certain chord progressions, psychoanalysts learn to notice markers of escalating anxiety and defenses. Even if neither were counted a science, each admits of systematic treatment. Nevertheless, in neither discipline does anybody lacking in the relevant praxis, no matter how comprehensive his theoretical education, attain mastery of either discipline's own brand of listening and doing (Lavin, 160).

He goes on to say that an ordinary person does not hear a succession of A, E, G, C notes as an Am7 arpeggio any more that an ordinary person notes escalations in a speaker's anxiety or shifts in an associative pattern as "arrivals of a defense" (Lavin, 162-3).

The analogy is meant to show that psychoanalysts are skilled and trained experts in their field, even if that field is not to be classified as "science." Likened to artists, they offer patients a service that is knowledge-generating and generally presumed to be liberating. Free association, if successful, leads to transference—"a stance towards his psychoanalyst that repeats, in broad outline, patterns of relating to central figures of his early life, especially in regard to the management of wishes, impulses, and their attendant emotions" (Lavin, 160). "If the project succeeds," Lavin says, "the patient replaces a stereotypic response from the past with a wider repertoire of responses." He is no longer prisoner to "reflexive, archaic responses." Even if that fails, he might find himself "better able to tolerate his ancient, unbreakable habit" (Lavin, 163).

One wonders how aidful the comparison of psychoanalysts with musicians is. It is indubitable that both psychoanalysts and musicians are trained artists that have auditory capacities for appreciating subtleties of expression, whether related to music or postures of defense. One obvious difference is that music, in the main, is appreciated for its own sake. Psychoanalysis, in contrast, is appreciated on account of its results. It is still, I believe, an open question whether psychoanalysis, even practiced as an avowed method for recognizing and ultimately breaking down a patient's defenses, is sufficiently valuable to warrant the time and expense that a patient often puts into it. Much hinges, I suspect, on Lavin's notion of transference, where past behaviors toward central figures of a patient's early life are repeated and where the therapist is in the place of any such figure. Following Nagel, one wishes to know why past figures hold the key to future psychoanalytic liberation and how "repressed" childhood wishes continue to operated without modification in one's conscious, if that is what Lavin has in mind.

Overall, by evaluating free association from an ego-psychology perspective, Lavin eschews some of the difficulties Freud faced—most troubling being the problem of free association as a viable tool for disclosing underlying pathogens of a sexual sort. Unlike Freud, however, Lavin's promise is modest—just that amount of liberation that can be gained by making what was once unconscious conscious. What a patient then does is largely up to him. Yet that sounds somewhat like the project Freud had in mind at the time of *Studies on Hysteria*. Freud writes about a conversation with an imaginary interlocutor:

> "Why, you tell me yourself that my illness is probably connected with my circumstances and the events of my life. You cannot alter these in any way. How do you propose to help me, then?" And I have been able to make this reply: "No doubt fate would find it easier than I do to relieve you of your illness. But you will be able to convince yourself that much will be gained if we succeed in transforming your hysterical misery into common unhappiness. With mental life that has been restored to health you will be better armed against that unhappiness" (1895, *S.E.* II: 305).

Notes

1. In "Autobiographical Study," Freud says queerly: "I must supplement what I have just said by explaining that from the very first I made use of hypnosis in another manner, apart from hypnotic suggestion. I used it for questioning the patient upon the origin of his symptom, which in his waking state he could often describe only very imperfectly or not at all. Not only did this method seem more effective than bald suggestive commands or prohibitions, but it also satisfied the curiosity of the physician, who, after all, had a right

to learn something of the origin of the phenomenon which he was striving to remove by the monotonous procedure of suggestion (1925, *S.E.* XX: 19).

2. See Strachey's fn. 1, 1895, *S.E.* II: 110.

3. Acknowledging the difficulty of time, Freud advocates guessing to expedite analysis. Whereas a correct guess would accelerate analysis, an incorrect guess would compel "the patient to take sides ... by enticing him into energetic denials which betray his undoubted better knowledge" (1895, *S.E.* II: 296). Either way, he boasts, no harm would be done.

4. Literally, "free irruption," in the sense of a sudden idea, freely popping into mind. For Freud's thoughts on the history of free association, see "Note on the Prehistory of the Technique of Analysis," (1920, *S.E.* XVIII, 263-5).

5. See also 1909, *S.E.*, X: 23.

6. In Freud's day, Oskar Pfister objected slightly to the neutrality of a therapist, when it comes to transference. He says, "according to my observations, it is also important that the analyst should transmit values which over-compensate for the patient's gain from illness or guilt feelings" (Freud et al., 1963, 112).

References

Brenner, Charles, *An Elementary Textbook of Psychoanalysis* (Garden City, NY: Anchor Books, 1984).

Brenner, Charles, *Psychoanalytic Technique and Psychic Conflict* (New York: International University Press, 1976).

Ellman, Steven, *Freud's Technique Papers: A Contemporary Perspective* (Northvale, NJ: 1991).

Fonagy, Peter, *Attachment Theory and Psychoanalysis* (New York: Other Press, 2001).

Freud, Sigmund, *The Standard Edition of the Complete Psychological Works of Sigmund Freud*, Vols. I-XXIV, ed. and trans. James Strachey (London: The Hogarth Press, 1976).

Freud, Sigmund and Oskar Pfister, *Psychoanalysis and Faith: The Letters of Sigmund Freud & Oskar Pfister,* eds. Heinrich Meng and Ernst L. Freud (New York: Basic Books, Inc., Publishers, 1963).

Gill, M.M., *Analysis of Transference, Vol. 1: Theory and Technique* (New York: International Universities Press, 1982).

Grünbaum, Adolf, *The Foundations of Psychoanalysis: A Philosophical Critique* (Berkeley: University of California Press, 1984).

Grunes, Mark, "The Therapeutic Object Relationship," *Psychoanalytic Review,* 71, 1984: 123-43/

Holowchak, M. Andrew, "The Problem of Unassailability: Analogy and the Adequacy of Constructions in Freudian Psychoanalysis," *Psychoanalytic Psychology* (forthcoming, 2011).

Kanzer, Mark, "Past and Present in the Transference," *Journal of the American Psychological Association* 1, 1953: 144-54.

Nagel, Ernest, "Methodological Issues in Psychoanalytic Theory," *Psychoanalysis, Scientific Method, and Philosophy,* ed. Sydney Hook (New York University Press, 1971).

Rudnytsky, Peter L., "A Psychoanalytic Weltanschauung," *Psychoanalytic Review,* 79(2), 1992, 295-302.

Salmon, Wesley. "Psychoanalytic Theory and Evidence," *Psychoanalysis, Scientific Method, and Philosophy,* ed. Sydney Hook (New York University Press, 1958), 252-267.

Chapter 16
Reply to Dr. Grünbaum

Michael Lavin

GRÜNBAUM'S CHAPTER CONTINUES EXTENDING his long-standing rejection of the adequacy of Freud's efforts to justify free association. His criticism of free association is more limited than some may have noticed. In particular, he contends that "he has established the multiple failure of Freud's therapeutic argument for the etiologic probativeness of free association in psychopathology"; however, he separates his rejection of free associations to identify latent causes of psychopathology from other uses free association may have. A psychoanalyst might, even if Grünbaum is right about the worthlessness of free association to identify the root cause of a patient's psychopathology, discover that a patient's free association's are revealing about "psychological preoccupations and personality dispositions." Of course Grünbaum does not go on to say that they are in fact revealing. In principle, he allows that they may be revealing, even if their role in identifying the "etiological probativeness" of a patient' psychopathology is worthless. My chapter defending free association did not hinge on its capacity to remove the trauma-induced pathogens that Freud believed to be the *sine qua non* of psychopathology in the early stages of his development of psychoanalysis. Instead, my chapter put other uses of free association front and center. Also, on my view, free association, as nowadays understood, was at most in the process of being invented in the 1890s.

Further Freud, by the end of his career, had moved away from the Therapeutic and Etiological hypotheses that Grünbaum attributes to him. In "Analyses Terminable and Interminable," Freud gives two views of when an analysis has come to an end. On the first view, two conditions are present at the end of a psychoanalysis: (1) the patient's principal symptoms shall have resolved and (2) the psychoanalyst shall have concluded that "so much repressed material has been made conscious, so much that was unintelligible has been explained, and so much internal resistance conquered that there is no need to fear a repetition of the pathological processes concerned." He goes on to offer a second sense of termination that is more ambitious than the first. In it, which he believes is limited to cases of traumatic neurosis, psychoanalysis, by having "strengthened the patient's ego," will replace an "inadequate decision" reached in the patient's immaturity with a "correct solution" (1937, *S.E.,* XXIII: 219-20). These characterizations of the goal of psychoanalysis in regard to psychopathology have moved a discernible distance from Freud's earlier view in *Studies of Hysteria*. There is no mention of simple cure via a patient's abreaction to recovered memories of traumatic events alleged to cause his specific symptoms. Moreover, at least two levels of "cure" are proposed.

These exegetical points leave intact Grünbaum's central contention that free association lacks the probative role in the establishment of the etiology of a patient's psychopathology. However, a trend toward understanding an analytic process emerges in Freud's writing as time passes. In my chapter, I, in agreement with Meehl and Grünbaum, conceded that free association does not suffice to establish latent causes. Nevertheless, what is striking is that it was presumably listening to what patients had to say, as well as to the reports and criticism of a growing cadre of psychoanalysts, that forced Freud away from his early, simplistic views of psychopathology.[1] And the march towards more complicated models of psychopathology has continued. Without argument, I'll assert that psychoanalysts, as well as psychiatrists and psychologist, have moved to more nuanced and biologically informed conceptions of psychopathology. Despite greater sophistication about the etiology of psychopathology, therapies that cannot provide an accurate etiology for whatever the real taxons of psychopathology are may still help in understanding a patient's expression of pathology, his experience of pathology, and how he comes to meaningful terms with his pathology, just to mention a few possibilities.

Even though free association may have emerged from and been initially justified by an utterly mistaken view of pathology that is not in itself lethal. One of the most enduring psychological tests is the MMPI. No psychologist would now have gone about constructing the test the way it was first constructed by gift Minnesota psychologist. For one thing, nobody accepts the diagnostic categories that guided the test's dust-bowl empiricism construction. All the, the MMPI has continued in use, albeit in revised forms. Its principal scales have been retained, even though psychologists, owing to research proving the diagnoses used to develop those scales were unreliable and of dubious validity at best. Nobody now uses the diagnostic categories of the late 1930s and early 1940s. Despite the MMPI's dubious beginnings, an avalanche of research on the MMPI has established a good measure of predictive validity for it in all manner of contexts. So, psychologists continue to use it, but not to diagnoses psychasthenia or hyopchondriasis. For better or worse, free association has also generated an impressive body of psychoanalytic theory and "results." It is improbable, it seems to me, that free association's justification hinges on any single lifeline.

Let me conclude with one final remark. I wish to pay tribute to Professor Grünbaum and his work. More than any person I can think of, he forced psychoanalysts and those friendly to the psychoanalytic enterprise to make their work more rigorous. I was much impressed when I read his *Foundations of Psychoanalysis*. He changed my complacent picture of the reputability of psychoanalysis. Psychoanalysis is a much better discipline because of the informed, original, and creative work he did on it.

Notes

[1] See also an early explanation of Freud's in the first footnote in "Dynamics of Transference" (1912, *S.E.*, XII: 99).

Bibliography

Sigmund Freud, *The Standard Edition of the Complete Psychological Works of Sigmund Freud*, Vols. I-XXIV, ed. and trans. James Strachey (London: The Hogarth Press, 1976).

PART V
The Unconscious

Freud states in his 1915 essay "The Unconscious", "Our right to assume the existence of something mental that is unconscious and to employ that assumption for the purposes of scientific work is disputed in many quarters. To this we can reply that our assumption of the unconscious is necessary and legitimate, and that we possess numerous proofs of its existence" (1915, *S.E.*, XIV: 166).

What precisely is Freud's view of "unconscious"? Are his "numerous proofs" incontrovertible? Can and should psychoanalysis do without it?

Pro: Grant Gillett, *University of Otago Medical School,* "Freud's *Wunderblock*: The Unconscious as Neural Palimpsest"

Con: Edward Erwin, Ph.D., *University of Miami,* "Freud's Greatest Failure: The Unconscious"

Chapter 17
Freud's *Wunderblock*
The Unconscious as Neural Palimpsest

Grant Gillett
University of Otago, New Zealand

FREUD PUBLISHED A PAPER IN 1925 on the "mystic writing pad" or "*Wunderblock*." He describes the apparatus in detail as a child's toy on which you write messages which then are erased by peeling off a two-layered film (of celluloid and waxed paper) attached to an underlying wax pad. The message is easily visible immediately after writing and is easily erased by lifting the top two layers, but it leaves a trace on the underlying wax. Freud likened this to the psyche in which the conscious ego and its contents based on perception ("system Pcpt.-Cs") are like the messages clearly visible in the film and the unconscious layers of the psyche are like the underlying wax. In his "A Note on a Mystic Writing-Pad," Freud has a theory about how this might work in the human neuro-cognitive system.

> [C]athectic innervations are sent out and withdrawn in rapid periodic impulses from within into the completely pervious system Pcpt.-Cs. So long as that system is cathected in this manner, it receives perceptions (which are accompanied by consciousness) and passes the excitation on to the unconscious mnemonic systems; but as soon as the cathexis is withdrawn, consciousness is extinguished and the functioning of the system comes to a standstill. It is as though the unconscious stretches out feelers, through the medium of the system Pcpt.-Cs., towards the external world and hastily withdraws them as soon as they have sampled the excitations coming from it (1925, *S.E.*, XIX: 231).

This theoretical interpretation resonates so well with contemporary work on the role of the self-related systems of emotive and motivational control that form the limbic system of the brain (and therefore in personality structure and function) that it is prescient on the part of Freud. As a neuro-philosopher of the psyche, he had clearly benefited from the lessons of his philosophical and neuro-scientific mentors.

A number of recent strands of work reveal the emotional markers of cognition and the self system and the patterns of neural excitation that influence a human being to act in ways guided by emotional relevance, remembered significance, and relevance to self (Northoff, 2007). These findings have supported Freud's thesis that the springs of human behavior lie deep within the primary associative and instinctive tracts of our own life stories and the traces that these have left on the brain. Some of our deepest feelings, important in reactions and motivational hierarchies, arise in ways that the conscious self barely comprehends. They are almost certainly a result of deeply ingrained and meaningful habits of the heart and the experiences that have inscribed them in the psyche (Damasio, 2000). Freud's mnemic residues and cathexes are a slightly dated way to refer to what are in effect distributed associational complexes, involving midline and limbic centers and the paralimbic cortex, itself involved in memory function. [Yes fine] The way that perception and thought reflect, obliquely and in sometimes inchoate ways, the activity in "older" circuits and assemblies in the brain, serving the central concerns and affects of the self, is neatly captured by the *Wunderblock* metaphor.

The *Wunderblock* has an underlying base of wax, contact with which creates a graphic image on the surface layers that allow it to be read. But the underlying wax develops grooves that are a reflection of what has been written and these in turn create an embossed pattern of criss-crossing traces that affect any new messages that are written on the surface film. They render some aspects of it a little broken and difficult to decipher a graphic analogy to the human associational neural network that is affected by successive conscious experiences but, over time, develops "grooves" or deeply inscribed traces (preferred patterns of excitation and inhibition) as a result of those same experiences (and not just what one remembers about them). Thus we also derive the metaphor of "the neural palimpsest"—a cumulative and interfering tracework of inscriptions contributed to by the lived experience of the individuals in ways that may not be obvious to the subject; and so to the Freudian psyche.

The Freudian Psyche and Its Construction

Freud offered us the first open-ended scientific exploration of the soul. It was premised on the idea that the soul/psyche was an aspect of a human being continuous with the nature of animals and realized by the brain so that, in principle, it could be studied as a natural system. Unlike Descartes, Locke, and other philosophical defenders of consciousness and responsibility, he went beyond reason alone to gain evidence about the subject's psychology and worked chiefly by inference from clinical observations, analytic interviews, and an underpinning knowledge of neurology and brain function.

Freud's compelling *Wunderblock* metaphor was invented when he saw his grandson playing with the new toy that was all the rage—a magic writing pad.

The *Wunderblock* or magic writing pad, a common children's toy of the last century, predated the wonders of electronic wizardry. It comprised three layers—a cellulose film, a waxed paper film, and an underlying wax block. A child used a stylus to write a message on the cellulose and it appeared as writing, readable until someone peels off the cellulose and erases it. The pad is now ready for a new message, which can also be written and just as easily erased. This goes on seemingly endlessly until the underlying score marks or grooves in the wax block disrupt and fragment the new messages so that the writer becomes frustrated and must re-melt the wax, or wipe the slate clean of the traces that have inscribed it.

Freud saw, in an instant, a metaphor for the psyche. Consciousness and its perceptual systems move from one experience to the next, apparently leaving the previous experiences behind. "The moving finger writes and, having written, moves on." A reference to Omar Khayyam. But despite the passing of those moments of experience, traces are left on the nervous system (the wax block beneath) that gradually, when the same pattern is traced and retraced, score grooves into it (or set up quasi-stable excitation and inhibition patterns) that will interact with the new messages that are being formed to hook up to memory and its systems of prompting and learned response (Freud's "mnemic residues"). Sometimes the interference is so pronounced that new perceptions are made confusing or even unreadable by subjects; they are apparently meaningless, but perhaps have an effect nonetheless. This metaphor, for Freud, illustrated the relationship between the underlying unconscious base of the psyche and the transitory conscious ego that paraded itself for public "reading." As the pad became scored by successive repeated patterns, so too the psyche would become scarred by repeated patterns of experience that laid down associations, which influenced a person's reaction to and feelings about everything that happened to him. Some of these scored grooves or scars would be so profound that they would make impossible the telling of a coherent and liveable story and any sense of ease or comfortable fit between the person and his life-world. Such disruptions, argued Freud, form the cathectic (emotive-motivational-cognitive) basis of various (he seems to have thought all) psychological disorders.

The picture is of successive messages from the world, transmitted to the psyche but not wounding it, unless they are deeply inscribed and connect with the strong needs that it meets. The psyche as it searches the environment uses its sensory/perceptual system to gather information (in ways that resonate with recent work on the ecological theory of perception and cognition and the genetic and cultural aspects of psychological evolution. That view also resonates with Foucault's striking remarks about the soul or psyche as "the present correlative of a certain technology of power over the body" (1984, 177) or as the cumulative result of inscriptions on the body "traced by language and dissolved by ideas" (1984, 83). Freud's psyche is here seen in terms of an archeology of collective and ontogenetic history, communicated to an individual by those around who are, in themselves and through their interactions with the individual, the representatives of culture.

Freud extended his use of the metaphor from the basic and very compelling picture of the psyche presented by the *Wunderblock* to a Victorian causal machinery of layers of neural function. The conscious layer of function obeyed the laws of reason and public endorsement and was the presentable face of the psyche—*the Ego*. Beneath that, two less principled and accessible systems worked their complex ways in the systems of association that constituted them and were constituted by them. *The Id* caught up into itself the instincts inherited from phylogeny and the intuitions and primary irrational affect-laden dispositions and associational complexes arising in infancy and childhood. These complexes embedded narcissistic and self-oriented ways of thinking and acting and a distorted view of the world in which the yearnings of a vulnerable and needy child dominated and negotiated life's challenges with an unwavering eye to self-defense and gratification. The Ego struggles to conform the psychology of the individual to an external and less indulgent, more culturally and socially acceptable way of being, often in the process, finding itself needing to wield powerful associative influences of its own as *the Super-ego*—stereotypically seen as the condensed parental voice striving with the wayward and headstrong Id. Together the three aspects of the psyche set up ways of conducting oneself in a world shared with others and dominated by their word as Law—enacted by the Father and supported (but also softened) by the Mother. This is the real structure of the Freudian psyche—sketched in metaphoric outline by the *Wunderblock* but operating in conative force as one take on the activity of the human brain as a complex neural system, reacting to the subject's being-in-the-world.

We can now pursue the metaphor of the *Wunderblock* and link it into a second metaphor—that of the palimpsest—in reconstructing an informative picture of the Freudian psyche sufficient to a post-structural or discursive psychology.

The Neural Palimpsest

A palimpsest is an historical curiosity. It dates from a time when writing materials were far more costly than would allow their use for just one message. The writer kept the manuscript and wrote a new message over the top of the old one. The new message could be in a different-colored ink or composed after the manuscript had been partially cleaned so that the page became a multi-layered text with different messages, each written on top of others. Therefore, at least potentially, the record of a correspondence could be reconstructed from the traces of text.

The human soul/psyche can be seen to be similar to a palimpsest in one important respect: It is, in part, the result of traces of multiple encounters and interactions that have inscribed it with messages directed to the addressee. These layers of inscription, if reconstructed, tell us much about the dynamic relationality that has played its part in forming the person who has participated. The soul thus carries inscriptions in two ways: through the metaphor of the *Wunderblock*, where grooves have been formed from repetition (we shall come to the technical terms later) and from reinforcement, and through over-writing that has combined together to form a unique pattern of markings which, in its totality, make the psyche a (quasi-artistic) texture of dealings between humans and their life-world.

The neural network that is the human brain is an almost perfect analogue of this type of construction whereby multiple markings, each change the character of the whole—line upon line, precept upon precept—until we are faced by a personality obeying all sorts of imperatives conveyed in the messages that have informed a person. The individual psyche thus formed carries in itself a record, however difficult to decipher, of what has happened to a person, of reactions and responses, things that have been done subsequently, and how the whole has developed as a result of the cumulative history of the individual in context. Innocence is overlaid with experience and fitted (or ill-fitted) the person for the human life-world in ways that reflect what has been enjoyed, endured, and initiated, and the result reflects the various encounters and relationships that make a human life. The brain accumulates and reshuffles these "inscriptions."

The human neocortex is the most sophisticated, extensive, and complex processing network in the animal kingdom and its fundamentally axial architecture is disposed as an extended thick slice with fibers, oriented along two axes—one in the plane of the cortex (call it "horizontal") and the other orthogonal to it (call it "vertical"). We see this in any standard diagram of the cortex where the layers of cells are arranged horizontally and the interconnecting fibers are of two types: short and intermediate length or "horizontal," connecting proximal or related cortical areas, and both long and short length or "vertical," connecting within cylinders of cortex and between the cortex to lower centers in the brain and spinal cord. Its layered structure occurs within the context of a more comprehensive layering able to provide the informational capacities to produce a soul or "psychic apparatus" with a complexity that makes it prone to an unending set of individual maladies similar to and differing from one another in important ways such that each person, in one sense, has a disorder of their own (Kristeva, 1995).

The layers of the cortex clearly have a pattern of connectivity whereby both the planar (or horizontal) and the vertical axes have both short and long connections receiving afferents and sending efferents. The net effect of most of the short connections is to transform the cortex into a series of stacks (or columns) and the long connections allow one area of the cortex to mix and meld its information with diverse (in terms of sensory modality and motor output) other areas of the cortex or with that arising from subcortical centers.

In general, the long fibers for reception and projection connect the subject to the world, via sensory surfaces and motor outputs, and the short fibers, for interconnection, allow ever more complex patterns of information, both internal and external, and residues of past experience to control patterns of activity. Russell's dictum—"Only connect"—can therefore be given both an internal cognitive-emotive meaning ("Connect diverse internal activations!") and an interactional or ecological meaning ("Connect to your environment in self-concerned ways!")

Among the cortico-cortical fibers in the human brain, many are in contact with speech and language information for reasons related to the function of language in human thought—a connection that some neuropsychologists realised over thirty years ago. "Whereas the relatively elementary forms of regulation of organic processes and even of the simplest forms of behaviour can take place without the aid of speech, higher mental processes are formed and take place on the basis of speech activity" (Luria, 1973, 93-94). This fact is very significant in the light of growing knowledge of neural plasticity. "Maps of the cortex apparently change, the apparent stability in them being a consequence of balanced competition. Changing the balance results in an orderly sequence of change that produces a new balance and a new organisation" (Kolb and Whishaw, 1990, 191).

Our best model of brain microprocessing and human cognitive function is provided by parallel distributed processing (PDP) or neural-network systems that use a number of parallel channels to create extended patterns of excitation in three cerebral dimensions, with an extended and horizontally interconnected surface level and a set of "vertical" connections feeding into and out of the former at myriad points. The resulting activity instances notional vectors in the overall flux of brain activity interacting in the way they deal with patterns in the incoming input according to preformed dispositions.

> [T]he brain's basic mode of occurrent representation is the activation vector across a proprietary population of neurons—retinal neurons, olfactory neurons, auditory neurons and so forth. Such activation vectors have a virtue beyond their combinatorially explosive powers of representation. They are ideally suited to participate . . . in a powerful mode of *computation*, namely, vector-to-vector *transformation*. An activation pattern across one neural population (e.g. at the retina) can be transformed into a distinct activation pattern (e.g. at the visual cortex) by way of the axonal fibres projecting from the first population to the second, and by way of the millions of carefully tuned synaptic connections that those fibres make with the neurons at the second or target population (Churchland *et al.*, 1998, 14).

From these "activation vectors" novel patterns of data detection and combination can be generated so as to register and make use of previously unused environmental contingencies. Thus the system as a whole can "learn" to "recognize" complex inner-outer patterns of related contingency even where these are non-obvious, embedded in a lot of incidental data, and may have no simple relation to salient instincts. The system, one could say, generates subtle regularities and correlations embedded in a cumulatively expanding array of possibilities that is unique to historico-cultural context, family and learning history, and the serendipity or catastrophes of infancy. This heuristic process responds to holistic patterns of activity, aspects of which may be inchoate, rather than to specific details with explicit roles. Minor details are not ignored, particularly if they capture some regularity associated with a significant environmental contingency and higher level patterns of excitation along with contextual, and other clues may disambiguate or problematize patterns at lower levels. By using both the level that picks out the elements in a presented array and the level that detects the overall pattern, the system "makes meaning of" what is being presented in terms of the concerns of the individual.

For instance, consider a system presented with an ambiguous stimulus array such as:

P # N (pun or pain?)

And if the context is:

"Your father made a P#N to make light of the situation."

Now a system task oriented to detecting English words will use the information that the context is one where humor is apt as a disambiguating cue (from a "higher" or more holistic level of information processing) and, as a result, take the sign as "pun" rather than "pain." The word then takes on feeling tone in a process that implicates many levels of complexity and clothes the words with semantic and emotive content.

The human neural network allows us to cognize the world as containing similar and repeated patterns of information and recognizable objects or patterns of events even when the information is partial or varies in its details. For instance, I may hear someone say "You are such a bad boy!" but in a context where I realize that the message is effaced somehow and that my actions are being commended in some way rather than condemned. I might report this as "Dad told me off; but only because mum told him to." My psyche works with a picture of the human life-world and what goes on in it, arising from dynamic cognitive activity, using multiple images gained at different times. It then constructs an understanding of myself that is true, but not in any objective or detached way, rather true in an intrapsychic way. Its intrapsychic truth reflects the layers of meaning and affect that Freud reifies in his causal mechanisms. Such mechanisms are based on a conception of neurophysiology that is deterministic and does not allow room for a dynamically interactive unconscious, affecting the world as much as it is affected by the world and constructing new realities that change the lives of kings, paupers, popes, believers, and captains of industry. Whatever its origins in imagination and wish fulfillment, the world as a human life-world is as real as war and climate change and, in that respect, worthy of serious study in terms of the values and instincts that underpin it.

A profound insight is available when we consider PDP systems, dealing with non-obvious patterns embedded in a stimulus array; here collateral cues or correlated teaching inputs can come into play (Rumelhart and McLelland, 1986, 184ff). The system uses the presence or absence of the cue and, on that basis, links together any associated data to form quasi-stable patterns. The application to human discourse and to the parallel or collateral patterns of body language and non-verbal affective "messages" is obvious and provides a very plausible basis on which to understand the inscription of the neural network of an infant by patterns of relationship and interaction within their primary socializing group. The infant, as a focus or topic of thoughts and attitudes for its own human group and the significant figures within it, receives (concerning itself) an extended and cumulative non-obvious data package. If we use Lacan's neo-Freudian terms, we can think of the result as an image or better imagistic quasi-object with an intrinsic set of associated emotive and evaluative associations based in the interactions that the infant has been part of (Lacan, 1977, 1-7). Humans are always "cueing" each other as to how things ought to be thought of and evaluated and thereby creating complex recognitional abilities that are robust in the face of varying input and are deeply inscribed in the layers of the psyche where instinct, intuition, and emotion are part of the neuro-cognitive maelstrom variably accessible to consciousness (or cognitively penetrable).

Linguistic signs occur in conversation and, *inter alia*, in combinations that forge diverse associations—connections not only between the features of the actual arrays of stimuli (in the raw, as it were) but also between related signs. These links enable cognitive and affective transitions to be established via the shared cognitive resource of language and idiosyncratic learning histories.

The cognitive structure that results extends and greatly complicates the flexibility and richness of human cognitive, affective, and conative processes to the extent that Luria gives a pervasive role to linguistic signs in human psychology. He notes that perception involves mapping on presented information to stable, reproducible, and associative structures so that "perceptual activity is not confined to the processes of visual perception, but necessarily includes the active formation of visual images corresponding to a single word meaning" (1973, 237-8).

Certain caveats apply to the "visual" of these "visual images" and I have extended the mapping of perceptual presentations to include principled means of grouping multi-modal stimuli and more subtle regularities associated with signs. Luria's emphasis on the active (or visual search) nature of perception (1973, 229) strengthens the idea that human subjects are *information gatherers* that use a repertoire of perceptual anticipations or schemata, some of which are motivated in quite inexplicit ways, to collect information from their environment.

Luria's insight that perception is influenced by (the top-down activation of lower assemblies by higher patterns associated with) discourse can usefully be picked up when we consider the role of speech and linguistic signs in attention. Targeted responding to a given item requires selective and flexible attention that favors some features of an array at the expense of others. Verbal instructions may be used to direct attention but they may also restrict the sampling that the subject does in order to codify or represent what is thought to be the case in a complex situation so that "voluntary attention is not biological in its origin but a social act" (1973, 262). Actions also "are dictated by intentions which are formed with the close participation of speech" (1973, 37). But all of this is explicit, accountable by the conscious and discursive subject, and many motivations, emotions, and reactions may not so easily be explicable even to the person who is their subject.

For Luria it is important that the cerebral neocortex or highest level of brain function is involved in all cognitive processes through its top-down influences on neural function. Freud, in contrast, is more interested in those influences of which no articulate account can be given by the naïve psychological subject. These are not, according to Freud, merely biological impulses, but also draw richly on the milieu of meaning and evaluation in which the subject participates, and often in confusing ways. Such interaction between processing levels is, as noted, a feature of a neural network/PDP systems in disambiguating deficient low-level data and in altering the tone and emphasis of higher level processing schemata.

According to the present account, any input data, and especially non-salient data, can be "lost" in the ongoing stream of brain activity if they are not picked out by a learning set or cognitive instruction condition. The way the data are dealt with, the affective and conative links that they make, changes of sensitivity channeled by contact with selected "mnemonic residues." Schema formation, sensitivity setting (particularly invoked by social influences in the human case), and other complex effects on every level of the human neuraxis create preferential processing paths that respond to perceptual clues and connections within the human psyche. Many of those paths are not evident to persons who are conscious psychological subjects, trying to keep in touch with "reality" and with their own identity and sense of worthwhileness.

On this account, signs and their meanings, associative complexes, linked by learning history and semantico-linguistic structure to life situations, are the very stuff and driving force of human cognition and behavior. But many of these connections are not fully understood by the individual and require informed reference to culture, history, and value as constructed by human beings and worked out in terms of sociological and interpersonal forces. In that sense alone, there is a great deal of work to be done by an updated notion of the unconscious which expands the crude Darwinism of the neuro-biological Freud and begins to take account of some of the complexity at which he and Charcot gestured in their studies of hysteria (see Gillett, 2009, esp. chap. 12).

Freud's theory of the unconscious causation of psychic states and disorders allowed hysteria to be classified as an affliction that, although psychic rather than neurological, was both causative and not subject to conscious construction by the person involved. Charcot himself seemed to be aware that his "demonstrations" of hysteria and hypnosis were not quite as they might appear to be.

> We must conclude that Charcot's orientation to the problem of hysteria was neither organic nor psychological. He recognized and clearly stated that problems in human relationships may be expressed in hysterical symptoms. The point is that he maintained the medical view in public, for official purposes, as it were, and espoused the psychological view only in private, where such opinions were safe (Szasz, 1962, 47).

No such irony is found in Freud's belief that unconscious psychic cathexes, usually erotic, produce symptoms of bodily dysfunction with symbolic links to their genesis. The key to hysteria as a phenomenon betraying the unconscious psyche is the evident meaningfulness of the symptoms and the patient's inability to comprehend that aspect or make the relevant connections to his or her own life history.

But Showalter remarks that the connections made by psychoanalysis, "the child of the hysterical woman" are created out of the union of suffering and unspeakability, but not necessarily in the way set out by the doctrine of the unconscious mind and its ideational contents (1987, 147). Charcot and his colleagues, she argues, could have heard the messages that his patients were trying to convey, albeit in an inchoate and unspeakable way, and noted that the unconscious is related in complex ways to the unspeakable. Instead Charcot pronounces, with the incontestability of the clinical ring-master "[Y]ou see how hysterics shout . . . much ado about nothing" (the Shakespeare is apposite to the dramatic impressions that hysterics make on others and on themselves). The language that speaks when speech is impossible (as in Dora's "complete loss of voice" [1987, 159]) was, despite not being completely ignored by the time psychoanalysis developed the "talking cure," misconstrued in terms of Freud's preferred account of deep neuro-psychic mechanisms that only partially surfaced in the conscious self-understanding of the psychological subject. Showalter adds, "Freud and Breuer saw the repetitive domestic routines, including needlework, knitting, playing scales, and sickbed nursing, to which bright women were frequently confined, as the causes of hysterical sickness (158). Despite their alleged recognition of aspects of the suffering in interpersonal and other woes, the doctrinaire language of the Ego, the Id, and the Superego, we could argue, obscured the real need for clinicians to probe beneath the stories of the self to expose the dynamics of the self produced by the intersection of social and interpersonal context, individual needs, vulnerabilities and aspirations, and the domain of shared language—the word as imperative and imagistic. We can do little better than to quote Lacan at this juncture.

> The psychoanalytic experience has rediscovered in man the imperative of the Word as the law that has formed him in its image. It manipulates the poetic function of language to give to his desire its symbolic mediation. . . . [I]t is in the gift of speech that all the reality of its effects resides; for it is by way of this gift that all reality has come to man and it is by his continued act that he maintains it (1977, 106).

The brain, I have argued, receives information from the world as presented and "illuminated" by human activity and language. Thus all stimulus arrays that we detect are linked to human activities and the words used in those activities. This social milieu picks out and draws a subject's attention to the relevant features and items in the world and then marks them for future use by attaching signs to them. The result is a grid which maps us on to the human life world and tells us the significance of things—what it means to be sick or well, what it is to desire, what is desirable and what forbidden and so on. The grid and the salient objects related to it comprise a cognitive, conative, and affective map of the world as rich as the representational system and developed sensitivities of the subject will allow. Many aspects of this mapping of self on to world are not evident to the person whose lived story is based on it and, in that sense, they are unconscious. They may even be said to form a system in which the self as self-conscious and the reality it relates to can be understood as being influenced in a dynamic way by the urges of instinct and the molding effects of the socio-cultural milieu. This is Freud without the Victorian neural machine, but what it means in terms of the psyche ought not to be obscured from us by throwing the (Freudian) baby out with the (deterministic neo-Darwinian) bathwater.

This model can be combined with (and indeed seems eminently suited to) the recent discussion of dynamic–systems-oriented approaches to cognition where psychological activity is viewed as comprising interactive partial programs designed to function in relation to a complex and socially articulated environment and to theorize human psychology as activity in which conception, imagination, desires, attitudes, and values are essentially relational. This position puts a contemporary gloss on Freud's case for the unconscious psyche—*System Ucs.*

Arguments for and against the Unconscious

Freud's arguments for the unconscious were relatively simple and rested on (1) the gaps in psychological explanation evident when one is limited to conscious phenomena, (2) the nature of post-hypnotic suggestion, and (3) the coherence and meaningfulness of dream interpretations (1986, *S.E.*, III: 135ff). The gaps in explanation are filled by two different types of psychic contents: those not present to consciousness at a given point in time and those later characterized as repressed. Such contents are uncontentious when we consider memories or beliefs not currently the focus of attention, but Freudian explanations of slips of the tongue, irrational behavior, and other "ideas keeping apart from consciousness in spite of their intensity and activity" (1912, *S.E.*, XII: 262) now have a much more neuroscientific flavor. Despite that shift, psychology still needs to attend to such things as the cathexes or meaningful/emotional loadings of generally innocuous or non-emotive remarks, events, and incidental thoughts or fixations and idiosyncratic tendencies to repeat or return to certain psychological foci in a quasi-obsessive way.

The dynamic thesis whereby unconscious contents have psychic content that explains otherwise inexplicable acts and attitudes is not merely the idea that there are unconscious informational processes explaining our cognitive performance in solving problems or in relation to thought in general. It is also the claim that these are continuous with our understanding of dynamic and interpersonal aspects of disorders such as Multiple Personality Disorder, Hysteria, and anorexia. In relation to these, mere neuro-cognitive anomalies will not do the explanatory work we need.

Freud appeals to the fact that we rationalize and minimize the significance of phenomena, such as "slips of the tongue" or our laughter at slightly "off" jokes. Nonetheless, such phenomena are deeply revealing. He notices that dreams often have recurring themes and are suggestively related to patterns of activity that show up in waking life and asks about the connection between those things. He also discusses hypnosis, post-hypnotic suggestion, and the feeble rationalizations to which hypnosis gives rise as evidence that the unconscious can affect conscious behavior in ways that are not evident to the agent. He mentions, *inter alia*, a patient who, under the influence of post-hypnotic suggestion, picks up a doctor's umbrella and holds it over the doctor's head to ward off the rain when the doctor comes to his ward. When challenged, the patient makes "some lame remark" about why he is doing that (1885, *S.E.* II: 188). Freud claims that such evidence indicates that contents in the psyche have behavioral effects without being accessible to the conscious awareness of the patient.

Sartre had some quite specific worries about Freudian theory—the most deep-seated of which was that descriptions of the human psyche as a deterministic system seemed to undermine human freedom and responsibility. The compatibilist claim that human free will reflects no more than acting as a result of inner states, comprising the desires and character of the psychological agent, for Sartre, neglected the fact that we are constantly and creatively interpreting the world in which we act. Thus conscious levels of psychological function—Freud's Ego—must (for an existentialist) influence the unconscious by shaping thoughts, desires, and actions which, by implication, cannot, therefore, be deterministic in their function (as in the remark by Lacan).

Sartre's critique has a certain cogency. We live in a world that is partly imagined and in which the interpretations of reality that we compose—for instance that children are innocent and vulnerable moral beings despite their inability to take part in the moral world of reasons and actions—significantly guide our behavior and attitudes. His own down-to-earth example makes the point *a fortiori*. Imagine that you intend to have coffee with your friend Pierre. You walk past a café that you commonly frequent and notice that he is not there. But what have you noticed? What is it in the physical information your sensory systems can pick up that tells you he was not there (rather than some other fact (that it was not painted purple, that there were crissants in the window)? In fact what we notice in the world depends on the projects we are involved in and the ways we search or look for relevant information in our context (as noted above). Each of us inhabits a world, relativized to what we seek and can do in it. We are active in the world and not just driven by stimulus conditions. Nevertheless, what we see and do are not merely products of choice. The scenario is more complex than that and reflects the many-faceted dynamic interaction between ourselves and a world in which we are active participants

Second, psychoanalysis aims to engage consciousness and conversation with the unconscious psyche so the conscious psyche must have some effect on "*System Ucs*." In any conversation, the conscious person is an active party (setting aside hypnosis or other altered states) so that "talk therapy" (e.g., psychoanalysis, cognitive behavioural therapy, narrative therapy, logotherapy, or counselling) is part of the process. But, insofar as any of these are successful, events going on between human beings as conscious interacting beings, affect the psyche as a whole. Sartre is therefore right as judged by evident human observation and reason.

Sartre also objects that the doctrine of the unconscious is in bad faith. It is all too convenient, he claims, to excuse behavior that is hard to justify by attributing it to inner forces over which one has no control. Consider a young woman who allows the young man she is dining with to lay his hand on hers and then later reacts indignantly when the young man makes a romantic overture. Sartre argues that this "ignorance" of the meaning of a gesture or touch is a kind of bad faith (1955, 55). This excuse becomes elevated to a global theoretical framework in Freudian theory so that people find it expedient to blame their unconscious for behavior for which they are too ashamed to take responsibility.

Sartre and the existentialists were alert to irrationality, passion, and angst at the heart of the soul, but unwilling to encourage the dishonest tendency to explain these away as a result of natural forces at work on us and within us. Human beings, replete with all the weaknesses that flesh and spirit are prone to, must learn to accept themselves and have the courage to be who they are rather than passively conforming to a static picture of the self, sketched in terms that excuse or diminish them,.

Jaspers' critique is more measured. "In Freud's work we are dealing in fact with *psychology of meaning* not *causal explanation* as Freud himself thinks." He both appreciates Freud's contribution and attacks his theory.

> Freud teaches us many new individual meaningful connections and does it in a convincing way. We understand how complexes repressed into unawareness re-emerge in symbolic form. We understand the reaction-formation to repressed instinctual drives, the differentiation between the primary real psychic events from the secondary ones which are merely symbols or sublimations. Freud . . . penetrates deeply into the unnoticed parts of psychic life which through him is brought into clear consciousness (1913, 91).

Jaspers' Freud unravels connections in the life stories of his patients and articulates them according to a psychologically realist interpretation. But these inner realities are as subject to interpretation and distortion as the outer complexities that often bedevil our attempts at truth. "An error in the Freudian teaching consists in the increasing simplification of his understanding which is connected with the transformation of meaningful connections into general theories. Theories tend to simplification. Understanding finds infinite variety and complexity" (1913, 92). Freudian theory aims at a general or relatively parsimonious science of the unconscious as a causal domain, but a post-structuralist view is less dogmatic about the psyche.

Neo-Freudian View of the Unconscious

Consciousness is plausibly seen as a story we tell to ourselves and about ourselves—a narrative that articulates what is happening to us on the basis of a dynamic brain-world interaction between the human body (and brain) and the world (none needed—it's the vibe of the thing) (Dennett, 1991). If that is so, then the conscious self, or Ego, is a reification of the complex activity of self-monitoring and self–reporting. That activity, arising from a human being's trajectory through the world, articulates what is happening in the brain.

That conclusion persuades Metzinger to argue that the self is nothing but a pattern of representation in neural circuits prominently involving deep midline structures of the brain (such as the insula and limbic system, including the cingulate gyrus, the anterior part of which seems critically involved in depression and severe anxiety related disorders such as 0bsessive-compulsive disorder). This is similar to the core Freudian thought that the ego is a construct based on psychically interpretable activity in the neural system. While less committed to neurobiological reductionism, Freud is also less obviously informed by phenomenology, but, when linked to the thought that our constructions comprise the human life-world and are thereby as real as peace treaties and life sentences, we can distance the insight from any unhelpful fictionalism (or eliminativism) about the psychological subject.

This conclusion allows that any person can be wrong about what is going on in his psyche (thus Lacanian *méconnaissance*). A person reads into his neurocognitive interaction with the world not just integrated perceptions, arising from stimuli in certain contexts, but also motivated interpretations or constructions, serving the need to retain a liveable self image or imago. We need to tell stories that accord with our desire to fit in with others and incorporate their values because they form the value frameworks which each of us inhabits. What they admire, we admire; what they desire, we desire (with allowance for individuals' learning histories). We live with what Ian Hacking calls "the looping effect of human kinds" (Hacking, 1995, 21). Each of us becomes or enacts in himself an image of what he believes such a person to be. If I think of myself and aspire to be an academic, I will do what academics do and learn to love what they love: I will read, I will debate, I will undertake systematic enquiries and enter into a milieu of scholarly exchange. These activities will be part of an accurate conception of who I am because they shape my life so that I reify, through self-creation, the image I have of myself and my aspirations to be that kind of person.

This process of imaginative creation influences and transforms us, but not always as the existentialists portray it. We bring to our world ancient tendencies to react and to seek things that appeal to us. We enact truths, disclosed by instinct and demanding allegiance in many ways, which we understand only slightly but deeply care about.

The imago, or imag-(eg)-o, is the self of our flawed self-understanding—our means of exploring and conducting ourselves in the human life-world. Its desires emerge from the intersection of our instincts and the stories and images we assimilate. Thus, for instance, the picture that a woman composes of her lover is an amalgam of the implied subject who mirrors her to herself in a way she likes, the actual person, and a construction from her own attraction to him and what she most admires or needs in a partner. Indeed, a further metaphor of the soul becomes helpful here.

The Soul as Palimpsest

The neural palimpsest, in Foucault's words, constitutes the body as "the inscribed surface of events (traced by language and dissolved by ideas) . . . a volume in perpetual disintegration" and the soul as "the present correlative of a certain technology of power over the body born out of methods of punishment, supervision and constraint" (1984, 176).

The words that are spoken to us affect us in ways that depend on the cultural and historical milieu of ideas in which they have a meaning or significance. If their effect is moderated by a new context, they inscribe or etch themselves into us differently. To be called "enthusiastic" may cause the soul to lift or the body to wince. The soul is fashioned by techniques applied to us when we are punished, made to conform to this or that norm, and encouraged or restrained in doing and saying certain things. This is how we learn to be what we are and come to feel good or bad about ourselves.

Imagine, for instance, that as a member of an indigenous group, I am told that the myths in which are found the roots of my being are all illusory. My cherished connection to the land that gave me birth and the ways that my people understand the seasons, the activities they should be about, and the way they do them, is belittled, marginalized, and dismissed. I may think that this is wrong—how can a social decision deny or seek to nullify something which is real, that is, the place of my birth and a connection with the spirits of a place that goes back beyond human memory? What is real is not arbitrary—to be changed by just saying so or by the stroke of a pen. But, in the presence of powerful people who are in the grip of their delusion and enforce it with violence, what can I do or say? When you live with mad people, sanity and reality become meaningless terms, of a piece with dreams and fantasies. This is the lived experience of many post-colonial people, who are not listened to and whose understanding of the world is sometimes even assimilated to the unreason of the unconscious mind.

The unconscious, even if no longer full-bloodedly Freudian, retains many features of Freud's system Ucs. It is the root of identity and the mediator of value. It blends the instincts of nature with the prescriptions of nurture and culture. It is the domain in which Hebb's law and the primary processes rule. Cathexes—psychic complexes of meaning, emotion, and will (or weakness thereof)—are created in the associational networks that arise within us as a result of cultural and interpersonal history. These associational networks obey laws of causality and psychic significance and not of rationality and conscious endorsement. We are redeemed from the impasse of existential anomie by the oral law within; the conversations and encounters that have formed us, and molded our expectations and aspirations, create incentives that are truthful in the light of our place of being.

The human "search for meaning" is given impetus by a potential chaos of subversive voices, from within—the clamour of the unconscious—and without—the clamour of the marketplace. It is also informed by the many layers of meaning and inscription that shape the neural palimpsest undergirding the life-story any person can tell about himself. The neural palimpsest deals with information that has shifting significance in the light of all the other patterns of excitation running through it—including political, social, and discursive engagement in close-kin relationships and friendships; biological needs; and commitments and identifications in the symbolic world. All these are stitched together by conversations where we relate to each other as whole beings and communicate verbally and through our body language—touching or not touching; picking up cues and leads from the words, gestures, and looks of others; and reshaping ourselves, perhaps ever so slightly in terms of each new level of writing that scores the wax block of the unconscious psyche.

The many-layered psyche has within it the sources of energy, both positive and negative, that guide a person's attitudes, beliefs, desires, thoughts, and feelings. These are all entwined with meanings and images that articulate what is urgent, primitive, and indistinct, and turn it into what is thinkable, subject to reflection and criticism, so that we can fashion ourselves in a way that can be indwelt with conviction. Reason and the ego are in constant negotiation with the reasons of which reason knows not—or only partially. We search within ourselves for the surreal montages that are our desires (Lacan, 1979, 169), patched together out of imagery, the urges of the body, and the deep things of the soul with the strongest roots and the most hold on us. Searching out these sources of meaning and motivation is hard and the results of our search may not be worthy or admirable in the light of our commitments and allegiances.

That search for the roots of our being, the things that mean most to us and do most to unify our plans and projects, as it is pursued, relate to self-critical work, which often needs a guide and companion to see it through. Our search rests on a conception of the human psyche that examines the myths, images, and symbols that inform our self-understanding in ways illuminated by three powerful metaphors, two of which—the *Wunderblock* and the palimpsest—we have explored so that it remains for us to reflect on a third—the braided river.

As the final metaphor of the psyche, Wittgenstein uses the metaphor of a river to understand the shifting patterns of human knowledge. Writes Wittgenstein in *On Certainty*: "The river bed of thoughts may shift. But I distinguish between the movements of the waters on the river-bed and the shift of the bed itself; though there is not a sharp division of the one from the other" (1972, 97-99).

The fluidity of the psyche is made vivid by comparing it with the braided rivers found in the South Island of New Zealand. These rivers have the characteristic of forming and reforming their channels as the water flow works on the shingles of the river bed. Boating on the braided river is both scenic and thrilling, but the river only reveals its overall pattern from a bird's eye view—an *Übersicht*. The ride, with many unexpected twists and turns that cause alarm or exhilaration, is unpredictable. The metaphor reminds us of the changeable channels of the psyche that direct our lives in varying ways. In particular it can be related to the multiple inscriptions of the palimpsest metaphor with its own relationships to language, culture, and community.

Wittgenstein argues that, in reality, human knowledge is fluid—a production of the human community based on our biology, our interactions with each other, their historico-cultural context, and our engagement with the world in which we live. The human psyche is, likewise, jointly produced by a human being, a society or culture and the relationships in which the person is formed, and the world around us.

These three metaphors—the *Wunderblock*, the palimpsest, and the braided river—resonate with our understanding of the mechanisms of the neuro-cognitive basis of the psyche and Freud's portrayal of the unconscious. The layers of the psyche are perhaps not best construed in the fairly fixed terms of Freudian theory. The conscious realm is, as he noted, the domain of the ego and the reality principle and keeps us in touch with the world and with others (thus *con-scio* or knowing with). The preconscious realm is the aspects of this world-as-known not actively before the mind.

The unconscious is more shadowy than the conscious or preconscious. It is engaged with the world, both inner and outer, past and present, but its engagement is not structured according to the rule-governed and validated public realm. Its connections and contours of significance are often inchoate, always moving (in both senses—motivating and mobile), and idiosyncratic. Its influence within a life-story, although discernible with skill and direction, is cumulative, continuous, and dynamically shifting. Brute causal associations between states of the body and psychic responses, sensitive to nuanced contexts, dynamically and cumulatively form a (partly inchoate) record of impingements on my body (some sensorimotor, some visceral, some mediated by sounds, and others by ill-formed, half apprehended impressions of this, that, or the other situation). Here is the primary process, replete with shifting and unprincipled liaisons between words, feelings, felt relationships, and experiences. That process, as Freud so clearly saw, is unstable and potentially life-altering. It sometimes produces explosive effects, but, throughout, it is in a dynamic interaction with the narrative that is my conscious life (my reconstructed trajectory through the human life-world).

What drops out of (or rises to the surface from) the kaleidoscopic world of the multi-layered psyche is fascinating. It is quickened by words and glances, icons and attention catching intrusions, facial expressions and tones of voice, and it has the capacity to pull my mind in this or that direction in ways that I may or may not feel in harmony with. That is "what-it-is-like-to-be" (Nagel, 1986) a neural network the size of a tennis court with shifting patterns of excitation ranging over and between multiple layers of complex computational circuitry the activity in which one has to learn to make sense of. That is the complex psych-somatic reality that Freud found he could only characterize by using the idea of an unconscious mind and the system of psychic forces that he described astutely and reified in an attempt to make it apt for the attentions of natural science.

References

Churchland, P. and P. Churchland, *On the Contrary* (Cambridge: MIT Press,1998).

Damasio, Antonio, *The Feeling of What Happens: Body and Emotion in the Making of Consciousness* (New York: Mariner Books, 2000).

Dennett, Daniel, *Consciousness Explained* (London: Penguin Press. 1991).

Foucault, M., *The Foucault Reader*, ed. P. Rabinow (London: Penguin, 1984).

Freud, Sigmund (1885), "Studies on Hysteria," *The Standard Edition of the Complete Psychological Works of Sigmund Freud*, Vol. II, ed. and trans. James Strachey (London: The Hogarth Press, 1955).

Freud, Sigmund (1912), "A Note on the Unconscious in Psycho-Anaylysis," *The Standard Edition of the Complete Psychological Works of Sigmund Freud*, Vol. XII, ed. and trans. James Strachey (London: The Hogarth Press, 1958).

Freud, Sigmund (1925), "A Note upon the Mystic Writing Pad," *The Standard Edition of the Complete Psychological Works of Sigmund Freud*, Vol. XIX, ed. and trans. James Strachey (London: The Hogarth Press, 1961), 227-32.

Gillett, Grant, *The Mind and Its Discontents,* 2nd ed. (Oxford: Oxford University Press, 2009).

Hacking, Ian, *Rewriting the Soul* (Princeton: University Press, 1995).

Jaspers, Karl, *General Psychopathology,* trans. J. Hoenig and M.W. Hamilton (Chicago: University of Chicago Press, [1913], 1963).

Kolb, B., and I. Wishaw I, *The fundamentals of Human Neuropsychology* (New York: W.H. Freeman & Co., 1990).

Kristeva, J. *The New Maladies of the Soul* (New York: Columbia University Press, 1995).

Lacan, J., *Écrits* (New York: Norton and Co. 1977).

Lacan, J., *The Four Fundamental Concepts of Psycho-Analysis*, trans. A Sheridan (London: Penguin Books, 1979).

Luria, Alexander R., *The Working Brain* (New York: Basic Books, 1973).

Metzinger, T. *Being No-One: The Self Model Theory of Subjectivity* (Cambridge: MIT Press, 2004).

Nagel, Thomas, *The View from Nowhere* (Oxford: University Press, 1986).

Northoff, Georg, "Psychopathology and Pathophysiology of the Self in Depression: A Neuropsychiatric Hypothesis, *Journal of Affective Disorders*, 104, 2007: 1-14.

Rumelhart, D.E., J.L. McClelland, and the PDP Research Group, *Parallel Distributed Processing Explorations in the Microstructure of Cognition* (Cambridge: MIT Press, 1986).

Sartre, Jean-Paul, *Being and Nothingness,* trans. H. Barnes (London: Methuen & Co., 1958).

Szasz, T. *The Myth of Mental Illness. Foundations of a Theory of Personal Conduct*. London: Secker & Warburg, 1962).

Wittgenstein, Ludwig, *On Certainty,* ed. G.E.M. Anscombe and G. H. von Wright (New York: Harper & Row, Publishers, 1972).

Chapter 18
Freud's Greatest Failure
The Unconscious

Ed Erwin
University of Miami, U.S.A.

"Our right to assume the existence of something mental that is unconscious and to employ that assumption for the purposes of scientific work is disputed in many quarters. To this we can reply that our assumption of the unconscious is necessary and legitimate, and that we possess numerous proofs of its existence" (Freud, 1915, *S.E.*, XIV: 166).

SIGMUND FREUD'S VIEWS ABOUT THE UNCONSCIOUS are interesting in their own right, but also because of their centrality to his theories about the meaning of dreams, slips of the tongue, the etiology and treatment of neuroses, the existence of repression, and the phenomenon of transference. At a minimum, Freud must be right in holding that there are unconscious mental states or events, or virtually all of his other main theories are wrong.

Although some have disputed Freud's theory of the dynamic unconscious, very few writing today have challenged this minimal thesis that unconscious mentality exists, but in an earlier day, at least two well known philosophers did press this challenge: William James (1950 [1890]) and Franz Brentano (1995 [1874]. As Rosemarie Sand points out (2011), the issue about the existence of any sort of an unconscious mental was quite contentious in the pre-Freudian period with unconscious mentality being questioned by Locke, the British associationists, and Mill, while it was supported by Leibniz, Herbart (Sand, 2002), Schopenhauer, and William Hamilton.[1]

The Arguments of James and Brentano

James and Brentano were trying to answer pro-unconscious mentality arguments, given by nineteenth-century philosophers and psychologists, such as Eduard von Hartmann and Hermann von Helmholtz, but some of their points are relevant to Freud's arguments as well and some of the issues they raised are still live ones.

Dispositions

Brentano points out that one common argument for the existence of an unconscious is that we possess a store of knowledge without consciously thinking of it. So, it is argued, the knowledge, or, more precisely, the beliefs associated with this knowledge, must exist in the unconscious. The sorts of examples that are commonly given include such beliefs as *Paris is the capital of France* and *7+7 = 14*. Brentano replies that there is a rival hypothesis that is at least as likely to be true: What we have are dispositions toward certain acts of thinking rather than mental states existing in the unconscious.

Mechanical Associations

One influential line of argument for an unconscious can be found in Helmholtz's work on perception. When we see a man in the distance, we infer that he is of normal size, but we are not conscious of any inference. So, the inference must be unconscious.

James replies that there is no basis here for concluding that there is any inference at all. Rapid judgments of size, shape, and distance are best explained as processes of mechanical associations. I see the man, but I need not have the unconscious thought that there is an appearance of a small man from which I unconsciously infer that he is likely to be a man of normal size. Instead, I might just automatically associate the percept of a man who looks small at a distance with the idea of a normal size man, so that when I entertain the one idea, I move quickly to the associated idea. I see a figure outside my window of something going by in a coat with an upturned collar, but I need not make an unconscious inference to the conclusion that there is a man wearing the coat. Instead, there is just an association of two ideas: something walking by wearing a coat and a man wearing the coat.

Brain Events

James considers the argument that in some cases we are conscious of thinking of A and C, but are not consciously thinking of a natural link between them, say B. I think that thirty people have confirmed that they are coming to the lecture and I also think immediately that this is greater than the maximum allowed, which is twenty people. The link that would logically bridge the gap and provide a basis for an inference is that thirty is greater than twenty, but this is not something I consciously think. Consequently, it is argued, the idea of link B must be in my unconscious mind.

James replies that we have two other choices. The first is that the linking idea, B, was in consciousness but in the next instant was forgotten. The second choice, the more plausible one, raises a more important philosophical issue.

James points out that we would need to rule out the workings of a "brain tract" that is adequate by itself to do the work of coupling A and B. No mental event outside of consciousness need be assumed.

Brentano raises the same issue, but he poses it as a general challenge to arguments for unconscious mentality. Whenever I act or think, there is something going on within me of which I am not conscious. Obviously there are many such things. I look at the seemingly small people below my 17th-story terrace and I am not conscious of any inference when I quickly conclude that they are normal sized people, but neither am I conscious of what is going on in my digestive track, or of my heart pumping blood, or of electrical discharges in my brain. Why believe that what lies within me outside of consciousness is ever *mental*? Why not just postulate brain events wherever we are inclined to postulate unconscious mental events?

It is true that we cannot generally specify exactly which neural events cause me to think or act, but given our lack of knowledge about the brain, it is rare that we can do this even where unconscious mentality is not an issue. We just do not know enough yet to say exactly which brain events are involved, but that by itself is no reason to postulate unconscious mental events. As Brentano phrases his general challenge to putative proofs of unconscious mentality: "The possibility of proof ends only at the point where the field of brain-physiology, which is so far inaccessible, begins" (1995, 116).

Evidential Standards

Brentano argues that certain evidential standards must be met, if the existence of the unconscious is to be demonstrated, nonetheless all such purported demonstrations fail to meet at least one of the standards. Here are two of the standards he discusses: differentialness and inference to the best explanation (IBE).

Differentialness

This is not a term that Brentano employs—it was introduced in Erwin and Siegel (1989)—but the idea is that in order for seeming evidence to support some hypothesis, it must "differentiate" the hypothesis from all competitors that are of equal or greater credibility. Many philosophers would see this as sheer scientific common sense, but some philosophers who defend Freud have raised objections. There are, furthermore, counter intuitive implications having to do with increases in probability. Finally, Brentano provides no argument for his differential standard. All of the aforementioned issues are addressed in either Erwin and Siegel (1989) or in Erwin (1996, 44-54; on the proof question, see 47-8).

IBE

Brentano does not discuss what is now called inference to the best explanation, but his view anticipates well know criticisms of IBE due to Bas van Fraassen (1980), Achinstein (1992), and others: "For the present, it is sufficient to have pointed out that the alleged consequences from unconscious inference cannot furnish any proof for the existence of unconscious mental activity, as long as the impossibility or extreme improbability of any other conception has not been established, and that so far no one has fulfilled this condition" (Brentano, 1995, 111).

What Brentano appears to be saying here is that it is not enough to rule out known plausible competitors to the existence of a mental unconscious; one also has to provide evidence of the improbability of any unknown rival.

In more contemporary terms, suppose that we meet the conditions for an inference to the best explanation as they are commonly set out. We consider all of the plausible known hypotheses that, if true, would explain certain facts and then we select the best of these by ruling out all of the others. This is still not enough; for, as van Fraassen puts it, the survivor may, for all we know, be the best of a bad lot. What we need is evidence that the set of hypotheses we are aware of contains the true one. Without this additional evidence, the inference from the claim that H is the best—i.e., the most likely—of the known explanatory hypotheses to the claim H is true, or even probable, is illicit.

Peter Lipton, in the second edition of his *Inference to the Best Explanation* (2004), tries to meet the standard objections, but he does not succeed (Erwin, 2011). Inference to the best explanation is not a legitimate form of inference.

Freud's Defense of the Unconscious

When Freud says that he possesses "numerous proofs" of the existence of the unconscious (Freud, 1915, *S.E.,* XIV: 166), what proofs is he referring to? Although arguments for unconscious mentality can be found scattered throughout his work, his main arguments appear in Chapter VII of *The Interpretation of Dreams* II (1900, *S.E.,* V), his important paper "The Unconscious" (1915, *S.E.*, XIV), and in his brief paper "A Note on the Unconscious in Psychoanalysis" (1912, *S.E.,* XII). Some of his arguments presuppose specific theoretical principles which in turn would have to be argued for in order for the proof of an unconscious mind to be convincing, but others are not like that.

In his 1912 paper, Freud, like others before him, appeals to hypnotism to establish an unconscious mind. He notes that in Bernheim's experiments, a subject is put into a hypnotic state and while in this state is ordered to execute a certain action at a specified time when he awakens. After waking up, the subject has no memory of his hypnotic state, but at the appointed time has an impulse to perform the assigned task and does so. It seems impossible, Freud says, to give any other account than to say that the experimenter's order had been present in the unconscious of the subject. But, contrary to what Freud says, it is not impossible.

William James (1950) suggests a rival hypothesis when he criticizes the "Fourth Proof" of an unconscious. According to the Fourth Proof, problems unsolved when we go to bed are sometimes solved when we wake up. Unconscious thinking must be responsible for these acts, it is claimed. James replies rather tersely: Consciousness forgotten, as in the hypnotic trance. What he means, presumably, is that the mental events responsible for the problem solving or the posthypnotic behavior were present in consciousness but we quickly forgot them.

Although James does not spell this out, he could have said the following. The hypnotist suggests to the subject that he or she do something at a certain time and not remember the original order. The act of suggestion creates in the subject a disposition both to perform the act and to forget the origin of the order. There is no need in such cases to speak of any unconscious mental states or processes.

Freud also discusses another commonly used argument for the unconscious in his 1912 paper. A conception is present to my consciousness, but then may become absent, and later still become present again when I remember it. I learn that Freud was born in 1856, but I do not consciously think of this for several months. Later, I recall the date of his birth and the idea becomes "present to consciousness."

Freud says of such thoughts that they are present in the mind even when outside of consciousness. They are *latent* in consciousness. He takes this to be a satisfactory common-sense proof of the existence of an unconscious—here he is counting the existence of preconscious ideas as sufficient for unconscious mentality—but not before he disposes of "the philosophical objection" that what we are calling unconscious mental ideas in these sorts of cases are not in the mind at all; what exists rather are dispositions to think or behave in a certain sort of way. Freud replies (1912, S.E. XII: 260) that this begs the question in asserting "conscious" to be an identical term with "psychical."

Freud is wrong here. When Brentano gives his dispositional reply, he is neither assuming that everything psychic is conscious, nor is he begging the question in some other way. Rather, his point is just that in order to appeal to the kind of case that Freud cites, one has to rule out an equally credible rival hypothesis: When we remember things that were formerly in conscious, there are dispositions toward certain acts of thinking rather than mental states existing latently in the unconscious (or, as Freud would say, the preconscious).

In a later paper, "The Unconscious" (1915, *S.E.* XIV), Freud has a section titled "Justification for the Concept of the Unconscious," but before he explains his justification, he gives a separate argument that appeals to repression. We have learnt from psycho-analysis, he says, that the essence of repression lies in preventing an idea from becoming conscious (166). When this happens, Freud continues, we say of this idea that it is in a state of being "unconscious." This is one of his arguments that go beyond common sense and presuppose one or more of his theories. The argument presupposes that repression occurs. This will seem like a harmless presupposition to most Freudians, but there is reason to doubt it. I am not speaking here of the doubt that repression explains in part the content of dreams, or slips of the tongue, or the origin of the psychoneuroses. I am saying something more radical: that there is no credible evidence that repression even occurs (see Erwin, 1996, 220-5).

Freud's next argument is the one that many Freudians have traditionally relied on: the "unintelligible gaps" argument. The data of consciousness, Freud says (1915, *S.E.* XIV, 166), have a very large number of gaps in them. Both in sick and healthy people, psychic acts often occur which can be explained only by presupposing other acts of which the subjects are not conscious.

These psychic acts include dreams and parapraxes in healthy people, and, Freud says, neurotic symptoms in the sick; in addition, our most personal experience acquaints us with ideas that come into our head from we know not where and with intellectual conclusions arrived at we do not know how. All these conscious acts, Freud argues, remain unconnected and unintelligible if we insist that all mental acts be conscious. They fall into a demonstrable connection, however, if we interpolate between them the unconscious acts we have inferred. "A gain in meaning ," Freud then says, "is a perfectly justifiable ground for going beyond the limits of direct experience" (1915, *S.E.* XIV: 166-7).

What does Freud mean here by a "gain in meaning"? If he does not mean a gain in explanatory power, then without some explanation of what he means, an appeal to gain in meaning is not a "perfectly justifiable ground" for postulating an unconscious. He would be leaving unexplained the connection between a gain in meaning and evidence. However, Freud makes clear that he is speaking of an increased power to explain when he says (1915, *S.E.* XIV: 166) that the assumption of an unconscious is necessary because the gaps in the data of consciousness can be explained *only by* appeal to other acts of which "consciousness affords no evidence."

Here, Freud runs squarely into the deepest of Brentano's objections. Freud's argument takes the form of an inference to the best explanation. He is proposing a theory, the theory of repression, that provides the only available and hence the best available explanation of dreams, parapraxes, and neurotic symptoms. Hence, Freud argues, there is good evidence for the unconscious. Brentano's objection, if I am interpreting him correctly, and, in any event my objection (Erwin, 1996, 62-73), and the objection of most critics of IBE, is that the inference is not warranted unless Freud does something else. It is not enough to present a theory that would explain the known facts, if only it were true; Freud also has to argue that the set of theories we are aware of contains the true theory. He does not do this. For this reason, his key argument fails.

This failure, however, is hardly decisive. Freud need not rely on this overarching argument. He has separate arguments for his theory of dreams, parapraxes, and the etiology of the psychoneuroses. These separate arguments can take the place of his very general "gaps" argument. Before commenting on these other arguments, I should say something about his arguments for the unconscious in Chapter 7 of his *Interpretation of Dreams*.

In explaining how the residues from daytime life can serve as the instigator of dreams, Freud makes the point that even where this happens, the motive force which the dream requires has to be provided by a wish, and the wish "invariably and indisputably" is a wish from the unconscious (1900, *S.E.*, V: 560-1).

Later in the same chapter, Freud recounts the response of a physician (presumably himself) who is assured by a philosopher that "consciousness is an indispensible characteristic of the psychical." Freud continues:

> [A]nd perhaps, if he [the physician] still feels enough respect for the utterances of philosophers, he may presume that they have not been dealing with the same thing or working at the same science. For even a single observation of a neurotic's mental life or a single analysis of a dream must leave him with an unshakable conviction that the most complicated and most rational thought processes, which can surely not be denied the name of psychical processes, can occur without exciting the subject's consciousness (1900, *S.E.*, V: 612).

Freud concedes (1900, *S.E.*, V: 612) that the physician cannot learn of these unconscious processes until they have produced some observable effect, but the physician "must feel at liberty to proceed by *inference* from the conscious effect to the unconscious psychical process."

Freud does not say at this point, however, what the basis is for the inference he is recommending. Both of his arguments, the earlier one appealing to the premise that the motive force of all dreams is an unconscious wish and the argument that we are warranted in inferring unconscious psychical processes from observations pertaining to dreams and neurotic symptoms presuppose arguments given elsewhere. Without these additional arguments, the arguments in chapter 7 add nothing to his case for unconscious mentality.

Before we take stock of all this, one more of Freud's arguments should be considered: his therapeutic argument. He argues that when the assumption of there being an unconscious enables us to construct a successful procedure—he means psychoanalytic therapy—by which we can exert an effective influence upon the course of conscious processes, this success will have given us an "incontrovertible proof" of the existence of what we assumed (1915, *S.E.* XIV: 167).

We have arrived at the following resting place. Freud has at least two arguments for unconscious mentality that do not presuppose any part of psychoanalytic theory, the first appeals to the phenomenon of hypnotism and the second is his commonsense proof that preconscious thoughts are "latent" in the mind,. Neither originates with Freud, and both appear to be vulnerable to the objections of James and Brentano, but at least their cogency does not stand or fall with the evidence for Freudian theory or therapy. That is not true of his other arguments for the unconscious. They all presuppose Freudian claims about dreams, neurotic symptoms, parapraxes, or psychoanalytic therapy. If the evidence for all of these claims is no good, then these other arguments for the unconscious are also no good.

Freud's therapeutic argument encounters several problems. In the 1970s, behaviorists in clinical psychology argued that the fact that effective behavior therapy techniques were based on behavioristic conditioning principles was confirmation of these principles. It was not (Erwin, 2010).The fact that a set of theoretical principles serves a heuristic function such that, by reflecting on them, therapists can develop effective techniques is no evidence that any of the underlying theoretical principles is true. False theoretical principles can serve this heuristic function just as true ones can. Freud faces the same problem. His theories obviously influenced him in developing his therapy, but even if his therapy works it might be for non-psychoanalytic reasons. Therapeutic effectiveness by itself is not evidence for Freudian theory.

In his 1917 lectures, Freud tries to strengthen his argument by adding the premise that his therapy will be successful in resolving a patient's conflicts only if the anticipatory ideas given by his analyst "tally with what is real"; i.e. they need to be true if the therapy is to work (1917, *S.E.*, XVI: 452). Assuming that the analyst's ideas purport to give insight into the origin of the neurosis, a successful cure will prove that the analyst's etiological theory is correct: "Whatever in the doctor's conjectures is inaccurate," Freud writes (1917, *S.E.*, XVI: 452), "drops out in the course of the analysis; it has to be withdrawn and replaced by something more correct." Adolf Grünbaum (1984) dubs Freud's assumption the "Necessary Condition Thesis" and then explains in detail why Freud's entire argument fails. One problem is that Freud has no way of proving his necessary condition thesis; another is that there is evidence that it is false.

Freud is even on shaky ground in assuming that his therapy is sometimes effective. After reviewing the evidence for the effectiveness of psychoanalysis, I reach the conclusion (Erwin, 1996, chapter 6; see also Erwin, 2009) that there is no credible evidence that psychoanalysis is ever effective. In 1999, the Research Committee of the International Psychoanalytic Association reviewed all of the evidence and reached essentially the same conclusion as mine. It concluded that existing studies failed to demonstrate that psychoanalytic treatment is efficacious relative to either an alternative treatment or an active placebo (see Erwin, 2009, 604).

As to Freud's theories about the meaning of dreams, the etiology of neuroses, and slips of the tongue, Grünbaum (1984 and 2002) has given the most incisive analysis of Freud's arguments for his repression theory, including his theory of dreams, neuroses, and slips, and concludes (1984, 278) that in so far as Freud's evidence is clinical evidence it is "remarkably weak ." That might leave hope for confirmation in the existing Freudian experimental literature, but none of the experimental studies, or all combined, provide any credible evidence for Freudian theory (Erwin, 1996). There has been some new evidence, including data from neuroscience, but none of this so-called "new evidence" is confirmatory either (Erwin, 2009).

Conclusion

Was Freud, then, right or wrong in assuming the existence of something mental that is unconscious? I believe he was right. Whatever verdict we reach on his arguments for an unconscious, there is evidence for Freud's assumption provided by later experiments on semantic priming and perception (Erwin, 1996).

Some have claimed that despite these later experiments, Freud was the first to demonstrate the existence of unconscious mentality. This was not, however, the view of Freud's editor, James Strachey, who gives credit not to Freud but Breuer (1915 *S.E.*, XIV: 164). It would be difficult to tell if Strachey is right. One would have to evaluate the arguments of those who argued for an unconscious mind before Breuer or Freud; then see who, if anyone, first overcame the obstacles raised by James and Brentano; and then do the same for the arguments of Breuer and Freud. Even this would not be enough. One would have to also examine the arguments of pre-19th-century scholars. In the end, the question might not be worth pursuing.

If we put aside the issue of who gets credit for first proving it, the minimal thesis is accepted by virtually all of Freud's critics, including Grünbaum (1984) and myself (1996). The question of whether there is something mental that is unconscious is generally not considered controversial today and it certainly does not generally divide Freud and his critics. What is still controversial, however, is Freud's own contribution to the subject: his theory of the dynamic unconscious.

When discussing the work of one of his contemporaries who also believed in unconscious mentation, Lipps (1897), Freud makes the point that what is disputed by Lipps and his critics is the thesis that apart from conscious there are also unconscious psychical processes (1900, *S.E.,* V: 614)—what I have been calling the "minimal thesis." But it was not to establish this thesis, Freud says, that we have summoned up the phenomena of dreams and the formation of hysterical symptoms. His "new discovery ," he says, taught by the analysis of psycho-pathological structures, is that in addition to a preconscious, there is also what he terms the *Ucs.*, the unconscious, which is *inadmissible* to consciousness (1900, *S.E.,* V: 614-615).

This inadmissibility claim is central to Freud's theory of the dynamic unconscious, but if this were the entirety of it, certain 20th-century cognitivist theories in psychology and linguistics would also qualify as theories of the dynamic unconscious. What are also important is Freud's theory about what keeps unconscious thoughts and wishes unconscious, namely his theory of repression, and his therapeutic theory of how to bring to consciousness what had been temporarily inadmissible to it. In brief, his theory of the dynamic unconscious includes the following: Unconscious ideas have a dynamic quality in that they have effects; they are also typically prevented from entering consciousness due to the operation of repression; and they can enter consciousness only when the repression is "lifted ," which requires overcoming the person's resistances through the use of psychoanalysis. Preconscious ideas may also have effects but they lack the other features of unconscious ideas.

Issues about the evidence for what on Freud's view is his distinctive contribution to the subject of the unconscious, his theory of the dynamic unconscious, are the same issues as arise about the evidence for his repression theory, which he called "the cornerstone" of the whole structure of psychoanalysis (1914, *S.E.*, XIV: 16), and his therapeutic claims about lifting repressions. Based on the work cited earlier (Grünbaum, 1984 and 2002; Erwin, 1996 and 2009), the verdict must be: not proven, i.e., there is no credible evidence for the theory of a dynamic unconscious.

Notes

[1] See as well Marcel Zentner's discussion of the views of Schopenhauer, Eduard von Hartmann, and Nietzsche on the unconscious (Zentner, 2002).

References

Achinstein, P., "Inference to the Best Explanations: Or, Who Won the Mill-Whewell Debate?" *Studies in History and Philosophy of Science* 23, 1992: 349-364.

Brentano, F., *Psychology from an Empirical Standpoint* (New York: Routledge, 1995 [1874]).

Erwin, E, *A Final Accounting: Philosophical and Empirical Issues in Freudian Psychology* (Cambridge MA: The MIT Press, 1996).

Erwin, E., "Is Freud Back?" *Logic, Methodology, and Philosophy of Science: Proceedings of the Thirteenth International Congress*, eds. C. Glymour, W. Wei, and D. Westerståhl (London: College Publications, 2009).

Erwin, E., *Behavior Therapy: Scientific, Philosophical, and Moral Foundations*, 2nd Edition (New York: Cambridge University Press, 2010 [1978]).

Erwin, E, and Siegel, H., "Is Confirmation Differential?" *British Journal for the Philosophy of Science* 40, 1989: 105-19.

Erwin, E., *Evidence-based Psychotherapy: Philosophical Foundations*, (Unpublished Manuscript, 2011), ch. 1.

Erwin, E, and Siegel, H. (1989). Is confirmation differential? *British Journal for the Philosophy of Science* 40: 105-119.

Freud, Sigmund, *The Standard Edition of the Complete Psychological Works of Sigmund Freud*, Vols. I-XXIV, ed. and trans. James Strachey (London: The Hogarth Press, 1976).

Grünbaum, A., *The Foundations of Psychoanalysis: A Philosophical Critique* (Berkeley, CA: The University of California Press, 1984).

Grünbaum, A., "Critique of Psychoanalysis," *The Freud Encyclopedia: Theory, Therapy, and Culture,* ed. E. Erwin (New York: Routledge, 2002).

James, W., *The Principles of Psychology* (New York: Dover Publications, 1950 [1890]).

Lipton, P., *Inference to the Best Explanation*, 2nd Edition (New York: Routledge, 2004).

Sand, R., Herbart, "Johann Friedrich (1776-1841)," *The Freud Encyclopedia: Theory, Therapy, and Culture,* ed. E. Erwin (New York: Routledge, 2002).

Sand, R. Personal correspondence, 2011.

Strachey, J., "Editor's Note," 1890, *S.E.*, XIV: 161-5.

Van Fraassen, B., *The Scientific Image* (Oxford: Oxford University Press, 1980).

Zentner, M. "Nineteenth-Century Precursors of Freud," *The Freud Encyclopedia: Theory, Therapy, and Culture,* ed. E. Erwin (New York: Routledge, 2002)

Chapter 19
Reply to Dr. Gillett

Ed Erwin

PROFESSOR GILLETT USES THREE METAPHORS, OR SIMILES, to explain Freud's theory of the unconscious: a *Wunderblock,* a palimpsest, and the movement of water in a channel.

There is first the idea of the *Wunderblock*, or mystic writing pad. As many children have learned, the pad has a two layered film and underlying wax. A child can write with a stylus on the outer layer and then erase the message by lifting the top two layers. After a certain amount of use, the underlying wax develops grooves due to the repeated writing, just as an individual's experiences register on the conscious mind, or writing pad, but traces are left in the unconscious, or, to continue the metaphor, in the underlying wax.

In his paper, "A Note upon the 'Mystic Writing Pad,'" Freud (1925 [1924], p. 230) draws additional analogies between the child's toy and the unconscious. The writing pad serves two functions: Its receptive surface can be used over and over again, and, like a slate, it also registers permanent traces of what has been written. The pad solves the problem of combining the two functions—the writing and leaving permanent traces—by dividing them between two separate but interrelated component parts or systems. This is analogous, Freud points out, to how the mental apparatus, on his theory, performs its perceptual function. The layer which receives the stimuli, the system *Pcpt.-Cs.*, forms no permanent traces; the foundations of memory come about in other adjoining, systems

Freud also likened the unconscious to a palimpsest, which is a parchment on which messages can be written and then erased, allowing for new inscriptions, much like the mystic writing pad. Gillett makes the following comparison: "The human soul/psyche can be seen to be similar to a palimpsest in one important respect: It is, in part, the results of multiple encounters and interactions that have inscribed it with messages directed to the addressee" (Gillett, 194). These layers of inscription, if reconstructed, tell us much, according to Gillett, about the dynamic "relationality" that has helped form the person.

Charles Baudelaire had earlier used the metaphor of a palimpsest but to describe the brain instead of the psyche: "My brain is a palimpsest and so is yours, dear reader. Innumerable layers of ideas, images, feelings have fallen successfully on your brain as softly as the light. It seemed that each had buried its predecessor. But none in reality has perished" (quoted in Kuberski, 1992, 9).

Gillett too compares a palimpsest to the brain when he speaks of the unconscious as the "neural palimpsest." This switch alters the metaphor considerably, changing the comparison of a soul/psyche to a palimpsest to a comparison of the brain to one. In terms of Freud's theory of the unconscious, there is a switch here from trying to illuminate a psychological theory to explaining a neuroscientific one.

The third metaphor Gillett employs is due to Wittgenstein, who likens the mind to the movement of waters and its underlying ground or channel. As a human processes more information, the person's thoughts shift, but so too does what lies beneath it move, as does the river water and its underlying bed.

The use of these and other metaphors and similes can be useful in thinking about the unconscious mind, as well as Freud's theory about it. However, none of these metaphors, quite obviously, can substitute for a detailed account of Freud's specific theory of the unconscious, nor do they add anything to the grounds for thinking that the theory is right, or wrong.

Gillett also discusses some findings in neuroscience, perhaps because he has shifted metaphors, moving from a mental palimpsest to a neural palimpsest, or perhaps to support Freud. Gillett explains, for example, how the layers of cells in the neocortex are arranged horizontally and how some of the interconnecting fibers connect to related cortical areas, while "vertical" ones link the cortex to lower centers in the brain and spinal cord. He also explains the idea of neural plasticity. Maps of the cortex change the balanced competition between forces resulting in a new balance and a new organization (Kolb and Whishaw, 1990, 191).

Gillett's discussion raises a general issue discussed recently in the psychoanalytic literature: How relevant is neuroscience to Freud's psychological theories? In an excellent discussion of the issues, two supporters of Freud, Blass and Carmelli (2007), give several arguments to show that neuroscience findings are irrelevant to the assessment of Freudian theory. Here is one of them: "Neuroscience can describe the neural networks underlying psychological phenomena, patterns, and tendencies, but these phenomena, patterns, and tendencies are recognized and their laws specified without any information regarding the neurons that function concomitantly. Only once these are recognized on the psychological level can neuroscience proceed with its description, but it does so without adding anything to the psychological knowledge already obtained" (Blass and Carmelli, 10).

In contrast, some psychoanalysts, such as Mark Solms (2004), argue that neuroscience is not only relevant but in some instances strongly supports Freud.

Given Gillett's discussion, I take it that he disagrees with the Blass-Carmelli position that neuroscience is always irrelevant to Freudian theory. If this is his position, I agree with him. However, it is quite another matter whether the neuroscience supports Freud, is neutral, or tells against his views (see my negative evaluation of Solms' pro-Freudian arguments, Erwin, 2009).

To support Freud, it is clearly not enough to show that recent neuroscience is consistent with Freud's theory of the unconscious. One needs to show in detail how the neuroscience findings support one or more specific postulates of Freud's psychological theory of the dynamic unconscious. Gillett does not attempt to do this.

Later, Gillett explains Freud's arguments for the unconscious. As he rightly points out, they rest on the gaps in psychological explanations of conscious phenomena; the nature of post-hypnotic suggestion; and the meaningfulness and coherence of dream interpretations. Here Gillett leaves Freud on his own. He cites the Freudian arguments but does not defend them. I examine these arguments in my main paper in this volume and conclude that they all fail to provide any credible grounds for Freud's theory of a dynamic unconscious.

What we have, then, is some useful metaphors, a discussion of neuroscience without any detailed attempt to show that the findings support Freud's theory of the unconscious, and citations of Freud's arguments without any attempt to defend them against criticisms. I conclude, therefore, with the same verdict as in my main paper concerning Freud's theory of the dynamic unconscious: not proven. Given the centrality of this theory to the Freudian corpus, the failure of his arguments deserves, in my view, to be called "his biggest mistake."

References

Blass, R. and Z. Carmelli, "The Case against Neuropsychoanalysis: On Fallacies Underlying Psychoanalysis' Latest Scientific Trend and Its Negative Impact on Psychoanalytic Discourse," *International Journal of Psychoanalysis,* Vol. 88, 2007, 1-15.

Erwin, E., "Is Freud Back?" *Logic, Methodology and Philosophy of Science: Proceedings of the Thirteenth International Congress,* eds. C. Glymour, W. Wei, and D. Westersthal (College Publications, King's College London), 599-612.

Freud, S., "A Note upon the 'Mystic Writing Pad,'" S.E. XIX, 1925 [1924], 227-32.

Kolb, B. and I. Wishaw, *The Fundamentals of Human Neuropsychology* (New York: W. H. Freeman and Co., 1990).

Kuberski, P., *The Persistence of Memory: Organism, Myth, Text* (Berkeley, CA.: University of California Press, 1992).

Solms, M., "Freud Returns," *Scientific American*, Vol. 290, 2004, 82-8.

Chapter 20
Reply to Dr. Erwin

Grant Gillett

ERWIN IS SURELY RIGHT TO NOTICE THE PHENOMENOLOGICAL critique of Freud's unconscious. What is more, his use of Brentano is both apt and appealing in the light of the close relation between phenomenology and current cognitive neuroscience. Brentano's thesis that the unconscious is not so much a domain of mental life as a set of dispositions to react thus and so at the level of conscious being-in-the-world has been most recently argued by Searle in his discussion of unconscious thought. Erwin is also quite correct to undercut the profligate use of inference to account for the vagaries of perception as the perceiver tries to settle to his satisfaction what exactly he is seeing. Erwin's idea of "differentialness" (such a horrible word that there must be a way of avoiding it) is very like a principle of economy which dictates that we do not multiply psychological entities and processes beyond that required for adequate explanation of a given phenomenon. A similar caveat applies to the production of entities and realities by means of inference to the best explanation as Erwin repeatedly stresses.

Erwin makes a telling point about the difference between the preconscious and the unconscious per se and himself hints at the existence of associations and connections in the brain that obviate the need to invoke a full panoply of mental states to populate the more inaccessible aspects of our own motivations. Such connections must lie beneath a person's extended task of forging a good enough life to live by.

A word is needed about "unintelligible gaps" in the account a person gives of him- or her-self and the "gains in meaning" that one achieves through positing system UCS.

The danger here is, as Jaspers—a phenomenologist and follower of Brentano in many respects—noted, to reify what emerges from "storying" a gap in intelligibility in an illuminating way (with perhaps an appeal to a conception of the primary process). The reification concerned, for a psychologist of the biological stripe, is in terms of a set of unconscious mentally configured causal processes and entities but the illumination falls far short of sustaining a metaphysical invention of that type. Explanation is not limited to those terms as any student of Aristotle is well aware. The gain in meaning that traces connections between symptom and life story may indicate points in one's personal history and character development where serious repair and emotional work need to be done rather than a cog in the biological psyche that is malfunctioning. The work required, a type of coaching in self understanding and the skills to deal with one's own shortcomings, may require that one bond, in a certain way, to a therapist or companion of the right kind. Is this the discovery of a cathexis and the development of transference? I, as mere neurosurgeon and philosopher, could not possibly say.

The tendency to erect a metaphysics of mind on the shifting sand of excitation in a neural network is almost irresistible, and not only for Freud. A nuanced approach to the relationship between the trajectory of a subjective human being through a world full of meanings that go beyond good and evil is likely to take a careful account of the human, all too human stories we tell about ourselves. Telling what is going on in that world and with ourselves is not always straightforward and, when the strain of doing so makes life unliveable, a *soupcon* of Freud's clinical acuity, uncluttered by faith in his theoretical commitments, goes a long way. The kinds of truth one discovers by adopting that approach perhaps do not deserve to be called a theory but they do embed an orientation to the work we all have to do in translating what happens between the human brain and the world in which it functions into terms that engage with the realm of meaning that as living, loving souls we all share.

I fear I am but a poor apologist for Freud in that, as a post-structuralist, I find myself condemned to wander forlorn through an ontologized world but, nevertheless, I will attempt to add some words of praise and not merely bury the great man and his key idea. The unconscious and inaccessible currents inadequately expressed in our conscious lives cannot be ignored. They are meaningful, of course, because we are creatures jointly formed by meaning and contingency. They are also often childish and narcissistic so that we struggle to come to grips with a world where we must act as reasonable, responsible adults without losing our innocence in the face of experiences that threaten to overwhelm us with cynicism every day. Learning to tell how it is as a being-in-the-world without losing a sense of wonder that it is so is a difficult task but one which must be undertaken if we are not to be left behind by the brave new world to which we are constantly readjusting ourselves.

PART VI
Psychoanalysis as *Weltanschauung*

Freud writes in "On the Question of a *Weltanschauung*", "Psycho-analysis … is incapable of creating a *Weltanschauung* of its own. It does not need one; it is a part of science and can adhere to the scientific *Weltanschauung* … [which] is not all-comprehensive, it is too incomplete and makes no claim to being self-contained and to the construction of systems. … A *Weltanschauung* erected upon science has, apart from its emphasis on the real external world, mainly negative traits, such as submission to the truth and rejection of illusions" (1933, *S.E.*, XXII: 181-2).

Freud here and elsewhere consistently argues that psychoanalysis is not a *Weltanschauung* in the primary sense of the term, but part of the scientific *Weltanschauung*. He also argues that the scientific *Weltanschauung* is radically different from the *Weltanschauung* of religion. Are his arguments cogent?

Pro: Andreas De Block, Ph.D., *University of Leuven, Belgium,* "Freud's Psychoanalysis: A Project for a Genuinely Scientific Psychology?"

Con: Douglas Kirsner, Ph.D., *Deakin University, Australia,* "Psychoanalysis as *Weltanschauung*"

Chapter 21
Freud's Psychoanalysis
A Project for a Genuinely Scientific Psychology?

Andreas De Block
Catholic University, Leuven, Belgium

THE MOST DISTINGUISHED PHILOSOPHERS OF SCIENCE have tried to find an answer to the questions concerning the distinction between good science and bad science and concerning what distinguishes science from pseudoscience. Despite all their efforts, there is no philosophical consensus. Most probably, the sciences are so heterogeneous that it is not possible to come up with a fixed set of features that define what science is—let alone good science.

However, the inability to provide undisputed and philosophically sound demarcation criteria has not hindered the emergence of a consensus among philosophers of science that psychoanalysis does not pass as good science. Psychoanalysis is featured as bad or pseudo-science in nearly all of the classic texts on the demarcation problem. For the logical empiricists, the explanatory concepts of Freud's psychoanalytic theory are nonsensical because they cannot be given any empirical meaning. In Popper's view, Freud's statements should not be seen as scientific, because they are not falsifiable. According to Lakatos, psychoanalysis is not a progressive research programme because it has long ceased to generate new predictions and because it is part and parcel of psychoanalysis' argumentative strategy to invoke *ad hoc* hypotheses whenever the facts seem to contradict the theoretical kernel of psychoanalysis (Lakatos, 1978, 88). For many of these critics, psychoanalysis is more a *Weltanschauung* or world-view than a science.

There are roughly three kinds of arguments that have been used to defend Freudian psychoanalysis against these allegations.

First, one can argue that the critics have misrepresented Freud's theory. This would mean, for example, that Freud's theory is falsifiable or that it constitutes a genuinely progressive research programme. Grünbaum, for instance, claims that Freud's Tally Argument makes psychoanalysis falsifiable because it forbids the therapeutic efficacy of non-analytic therapies for psychoneuroses (1980, 343).

Second, some proponents of psychoanalysis argue that psychoanalysis is much of what its critics have claimed it to be, but that the critics are wrong in claiming that these features and properties of psychoanalysis are enough to label it a pseudoscience or to qualify it as bad science. Not surprisingly, this type of defense usually builds upon the idea that the demarcation problem is an intractable problem, and that all the attempts to draw clear boundaries between science and pseudoscience have come up short.

Third, some scholars claim that the criticisms are completely off the mark, because it is wrong to assume that psychoanalysis is primarily meant to be a scientific enterprise. For example, Paul Ricoeur explores and defends Freud's psychoanalysis as a philosophical theory of interpretations. According to Ricoeur, Freud understood that an interpretation is both archeological and teleological. An interpretation is archeological because it searches for hidden origins, and it is teleological because it hints at a purpose. The interpretation tries to articulate a *telos* of the subject that Ricoeur identifies as the meaning of desire (1970). In this hermeneutic interpretation, Freud's main contribution to our understanding of the human psyche is the development of the "semantics of desire," rather than the construction of a scientific theory of the mind.

Ironically, it was Popper himself who offered psychoanalysis this last escape route. He suggested that, although psychoanalysis was unfalsifiable and hence not a scientific theory in the strict sense, it may constitute a valuable metaphysical research program. According to Popper, such a *Weltanschauung* is valuable and can even function as a source for viable scientific theories. "This does not mean that Freud and Adler were not seeing certain things correctly: I personally do not doubt that much of what they say is of considerable importance, and may well play its part one day in a psychological science which is testable" (2002, 49). Yet that does not alter the unscientific status of psychoanalysis. After all, many of the current scientific theories and hypotheses are anticipated in myths or even influenced by mythical thinking, but that is far from saying that mythical thinking is equivalent to scientific thinking.

In this paper, I will argue that Freudian psychoanalysis is not a *Weltanschauung*.

A first and pretty straightforward argument is that Freud himself would agree. In his view, psychoanalysis, "[a]s a specialised science, a branch of psychology—"depth-psychology": or psychology of the unconscious— . . . is quite unsuited to form a *Weltanschauung* of its own; it must accept that of science in general" (Freud, 1933, *S.E.*, XII: 158). Moreover, Freud is convinced that the scientific *Weltanschauung* is not really a *Weltanschauung* or, at least, that the scientific *Weltanschauung* differs quite dramatically from other *Weltanschauungen*. He contends that the main differences have to do with epistemological issues: Only the scientific methodology can give us genuine knowledge.

Unfortunately, this straightforward answer—"Psychoanalysis is not a *Weltanschauung* because Freud said so"—will not suffice because Freud could be mistaken about the nature of his own theory. Maybe Freud's psychoanalysis has much more in common with the therapy of desire offered in ancient philosophy (Nussbaum, 1996) and with Spinoza's naturalistic ethics than with today's sciences. Maybe Freud unknowingly developed a metaphysical research program that comes *dangerously* close to the *Weltanschauungen* of philosophy and religion. At least, the structure and functioning of the psychoanalytic community seem to point in that very direction. For instance, many psychoanalysts still regard Freud's writings as a privileged source of "Truth," and many other sectarian tendencies plagued psychoanalysis from its early days onwards (Weisz, 1975, 352-4). Thomas Szasz has defended the position that psychoanalysis is a religion-like *Weltanschauung*. In *Schizophrenia: The Sacred Symbol of Psychiatry*, he writes, "The gist of my argument is that men like Kraepelin, Bleuler and Freud were not what they claimed or seem to be—namely, physicians or medical investigators; they were, in fact, religious-political leaders and conquerors" (1979, 35).

Nevertheless, I think that Freud was not mistaken on this point. Psychoanalysis should be seen as a project for a genuinely scientific psychology.[1] That is not to say that psychoanalysis has nothing in common with philosophy. Actually, Freud's own ideas about the relation between knowledge, philosophy, and science are quite "Quinean," even though these ideas are obviously much less sophisticated than Quine's. First, Freud thinks that, in the end, only science can tell us what the world is like. Second, he contends that there is no essential difference between science and ordinary thinking. The sort of knowledge that science produces does not fundamentally differ from ordinary knowledge, even though scientific thinking does a much better job in generating true beliefs. Third, although Freud believed that Hegelian idealism was gibberish, he would probably not have objected to the kind of metaphysical project that Quine proposed. This metaphysics is scientifically well-informed and accords with scientific standards of clarity, evidence, and explanatoriness (Quine, 1990).

In short, when I take side with Freud against the view that psychoanalysis is primarily a *Weltanschauung*, I do not have to argue that there are no points of contact between Freud's psychoanalysis and philosophy. I agree with Freud and with many of the most distinguished philosophers of science that there no clear-cut boundaries between ordinary knowledge, science, and philosophy (e.g., Williamson, 2007). Since there are no such clear-cut boundaries, it would come as a big surprise if there were no philosophical issues upon which a scientific discipline like psychoanalysis would touch. But despite the numerous overlaps between philosophy and science, I maintain that the two are clearly not the same and that psychoanalysis is not a *Weltanschauung*.

In this essay, I will proceed as follows. In the first section, I will argue that many aspects of Freud's psychoanalysis are indisputably scientific. More precisely, I will show how Freud emphasized the manner in which his psychoanalytic theory subscribes to the scientific *Weltanschauung*. The concepts Freud borrowed from philosophy and mythology were profoundly transformed in Freud's scientific framework. In the second section, I will argue that Freud's psychoanalysis is not—or at least not primarily—a philosophical anthropology. This section explicates one of Freud's seemingly most philosophical claims, namely that man is a neurotic animal and that mental health is not within the reach of human beings. I will show how this "contribution" or "insight" can indeed be fruitful for philosophy, but that it was first and foremost a scientific idea. So even in his more philosophical moments and writings, Freud remained the scientist he wanted to be. To make this point as strong as possible, I will compare Freud's scientific claim "Man is a neurotic animal" with Nietzsche's philosophical slogan that "Man is an insane animal." In the concluding section, I explore how the revolutionary character of psychoanalysis as a science is connected to the emergence of a psychoanalytic *Weltanschauung*.

Physicalism and Naturalism

Philosophy was the cradle for most of the current sciences. This is not different for psychology, which emerged as a discipline distinct from philosophy only late in the 19th century. Sigmund Freud's path to psychology, however, did not originate in philosophy. Freud's pre-psychoanalytic period was through and through biomedical. Of course, Freud read a many philosophical essays—he was especially fond of Nietzsche—and some of them undoubtedly had an influence on his theorizing, but his biomedical theorizing always tended to naturalize the philosophical ideas.

There are many books and articles devoted to Freud's neurological writings, so I will not go into the details of his pre-psychoanalytic work. Still, it remains important to know that Freud's scientific ambition did not substantially change after he abandoned his neurological research. This ambition was the development of a theoretical framework that allowed for the mechanistic explanation of mental states and human behavior. In his *Project for a Scientific Psychology* (1895, *S.E.*, I: 295), Freud gave a materialistic twist to this ambition, as is obvious from this oft-cited passage: "The intention is to furnish a psychology that shall be a natural science: that is, to represent psychical processes as quantitatively determinate states of specifiable material particles, thus making those processes perspicuous and free from contradiction."

Immediately after Freud had completed this "Project," he turned his attention away from the scientific study of the neurons and started to analyze dreams and symptoms of his patients to get a grip on "unconscious" factors that determine our thinking and behavior. But in his view, the new psychoanalytic theory was just another and more promising way to realize the original scientific project. This new psychoanalytic model of the mind could explain both normal and pathological behavior and was, according to Freud, much better at it than the then-still immature brain science (Ellenberger, 1970).

But even after Freud abandoned the physicalist project, the main sources of inspiration for his psychological model of the mind remained medical and biological theories, rather than philosophical speculations. Freud took from the psychophysicist Fechner so many concepts and principles that Ellenberger could write that "a large part of the theoretical framework of psychoanalysis would hardly have come into being without the speculations of the man who Freud called the great Fechner" (1970, 218). The main inspirations for his sexual theory were obviously Richard von Krafft-Ebing and Albert Moll. His theory of the neuroses was built upon the preliminary work of Breuer, Charcot, and Janet. Darwinian evolutionary theory—especially Haeckel's recapitulationist version of it—pervades almost any aspect of Freud's metapsychology. So, although Freud abandoned the physicalist project of understanding the mind solely on the basis of the interaction between nerve cells, he never stopped believing in the possibility of naturalizing the mind. Freud continued to use tools from the natural sciences to inform, correct, and complement his methods and theories, but this time without aiming at a reduction of psychology to, say, neurology and/or evolutionary biology. In that regard, the title of Frank Sulloway's masterpiece *Freud: Biologist of the Mind* is very well chosen for two reasons. First, Freud thought of the mind as part of biology. Second, Freud focused on the mind, rather than on the brain (Sulloway, 1979).

Freud and the Philosophers

Freud compared himself to the greatest of all scientists. He saw himself as the Copernicus or the Darwin of the mind (1917, *S.E.*, XVI: 285). Of course, that is not to say that the widely discussed *Weltanschauung* of Freud's time did not have an influence on Freud's work. Goethe's Spinozistic philosophy inspired Freud and certain parallels between Freud and Schopenhauer are absolutely striking. But Freud transformed the philosophical and/or mystical ideas by incorporating these ideas into a scientific framework. For example, though Schopenhauer's psychological doctrines played a role in Freud's work, the influence of Schopenhauer's metaphysical and epistemological ideas on Freud's metapsychology remained very limited. Although Schopenhauer was certainly much more than just "an ancestor of modern dynamic psychiatry" (Ellenberger, 1970), that was exactly how Freud dealt with him.[2]

Freud was exposed to Schopenhauer's ideas mainly through the work of another philosopher, Karl von Hartmann. Karl von Hartmann's *Philosophy of the Unconscious* (2000) presents a curious blend of Schopenhauer and Darwin and it has often been pointed out that von Hartmann was a precursor of Freud's psychoanalysis. Indeed, many Darwinian and Schopenhauerian elements in von Hartmann's philosophy are also central to Freud's psychoanalysis. But whereas von Hartmann constructs a *Weltanschauung* upon these foundations,[3] Freud tries to erect a scientific psychology upon the same—or, at least, upon very similar—foundations. This results in a dramatically different understanding of the unconscious, the pivotal notion in both theories. For von Hartmann, the unconscious was an almost god-like principle of the whole universe. He talked about the "Unconscious Will of Nature," and argued at length for the fundamental unity of the Unconscious Will of Nature, the total sum of individual unconscious wills, and the Immanent Divine (Jensen 2006). One will look in vain for similar claims or arguments in Freud's work. For Freud, the unconscious was not the steering force behind cosmological and biological evolution, but rather the opposite; the unconscious was itself the by-product of biological evolution. In Freud's view, the personal unconscious originates in the organic repression of infantile sexuality and there is no need for a collective unconscious or an unconscious we share with all animate and inanimate beings. Unlike von Hartmann, Freud never thought that direct or indirect introspection would be the ideal method to come to a complete understanding of the world. If Freud's biopsychological psychoanalytic project shed a light on metaphysics and religion, it was an overtly critical light because he assumed that psychoanalysis uncovered the instinctual and infantile roots of metaphysical and religious systems.

Nevertheless, it is hard to deny that there are religious or semi-religious undercurrents in some of Freud's theories and concepts. This is probably nowhere truer than in the case of the death instinct. Sections IV to VII of *Beyond the Pleasure Principle* (1920, *S.E.* XVIII) are full of confusing and—even according to the author himself—far-fetched speculations, centered on biology, Schopenhauerian and Platonist philosophy, and Greek mythology. In "Analysis Terminable and Interminable," Freud continued on the same mythologico-philosophical path by comparing the death instinct to Empedocles' *neikos*, a destructive force that pervades and constitutes the universe (1937, *S.E.*, XXIII: 244-247).

Is this not enough evidence that Freud's theory is really a *Weltanschauung*, despite Freud's claims to the contrary?

I think this evidence is weak at best. First, it is important to note that *neikos* is a mechanical and naturalistic cause for both Empedocles and Freud. Even though *neikos* means "hate" or "strife," it was not Empedocles' (or Freud's) intention to suggest that the universe could feel anything or that the ultimate principle of the universe was a teleological one. Inasmuch as Freud relied on a *Weltanschauung* in *Beyond the Pleasure Principle* or in "Analysis Terminable and Interminable," it is obviously a mechanistic worldview—i.e., the worldview of science in general. Second, Freud started his speculations in *Beyond the Pleasure Principle* with a kind of disclaimer: "What follows is speculation, often far-fetched speculation, which the reader will consider or dismiss according to his individual predilection." (1920, *S.E.*, XVIII: 24) He clearly knew that he was leaving the firm ground of science and he did not expect his fellow-psychoanalysts to accept outright the ideas and conjectures tossed in the speculative sections. Thirdly, the main purpose of the writings on the death instinct was certainly not the construction of an all-encompassing worldview. Freud did not want to write a new *The World as Will and Representation*. What he did aim at was a deep (i.e., biological) understanding of certain clinical phenomena, such as masochism and war neuroses. I agree with Richard Wollheim, who writes, "Freud required of even the most abstract or speculative of his hypotheses that it should not be assessed otherwise than as part of a theory that is, in its overall intentions, empirical" (1995, 206).

Freud's scientific aim can be summarized as follows: A wide range of clinical and socio-cultural phenomena can be explained by unifying them in a single causal pattern. Mythological, philosophical, or religious notions can fit into this framework, but not in the same manner as they do in mythological, philosophical, or religious systems. If they play an explanatory role, they only can do so insofar as they have been naturalized. Furthermore, psychoanalysis contributes to a more general naturalizing project, because it sees philosophical and religious systems as belonging to the set of socio-cultural phenomena for which it provides its own causal explanations.

In this section, I have tried to argue with Freud that psychoanalysis is not a metaphysical theory about the ultimate nature of all things. However, when scholars write of Freud as the founding father of a particular *Weltanschauung*, this usually means that they consider Freud to be a theorist of human nature, whose theory has more in common with philosophical anthropology than with other branches of, or approaches in, psychology (Lear, 2005, 17). Hence, arguing that Freud's psychoanalysis is not a *Weltanschauung* must go further than just showing that Freud's aims were scientific and that his world view was naturalistic. I will also have to show that psychoanalysis is not primarily a philosophical anthropology.

The Insane Animal

Philosophical anthropology is a philosophical sub-discipline that deals with the phenomenology, metaphysics, and ethics of the human condition. Of course, a philosophical understanding of human beings often requires scientific input from anthropology, psychology, and biology, if only not to contradict other genuine sources of knowledge on the human. This explains why traditional overviews of philosophical anthropology such as Landmann's (1974) are not limited to extensive descriptions of philosophical theories and authors (e.g., Rousseau, Ortega y Gasset, and Scheler), but also include discussions of scientific theories and hypotheses, including Darwin's theory of evolution, Skinner's behaviorism, and the Sapir-Whorf hypothesis. The issue here is where to place Freud in the project of a philosophical anthropology. Was Freud on a par with Rousseau and Scheler, and was he—probably unknowingly—one of the greatest philosophical anthropologists ever? Or should his theory rather be seen as a scientific theory that is of likely importance for philosophical anthropology? I will tackle these questions by focusing on one of Freud's most "philosophical" claims regarding the human condition—namely that man is a neurotic animal.

The idea that an ontology of what is human has to be reconsidered from the perspective of psychopathology can be found in the work of many philosophers. Rousseau called modern man a corrupt and degenerate animal. Lessing taught that the human condition was an incurably illness. Montaigne classified our species as the weakest in nature (for an overview of these and similar philosophical claims, see Landmann, 1974, 177-9). But perhaps the most influential formulations of this idea came from Nietzsche. He expressed his contempt for modern man by comparing the latter to an ailing animal (*das kranke Tier*) and even to an insane animal (*das wahnsinnige Tier*). As he explained himself: "For man is more ill, uncertain, changeable and unstable than any other animal, without a doubt,—he is the sick animal" (Nietzsche, 1994, 88). In *The Gay Science*, Nietzsche even sees insanity as a defining and essential property of our nature: "the animals see man as a being like them who in a most dangerous manner has lost his animal common sense—as the insane animal" (Nietzsche, 2001, 145). And in *Thus spoke Zarathustra*, Nietzsche writes: "The earth . . . hath a skin; and this skin hath diseases. One of these diseases, for example, is called 'man'" (Nietzsche 2006, 122).

A very similar image of humanity is sketched in Freud's work. Like Nietzsche, Freud rejects the idea that man is superior to non-human animals: We may pride ourselves in thinking that our rationality makes us better than all other creatures, but this is only pride. In fact, Freud and Nietzsche tell us, the ultimate motivations have to do with instincts and the power of human rationality is only very superficial. On the whole, Freud agrees with Nietzsche that, unlike the instincts of other animals (*Instinkten*), our human instincts (*Triebe*) are a source of inner conflicts, self deception, and other problems that cannot be solved rationally. As some sort of conclusion, Freud writes in his *Introductory Lectures on Psycho-Analysis* that neurosis is one of the most important "prerogatives" of human beings over other animals (1917, *S.E.*, XVI, 414).

Why is Nietzsche a philosopher and Freud a psychologist, if they have such similar views on the human condition? To understand this, we have to take a closer look at how Freud deals with the issue of human vulnerability to mental disorders. This closer look will reveal that we call Freud a psychologist because Freud's method and goal is scientific, while Nietzsche is a philosopher because he subscribes to a philosophical goal and method.

According to Freud, the "prerogative" of humans over other animals is neurosis and not Nietzsche's insanity. Freud's claim is more specific than that of Nietzsche, even though "neurosis" is in Freud's work a taxon that covers a wide range of mental disorders, including the psychoses or "narcissistic neuroses." Quite unlike Nietzsche, Freud spent the largest part of his career figuring out which biopsychological factors cause these diseases. His main hypothesis was that all neuroses had to do with the interplay of defense mechanisms with infantile sexual problems. Freud constantly refined this overarching hypothesis by listening carefully to his patients and by discussing "cases" with his followers and colleagues. This resulted in a number of sub-hypotheses that were all aimed at an explanation of individual differences. For example, Freud held that obsessional neurosis was due to the interaction between anal-sadistic desires and reaction formation, that paranoia resulted from a projection of homosexual urges, and that the disavowal of female castration caused fetishism.

A fine-grained etiological theory of different mental disorders that tried to make sense of individual differences is totally absent from Nietzsche's work. The reason is that Nietzsche was not primarily a psychologist and, consequently, not very interested in individual differences and pathogenic or risk factors for the different kinds of neuroses. For the very same reason, Nietzsche never discussed or interpreted the associations, the postures, and the comments of individuals with mental problems. In short, the "human insanity" Nietzsche is talking about is not a medical insanity, but an ontological or existential one. It is a medical metaphor to illuminate a philosophical point. A similar medical metaphor can be found in Kierkegaard's *The Sickness unto Death*:

> Just as a physician might say there isn't a single human being who enjoys perfect health, so someone with a proper knowledge of man might say there is not a single human being who does not despair at least a little, in whose innermost being there does not dwell an uneasiness, an unquiet, a discordance, an anxiety in the face of an unknown something, or a something he doesn't even dare strike up acquaintance with, an anxiety about a possibility in life or an anxiety about himself (1989, 52).

But Freud is not talking about despair, uneasiness, discordance, or an existential anxiety. He is talking about mental disorders and not as a philosopher, but as a psychologist and as a physician.

The Dimensional View

Is not Freud making a similar "ontological" turn by claiming that psychopathology reveals human nature? (Geyskens, 2001) In Freud's view, normality is a neurosis (Verhaeghe, 2004) and mental health is not something within our human reach. Freud argued that all human beings are vulnerable to mental disorders and this is the main difference between humans and non-human animals. Thus, one seems to be forced to conclude that, at a certain point in his intellectual career, Freud built a philosophical anthropology upon his psychoanalytic hypotheses.

However, I think that this conclusion is too hasty. Although Freud's claims about the relation between the normal and the pathological may be important for the philosophical study of our human condition—at least, if they are true—these claims are not philosophical in themselves. It is not—or not primarily—an anthropological or metaphysical pessimism that gave rise to these claims, and these claims are not rooted in a rejection of a Cartesian view of human rationality. What Freud mainly did was argue for a dimensional rather than a categorical approach to mental disorders.

In the case of neuroses—but not necessarily in the case of other mental disorders, such as mental retardation—the dimensional approach is to be preferred over the categorical approach because there is a continuum between "normal" individuals and mentally ill individuals on three different, but interacting, levels.

First, the infantile, polymorphously perverse sexuality is the source of everyone's sexuality and not only the breeding ground for neurotic problems. In the *Three Essays on the Theory of Sexuality*, Freud writes, "[T]here is indeed something congenital at the basis of perversions, but it is something *which is congenital in all persons*" (1905, *S.E.*, VII: 171). Second, all of us have to defend ourselves against problematic components of this infantile sexuality and the defense mechanisms normal neurotics rely on do not differ in kind from the mechanisms that cause heavy neuroses. Again in the *Three Essays on the theory of Sexuality*, Freud says: "[T]he infantile amnesia gives us a new point of comparison between the psychic states of the child and those of the psychoneurotic. . . . The hysterical amnesia which serves the repression can only be explained by the fact that the individual already possesses a sum of recollections which have been withdrawn from conscious disposal and which by associative connection now seize that which is acted upon by the repelling forces of the repression emanating from consciousness" (1905, *S.E.*, VII: 175). Third, the symptoms of neurotic patients showed parallels with so-called normal behavior, as Freud abundantly illustrated in his *Psychopathology of Everyday Life* and all of his studies in applied psychoanalysis. According to Freud, the continuum between the "normal" and the pathological behavior is due to the continuum between the causes of that behavior.

The supporting evidence Freud presented for these continua did not draw on ingenious philosophical thought experiments or sophisticated conceptual analyses. It mainly came from a series of pediatric, psychiatric, and sexologist observations, evolutionary theory, and anthropological material, complemented by anecdotic evidence gathered through introspection, dream interpretations, and other "psychoanalytic investigations," including self-analysis. The analytic method itself was seen as a scientifically reliable method, because its findings could (often) be verified or corroborated by direct observation:

> The above-mentioned assertions concerning the infantile sexuality were justified in 1905, in the main through the results of psychoanalytic investigations in adults. Direct observation of the child could not at the time be utilized to its full extent and resulted only in individual indications and valuable confirmations. Since then it has become possible through the analysis of some cases of nervous disease in the delicate age of childhood to gain a direct understanding of the infantile psychosexuality. . . . I can point with satisfaction to the fact that direct observation has fully confirmed the conclusion drawn from psychoanalysis, and thus furnishes good evidence for the reliability of the latter method of investigation (Freud, 1905, *S.E.*, VII: 193-4).

Neurosis and Human Nature

Usually, a dimensional view argues that there is only a quantitative difference between mentally healthy and mentally unhealthy individuals. Such dimensional views of mental disorder must emphasize the existence of imprecise cut-off points: There are cases in which one cannot say with certainty whether a person is mentally ill or not. Freud situated the vagueness elsewhere. Freud's dimensional view entails that the severity of mental disorders varies and that individuals differ in how much they suffer from their mental disorder(s). But since everyone uses defenses against their infantile polymorphously perverse urges, Freud argues that everyone has symptoms and everyone is neurotic, albeit in different degrees. This is not some sort of philosophical turn in Freud's work. It is just the logical consequence of the dimensional view on which Freud had built what he thought was good scientific evidence.

But how could Freud know that the similarities between normal behavior and neurotic symptoms were more than superficial? How did Freud exclude the possibility that there are mentally healthy individuals? One cannot rely on observation alone to deal with these issues and Freud seemed to have been well aware of that. Thus, in order to show that everyone is neurotic (or mentally ill), Freud had to complement the above-mentioned evidence with other arguments. These arguments were not primarily philosophical. Freud did not try to define or redefine "mental illness" or "mental health," nor did he dwell on how to conceive of similarity and resemblance. Instead of seeking help from philosophy, Freud turned to biology to legitimate the unification of many psychological phenomena under the umbrella of the neuroses.

The biological cornerstone of Freud's argument was organic repression. Biological and not psychological factors make it impossible to gratify our instinctual urges and necessitate their repression. In general, human anatomy, the endocrinologically determined diphasic character of sexuality, and our bisexual constitution make human sexuality into something inherently pathogenic. In Freud's view, the human upright posture seemed to be particularly problematic.[4] This is how he puts it in *Civilization and its Discontents* (1930, *S.E.*, XXI: 106, note 3):

> It is to the effect that, with the assumption of an erect posture by man and with the depreciation of his sense of smell, it was not only his anal erotism which threatened to fall a victim to organic repression, but the whole of his sexuality; so that since this, the sexual function has been accompanied by a repugnance which cannot further be accounted for and which prevents its complete satisfaction.

Although Freud saw an intimate connection between the organic repression and coprophilic instincts, other instincts were equally subject to this biologically anchored mechanism. In "A Child Is Being Beaten" (1919, *S.E.*, XVII: 188), he writes:

> Most probably they pass away because their time is over, because the children have entered upon a new phase of development in which they are compelled to recapitulate from the history of mankind the repression of an incestuous object-choice, just as at an earlier stage they were obliged to effect an object-choice of that very sort.

The biological "schemata" of human sexual development lead automatically to the repression of certain sexual drives, which leaves traces of *Unlust* in the human psyche. In adolescence, repression and other defense mechanisms are triggered by the hormonally reactivated perverse and incestuous representations, because biological maturing has already made these representations disgusting or otherwise unpleasurable. In Freud's view, a severe hysteria is to be expected whenever this interaction between regression and repression hits the voyeuristic and genital drives. But even if only the oedipal, coprophilic, and sadistic drives are being repressed, neurotic symptoms will emerge.

I surmise Freud appealed here to biology for two different reasons. First, if culture, rather than biology was the main determinant of neurosis, neurosis would probably not have been as universally human as Freud had claimed it to be. Second, evolutionary biology had much more academic credibility than psychoanalysis and the claim that we are all mentally ill seemed difficult to reconcile with Darwinian evolutionary theory and the pivotal role of adaptation in that theory. Hence, in order to boost or to preserve the academic credibility of his psychoanalytic views, Freud had to give a plausible explanation for why the neurotogenic aspects of human sexuality were preserved during the course of evolution.

In short, we should call Freud a psychologist, and not a philosopher, because his interests were in particular things, primarily in dynamic psychology—i.e., in how one part of the psyche produces and/or interacts with another part of the psyche and how this brings about neurotic suffering. Nietzsche, on the other hand, may have been an anti-philosopher in some respects, but his anti-philosophy had a distinctively philosophical goal. His main aim was to evaluate and attack the systematic world views that other philosophers had constructed. Methodologically, the differences between Freud and Nietzsche are equally dramatic. Nietzsche defined or redefined concepts and evaluated assumptions. Freud, on the other hand, used clinical observation and tried to interpret what his patients said.

Some might object to this last argument that although Freud's goal may have been scientific, his methods certainly were not exactly prototypically scientific. Even one of the most influential proponent of Freud, Nobel Prize winner Eric Kandel, has criticized Freud for using the wrong, unscientific tools, "[A]lthough psychoanalysis has historically been scientific in its aim, it has rarely been scientific in its methods; it has failed over the years to submit its assumptions to testable experimentation" (1999, 506). This is true, at least to some extent. But the important point here is not that Freud could have used other, more scientifically fruitful methods than the ones he did use. The important point is that Freud used a hypothetico-deductive approach and that he tried to test his hypotheses on observable data, gathered in his psychoanalytic practice. Freud strived for an objective kind of insight, achieved by systematic unification and by exhibiting the phenomena as manifestations of common, underlying structures and processes that conform to specific principles. He did not aim at an intuitive or highly subjective kind of understanding (cf. Hempel, 1966, 83).

The Psychoanalytic Revolution and Its Philosophical Recuperation

Freud compared himself to the most revolutionary of all scientists, including Darwin, Galileo, and Copernicus. Freud's ambition was to bring about a fundamental change in our understanding of the mind. Now, scientific revolutions tend to have a bearing on our world-view and on our understanding of what it means to be a human being. Freud's psychoanalytic revolution is no exception to that rule. What might be exceptional, however, is that Freud's influence on our self-understanding is probably much greater than his (direct) influence on scientific theorizing. So even though psychoanalysis developed as a scientific theory, the reception of Freudian psychoanalysis may have transformed it into a *Weltanschauung*, though a peculiar one. As I have explained in the introduction of this chapter, this transformation has much to do with the philosophical criticisms on psychoanalysis as a science. One can even see this as a strategy of immunization. What is certain is that the growing implausibility of Freud's etiological hypotheses and interpretations did not have a negative impact on the claims of psychoanalysis to philosophical interest, at least not in continental philosophy.

As a conclusion, however, I want to consider another reason for this transformation. I will briefly examine how the revolutionary character of psychoanalysis as a science required a convincing "philosophical back-up" that paved the way for the recuperation of psychoanalysis as a *Weltanschauung*.

Freud shifted the focus of psychology to self-deception and self-manipulation, without changing any of the crucially *scientific* elements of psychology. However, as many philosophers have pointed out, the mere definition of self-deception is paradoxical: How can a person be the dupe of a deceitful strategy he deploys? In Freud's view, this dynamic problem could only be solved by a division in the psyche where one part of the psyche deceives the other part (Rorty, 1988, 16). Moreover, the parts of the psyche involved in self-deception and self-manipulation cannot both be conscious, for that would revive the very same paradox. In order to make self-deception and self-manipulation less paradoxical—and thus much easier to understand—Freud developed his topographical model of the mind.

Freud's reasons to shift the focus of psychology in the direction of self-deception are obviously related to his interest in hypnosis and much of the evidence he gathered for the existence of unconscious mental states came from Bernheim's and Charcot's hypnotic experiments. Nonetheless, Freud was convinced that this "scientific" evidence had to be complemented by a philosophical argument that unconscious mental states were truly mental. Time and again, Freud explains why the unconscious is mental and not a physiological state that interacts with consciousness. His main philosophical argument is that unconscious mental states are mental because they are intentional. Jerome Wakefield summarizes Freud's position as follows:[5]

> Briefly, mental representations refer to objects outside themselves and so appear to have meaning, which provides plausibility to the claim that they are mental, and representationality appears to be potentially independent of consciousness because a representational structure can be instantiated in brain tissue even when outside awareness, just as it is instantiated in other kinds of physical structures outside of awareness, such as a sentence in a book or a painting in a vault (1992, 80).

So Freud redefined psychology as a science by showing that unconscious mental states are logically possible—i.e., not conceptually excluded. This required a genuinely philosophical effort, but this philosophical effort was for Freud primarily a stepping stone for his real scientific aim: the development of a psychodynamic psychology.

Nonetheless, the development of a conceptual framework for psychology in which unconscious meanings occupy a pivotal place may have made psychoanalysis ready for its subsequent adoption as a *Weltanschauung*. For suddenly, each aspect of human behavior was pregnant with meaning. Even more importantly, these meanings were meanings that originated in one's own unconscious. Every seemingly unintentional act could now be interpreted as a parapraxis. Since Freud, forgetting an umbrella is for many people more than just forgetting an umbrella, and even intentional actions such as cigar smoking and writing a novel have much more meaning than one is aware of.

Freud's emphasis on unconscious meaning is usually understood as an emphasis on deep meanings. These meanings are not only deep because Freud used a topographical model to conceive of them, but also because they relate to existential issues, such as sexuality, intra-familial conflict, and death. Hence, Freud's psychoanalysis seems to be an antidote to the contingency and arbitrariness that is emphasized in other sciences. While other sciences tend to sketch a view of man and world in which there is no place for purpose or meaning, psychoanalysis suggests otherwise. Of course, this meaning is to a great extent naturalized and connected to the most feral instincts, but at the same time it builds bridges between scientific objectivity and our individual narratives about existential meaning. More precisely, the existence of unconscious mental states and unconscious mental meanings seem to imply that our choices and preferences are not contingent or arbitrary after all. The omnipresence of neurotic symptoms is at the same time the omnipresence of deep meaning.

Notes

1. Of course, I am certainly not the first person to argue for this view. A member of the Vienna Circle, Else Frenkel-Brunswick, has argued in the1950s that psychoanalysis was a serious part of a "*wissenschaftliche Weltauffassung*." In her view, Freud's conceptual methodology is perfectly compatible with the methods of the main scientific theories. See Borchers, 2003.

2. Freud always denied any direct influence: "The theory of repression quite certainly came to me independently of any other source; I know of no outside impression which might have suggested it to me, and for a long time I imagined it to be entirely original, until Otto Rank showed us a passage in Schopenhauer's *World as Will and Idea* in which the philosopher seeks to give an explanation of insanity. What he says there about the struggle against accepting a distressing piece of reality coincides with my concept of repression so completely that once again I owe the chance of making a discovery to my not being well-read. Yet others have read the passage and passed it by without making this discovery, and perhaps the same would have happened to me if in my young days I had had more taste for reading philosophical works. In later years I have denied myself the very great pleasure of reading the works of Nietzsche, with the deliberate object of not being hampered in working out the impressions received in psycho-analysis by any sort of anticipatory ideas. I had therefore to be prepared—and I am so, gladly—to forgo all claims to priority in the many instances in which laborious psycho-analytic investigation can merely confirm the truths which the philosopher recognized by intuition" (1914, *S.E.*, XI: 15-6).

3. Hartmann himself called his speculative psychology a "psychological *Weltanschauung*." See Jensen, 2006, 42.

4. Freud primarily developed this view in his study of the Rat Man (1909, *S.E.* X: 155-318) and in his letters to Fliess.

References

Borchers, D., "No Woman, No Try? Else Frenkel-Brunswik and the Project of Integrating Psychoanalysis into the Unity of Science," *The Vienna Circle and Logical Empiricism: Re-evaluation and Future Perspectives*, ed., Stadler (Dordrecht: Kluwer Academic Publisher, 2003), 323-38.

Ellenberger, H., *The Discovery of the Unconscious: The History and Evolution of Dynamic Psychiatry* (New York: Basic Books, 1970).

Freud, Sigmund, *The Standard Edition of the Complete Psychological Works of Sigmund Freud*, Vols. I-XXIV, ed. and trans. James Strachey (London: The Hogarth Press, 1976).

Grünbaum, A., "Epistemological Liabilities of the Clinical Appraisal of Psychoanalytic Theory," *Nous*, Vol. 14, 1980: 307-85.

Geyskens, T., "Freud's Letters to Fliess: From seduction to sexual biology, from psychopathology to a clinical anthropology," *The International Journal of Psychoanalysis*, Vol. 82, 2001: 861-76.

Hempel, C., *Philosophy of Natural Sciences.* (Englewood Cliffs: Prentice Hall, 1966).

Jensen, A.K. "The Rogue of All Rogues: Nietzsche's Presentation of Eduard von Hartmann's *Philosophie des Unbewussten* and Hartmann's Response to Nietzsche," *The Journal of Nietzsche Studies*, Vol. 32, 2006, 41-61.

Kandel, E., "Biology and the Future of Psychoanalysis: A New Intellectual. Framework for Psychiatry Revisited," *American Journal of Psychiatry*, Vol. 156, 1999: 505-524.

Kierkegaard, S., *The Sickness Unto Death: A Christian Psychological Exposition for Edification and Awakening*. (London: Penguin Books, 1989).

Lakatos, I., "Falsification and the Methodology of Research Programme," *Imre Lakatos: The Methodology of Scientific research Programmes, eds. J. Worrall and G. Currie.* (Cambridge: Cambridge University Press, 1978), 9-101.

Landmann, M., *Philosophical Anthropology* (Philadelphia: Westminster Press, 1974).

Lear, J., *Freud* (New York: Routledge, 2005).

Nietzsche, F., *The Gay Science* (Cambridge: Cambridge University Press, 2001).

Nietzsche, F., *On the Genealogy of Morality* (Cambridge: Cambridge University Press, 1994).

Nietzsche, F., *Thus Spoke Zarathustra* (Cambridge: Cambridge University Press, 2006).

Nussbaum, M., *The Therapy of Desire: Theory and Practice in Hellenistic Ethics* (Princeton: Princeton University Press, 1996).

Popper, K. *Conjectures and Refutations* (London: Routledge, 2002).

Quine, W.V.O. *Pursuit of Truth* (Cambridge: Harvard University Press, 1990).

Ricoeur, P., *Freud and Philosophy: An Essay on Interpretation* (New Haven: Yale University Press, 1970).

Rorty, A.O., "The Deceptive Self: Liars, Layers, and Lairs," *Perspectives on Self-Deception*, eds. B.P. McLaughlin and A. O. Rorty (Berkeley: University of California Press, 1988), 11–28.

Smith, D.L., *Freud's Philosophy of the Unconscious* (Dordrecht: Kluwer, 1999).

Sulloway, F., *Freud, Biologist of the Mind* (New York: Basic Books, 1979).

Szasz, T., *Schizophrenia: The Sacred Symbol of Psychiatry* (New York: Syracuse University Press, 1979).

Verhaeghe, P., *On Being Normal and Other Disorders: A Manual for Clinical Psychodiagnostics* (New York: Other Press, 2004).

Von Hartmann, E., *The Philosophy of the Unconscious* (London: Routledge, 2000).

Wakefield, J., "Freud and Cognitive Psychology: the Conceptual Interface," *Interface of Psychoanalysis and Psychology*, eds. J. Barron, M. Eagle and D. Wolitzki (Washington: American Psychological Association, 1992), 77-98.

Weisz, G., "Scientists and Sectarians: The Case of Psychoanalysis," *Journal of the History of the Behavioral Sciences*, Vol. 11, 1975: 350–64.

Williamson, T., *The Philosophy of Philosophy* (Oxford: Blackwell, 2007).

Wollheim, R. *Sigmund Freud* (New York: Cambridge University Press, 1995).

Chapter 22
Psychoanalysis as *Weltanschauung*

Douglas Kirsner
Deakin University, Australia

In "On the Question of a *Weltanschauung*", Freud writes, "Psychoanalysis . . . is incapable of creating a *Weltanschauung* of its own. It does not need one; it is a part of science and can adhere to the scientific *Weltanschauung* . . . [which] is not all-comprehensive, it is too incomplete, and makes no claim to being self-contained and to the construction of systems. . . . A *Weltanschauung* erected upon science has, apart from its emphasis on the real external world, mainly negative traits, such as submission to the truth and rejection of illusions" (1933, *S.E.*, XXII: 181-2).

Freud here and elsewhere consistently argues that psychoanalysis is not a *Weltanschauung* (roughly, world-view) in the primary sense of the term, but part of the scientific *Weltanschauung*. He also argues that the scientific *Weltanschauung* is radically different from the *Weltanschauung* of philosophy or religion. Are his arguments cogent?

Although Freud rejected the notion of psychoanalysis as a *Weltanschauung* in the primary sense, he "protested too much." First, his discovery about the meaning of psychological or psychologically related symptoms is a semantic, not an etiological discovery. He began with the idea of causal explanations being necessary for psychoanalysis in *Studies on Hysteria*, but his mature ideas involved the language of motives, meaning, and intentions. Second, though Freud always insisted that psychoanalysis works at the descriptive level, there is an undeniable normative aspect to it, as the novelty of his psychoanalytic discoveries in mature works lies in the different normative realm of how best to live—a realm shared by religion and philosophy. Third, at the same time that he develops a deconstructive critique of organized religions, he initiates a movement with many of their accoutrements. Finally, Freud's seems hell-bent on finding an overarching, single theory that could explain all psychically related behavior and that seems more characteristic of religiosity and a *Weltanschauung* in the primary sense than of science.

Freud on *Weltanschauung*

The question of a *Weltanschauung* was sufficiently important for Freud that he devoted an entire lecture to the topic out of seven in his *New Introductory Lectures on Psychoanalysis* (1933). Moreover, it was the concluding one.

The *New Introductory Lectures* is the sequel to his *Introductory Lectures on Psychoanalysis*—a series of lectures he delivered to University of Vienna medical students from 1915 to 1917. The *New Introductory Lectures* were written and not delivered, but modeled on the format of the earlier lectures. Taken together, these two collections of essays, comprising 35 lectures, provide an important introduction to what Freud saw as his main ideas and contributions over much of his psychoanalytic career. His lecture on *Weltanschauung* addressed the charges from many quarters that psychoanalysis was a *Weltanschauung*. In that lecture. Freud defines a *Weltanschauung* as "an intellectual construction which solves all the problems of our existence uniformly on the basis of one overriding hypothesis, which, accordingly, leaves no question unanswered and in which everything that interests us finds its fixed place. It will easily be understood that the possession of a *Weltanschauung* of this kind is among the ideal wishes of human beings. Believing in it one can feel secure in life, one can know what to strive for, and how one can deal most expediently with one's emotions and interests" (1933, *S.E.*, XXII: 158).

Thus a belief in a *Weltanschauung*, while emotionally comforting, is inconsistent with a more objective or dispassionate view of the human condition. Rather than accepting such views, Freud deconstructs them through investigating the psychological sources of such beliefs as needs to be understood so as to move beyond the conditions that produce them.

For Freud, the paradigm case of a *Weltanschauung* is religion, which he pits against science. Freud dismisses religion because it takes responsibility away from human beings and provides a sense of false security. For Freud, the mistaken beliefs of a religious *Weltanschauung* are the results of our emotional need for protection and reassurance instead of our facing the truth. In contrast, at least in principle, science provides an objective and critical approach.

Yet, despite his self-definition as scientist, Freud's novelty lay in his philosophical discovery in another realm that shared the neighborhood of religion—the realm of how we could best live our lives. In his *The Future of an Illusion* (1927, *S.E.*, XXI: 5-56), Freud says religion as is an illusory system that simply prevents one from seeing and acting on reality. Freud's deconstruction of religion comprises its illusory emotional rewards. According to Freud, religion brings illusory consolation whose psychological attraction—inculcated as "poison" from childhood—is that it helps us feel less vulnerable to the exigencies of life and death. But this childlike dependence on illusion cannot last forever. "Men cannot remain children for ever; they must in the end go out into 'hostile life.' We may call this '*education to reality*'" (1927, *S.E.*, XXI: 49). For Freud, religion is a *Weltanschauung* complete with solutions to the problems of human existence, known in advance, whereas science is an open and critical system of inquiry. In making life appear more bearable, religion has the opposite effect of making it harder. Science, in contrast, is dependent on reason. However, the special role Freud grants to reason, as we shall see below, is scarcely a ringing endorsement of it. But at least Freud grants it the quality of insistence:

> The voice of the intellect is a soft one, but it does not rest till it has gained a hearing. Finally, after a countless succession of rebuffs, it succeeds. This is one of the few points on which one may be optimistic about the future of mankind. . . . The primacy of the intellect lies, it is true, in a distant, distant future, but probably not an infinitely distant one (1927, *S.E.*, XXI: 53).

The double negative of the "not infinitely distant" is as optimistic as Freud gets. It demonstrates how little hope he had for mankind. He regards "our best hope for the future" as lying in the intellect or reason being able to establish in time "a dictatorship in the mental life of man." Freud postulates the crucial role for "such a domain of reason" as proving "the strongest uniting bond among men and [leading] the way to further unions." In contrasting religion with this liberating role, which would bring people together, Freud shows us why he sees religion in such a negative light. "Whatever, like religion's prohibition against thought, opposes such a development, is a danger for the future of mankind" (1933, *S.E.*, XXI: 171-2). In this world, where a religious *Weltanschauung* is so attractive and reason so demanding, how is it possible to bear with reality? One way is the very long-term scientific faith that everything can be explained.

I have suggested elsewhere that Freud was influenced by Greek philosophy, especially Stoicism, which helped him bear with such hard realities. The Stoics wanted to be therapists of the mind or soul *(psyche)*, just as physicians cared for the body and just as in the twentieth century psychoanalysts have also set themselves this task. For both Freud and the Stoics, reason was in battle with the passions and required clear sight to have a chance of prevailing over them. Freud's belief that a therapist should be removed from patients—i.e., therapist neutrality (G., *Indifferenz*)—is in line with the Stoic idea of *apatheia*. So too is his belief that experimenters ought to attempt to distance themselves from the experimental field. Freud often conflates ethics and science. His scientific approach is often colored by an unrecognized ethical stance (Kirsner, 2006). Moreover, Freud essays to make the human mind, not the brain, to be the object of scientific investigation and the mind to many philosophers is inescapably subjective. Subjectivity is more in line with philosophy, literature, and linguistics.

The "Sense" of Symptoms

In an early lecture in his *Introductory Lectures*, Freud refers to *Weltanschauung* as he attempts to explain what seem to be marginal phenomena in our lives: dreams, slips, jokes, and myths. He believes a scientific explanation of these phenomena would help explain central aspects of our lives, including the nature of our minds and neurosis. For Freud, these "marginalia," so to speak, are breaks that are indications that should not be missed so as to take a different approach to understanding human subjectivity.

The *Introductory Lectures* are divided into three sections: "Parapraxes," "Dreams," and "A General Theory of Neuroses." First, parapraxes—which include slips of the tongue, pen, bungles, etc.—demonstrate to Freud that there is psychic conflict. Parapraxes have meaning and sense in everyday events that we often do not even notice. Describing and explaining them invariably involves unconscious mental life. Next, dreams demonstrate a deeper notion of unguarded unconscious activity with a broader explanatory power about realms of our being to which we have no conscious access. Finally, neuroses build upon the concept of the unconscious further by explaining phenomena, ranging from psychological symptoms to the nature of civilization. Assuming that every event has a cause—for the mind, that there is no such thing as an uncaused mental event—Freud aims to explain even the smallest fact or event. He writes:

> Let us now call in someone who knows nothing of psychoanalysis, and ask him how he explains such occurrences. His first reply will certainly be: 'Oh! That's not worth explaining: they're just small chance events.' What does the fellow mean by this? Is he maintaining that there are occurrences, however small, which drop out of the universal concatenation of events—occurrences which might just as well not happen as happen? *If anyone makes a breach of this kind in the determinism of natural events at a single point, it means that he has thrown overboard the whole* Weltanschauung *of science.* Even the *Weltanschauung* of religion, we may remind him, behaves much more consistently, since it gives an explicit assurance that no sparrow falls from the roof without God's special will. I think our friend will hesitate to draw the logical conclusion from his first reply; he will change his mind and say that after all when he comes to study these things he can find explanations of them (1915-16, *S.E.*, XVI: 27-28; emphasis added).

In declaring that parapraxes have a meaning and are not just "small chance events," Freud is assuming that nothing occurs by chance, that all events are etiologically concatenated, and thus, that everything in the world and in our conscious life can be explained. We cannot say, "It was just a slip, just an accident, and I cannot explain it."

Freud seems to identify the position that everything in the world can be explained with the position of scientific determinism, namely that everything can be explained causally in terms of antecedent factors (e.g., the way we explain a physical event like a jug boiling) and relevant laws. The idea that everything can be explained does not mean that everything needs to be explained *causally.* There are other kinds of explanations than causal or scientific ones. Nonetheless, Freud says that if we were to admit that parapraxes are inexplicable chance events, a breach would be made "in the determinism of natural events" and this would mean overthrowing the whole *Weltanschauung* of science.

Freud, insisting on causal explanations for all psychical or psychically related events, goes too far here on a number of grounds. Science need not claim a rigid relationship between events as cause and effect. To begin with, this relation may vary from field to field, especially between psychology and the physical sciences. Moreover, the claim that determinism has to be true or else these relationships would be haphazard and meaningless is questionable if only because the relationships need not be invariable but may be only probabalistic. As Salmon explains in a classic paper,

> There would hardly be grounds for complaint if psychoanalytic theories could be shown to be well-confirmed statements of probabilistic relations which would enable us to explain any event as following from certain predecessors with a high degree of probability. In such a case we would have every right to deny that events such as slips, dreams, and neurotic symptoms are haphazard and meaningless, and this is what the psychoanalytic principle of determinism is concerned to deny (1957, 257).

All Freud needs to show, and perhaps all that he does show, is that the parapraxes are motivated and intentional acts have a sense or meaning. Parapraxes need to be understood within a psychic context. Yet for Freud, we cannot stop until we have reached the explanation of the specific instance of each parapraxis. General explanations such as something was caused by inattention and fatigue are not good enough. They do not explain why a person makes a slip using one particular word rather than another.

If we allowed for any chance event, such as an uncaused parapraxis, a "breach of this kind in the determinism of natural events at a single point" would mean having "thrown overboard the whole *Weltanschauung* of science" (1915-1916, *S.E.* XVI: 27-8). Such hyperbolic language reveals a fundamental belief system on Freud's part, which involves a basic guiding faith and conviction that everything has to be explicable. But does it have to be *causally* explicable?

Freud has shown a couple of things, I suspect, but he has not shown that that every psychic event has a cause. Instead he seems to have shown, first, that every psychic event has a meaning to be discovered—something heuristic, not causal. Parapraxes have a sense, but this does not amount to them having a causal explanation in keeping with determinism. Secondly, he has shown that psychophysiological explanations do not seem adequate to explain parapraxes. As well as demonstrating that there are purposes at work of which we are not conscious, parapraxes seem to have a purpose. They are symbolic in that they point beyond themselves. They are communications, pieces of language to be interpreted on the model of a text to be deciphered. Overall, this idea seems not to be on the model of natural science but rather on the model of how we interpret a language or text—a hermeneutic approach. That Freud writes "The Sense of Symptoms" in *Introductory Lectures,* not "The Cause of Symptoms," and writes *The Interpretation of Dreams*, not *The Causation of Dreams*, indicates that his discovery is more linguistic than being akin to physics and chemistry.

In his lecture "The Sense of Symptoms," Freud says that psychoanalysis "established in the first place the fact that symptoms have a sense and are related to the patient's experiences." He attributes the discovery to Breuer but adds, "The great psychiatrist Leuret gave it as his opinion, before Breuer and Janet, that even the delusional ideas of the insane would certainly be found to have a sense if only we understood how to translate them" (1915-1916, *S.E.*, XVI: 257). As Charles Rycroft states, Freud "made a revolutionary discovery in semantics, viz. that neurotic symptoms are meaningful disguised communications, but that owing to his scientific training and allegiance, he formulated his findings in the conceptual framework of the physical sciences" (Rycroft, 1968, 13).

Freud's Normativism

According to University of Chicago philosopher and psychoanalyst, Jonathan Lear, Freud's approach is essentially normative. Lear asserts that for Freud neurotics are gripped by a "psychologically organized orientation that actively distorts their ability to understand the world and their place in it." Freud is trying to explain "psychological perturbations" related to how neurotics live. He sees people who are failing to flourish, and he sets out to give a psychological account of why that is. On his account, neurotics fail to live well because they themselves "turn away from reality" (2005, 153).

Lear suggests that for Freud neurotics are gripped by a "psychologically organized orientation that actively distorts their ability to understand the world and their place in it." Freud does not see pure cases of abstract principles as, for example, the pleasure principle or the reality principle at work. Instead he says: "[T]heoretical posits, whose joint and conflicted workings are supposed to explain what he does see: people living structured unhappy lives. The pleasure principle and the reality principle are there to explain why people are doing such a poor job answering the question of how to live" (2005, 153). They act as heuristics. Lear asserts that the master-complaint of Freud's patients was this: "In my own attempt to figure out how to live, something is going wrong." He adds:

> Freud was not well-placed to hear this master-complaint. He was a doctor and he conceived himself as engaged in scientific research. Just as a doctor probes for the hidden causes of physical diseases, so Freud took himself to be probing the unconscious for hidden meanings making the patient ill. With the benefit of hindsight, we can now see that a certain clinical brutality flows from this self-understanding. . . . It also blinds him to profound philosophical and ethical significance of his discoveries (2005, 10).

The complex issue of Freud's scientific approach is traditionally taken as Freud would have had use take it: non-normative—i.e., as a science without extra-scientific claims. Freud traditionally has been seen as somehow caught up as a child of his time in the flow-over of the burgeoning of science in the nineteenth century in that his discoveries used the aegis of science for his discoveries in different realms. There seems to be more to the picture than this, however.

According to Gödde, three nineteenth-century traditions represented philosophical sources for Freud's concept of the unconscious. First there was the cognitive unconscious source—deriving from the philosophical Enlightenment and including thinkers like Leibniz, Fechner, and von Helmholtz. Second there was the romantic, vitalist, and storm-and-stress source—comprising aesthetic theories of romanticism and *Naturphilosophie* and including thinkers like Goethe and Schelling. Third, there was the drive-related, irrational source—opposing the other two developments of Post-Kantian idealism, concentrating on dangerous and destructive inner urges, and including Schopenauer and Nietszche (Gödde, 2010, 262-3). A wide range of influences, ably documented by Makari (2009), included the philosopher Franz Brentano, with whom he studied in the only nonscientific discipline he studied in his medical degree at the University of Vienna.

Freud's interest in philosophy, humanities, and the ancient world went back to his school days. Freud's attitude toward science had a distinct ethical slant, taken from the ancient world, via Freud's classical education. He had a lifelong passion for antiquity and was profoundly interested in Egyptian, Greek, and Roman civilizations. Richard Sterba, a close colleague of Freud, notes the early influence of humanistic studies on Freud's character, values, and attitude. From 1868 to 1873, Freud attended a humanistic *Gymnasium* where he intensively studied Greek and Latin together with the major literary works of the ancient period. Eight hours a week was devoted to Latin for over eight years, while six hours a week were devoted to Greek for over six years. All the major authors—such as Homer, Sophocles, Plato, Tacitus, and Seneca—were studied (1974, 170).

The ancient world had considerable impact on the development of Freudian psychoanalysis. Think of Freud's terms that derive from Greek mythology, including the Oedipus and female Oedipus complexes, *Eros*, and his theory of narcissism (Kirsner, 2006). Freud's interest in philosophy and the ancient world continued throughout his life. He had an estimable collection of ancient artifacts (Burke, 2006) and even considered psychoanalysis metaphorically a type of archeology.

Freud's interest in and commitment to philosophy are well-documented in Tauber's recent aptly titled book, *Freud: The Reluctant Philosopher* (2010). Tauber, combining both a biological view of human behavior and a humanistic view of the *psyche*, notes the continuing tension between empirical science and moral philosophy throughout Freud's work. By never describing these positions explicitly, Freud "eschewed significant self-reflection on his own intellectual commitments" (2010, xiv). Throughout, from his early musings about the centrality of philosophy to his increasing social and cultural foci, philosophy was always part of Freud's approach. Perhaps he did not want to be identified with speculative philosophy, especially of the German variety, that was so abstract and did not explicitly focus on empirical and current social issues. It was too general for Freud, who concentrated on specific instances, vignettes, cases, or counter-examples in a systematic approach that was not dry or "academic" in the abstract sense of the term. Freud constantly moved between individual concrete example and generalizations. Such an approach did not fit easily with his prior disciplines. There was a lag of self-understanding of the nature and basis of Freud's new field.

Psychoanalysis as a Movement

One problem with tracing Freud as a scientist who was just building upon other investigations is that the novelty did not lie in new data as much as the object of investigation—the unconscious. The significance lay in the new beginning in the way data were organized to understand the unconscious and the study of sexuality in relation to neurosis. Psychoanalysis as a paradigm shift involved a transformation of perspective that was not explicable by early work in psychology. It was a creative admixture of approaches—derived from a wide range of humanities, social sciences, and natural sciences—with a new object, which included new methods, such as free association and psychotherapy, with new concepts, such as transference, resistance, and repression. The systematized idea that intentions, as unconscious, could be both determinate and determining was not consonant with previous ways of thinking.

This novelty had a major downside. Who would review and assess this new approach? How would it be done? A significant and famous aspect of Freud's new science was its movement aspect. Freud founded the movement that was controlled by him and his epigones. The specific route was via gate-keeping by the leaders. It was implemented and transmitted through training new members. The training was more akin to anointing new disciples. Politics often masqueraded as science and often supervened over open inquiry. Increasingly, it became a closed world, often with cultic dimensions (Kirsner, 2009). Jones set up a secret "committee" to protect and sustain the psychoanalytic cause that gave its most Freud-loyal members, a band of brothers, rings. It also excluded from the movement all who disagreed with Freudian dogma—e.g., Adler, Jung, and Reich (Eisold, 1994, 794).

The *New Introductory Lectures* was published in 1933, in the dark period that followed World War I and with the Great Depression and the rise of Nazism. The contrast between the attractions of emotionally charged religious and ideological *Weltanschauungen* and a rational scientific approach was understandably foremost in Freud's mind. But in contrasting these approaches and putting psychoanalysis clearly into the category of science, he arguably stopped his critique too soon. Freud did not inquire into what happens to a science that has morphed into a "movement," plagued by insularity and self-certainty, and which came to share significant characteristics with religion, which he characterized as dogmatic, parochial, and authoritarian—a *Weltanschauung* in the true sense.

Freud's Desire for Fame

What are the consequences of psychoanalysis, which is not just a method, body of knowledge, and form of psychotherapy but also a movement, a set of professional associations, a group of hypotheses about human nature and culture, and a collection of educational institutions—i.e., a philosophy and not a natural science?

Louis Breger suggests that Freud's desire for an overarching single theory, his rejection of colleagues' views that were critical of his, his focus on the Oedipus complex as a shibboleth, and other cult-like behaviors were based on his personal "need to be a great man; it was the basis of all the other problems with his theories and approaches to therapy" (2009, 117). Breger says:

> Freud's childhood identification with military leaders was crucial to the way he shaped the movement. He envisioned himself as the commander of a psychoanalytic army that was surrounded by enemies against whom he and his loyal lieutenants must battle. How different things would have been if, instead of a cult-like 'cause', psychoanalysis had really been the science that it claimed to be, a field in which new ideas and methods were examined, tested against observations, and welcomed when they proved fruitful in producing further research and more effective therapy. But that was not to be (2009, 114).

Moreover, Freud's drive for undying fame differed from celebrity. He did not want to be famous only for the sake of being lauded. He wanted to achieve something beyond celebrity that merited being famous. He wanted recognition for achievement, as having deliberately and determinedly sustained and shaped a revolutionary new understanding of the self and the world that would make a significant difference. But he set himself an almost impossibly high standard—that of those few who had transformed and revolutionized our understanding of the world. Freud's scientific quest is overwhelmingly about a single theory that explains all by going beyond psychophysics, biophysics, and sexology. He lists two major psychoanalytic hypotheses in the *Introductory Lectures* that are "an insult to the entire world and have earned its dislike." The first hypothesis is twofold—"that mental processes are in themselves unconscious and that of all mental life it is only certain individual acts and portions that are conscious." The second hypothesis is about sexuality—how it causes neurosis, how it created civilization, and how it maintains civilization. Freud asserts that sexual drives "play an extremely large and never hitherto appreciated part in the causation of nervous and mental diseases." That hypothesis implies that those very same sexual drives contribute to "the highest cultural, artistic and social creations of the human spirit" (1915-16, *S.E.*, XVI: 21-2).

As to the first hypothesis, Freud correctly sensed that his *Interpretation of Dreams* would be so significant for the new century that he had the date 1900 published on the frontispiece, even though it was published on October 22, 1899. Although Freud benefited greatly from traditions before him in both science and humanities, he transformed previous material into a new focus and pioneered a fresh way of thinking about these issues. There was certainly work on the unconscious before Freud, but he took a giant step in making the unconscious the object of psychoanalytic investigation with respect to meaning and intention. Again, in relation to the second hypothesis about sexuality, Freud transcended the approach of previous researchers: Although there were many precursors, Freud changed the entire approach of investigation. As Eli Zaretsky puts it, sexology was not so much a source *for* psychoanalysis but became rather an *object* of analytic reflection. This point is critical to understanding Freud's approach to gender. The sexologists believed that the mind was dominated by bisexuality, by which they meant the distinction between masculine and feminine characteristics. In *Three Essays on Sexuality*, Freud rejected this approach, substituting—in his words—the conflict of libido and repression for the conflict of masculine and feminine. Instead of viewing the mind as divided between masculine and feminine currents, he described men and women as the targets of originally non-gendered sexual drives such as masochism or orality (2010, 275-76).

Zaretsky aptly summarizes the epoch-making nature for the new century of Freud's new approach, how it transcended previous approaches and could not be reduced to them.

> Freud had stood at the confluence of two great currents, scientific and humanistic, from which he forged a powerful synthesis. What made this synthesis compelling was the discovery of a new object: the idiosyncratic, meaning-saturated, morally-inflected psychical life of the human being, and a new ethic that assumed that a meaningful life necessitated self-reflection in depth (2011).

That new understanding was so immensely significant in Freud's eyes that it inflicted a still greater blow to human narcissism than had the revolutions of Copernicus and Darwin. That considerable claim was built upon a big wish. That was the league in which Freud wanted to be. It necessitated a major idea that brought about a paradigm shift. This search involved a mindset that would implement a broad-ranging campaign, akin to a military campaign on a number of fronts, including public relations and the development of world-wide centers. Unlike the revolutions of Copernicus and Darwin, however, Freudian psychoanalysis became a movement that was more like the foundation of a church and the slow advances of science. It involved a movement of like-minded visionaries who practiced Freud's "science." Holowchak argues in his *Freud and Uto-*

pia that Freud wished to effect a Newton-like synthesis for psychology. He suggests that Freud, initiating the final and most wounding blow to human narcissims, saw himself standing above Copernicus and Darwin, as Newton stood above Kepler and Galileo (2011, 2-5).

Singular universal explanations and shibboleths are critically assessed in universities, at least in principle. Given Freud's big wish, it is not surprising that he rejected the academic route, where he might have been first among equals and not in command with a single, overarching all-encompassing theory in the psychological sciences. Instead he established a freestanding movement of internally focused cliques run by his own secularized "cardinals." From the Wednesday Society onward, there was a kind of university atmosphere within the societies, but only on certain conditions. This atmosphere could sometimes exist provided that the Professor or loyalists had the last word and that certain established ideological boundaries or shibboleths were not violated—such as the central importance of sexuality or the Oedipus complex—where sorting the "ins" from the "outs" then overrode freedom and became paramount. The role of humanistic education is not incompatible with such narrowness. For example, seminaries can be scholarly institutions and can entertain debate, especially around the interpretation of given texts or doctrine. Such debate, however, is not scientific (Kirsner, 2009).

A much neglected work of Freud's last years, *Moses and Monotheism* (1939, *S.E.,* XXIII: 1-138), narrates Freud's long interest in Moses whom he postulates was an Egyptian prince and not Jewish. In Freud's speculations, Moses was murdered by some of his followers, who, years afterwards, regretted their action and created the idea of a messiah. According to Freud, their sense of guilt in recognizing they deserved punishment ended up creating additional ethical commandments and regulations in an obsessive-compulsive reaction-formation to the murderous deed that Freud saw as founding the father religion (1939, *S.E.,* XXIII: 134-5). Perhaps Freud was identifying himself with Moses in the movement aspect of psychoanalysis and the creation of a psychoanalytic *Weltanschauung*.

References

Breger, L. *A Dream of Undying Fame: How Freud Betrayed his Mentor and Invented Psychoanalysis* (New York: Basic Books, 2009).

Burke, J., *The Gods of Freud: Sigmund Freud's Art Collection.* Sydney: Knopf, 2006).

Eisold, K., "The Intolerance of Diversity in Psychoanalytic Institutes," *International Journal of Psycho-Analysis,* 75. 1994, 785-800.

Freud, Sigmund, *The Standard Edition of the Complete Psychological Works of Sigmund Freud,* Vols. I-XXIV, ed. and trans. James Strachey (London: The Hogarth Press, 1976).

Gödde, G., "Freud and nineteenth-century philosophical sources on the unconscious," *Thinking the Unconscious: Nineteenth-Century German Thought,* eds. A. Nicholls and M. Leibscher (Cambridge: Cambridge University Press, 2010), 261-86.

Holowchak, M. Andrew, *Freud and Utopia: From Cosmological Narcissism to the "Soft Dictatorship" of Reason* Lanham, MD: Lexington Books, 2011).

Kirsner, D., "Psychoanalysis and its Discontents," *Psychoanalytic Psychology*, Vol. 21, 2004, 339–52.

Kirsner, D., "Politics Masquerading as Science: Ralph Greenson, Anna Freud and the Klein Wars," *Psychoanalytic Review*, Vol. 92, No. 4, 2005, 907-927.

Kirsner, D., "Freud, Civilization, Religion and Stoicism," *Psychoanalytic Psychology*, 23: 2006, 354-66.

Kirsner, D., *Unfree Associations: Inside Psychoanalytic Institutes. Updated Edition* (New York: Jason Aronson, 2009).

Lear, J., *Freud* (New York: Routledge, 2005).

Lipton, S., "The Advantages of Freud's Technique as shown in his Analysis of the Rat Man," *International Journal of Psycho-Analysis*, Vol. 58, 1977: 255–73.

Makari, G., *Revolution in Mind: The Creation of Psychoanalysis* (New York: Harper/Collins, 2009).

Rycroft, C., "Causes and Meaning," *Psychoanalysis Observed*, eds. C. Rycroft, G. Gorer, A. Storr, J. Wren-Lewis, and P. Lomas (Harmondsworth: Penguin, 1966).

Salmon, W., "Psychoanalytic Theory and Evidence," ed. S. Hook, *Psychoanalysis, Scientific Method and Philosophy* (New York: New York University Press, 1964), 252-267.

Sterba, R. "The Humanistic Wellspring of Psychoanalysis," *Psychoanalytic Quarterly*, 43, 1974, 167–76.

Tauber, A., *Freud: The Reluctant Philosopher* (Princeton: Princeton University Press, 2010).

Zaretsky, E., "Review of George Makari," *Revolution in Mind: The Creation of Psychoanalysis, The Journal of Modern History*, 82, 2010, 675-6.

Zaretsky, E., "Why the Freudian Century" Unpublished, French translation, "Pourquoi le XXe siècle fut freudien," *Freud: Droit d'Inventaire, Sciences Humaines*, 21, Dec. 2010-Jan. 2011.

Chapter 23

Reply to Dr. De Block

Douglas Kirsner

IS PSYCHOANALYSIS A SCIENCE OR AN IDEOLOGY? Dr. De Block gives many good reasons for arguing that psychoanalysis has much to contribute to genuine scientific knowledge. I agree with him. But Dr. De Block goes further, however, in arguing that psychoanalysis is neither a pseudo-science nor a philosophy, but a science. The problem then arises: What is a science? As De Block suggests, there is scant agreement among philosophers of science as to the nature of science, and this may be because the sciences are so heterogeneous. As De Block observes, Freud was very specific in his focus on mental disorders and on a technique for uncovering their psychodynamic bases and that suggests Freud was a chiefly a psychologist, not chiefly a philosopher. I cannot focus on many issues in De Block's rich paper, but I will make a few comments on some of the issues developing from it.

I agree with Dr. De Block that Freud is a premier psychologist and that, if he is a philosopher, he is not a "normal" philosopher (perhaps that's an oxymoron anyway). Freud's methods seem more akin to philosophy—finding a single unified causal explanation for all psychical phenomena. I also agree that Freud attempts to surpass Copernicus and Darwin as delivering the greatest blow to human narcissism (though perhaps not to his). He was searching for the single answer that would unlock the secrets of at least the human psychical universe—a quest that is discussed very well indeed in Louis Breger's book on Freud's "dream of undying fame" (2009). Freud wanted to uncover the building blocks in discovering the root cause of all human behavior. This he did via experience and examining data in a different way with a different technique—free association. He developed many tools for understanding and made numerous "discoveries" along his journey, such as transference, resistance, repression, drives, and interpretation. He used and analyzed uniquely qualitative clinical data.

While no doubt he was trying to be a scientist, Freud did not stick to scientific protocols—certainly not received ones. If there is one matter scientists are keen on, it is the possibility of robust debate that critically questions propositions and revises or casts aside those that prove false. That is not something Freud encouraged. Instead, he wended his own path. Freud's generalizations became psychoanalytic dogma. In time, he formed his own closed panoply of loyal psychoanalysts. Dissenters left or were encouraged to leave. Such intolerance of dissent is characteristic of a *Weltanschauung,* not science.

At all events, I believe Freud's theory is in principle scientific as an exploratory method and open system that challenges presuppositions. As the lifelong work of the most prolific writer in psychoanalysis today, Leo Rangell, Honorary President of the International Psychoanalytical Association, testifies, it is quite legitimate to say that psychoanalysis can be approached scientifically in an open, yet critically and rigorously investigative manner (Rangell, 2006). There are researchers in the psychoanalytic field that are trying to move the field forward in a more interdisciplinary and open way.

Nonetheless, psychoanalysis does not easily fit into "art" or "science," especially since it involves data that are in some sense normative. For instance, it is difficult to see how psychoanalysts can practice their craft with the dispassion of a surgeon. Therapy has to be guided by ethical ideals, whether cultural or absolute. Thus, it is arguably best dubbed a science-based art, where there is a scientific foundation to what is in every patient's hour a unique experience.

Freudian psychoanalysis need not be an ideology and it is a comforting all-encompassing explanation for all human behavior. Psychoanalysis, as Freud emphasized, is first and foremost a *method of inquiry* in that it shares its platform with science rather than ideology or religion. As a method of inquiry, psychoanalysis has made revolutionary contributions to the study of human unconscious thinking and behavior, not the least of which is a thorough repositioning of understanding the identity of the human subject as decentered. Psychoanalysis is also a thoroughgoing critique of the nature of thinking, deconstructing ideological or dogmatic religious panaceas as our seeking security and comfort in a heartless world.

Freud's world is not only the world of nature with its relentless calamities such as earthquakes, tsunamis, floods, fires, and droughts, but also the world comprising the biological vulnerabilities of our bodies. Yet the worst fear is of the threat posed by other people, as the daily news stories of terror, brutality and oppression ineluctably remind us. Freud was close, both geographically and temporally, to the ruthless totalitarianism of the Nazis and Communists, who offered chimeric, brutal, and inhuman solutions to human problems. At the same time, he rejected religious solutions, which offered answers in the next world to human problems while playing no part in solving the issues in this one, except in counter-productive consolation.

Freudian psychoanalysis, as a method of inquiry, opposes *closed systems.* Insofar as psychoanalysis is a method, it is an *open system.* There are no preordained or logically inevitable answers based on the assumptions, such as in a *Weltanschauung*.

De Block is perhaps correct in stating that psychoanalysis, as a method of inquiry, is no pseudo-science, but much hinges on what a "science" is. We can get too bogged down in this issue. Psychoanalysis cannot be reduced to causal explanation. There is more to it than quantitative, "testable" data. If a science, it is not a science on the model of natural sciences.

I think one way through these thickets to broaden the concept of science to involve a new science of persons. If a science is a method which deals with a field that is appropriate to it, as the psychoanalyst, R.D. Laing suggests in his classic book about existential psychiatry, *The Divided Self,* then psychoanalysis can be seen as "a science of persons." For Laing, one's relationship with the other as organism is generically different from the relationship with the other as person. "One acts towards an organism differently from the way one acts towards a person. The science of persons is the study of human beings that begins from a relationship with the other as person and proceeds to an account of the other still as person" (Laing, 1960, 21). A thoroughgoing understanding of ourselves as persons, both inter- and intra-personally, goes far beyond given views of a model of science that needs to be fitted into.[1] I believe that such a "science of persons" significantly includes intentionality and meaning.

Overall, Freud aimed at a singular explanation of humans and used an amalgam of untried methods to try to achieve this. Thus, psychoanalysis seems to be a *Weltanschauung.* Yet in theory, at least, he preferred the "nostrum" of science, which was in principle open to outcomes, to religion, which was closed in advance. In that, psychoanalysis seems to be science. Since his discoveries and methods do not easily fit into received scientific approaches, perhaps it is best to say that he has methodologically broadened our notion of "science".

Notes

1. Perhaps Laing, along with almost everyone, makes the wrong division, and organisms can be included along with persons as opposed to inorganic entities that are governed by causal laws. Elliott Jaques suggests that the divide need not simply be between persons on the one hand and inorganic and organic entities on the other, whereby organisms are causally understood on the same basis as inorganic entities. Perhaps organisms are intentional and make decisions like us, though on a different level. The divide should be organisms (including persons) that have intentions versus inorganic entities that are governed by causal laws. Organisms, including persons, make *decisions* whereas we can understand inorganic entities (including computers) through calculation. "Organical work" involves decisions and judgment whereas mechanical work pertains to the physical world (Jaques, 2002, 21). If this view has any merit, it implies a shift that brings assumptions of natural science about animals into a different sphere, closer to humans, while the division between biological entities and inanimate entities is sharply divided further.

References

Breger, L. *A Dream of Undying Fame: How Freud Betrayed his Mentor and Invented Psychoanalysis* (New York: Basic Books, 2009).

Jaques, E., *The Life and Behavior of Living Organisms* (Westport CT: Praeger, 2002).

Kirsner, D., "Is There a Future for American Psychoanalysis? *Psychoanalytic Review,* 77, 1990: 175-200.

Laing, R.D., *The Divided Self: An Existential Study in Sanity and Madness* (Harmondsworth: Penguin, 1960).

Rangell, L., *The Road to Unity in Psychoanalytic Theory* (New York: Jason Aronson, 2006).

Chapter 24
Reply to Dr. Kirsner

Andreas De Block

I AM SYMPATHETIC TO MANY OF THE ARGUMENTS that Douglas Kirsner develops in his insightful contribution to this volume. In my own contribution, I made some very similar points, for instance regarding the philosophical influences on Freud's theory of the unconscious and the sectarian aspects of the psychoanalytic movement. Moreover, I wholeheartedly agree with Kirsner that there are quite a few other, theoretically important points of contact between Freud's psychoanalysis and naturalistically conceived philosophies. Nonetheless, there are points to which I am inclined to take issue. The first point is concerned with the kind of explanations that Freud gives. The second point is concerned with the normative aspects of Freud's theory and why these normative aspects do not undermine or reduce the scientific nature of Freud's project.

Meaning and Causal Explanation

According to Kirsner, Freud's psychoanalysis is a *Weltanschauung*. Kirsner calls the psychoanalytic project a philosophical project partly because Freud focuses on the mind and not the brain. And indeed, it is undeniably so that after 1895 Freud almost completely abandoned the physiological approach he had endorsed before that time. But the very fact that Freud studied the mind rather than the brain does not make him a philosopher, nor does it commit him to a dualist position or any other metaphysical view regarding the mind-body relationship. Of course, philosophers do have a special interest in the mind, but the same can be said of psychologists and psychiatrists.

In other words, the fact that Freud studied the mind is insufficient to establish that he was a philosopher in disguise. If we want to unmask him as a philosopher, we have to show that he studied human behavior and thinking in a philosophical manner. In Kirsner's view, this is precisely how Freud approached the phenomena he studied: symptoms, dreams, and parapraxes. Or more precisely, Kirsner argues that Freud might have started as a would-be scientist, but that his more mature ideas about these phenomena were philosophical. But what would be so distinctively philosophical about Freud's approach? What is the difference between a philosophical study and a scientific study of these phenomena? According to Kirsner, the main difference has to do with the kind of explanation that is offered by the two approaches. Philosophy—or at least the subset of philosophy that psychoanalysis belongs to—is about discovering meaning by deciphering symbols, while scientists attempt to give a causal explanation that refers to laws or to law-like regularities. Kirsner writes, "He [Freud] began with the idea of causal explanations being necessary for psychoanalysis in *Studies on Hysteria*, but his mature ideas involved the language of motives, meaning, and intentions" (Kirsner, 247).

Kirsner's argument hinges upon the idea that Freud has shown that the parapraxes, symptoms, and dreams have a sense, but that he has not shown that every psychic event has a cause: "Parapraxes have a sense, but this does not amount to them having a causal explanation in keeping with determinism" (251). I think that this position is untenable: Parapraxes only have a sense because they can be causally explained. The sense of a symptom/slip/dream is determined by its unconscious motives, beliefs, or intentions. Freud gives the agent's reason for producing the symptom or for having the dream. The correctness of the analysts interpretation depends solely on getting the reasons right that led to the production or continued presence of a symptom or a slip. Here, admittedly, the therapeutic efficacy of the interpretation should not be confused with the accurateness of the interpretation. Hence, insofar as the psychoanalytic practice is a hermeneutic practice, it is a hermeneutic practice that is seriously constrained by a theory that tries to discover how different symptoms are caused by different unconscious motives and representations. In short, symptoms have no psychoanalytically relevant sense apart from the unconscious reason(s) that a person has for producing, or holding on to, this symptom.

Now suppose someone argues that reasons are not causes, or that intentional action explanations are not causal explanations. Would that not be fatal for my claim? Well, if the argument is compelling (but see Davidson, 1963), I would have to agree that Freud's explanations are not causal explanations. But even then, I could hold on to the view that this compelling argument is not problematic for my claim, because many, if not most, of the explanations in the social sciences are of this species. Reasons are what many social scientists are interested in. My main aim was to argue that Freud's psychoanalysis had much more to do with social sciences than with philosophy, not that the explanations of the social sciences belong to the same species of explanations as the explanations of the natural sciences.

Psychiatry and the Good Life

Freud's psychoanalysis may have profound philosophical and ethical significance. However, a theory's philosophical or ethical significance is in itself insufficient to conclude that this theory is first and foremost a philosophical or a moral theory. After all, Darwin's theory of evolution has obvious and important philosophical implications. Nonetheless, Darwin's theory remains a scientific theory. However, there is a difference between claiming that Freud's theory has a normative/ethical significance, and claiming that Freud's approach is essentially normative. If the latter claim turns out to be correct, one would have a much more difficult time to defend that the theory is not an ethical or philosophical theory. Or not? I believe that this crucially depends on what this normativity is. I also believe that the normativity of psychoanalysis is not the kind of normativity that makes psychoanalysis an ethical theory.

Together with Jonathan Lear, Douglas Kirsner defends the view that Freud's approach is essentially normative (252). The main reason for defending this view is that Freud deals with neurotic patients and their failure to live flourishing lives. In short, Freud's patients are all unhappy, and Freud tries to use his psychoanalytic techniques to aid his patients in problems that make them unhappy. Now it is hard to deny that Freud's patients were neurotics and that they failed to flourish. But what Lear and Kirsner write about Freud's theory is obviously also true for current psychiatric theories and psychiatric practices. Psychiatric therapies aim—directly or indirectly—at a reduction of their patients' distress. And part of psychiatry as a theoretical discipline aims to understand what the DSM IV calls "the clinically significant distress or impairment in social, occupational, or other important areas of functioning" (American Psychiatric Association, 2000). Does this make psychiatry a normative discipline? Maybe, but it surely does not imply that psychiatry is not a scientific discipline. After all, it is part and parcel of most medical disciplines that they try to understand and to alleviate people's suffering or impairment, but few would argue that this entails that medicine stops being a scientific discipline. Moreover, the unhappiness that Freud aims to reduce is pathological unhappiness. Whereas the typical *Weltanschauung* is interested in a cure for unhappiness, Freud merely aims at transforming "hysterical misery into common unhappiness" (1895, *S.E.*, II: 305). Hence, Freud obviously focuses on mental dysfunctions rather than on problems in living, even though his views about the etiology and structure of mental disorders may have implications for how we should take care of our problems in living. The Stoics and Epicurus constructed arguments and techniques to assist people in handling their fear of death or their ruminations about the meaning of life. Freud's psychoanalysis explains the fear of horses and the meaning of jokes. And that is precisely one of the reasons why Freud is more a psychiatrist (and a scientist) than a philosopher.

References

American Psychiatric Association, *Diagnostic and Statistical Manual of Mental Disorders*, 4th ed. (Washington, D.C.: APA, 2000).

Davidson, D., "Actions, Reasons, and Causes," *The Journal of Philosophy*, Vol. 60, 1963: 685-700.

Freud, Sigmund, *The Standard Edition of the Complete Psychological Works of Sigmund Freud*, Vols. I-XXIV, ed. and trans. James Strachey (London: The Hogarth Press, 1976).

List of Contributors

John Cottingham is Professor Emeritus of Philosophy at the University of Reading, Professorial Research Fellow at Heythrop College, University of London, and an Honorary Fellow of St John's College, Oxford. His is an authority on early-modern philosophy, especially Descartes, and has published widely on moral philosophy and the philosophy of religion. His books include *Philosophy and the Good Life: Reason and the Passions in Greek, Cartesian and Psychoanalytic Ethics* (Cambridge University Press, 1996), *On the Meaning of Life* (Routledge, 2003), The *Spiritual Dimension* (Cambridge University Press, 2005), *Cartesian Reflections* (Oxford University Press, 2008), and *Why Believe?* (Continuum, 2009). He is editor of the international philosophical journal *Ratio.*

Andreas De Block is an assistant professor of philosophy at the University of Leuven. His doctoral dissertation, from the University of Leuven, was on Freud's theory of sublimation. Since then his research has included topics in the philosophy of biology and philosophical psychology. He has published his work in journals such as *Biology & Philosophy*, *Philosophical Psychology*, *Environmental Values*, *Journal for Medicine and Philosophy*, *Biological Theory*, *Philosophy, Psychiatry, & Psychology*, *Perspectives in Medicine and Biology*, and *History of Psychiatry*.

Edward Erwin is Professor of Philosophy at the University of Miami and the author of *Natural Science Approaches to Psychotherapy* (due March, 2010), *Behavior Therapy: Scientific, Philosophical and Moral Foundations*, 2nd ed. (due June, 2010), *Philosophy and Psychotherapy: Razing the Troubles of the Brain* (1997), *A Final Accounting: Philosophical and Empirical Issues in Freudian Psychology* (1996), and is the Editor of *The Freud Encyclopedia: Theories, Therapy, and Culture* (2002).

Grant Gillett is a qualified neurosurgeon and practiced until 2006. He is now a Professor of Medical Ethics at the Bioethics Centre of the Medical School, and teaches in the Psychology department at Otago University. He is author of *The Mind and its Discontents* (2009), *Subjectivity and Being Somebody: Human Identity and Neuroethics* (2008), *Bioethics in the Clinic: Hippocratic Reflections* (2004) and numerous articles in philosophy, bioethics, and philosophy of psychiatry.

Adolf Grünbaum is the Andrew Mellon Professor of Philosophy of Science, Primary Research Professor in the Department of History and Philosophy of Science, Research Professor of Psychiatry, and Chairman of the Center for Philosophy of Science at the University of Pittsburgh. He has written on the philosophy of physics, the theory of scientific rationality, the philosophy of psychiatry, and the critique of theism. His 12 books include *The Foundations of Psychoanalysis: A Philosophical Critique* (1984) and *Validation in the Clinical Theory of Psychoanalysis: A Study in the Philosophy of Psychoanalysis* (1993). He has contributed nearly 400 articles to anthologies and to philosophical and scientific periodicals.

M. Andrew Holowchak teaches philosophy at Rider University. He is contributing editor to this compilation and has published 17 books and over 60 articles in peer-reviewed journals, including *Freud and Utopia,* "The 'Soft Dictatorship' of Reason: Freud on Science, Religion, and Utopia", "The Problem of Unassailability: Freud, Analogy, and the Adequacy of Constructions in Analysis", and "Technology and Freudian Discontent: Freud's 'Muffled Meliorism' and the Problem of Human Annihilation".

Douglas Kirsner is professor of philosophy at Deakin University. His research interests are in history and philosophy of psychoanalysis and its institutions. He is the author of *Unfree Associations: Inside Psychoanalytic Institutes* and "Fresh Freud", "Freud, Civilization, Religion, and Stoicism", "Psychoanalysis and Its Discontents", "Psychoanalysis Gone Wrong", "The Future of Psychoanalytic Institutes", and many other articles on psychoanalysis. He serves as editorial advisor or associate editor to several psychoanalytic journals.

Joel Kupfersmid is a semi-retired psychologist. He worked with children and adolescents for most of his 30 years employment with Ohio Department of Mental Health. He has co-authored two books in psychology and over 25 peer-reviewed articles. Three publications focus on the legitimacy of the Oedipal complex and challenge the traditional psychoanalytic view and Masson's position on how this complex was "discovered."

Michael Lavin is a psychologist in private practice in Iowa. He has previously had private practices in Washington, D.C., and Arlington, Virginia. Before training as psychologist, he taught philosophy for 11 years at the University of Tennessee. He has published numerous articles, book chapters, and reviews on philosophical topics in medicine, sport, mental health, and psychology, especially in relation to ethics.

Michael Michael is Assistant Professor at Underwood International College in Yonsei University, South Korea. Writing his doctoral thesis on *akrasia,* he studied mathematics, cognitive science, and biology, before completing a Ph.D. in philosophy at Cambridge University. His main research interest is philosophy of action. He has published on Freud's dream theory and his use of free association.

Rosemarie Sand is psychoanalyst, who has retired after 25 years of practice in Manhattan. She is a member of the Institute for Psychoanalytic Training and Research and the International Psychoanalytical Association. She has published "Early Nineteenth Century Anticipation of Freudian Theory," "Confirmation in the Dora Case," "Pre-Freudian Discovery of Dream

Meaning: the Achievements of Charcot, Janet, and Krafft-Ebing," "On a Contribution to a Future Scientific Study of Dream Interpretation," and "Freud and the Western Dream Tradition." Her special interests are in antecedents to Freudian theory. She is preparing two books, *Dreaming Before Freud* and *The Unconscious: History of a Concept,* for publication.

Paul C. Vitz is Professor of Psychology at New York University and Adjunct Professor at John Paul II Institute for Marriage and Family, Washington, D.C. Vitz has published over 100 articles and essays. His books include *Psychology as Religion: The Cult of Self-Worship* (2nd ed., 1994), *Modern Art and Modern Science* (1984), and *Sigmund Freud's Christian Unconscious* (1988).

Further Reading

John Cottingham (selected publications):

Philosophy and the Good Life: Reason and the Passions in Greek, Cartesian and Psychoanalytic Ethics (Cambridge: Cambridge University Press, 1998), esp. ch. 4.

The Spiritual Dimension: Religion, Philosophy and Human Value (Cambridge: Cambridge University Press, 2005, esp. ch. 4.

Cartesian Reflections (Oxford: Oxford University Press, 2008), chs. 1 and 6.

"A Triangle of Hostility? Psychoanalysis, Philosophy and Religion," *The Academic Face of Psychoanalysis,* eds. L. Braddock and M. Lacewing, (London: Routledge, 2007), 92-110.

"Conscience, Guilt and Shame," forthcoming in R. Crisp (ed.), *The Oxford Handbook of the History of Ethics* (Oxford: Oxford University Press, 2012).

Andreas DeBlock (selected publications):

With P. Adriaens, "Why We Essentialize Mental Disorders (forthcoming). *The Journal of Medicine and Philosophy,* Vol. 35.

With P. Adriaens, P., "The Evolutionary Turn in Psychiatry: A Historial Overview," *History of Psychiatry,* Vol. 21, No. 2, 2010, 131-43.

"Why Mental Disorders are Just Mental Dysfunctions (and Nothing More): some Darwinian arguments," *Studies in History and Philosophy of Biological and Biomedical Sciences,* Vol. 39, No. 3. 2008, 338-46.

"Applied Darwinism: Lessons from the History of Applied Psychoanalysis," *Culture and Organization,* Vol. 12, 2006, 293-305.

"Freud as an 'Evolutionary Psychiatrist' and the Foundations of a Freudian Philosophy. *Philosophy, psychiatry & psychology,* Vol. 12, No. 4, 2006, 315-24.

"Creatief met seksualiteit: over de onmogelijkheid van een freudiaanse sublimeringstheorie," *Tijdschrift voor Filosofie,* Vol. 65, Vol. 3, 2003, 415-37.

"Drift en ziekte: over het waarom van Freuds antropologische wending," *Tijdschrift voor filosofie,* Vol. 64, No. 2, 2002, 325-52.

"Culturele instincten: een alternatief voor de psychodynamica van de sublimering," *Tijdschrift voor Psychoanalyse,* Vol. 8, No. 4, 2002, 222-233.

With P. Moyaert, P. "Freuds theorie van de mannelijke homoseksualiteit," *Tijdschrift voor psychoanalyse,* Vol. 7, No. 2, 2001, 64-75.

Ed Erwin (selected publications):

"Psychoanalytic Therapy: The Eysenck Argument," *American Psychologist* (1980)

"The Truth about Psychoanalysis," *Journal of Philosophy* (1981)

"Psychotherapy, Placebos, and Wait-list Controls," *The Behavioral and Brain Sciences*, Vol. 6, (1983), 289-90.

"To What Degree Was Freud Wrong—and How Much difference Does it Make in Psychotherapy?" *Journal of Contemporary Psychotherapy* (1985)

"Psychotherapy and Freudian Psychology," *Hans Eysenck: A Psychologist Searching for a Scientific Basis for Human Behavior*, eds. S. Modgil and C. Modgil (Falmer Press, 1986).

"Special Review: H.J. Eysenck, "The Decline and Fall of the Freudian Empire," *Personality and Individual Differences*, 1986.

"Psychoanalysis: Clinical vs. Experimental Evidence," *Mind, Psychoanalysis and Science*, eds. P. Clark and C. Wright (Basil Blackwell, 1988).

"Philosophers on Freudianism: An Examination of Replies to Grunbaum's Foundations," *Philosophical Problems of the Internal and External Worlds: Essays Concerning the Philosophy of Adolf Grunbaum*, eds. J. Earman, A. Janis, G. Massey, and N. Rescher (University of Pittsburgh Press, 1993).

"The Effectiveness of Psychotherapy: Epistemological Issues," *Philosophical Psychopathology*, eds. G. Graham and G. Stephens (M.I.T. Press, 1994).

A Final Accounting: Philosophical and Empirical Issues in Freudian Psychology (Cambridge MA: The MIT Press, 1996).

"The Effectiveness of Psychoanalytic Therapy: A Question of Standards," *Psychology and Philosophy: Interdisciplinary Problems and Responses*, eds. W. O'Donahue and R. Kitchener (Sage, 1996).

Philosophy and Psychotherapy: Razing the Troubles of the Brain (Sage, 1997).

"Psychoanalysis: Past, Present, and Future," *Philosophy and Phenomenological Research* (1997)

The Freud Encyclopedia: Theories, Therapy, and Culture (Routledge, 2002).

"Did the Boy Come to Nothing?" Critical Discussion of *The Annual Review of Psychoanalysis*, Volume XXIX, *Contemporary Psychology* (2003).

"Cognitive-Behavior Therapy" in J. Radden (Ed.) *The Philosophy of Psychiatry* (Oxford University Press, 2004).

"Psychoanalysis", in D. Borchet (Editor) *Encyclopedia of Philosophy*, Second Edition, Macmillan, (2006).

"Randomized Clinical Trials in Psychotherapy Outcome Research", *Philosophy of Science* (2006).

"Freud's The Interpretation of Dreams", Internet publication, Scattergood Ethics.org., Applied Ethics of Behavioral Health (University of Pennsylvania, 2008).

"Is Freud Back?" *Logic, Methodology, and Philosophy of Science: Proceedings of the Thirteenth International Congress*, eds. C. Glymour, W. Wei, and D. Westerståhl (London: College Publications, 2009).

"Research Methods in Psychoanalysis," *Philosophy of Religion, Physics, and Psychology: Essays in Honor of Adolf Grunbaum,* ed. A. Grünbaum and A. Jokic (Prometheus, 2009).

"Which Way American Psychology? A Discussion of Barbara Held's Psychology's Interpretative Turn", *Philosophy of Social Science* (2009).

The Rejection of Natural Science Approaches to Psychotherapy (VDM Publishing, 2010).

"Not Proven: Reply to M. Lacewing's "Inferring Motives," *Psychology and Psychoanalysis: Philosophy, Psychiatry, and Psychology*, forthcoming, 2011.

Grant Gillett (selected publications):

The Mind and Its Discontents, 2nd ed. (Oxford: Oxford University Press, 2009).

"Intentional Action, Moral Responsibility and Psychopaths," *Responsibility and Psychopathy: Interfacing Law, Psychiatry and Philosophy*, ed. in Luca Malatesti and John McMillan (Oxford: Oxford University Press, 2009).

"Autonomy Intention and Brain Events," *Bioethics*, 2009.

Subjectivity and Being Somebody: Neuroethics and Human Identity (Imprint Academic, 2008).

"Clinical Medicine and the Quest for Certainty," *Social Science and Medicine* 58, 2004, 727-38.

Bioethics in the Clinic (John Hopkins University Press, 2004).

"Consciousness and Lesser States: The Evolutionary Foothills of the Mind," *Philosophy*, 74 (1999) 331-360.

"Moral Authenticity and the Unconscious," *The Analytic Freud,* ed. M. Levine (London: Routledge, 2000), 177-92.

Adolf Grünbaum (selected publications):

"Epistemological Liabilities of the Clinical Appraisal of Psychoanalytic Theory," *Noûs XIV* (3) (1980): 307-85.

"Freud's Theory: The Perspective of a Philosopher of Science," Presidential Address to The American Philosophical Association (Eastern Division) on December 28, 1982, in *Proceedings and Addresses of The American Philosophical Association*, Vol. 57, No. 1, 1983, 5–31.

"Retrospective Versus Prospective Testing of Aetiological Hypotheses in Freudian Theory," *Testing Scientific Theories*. Minnesota Studies in the

Philosophy of Science, Vol. X, ed. John Earman (Minneapolis, MN: University of Minnesota Press, 1983), 315–47.

"The Foundations of Psychoanalysis: A Philosophical Critique," *Mind and Medicine: Problems of Explanation and Evaluation in Psychiatry and the Biomedical Sciences,* Pittsburgh Series in the Philosophy and History of Science, Vol. 8, ed. L. Laudan (Berkeley, CA: University of California Press, 1983), 143-309.

The Foundations of Psychoanalysis: A Philosophical Critique (Berkeley, CA: University of California Press, 1984).

"The Hermeneutic Construal of Psychoanalytic Theory and Therapy: An Ill-Conceived Paradigm for the Human Sciences," *Science and Reality: Recent Work in the Philosophy of Science: Essays in Honor of Ernan McMullin,* ed. J.T. Cushing, C.F. Delaney, and G.M. Gutting (Notre Dame, IN: University of Notre Dame Press, 1984), 54–82.

"*Précis* of *The Foundations of Psychoanalysis: A Philosophical Critique*" and "Author's Response" to 40 Reviewers: "Is Freud's Theory Well-Founded?" *Behavioral & Brain Sciences*, Vol. 9, No. 2, 1986, 217–28; 266–84.

"The Placebo Concept in Medicine and Psychiatry," *Psychological Medicine*, Vol. 16, 1986, 19-38.

"Psychoanalysis and Theism," *The Monist*, Vol. 70, No. 2, 1987, 152–92

"The Role of the Case Study Method in the Foundations of Psychoanalysis," *Die Philosophen und Freud*: *Wiener Reihe, Themen der Philosophie,* Vol. 3, ed. H. Vetter and L. Nagl (Vienna, Austria: R. Oldenbourg Verlag, 1988), 134–74.

"The Role of the Case Study Method in the Foundations of Psychoanalysis," *Canadian Journal of Philosophy* Vol. 18, No. 4, 1988, 623–58.

"The Placebo Concept in Medicine and Psychiatry," *Non-Specific Aspects of Treatment*, World Health Organization, ed. M. Shepherd and N. Sartorius (Toronto: Hans Huber Publishers, 1989): 7–38.

"'Meaning' Connections and Causal Connections in the Human Sciences: The Poverty of Hermeneutic Philosophy," *Journal of the American Psychoanalytic Association,* Vol. 38, No. 3, 1990, 559–77.

"The Psychoanalytic Enterprise in Scientific Perspective," *Scientific Theories*, Minnesota Studies in the Philosophy of Science, Vol. XIV, ed. C.W. Savage (Minneapolis, MN: University of Minnesota Press, 1990), 41–58.

"Why Thematic Kinships between Events Do NOT Attest Their Causal Linkage," *Epistemologia* Vol. 13, No. 2, 1990, 187-207.

"Author's Response, Etiology and Therapy in Psychoanalytic Theory," *Behavioral & Brain Sciences,* Vol. 14, No. 4, 1991, 729-732.

"Two Major Difficulties for Freud's Theory of Dreams," *Freud and the History of Psychoanalysis*, ed. T. Gelfand and J. Kerr (Hillsdale, NJ: Analytic Press, 1992), 193–213.

"A New Critique of Freud's Theory of Dreams," *Scientific Philosophy: Origins and Developments,* ed. F. Stadler (Dordrecht, The Netherlands: Kluwer Academic Publishers, 1993), 169–191).

Validation in the Clinical Theory of Psychoanalysis: A Study in the Philosophy of Psychoanalysis (Madison, CT: International Universities Press: 1993), 257-309.

"Psychoanalytic Theory and Therapy After 100 Years, and Its Future," Keynote Address at the Awards Ceremony of the Prix Latsis Universitaires (Geneva, Switzerland: Fondation Latsis Internationale, 1994), 1–34.

"Freud, in Full View," *The Pittsburgh Post-Gazette* (January 7, 1996): B1 and B4.

"Is Psychoanalysis Viable?" *The Philosophy of Psychology*, ed. W. O'Donohue and R.F. Kitchener (London: Sage Publications, 1996), 281–90.

"Is the Concept of 'Psychic Reality' a Theoretical Advance?" *Psychoanalysis and Contemporary Thought,* Vol. 20, No. 2, 1997, 245–267.

"One Hundred Years of Psychoanalytic Theory and Therapy: Retrospect and Prospect," *Mindscapes: Philosophy, Science, and the Mind*, ed. M. Carrier and P. Machamer (Pittsburgh, PA/Konstanz, Germany: University of Pittsburgh Press/University of Konstanz Press, 1997), 323–60.

"A Century of Psychoanalysis: Critical Retrospect and Prospect," *Freud: Conflict and Culture,* M.S. Roth (New York: Alfred A. Knopf, 1998), 183–95.

"The Failure of Freud's Explanation of Counter-Wish Dreams," *Philosophy and the Many Faces of Science*, ed. D. Anapolitanos, A. Baltas, and S. Tsinorema (Lanham, MD: Rowman & Littlefield Publishers, Inc., 1998), 273–85.

"The Hermeneutic Versus the Scientific Conception of Psychoanalysis: An Unsuccessful Effort to Chart a *Via Media* for the Human Sciences," *Einstein Meets Magritte, an Interdisciplinary Reflection: The White Book of Einstein Meets Magritte,* eds. D. Aerts, J. Broekaert, and E. Mathijs (Dordrecht, The Netherlands: Kluwer Academic Publishers, 1999), 219–39.

"Does Freudian Theory Resolve 'The Paradoxes of Irrationality'?" *Proceedings of the 20th World Congress of Philosophy*. Philosophy of Mind and Philosophy of Psychology, Vol. 9, ed. B. Elevitch (Bowling Green, OH: Philosophy Documentation Center, 2000), 203–18.

"Reply to Symposium on the Grünbaum Debate," *Psychoanalytic Dialogues*, Vol. 10, No. 2, 2000, 335–42.
"Critique of Psychoanalysis," *The Freud Encyclopedia; Theory, Therapy, and Culture*, ed. E. Erwin (New York: Routledge, 2002), 117-36.
"The Hermeneutic Versus the Scientific Conception of Psychoanalysis," *Psychoanalysis at the Limit: Epistemology, Mind, and the Question of Science*, ed. J. Mills (New York: State University of New York Press, 2004), 139–60.
"Critique of Psychoanalysis," *Who Owns Psychoanalysis?* ed. A. Caseman (London: Karnac Books Ltd., 2004), 263-305.
"Freud, Sigmund," *Encyclopedia of Philosophy*, 2nd ed., Vol. 3, ed. D. Borchert (Farmington Hills, MI: Macmillan Reference, Gale Group/Thomson, 2005), 736–48.
"Is Sigmund Freud's Psychoanalytic Edifice Relevant to the 21st Century?" *Psychoanalytic Psychology,* Vol. 23, No. 2 (150th Freud Anniversary Issue), 2006, 257–84.
"The Reception of my Freud-Critique in the Psychoanalytic Literature," *Psychoanalytic Psychology* Vol. 24, No. 3, 2007, 545-76.
"Popper's Fundamental Misdiagnosis of the Scientific Defects of Freudian Psychoanalysis, and of Their Bearing on the Theory of Demarcation," *Psychoanalytic Psychology*, Vol. 25, No. 4, 2008, 574-89.
"Sigmund Freud," *History of Western Philosophy of Religion*, eds. Graham Oppy and Nick Trakakis (London: Acumen/New York: Oxford University Press, Vol. 4, 2009), 263-85.
"Freud's Theory: The Perspective of a Philosopher of Science," Centenary Celebration Volume of the *Presidential Addresses of the American Philosophical Association, 1901-2000*, Vol. 9, 1981-1990, ed. R.T. Hull, 138-180 (forthcoming).

M. Andrew Holowchak:

Freud and Utopia: From Cosmological Narcissism to the 'Soft Dictatorship' of Reason", Lexington Books, 2011.
"When Freud (Almost) Met Chaplin", *Perspectives on Science* (forthcoming)
"What Games, Play, and Sport Reveal about Games, Play, and Sports Fanatics: A Freudian Analysis", *The Journal of the American Academy of Psychoanalysis and Dynamic Psychiatry* (forthcoming)
"Freud on Philosophy and Philosophers: Patching the Gaps in the Universe with Nightcaps and Dressing-Gown Tatters", *International Forum for Psychoanalysis* (2011, 1-12)
"The Problem of Unassailability: Freud, Analogy, and the Adequacy of Constructions in Analysis", *Psychoanalytic Psychology* (forthcoming)

"The 'Soft Dictatorship' of Reason: Freud on Science, Religion, and Utopia", *Philo*, Vol. 13, No. 1, 2010

"Technology and Freudian Discontent: Freud's 'Muffled Meliorism' and the Problem of Human Annihilation", *Sophia*, Vol. 49, No. 1, 2010

"Freud's Debt to Stoicism? A Reply to Kirsner", *Psychoanalytic Psychology,* Vol. 27, No. 1, 2010.

Doug Kirsner:

Kirsner, D., "Psychoanalysis and its Discontents," *Psychoanalytic Psychology,* Vol. 21, 2004, 339–52.

Kirsner, D., "Politics Masquerading as Science: Ralph Greenson, Anna Freud and the Klein Wars," *Psychoanalytic Review,* Vol. 92, No. 4, 2005, 907-927.

Kirsner, D., "Freud, Civilization, Religion and Stoicism," *Psychoanalytic Psychology,* 23: 2006, 354-66.

Kirsner, D., *Unfree Associations: Inside Psychoanalytic Institutes. Updated Edition* (New York: Jason Aronson, 2009).

Joel Kupfersmid:

"The 'Defense' of Sigmund Freud," *Psychotherapy,* Vol. 29, 1992, 297-309.

"Freud's Rationale for Abandoning Seduction Theory," *Psychoanalytic Psychology.* Vol. 10, 1993, 275-90.

"Does the Oedipus Complex Exist?" *Psychotherapy,* Vol. 32, 1995, 535-47.

Michael Michael:

"On the Validity of Freud's Dream Interpretations." *Studies in History and Philosophy of Biological and Biomedical Sciences*, 39, 2008, 52-64.

Rosemarie Sand:

"Confirmation in the Dora Case," *International Review of Psycho-Analysis,* Vol. 10, 1983, 333-357

"Early Nineteenth Century Anticipation of Freudian Theory," *International Review of Psycho-Analysis,* Vol. 15, 1988, 465-79

"Pre-Freudian Discovery of Dream Meaning: The Achievements of Charcot, Janet, and Krafft-Ebing," *Freud and the History of Psychoanalysis,* eds. T. Gelfand and J. Kerr (New York: The Analytic Press, 1992), 215-29.

"On a Contribution to a Future Scientific Study of Dream Interpretation," *Philosophical Problems of the Internal and External Worlds: Essays on the Philosophy of Adolf Grünbaum* (Pittsburgh: University of Pittsburgh Press, 1993), 527-47.

"The Interpretation of Dreams: Freud and the Western Dream Tradition," *Psychoanalytic Dialogues*, Vol. 9, No. 6, 1999, 725-48.

"Herbart, Johann Friedrich (1776-1841)," *The Freud Encyclopedia: Theory, Therapy and Culture*, eds. Edward Erwin and Coral Gables (New York: Routledge, 2002), 254-6.

Paul Vitz:

Sigmund Freud's Christian Unconscious Grand Rapids, MI: Wm. B. Eerdmans Publishing Co., 1993).

Faith of the Fatherless: The Psychology of Atheism (Dallas, TX: Spence, 1999).